THE OXFORD HISTORY OF THE BRITISH EMPIRE

COMPANION SERIES

Blackburn
College

Library
01254 292120

Please return this book on or before the last date below

THE OXFORD HISTORY OF THE BRITISH EMPIRE

Volume I. *The Origins of Empire*
EDITED BY Nicholas Canny

Volume II. *The Eighteenth Century*
EDITED BY P. J. Marshall

Volume III. *The Nineteenth Century*
EDITED BY Andrew Porter

Volume IV. *The Twentieth Century*
EDITED BY Judith M. Brown and Wm. Roger Louis

Volume V. *Historiography*
EDITED BY Robin W. Winks

THE OXFORD HISTORY OF THE BRITISH EMPIRE

COMPANION SERIES

Wm. Roger Louis, CBE, D.Litt., FBA

*Kerr Professor of English History and Culture, University of Texas, Austin
and Honorary Fellow of St Antony's College, Oxford*

EDITOR-IN-CHIEF

Ireland and the British Empire

Kevin Kenny

Professor of History, Boston College

EDITOR

OXFORD

UNIVERSITY PRESS

*This book has been printed digitally and produced in a standard specification
in order to ensure its continuing availability*

OXFORD
UNIVERSITY PRESS

Great Clarendon Street, Oxford OX2 6DP

Oxford University Press is a department of the University of Oxford.
It furthers the University's objective of excellence in research, scholarship,
and education by publishing worldwide in

Oxford New York

Auckland Cape Town Dar es Salaam Hong Kong Karachi
Kuala Lumpur Madrid Melbourne Mexico City Nairobi
New Delhi Shanghai Taipei Toronto
With offices in
Argentina Austria Brazil Chile Czech Republic France Greece
Guatemala Hungary Italy Japan South Korea Poland Portugal
Singapore Switzerland Thailand Turkey Ukraine Vietnam

Oxford is a registered trade mark of Oxford University Press
in the UK and in certain other countries

Published in the United States
by Oxford University Press Inc., New York

© Oxford University Press 2004

The moral rights of the author have been asserted

Database right Oxford University Press (maker)

Reprinted 2010

ISBN 978-0-19-925184-1

EDITOR-IN-CHIEF'S FOREWORD

The purpose of the five volumes of the Oxford History of the British Empire was to provide a comprehensive survey of the Empire from its beginning to end, to explore the meaning of British imperialism for the ruled as well as the rulers, and to study the significance of the British Empire as a theme in world history. The volumes in the Companion Series carry forward this purpose. They pursue themes that could not be covered adequately in the main series while incorporating recent research and providing fresh interpretations of significant topics.

Wm. Roger Louis

FOREWORD

NICHOLAS CANNY

A book entitled *Ireland and the British Empire* might well have been published any time between 1880 and 1904. Then the character of its author
and the nature of its contents would have been entirely predictable. Our
likely author would have been a public man-of-letters of Protestant background and sympathy who harboured grave reservations concerning the
various Home Rule measures that were then in prospect for Ireland. In
writing his book he would have been seeking to persuade his readers—
men and women of leisure and influence—to oppose any weakening of
Ireland's constitutional ties with Britain. He would have done this by
extolling the benefits that Ireland had derived from its long association
with Britain and its Empire, and by praising the contribution that people
of Irish birth or interest had made to Britain's imperial achievements from
the moment of the supposed conception of Empire during the reign
of Elizabeth I to the pinnacle of its achievement during that of Queen
Victoria.

The conceiver of this actual book of 2004 is an editor rather than a sole
author, and while, like his putative predecessor of a century ago, he is a
man, this cannot be taken as either necessary or predictable since three of
the nine essayists are women. Neither the editor's politico-religious preferences, nor those of his contributors, appear relevant to what is being discussed, and they seem to foster no illusions that what they write will
influence those who make political decisions today. None the less our
editor and his contributors are just as involved in polemic as our imagined
author of the Victorian era, and they too seek to uphold their position by
rehearsing Ireland's association with England and with Britain's imperial
achievements from the close of the sixteenth century to the present.

The issues being pursued by the several authors, as well as the editor,
are evident enough, even if the combatants to the debate are less clearly
identified. The most pressing question, which recurs in each succeeding
chapter, deliberates whether Ireland's relationship with England (after 1603
Britain) through the centuries can properly be described as colonial, and,

if so, when this inferior status was established and by whom. Then successive authors ponder why some of those Catholics of Ireland (and their descendants) who were displaced from their lands and positions by English and Scottish interlopers, subsequently became active participants in colonial ventures both in Britain's overseas possessions and in other foreign empires. This raises the further question of the motivation of those many Irish people in every century who attached themselves to Britain's overseas enterprises: were they as ideologically committed as, for example, the English and Scots participants, or did some Irish engage for purely mercenary motives while they awaited their opportunity to strike against Britain in the name of Ireland's cause? Another recurring issue is the extent to which Ireland was used as a laboratory in which imperial experiments were first tested before they were later applied on a broader canvas. This, it is suggested, might have been the case when colonies were being established during the earlier centuries, with their governance during the eighteenth and nineteenth centuries, and at the moment of their dissolution in the twentieth. Related to this is the issue of the 'gendering' of Empire and how the representation of imperial service in masculine terms impacted upon the behaviour of Irish people who served the cause. Another, fundamental question concerns the motivation behind England's (later Britain's) involvement with Ireland, and the issue of profit and loss to Britain from that engagement down through the centuries. Finally, and related to many of the foregoing, is the question of Irish communal allegiance. In crude terms this amounts to asking if those Irish people, both Protestant and Catholic, who served the British interest whether in Ireland or overseas can be regarded as true Irish people, or whether they became hybridized Britons.

Once the principal issues raised in this book have been discerned it remains to identify those with whom the authors are engaging in debate. The question whether, at various times, Ireland is better described as a kingdom or a colony has been hotly contested by historians of Ireland for several decades, and the authors here are obviously seeking to settle within an imperial frame that for which no resolution could be found when it was deliberated in a purely national context. The issue of balancing the profit against the losses that accrued to Britain as a result of its involvement with Ireland is also a historians' one, and most would agree with the various contributors who conclude that the ultimate consideration for rulers in Britain was that of ensuring that Ireland did not fall prey to

Britain's continental enemies. It strikes one that, as with the analogous issue of England's involvement with the Hundred Years War, a counter-factual question might have gone some way to exposing another dimension to this question. For the seventeenth century, for example, what would have been the political and social consequences for Britain if it had not been able, at the conclusion of each of its major military engagements, to offload many of its officers and fighting men in Ireland? Equally, what would have been the demographic and economic consequence for Scotland, as well as for England, if together they had not been able to discharge as many as 350,000 people to settle in Ireland over the course of that same century?

The issue concerning the morality of the colonized Irish becoming active colonizers is one that has been raised principally by scholars in other disciplines, and by those historians who, in the context of the history of the United States, ask whether, or when, the Irish became 'white'. The contributors to this volume make it clear that when located in the much wider context of the British Empire the issue is altogether more complex than the originators of the question assume it to be. They also suggest—although, to my mind, with insufficient insistence—that if people are to be judged by moral standards, it must be by those they themselves cherished rather than by those of the present generation. Essentially, as members of a Christian community, Irish Catholics of the early-modern centuries—no less than English and Irish Protestants—believed themselves, like Christians everywhere, to be duty bound to spread their faith to all humanity, and as European inheritors of the classical tradition—as educated members of the Old English community in Ireland conspicuously were—they would have accepted that civil standards had always made their principal strides forward when imposed forcefully in the wake of conquest. Those who spoke for the Old English community objected to plantations in Ireland on pragmatic rather than principled grounds: they had objected originally because they were not admitted as equals with English-born (and later with lowland Scots) people as participants in the settlement of lands that had once belonged to the Gaelic Irish, and they objected from the 1630s onwards because they themselves, like the Gaelic Irish before them, had became targets of the plantation programme sponsored by successive governments.

The question of whether Irish people who participated in many of Britain's imperial projects were truly committed to the cause or were

some type of fifth column is one that—like the 'gendering of Empire'—
has been brought to the fore by literary scholars and exponents of
post-colonial studies. The proposition that imperial service encouraged
subversion also derives from present-day politics in Northern Ireland, and
some of the answers hinted at here are an outgrowth of the polemics
associated with that conflict. In so far as the authors cite historical evidence, it relates first to the relative decline in the numbers of Irishmen
who volunteered for British service from the 1880s forward; second to
Roger Casement's belief that he might recruit a subversive regiment from
among those Irish who did fight at the front during the First World War;
third to the so-called mutiny of the Connaught Rangers in India in 1920
and to the supposed brutality and insensitivity of that regiment in India;
fourth to the numbers of Irish soldiers within British forces during the
First World War who subsequently fought for an Irish Republic both in
the Irish war for independence and in the subsequent Irish civil war; and
finally to the numbers of Irish people, Protestant as well as Catholic, who,
having served in the British Army, are thought to have engaged in subversive activity on both sides in the recent struggle in Northern Ireland.

There is a certain plausibility and appeal to this proposition, although it
lacks narratives from the experiences of real Irish people of humble backgrounds to match the vivid accounts of unflinching service to the Crown
that is rehearsed here from the career of Brigadier-General Reginald Dyer,
the hero or anti-hero in 1919 of the massacre at Amritsar, from that of
Tipperary-born Sir Michael O'Dwyer, the draconian Governor of the
Punjab, and from that of Field-Marshal Sir Henry Wilson from County
Longford, who rose to become Chief of the Imperial General Staff before
he was assassinated in 1923 by two agents of Michael Collins who pur-
ported to be executing orders that had been issued before the Anglo-Irish
Treaty had been signed. Our authors are, for the most part, rehearsing such
evidence as has been cited in the secondary literature which hints that Irish
people (whether Protestant or Catholic) from comfortable circumstances
did not forget either their local origins or allegiances during their military
careers but seldom permitted such loyalties to hinder their commitment to
being exemplary officers of the Crown. Thus, to the extent that there is any
substance to the allegation that people of Irish birth were natural subversives within Crown forces, it rests on the behaviour of those whose poverty
left them with no option but to enlist. In so far as it is appropriate
for the writer of a Foreword to engage in such a debate, I can cite the

experiences of two Irish people from humble backgrounds who engaged in imperial service and whose life stories might occasion pause before we give final endorsement to the model now gaining favour in the current literature.

The first narrative concerns the career of P.[atrick] F.[estus] Joyce, a younger child of a large family from Cashel in County Galway, where the Connemara rock is so inhospitable that one can hardly grace those who rented holdings in the nineteenth century with the description farmer. After he had completed his primary schooling, Joyce was faced with the prospect of seeking a livelihood outside Ireland. Emigration to the United States, where a sister, Bridget, had settled in Boston, was theoretically possible but not in the 1890s, a decade of recession there. The solution came when the local landlord, who had been providing Joyce with occasional employment while he waited to make a career move, alerted him to the possibility of applying for admission to the British police force being recruited to maintain order in the increasingly important port of Singapore. His application proved successful. Joyce was provided with the necessary rudimentary training for police work, and he was reasonably satisfied with his posting until he was denied promotion to the rank of sergeant after he had passed the requisite examination. At that point he was assured that career advancement would be available to him if he volunteered to serve in any one of the police forces then being recruited by the British government to be put at the disposal of the various sultans who ruled over the independent provinces of the Malaya peninsula, where Britain had established substantial economic interests, notably in sugar and rubber, and where commercial activity was handled principally by a settler Chinese population rather than the native Malays. Joyce was attracted by the opportunity, and the promised promotion duly came his way, ostensibly in the service of the Sultan of Kedah in north-western Malaya but with his salary actually being paid from London.

Consequently, in 1905, P. F. Joyce, by then a Police Inspector, was able to return to Ireland on a long vacation, where he enlisted the parish priest of Clifden, the market town closest to his native Cashel, to arrange a marriage for him so that he might return to Kedah with an Irish bride. Negotiations were entered into with Margaret Connolly of Clifden who, after a short courtship, became the wife of P. F. Joyce. She was to be treated to an exotic honeymoon on the return journey from Clifden to Malaya, initially to London by train and boat via Galway, Dublin, and

Holyhead, and then from London by P&O liner via Suez, Aden, and Singapore. Life in a remote police station in the intensely humid and malaria-infested jungle of Malaya was even more exotic, not to say uncomfortable. The hazards of living there were brought home to the couple when, in 1906, Margaret had to be conveyed by elephant through the jungle in search of Western medical help when she experienced difficulty in child-birth. The assistance which was eventually found was sufficient to save her life but not that of the infant, who was either born dead or expired soon after delivery. Whichever, a baptismal service was conducted and the couple displayed their political as well as their religious attachments when the infant was christened Redmond Joyce, after John Redmond, leader of the Irish Parliamentary Party.

After this trauma the couple sought to resume a normal life together but when Margaret became pregnant for a second time she returned to her native Clifden, where a daughter, Helen Joyce, was born on 16 June 1908. Remittances from Malaya, via London, were sufficient to keep wife and child in relative comfort, while P. F. Joyce persisted in Kedah until 1919 when he retired from the Sultan's service, at the rank of Assistant Commissioner, and was permitted a special pension and gratuity on grounds of ill health, given that he had suffered from acute malaria for many years. In the meantime, in 1911, he had taken advantage of a long vacation to re-unite with his wife in Clifden, where he had the opportunity to see, and be photographed with, his three-year-old daughter. Otherwise he knew of what was happening in Ireland during those tumultuous years through personal and official correspondence (until that was disrupted by the First World War), and through the newspapers. However, the political changes that were underway in Ireland did not divert him from the decision he had previously taken with his wife to live out his retirement in Clifden. From the time of his return to Ireland in 1919 until his death in 1942, the family lived on his pension augmented by the proceeds of a small retail business he established in the town of Clifden.

This story of P. F. Joyce might be a Victorian tale of modest success through service to Empire, but, on a superficial level it also seems to endorse what has been said of the loyalty of those from poor backgrounds in Ireland who made their careers by that path. P. F. Joyce became a policeman in both Singapore and Malaya by happenstance rather than out of any ideological commitment, and what we know of him suggests that his primary loyalty was to himself, to his family, to his religion, to his local community in Ireland, and to Ireland, where he had always aspired to retire whenever he had the means to do so. However, his rapid promotion, the special pension he was granted in 1919, the lavish illuminated address and silver casket with which he was presented by the Sultan of Kedah on behalf of the Chinese community of the town of Lunas, all suggest that he was diligent, punctilious, honest, ambitious, and dedicated to his duties. The final proof of what loyalty to Empire meant to him comes from his years of retirement. When the Second World War was underway, Joyce offered himself for emergency police service in London because he believed it was his duty to do so, and it came very much as a relief to his wife and daughter, who did not share his sense of obligation, that his record of ill health resulted in his offer being declined. Thus, if the Empire served P. F. Joyce well, he gave loyal service in return and always displayed gratitude for the livelihood and social uplift with which it had provided him.

It has proved possible for me to provide these details on the career of P. F. Joyce because he was my maternal grandfather, and the crucial turning points in his career have been rehearsed to me by family members as well as by the photographs and memorabilia from his imperial service that have survived. The second person whose imperial service can be detailed is J.[osephine] M.[ary] Canny, my aunt on my father's side, and I learned these details from her own personal narrations since she survived to the age of ninety-four. Josephine Canny was one of nine children raised on a thirty-acre sheep-farm of limestone land in Roundfort, Hollymount, County Mayo. After the completion of primary schooling in Roundfort she considered a career in nursing but during the early 1920s this aspiration became a possibility for her only because an older sister, Delia, who had emigrated to Australia, and some cousins in that country, advised her to take advantage of assisted passage to Australia where, without any charge to herself, she would be able to train as a certified nurse in St Vincent's Hospital, Melbourne. Having completed her training in Melbourne, however, Josephine Canny found that there was no prospect of permanent employment in Australia, which had been hit harder than most countries by the Great Depression.

Confronted with this grim reality, Josephine Canny earned sufficient money from nursing private patients in their own homes to meet the cost of a return journey to Europe, where prospects of salaried employment were somewhat better. She recalled that on the journey home she became acquainted with a fellow passenger who advised her to make application for employment in the Queen Alexander Nursing Corps (QAs) of the British Army after she had earned a further qualification in midwifery, which was necessary in peacetime for an application to succeed. With this in mind she undertook a one-year course in midwifery at the Rotunda Hospital in Dublin and the following year she was interviewed for and accepted into the QAs. She was barely established in her post when Britain entered into the Second World War, and J. M. Canny was to serve right through the war in a variety of Western theatres, retaining pleasant memories of some, and horrific ones of others. Dedicated service brought its rewards in the shape of rapid promotion, ultimately to the rank of major, and a decoration for bravery.

After the war J. M. Canny continued in service and was posted variously in West Africa, in Berlin during the airlift, and as matron in charge of a military hospital in the south of England. My first meeting with her was when she was home on long leave in between some two of these assignments. I distinctly remember being the grateful recipient of all her Irish coins as she prepared for her return journey to England, and I recall being puzzled that she had to pack her very bulky grey-blue uniform and great coat as she made her way to the boat in Dublin with a view to unpacking and wearing it once she reached Holyhead. Her career in the post-war years, and especially those spent in England, were obviously more placid than what she had previously endured but when she was confronted with yet another foreign posting (this time probably to Aden) she decided to take early retirement and, with two sisters who were also able to retire, she purchased a house in suburban Dublin, where she lived until advancing years and declining health forced her to find refuge in a sequence of nursing homes.

As with the previous narration, service in the British forces was the outcome of need and chance rather than of vocation. However, J. M. Canny was always grateful for the career the British Army had provided, and while she was conscious that she had given of her best to what had proven a difficult life's assignment, she was also satisfied that she had been treated equitably. During her years of service she maintained regular correspondence with her family members when the mails were not interrupted by war, but equally well after her retirement to Dublin she maintained correspondence with many of her former colleagues in Britain. Moreover, she enjoyed occasional visits from other QAs who had retired to Ireland, and, while her health permitted, she attended the annual reception provided by the British ambassador to Ireland for retired officers of the British forces resident in Ireland.

While in service, Josephine Canny always remained conscious of being Irish, she took a lively interest in Irish affairs, and, despite their incompatibility, she had as much admiration for Mr de Valera as for Mr Churchill in their separate spheres. She was able to reconcile conflicting loyalties as long as she could keep them separate, and it was only in the spiritual sphere that such compartmentalization failed her. This conflict resulted from a marriage proposal she received, towards the end of her career and after her child-bearing years were past, from an Irish colonel in the British Army. She was satisfied that the officer in question would make an agreeable husband in every way, except that he was a divorced man and she a practising Catholic. The spiritual counsel she received, including that from her Army chaplain, was firmly against marriage, and the more sympathetic hearing she received from family members did not outweigh her respect for official Catholic teaching. This traumatic personal struggle may well have been more responsible than the prospect of another overseas posting in deciding J. M. Canny to take early retirement from Army service.

These two studies of two Irish people of humble origins who made their careers in British service at different times and in different capacities indicate that each experienced conflicts of loyalty and allegiance but in neither instance is there the slightest hint that such conflicts tempted them to become subversives. Neither person can be considered typical, any more than Dyer, O'Dwyer, or Wilson is typical of those from comfortable Irish backgrounds who joined the officer corps from the outset. The point is that case studies of the humble in origin can be constructed, and it is only when many careers are thus pieced together that we can move more closely to advancing firm judgements about the reception, behaviour, and loyalty of Irish people from poor or modest circumstances who made careers in the various official services of the British Empire.

This conclusion also makes the point that the real strength of this book is that each of the essayists points to where fresh research is required while also offering an assessment of current knowledge on the Irish experience with the British Empire over several centuries. Another strength is that it relates events in Ireland to those that the same British authorities had to deal with in other parts of the Empire, and indicates that solutions that might have appeared easy when looked at from an Irish perspective were altogether more difficult of resolution for those government officials who had to assess the impact decisions made concerning Ireland might have in other parts of a vast Empire. In so far as an opportunity has been lost it is in comparing issues and tensions that were peculiar to the Irish experience with the British Empire with analogous tensions in other European Empires of the same time. One such comparison that comes to mind relates to the position and activities of Catholic missionaries in different European Empires. For the moment one might reflect on the image of the Irish missionary priest seeking to spread British civility as well as Catholicism in Africa compared with that of Dutch-speaking priests from Flanders and the southern Netherlands seeking, in the Congo, to advance Francophone Belgian culture along with the Christian message in a language which was not their own. The ease with which it is possible to point to such comparisons is the best proof that the editor and authors of this collection on Ireland and the British Empire have done their work well.

Nicholas Canny
National University of Ireland, Galway

PREFACE

This book presents a history of Ireland and the British Empire from the origins of the Empire in the early modern era through its demise in the contemporary period. The course of modern Irish history was largely determined by the rise, expansion, and decline of the British Empire. And the course of British imperial history, from the age of Atlantic expansion to the age of decolonization, was moulded in part by Irish experience. The authors of this book seek to determine the shifting meanings of Empire, imperialism, and colonialism in Irish history over time. They examine each phase of Ireland's relationship to the Empire: conquest and colonization in the sixteenth and seventeenth centuries; consolidation of Ascendancy rule in the eighteenth century; formal integration under the Act of Union in the period 1801–1921; and, thereafter, independence and the eventual withdrawal of Ireland from the Commonwealth in 1949. In addition, several of the contributors examine the participation of Irish people in the Empire overseas, as merchants and migrants, as soldiers and administrators, and as missionaries. The book also considers the ways in which British policies in Ireland served as a laboratory for social, administrative, and constitutional policies subsequently adopted elsewhere in the Empire, and how Irish nationalism provided inspiration for independence movements in other colonies.

The nine chapters of the book are arranged in a flexible chronological framework with common themes interwoven throughout the narrative. After an opening chapter that surveys the topic as a whole, the second chapter examines English colonial expansion in Ireland in the early modern era, from the early sixteenth century through the end of the seventeenth. The third chapter considers Ireland's position and role in the British Empire from the 1690s through the Act of Union. The fourth chapter is devoted to the story of the Irish in the Empire at large over the full period covered by the book. Chapter 5 examines Ireland's, and then Northern Ireland's, colonial status and imperial involvement from the Act of Union to the outbreak of the 'Troubles' in Northern Ireland in the 1960s, while the sixth chapter considers the relationship between Irish fiction and Empire under the Union and in its aftermath. Chapter 7 offers a history of Irish politics and nationalism in an imperial context, from the Home Rule movement of the 1880s to Ireland's departure from the Commonwealth and subsequent reorientation toward the European Union. The eighth chapter examines the writings of historians and cultural critics on Ireland and the Empire. The final chapter considers postcolonial Ireland, with particular reference to politics, culture, and the construction of a new nation state.

I would especially like to thank Wm. Roger Louis for inviting me to produce this volume and for providing, through his own work, an extraordinary example of how to go about the task. I am grateful also to Ruth Parr, Anne Gelling, and the editorial team at Oxford University Press for guiding the book from inception to completion. I spent several months carefully planning the book with prospective authors in mind. Once the structure of the book was clear, I wrote to the prospective authors; each of them signed on enthusiastically, a clear sign of how large and important a gap in scholarship the book would fill. During the three years of writing, editing, re-rewriting, and re-editing, all of the authors responded promptly, graciously, and instructively to my criticisms and suggestions, and for this I salute them. I am also grateful to Craig Bailey, Elizabeth Butler Cullingford, Geoffrey Parker, and Paige Reynolds for their help with aspects of particular chapters. Above all, I want to thank my colleagues and students in the History Department and the Irish Studies Program at Boston College—Kristen Adrien, Christopher Caradec, Adam Chill, Claire Connolly, Kate Costello-Sullivan, Mike Cronin, Anthony Daly, Mark Doyle, Robin Fleming, Burke Griggs, Ruth-Ann Harris, Marjorie Howes, Ely Janis, Margaret Kelleher, Vera Kreilkamp, Niamh Lynch, Timothy Lynch, Damien Murray, David Northrup, Breandán Ó Buachalla, Philip O'Leary, Prasannan Parthasarathi, Rob Savage, James Smith, Nadia Smith, Andy Storey, and Peter Weiler. Their criticisms significantly improved every aspect of this book and their companionship provided an ideal setting in which to produce it.

Kevin Kenny
Boston College

CONTENTS

ABBREVIATIONS AND LOCATION OF MANUSCRIPT SOURCES

BL   British Library

National Archives, Public Record Office (PRO), London:

CAB	Cabinet office
CO	Colonial Office
CRO	Commonwealth Relations Office
DO	Dominions Office
PREM	Prime Minister's Office
PROB	Probate
WO	War Office
PRO	Documents acquired by the Public Record Office by gift, deposit, or purchase

Public Record Office of Northern Ireland (PRONI), Belfast

CAB	Cabinet office

LIST OF CONTRIBUTORS

THOMAS BARTLETT (Ph.D., Queen's University, Belfast) is Professor of Modern Irish History at University College Dublin and a member of the Royal Irish Academy. His publications include *The Fall and Rise of the Irish Nation: The Catholic Question, 1690–1830* (1992) and an edition of *The Life of Theobald Wolfe Tone* (1998). He is co-editor, with Keith Jeffery, of *The Cambridge Military History of Ireland* (1996).

NICHOLAS CANNY (Ph.D., Pennsylvania) is Professor of History and Director of the Centre for the Study of Human Settlement and Historical Change at the National University of Ireland, Galway. A member of the Royal Irish Academy and *Academia Europaea*, he is author of *The Elizabethan Conquest of Ireland: A Pattern Established, 1565–76* (1976), *Kingdom and Colony: Ireland in the Atlantic World, 1560–1800* (1988), and *Making Ireland British, 1580–1650* (2001); and editor of *Europeans on the Move: Studies on European Migration, 1500–1800* (1994) and *The Oxford History of the British Empire*, Volume I.

JOE CLEARY (Ph.D., Columbia) is Lecturer in English at the National University of Ireland, Maynooth. His research interests are in twentieth-century Irish literature and cinema, colonial and post-colonial literature and theory, and Renaissance drama. His publications include *Literature, Partition and Nation-State: Culture and Conflict in Ireland, Israel and Palestine* (2001). He is co-editor, with Claire Connolly, of the forthcoming *Cambridge Companion to Modern Irish Culture*.

STEPHEN HOWE (D.Phil., Oxford) teaches contemporary history at Ruskin College, Oxford. He has been Research Fellow at Corpus Christi College, Oxford and a *New Statesman* columnist. He is editor of *Lines of Dissent: Writing from the New Statesman, 1913–1988* (1988); and author of *Anticolonialism in British Politics: The Left and the End of Empire, 1918–1964* (1993), *Afrocentrism: Mythical Pasts and Imagined Homes* (1998), *Ireland and Empire: Colonial Legacies in Irish History and Culture* (2000), and *Empire: A Very Short Introduction* (2002).

ALVIN JACKSON (D.Phil., Oxford) is Professor of Modern History at Queen's University, Belfast. He was a British Academy Research Reader in the Humanities in 2000–02. His publications include *The Ulster Party: Irish Unionists in the*

House of Commons, 1884–1911 (1989); *Sir Edward Carson* (1993); *Colonel Edward Saunderson: Land and Loyalty in Victorian Ireland* (1995); *Ireland, 1798–1998: Politics and War* (1999); and *Home Rule: An Irish History, 1800–2000* (2003).

KEVIN KENNY (Ph.D., Columbia) is Professor of History at Boston College. His specialty is the history of migration, diaspora, and labour in the Atlantic world in the eighteenth and nineteenth centuries. He has published in the *Journal of American History, American Quarterly,* the *Journal of American Ethnic History,* and *Labor History.* He is author of *Making Sense of the Molly Maguires* (1998) and *The American Irish: A History* (2000), and editor of *New Directions in Irish-American History* (2003).

VERA KREILKAMP (Ph.D., City University, New York) is Professor of English at Pine Manor College and Visiting Professor in the Irish Studies Program at Boston College. Her research fields are Irish art and landscape and Ascendancy fiction. She is author of *The Anglo-Irish Novel and the Big House* (1998), editor of the catalogue for the exhibition *Éire/Land* (2003), and co-editor of *America's Eye: Irish Painting from the Collection of Brian P. Burns* (1996). She is also co-editor of *Éire-Ireland: An Interdisciplinary Journal of Irish Studies.*

DEIRDRE McMAHON (Ph.D., Cambridge) is Lecturer in History at Mary Immaculate College, the University of Limerick. She is a Research Associate of the Centre for Contemporary Irish History at Trinity College, Dublin and author of *Republicans and Imperialists: Anglo-Irish Relations in the 1930s* (1984), along with several articles on Ireland and the Commonwealth. She is currently working on a two-volume biography of Eamon de Valera.

JANE H. OHLMEYER (Ph.D., Trinity College, Dublin) holds the Erasmus Smith Chair of Modern History at Trinity College, Dublin. She is the author of *Civil War and Restoration in the Three Stuart Kingdoms: The Career of Randal MacDonnell, Marquis of Antrim, 1609–1683* (1993; 2001). She is editor of *Ireland from Independence to Occupation, 1641–1660* (1995) and *The Civil Wars: A Military History of England, Scotland and Ireland, 1638–1660* (1998; 2002); and co-editor of *Political Thought in Seventeenth-Century Ireland: Kingdom or Colony?* (2000) and *The Stuart Kingdoms in the Seventeenth Century: Awkward Neighbours* (2002).

1

Ireland and the British Empire: An Introduction

KEVIN KENNY

Ireland has often been described as both the first and the last colony of the British Empire. Just as often, historians have omitted the Irish case from British imperial history altogether. How, then, is one to write the history of Ireland and the British Empire? Was Ireland a sister kingdom, or equal partner, in a larger British archipelagic state? Was it, by virtue of its location and strategic importance, the Empire's most subjugated colony? Or was it both simultaneously, its ostensible constitutional equality masking the reality of its colonial status? Questions of this sort can only be answered historically: Ireland's relationship with its more powerful neighbouring island—and with the global Empire which that island eventually produced—developed and changed over time. So too did the form, extent, and meaning of the British Empire. Modern Irish history unfolded in tandem with the rise, unprecedented expansion, and eventual decline of the Empire; and, just as Irish history does not make sense without this imperial entanglement, British imperial history assumes its full dimensions only if Ireland is included.[1]

This book offers a history of Ireland's relationship to the British Empire from the early modern era through the contemporary period. In seeking to determine the nature of this historical relationship, it moves beyond two conceptions that stand at opposite extremes in much popular and academic discourse. The first of these holds that Ireland was never,

---

[1] Whether, why, and how to include Ireland were the subject of much discussion during the planning stages of the five-volume *Oxford History of the British Empire* (hereafter *OHBE*). In the end, Ireland became the subject of six chapters: *Vol. I,* Jane H. Ohlmeyer, 'Civilizinge of those rude partes: Colonization within Britain and Ireland, 1580s–1640s' and T. C. Barnard, 'New Opportunities for British Settlement: Ireland, 1650–1700'; *Vol. II,* Thomas Bartlett, '"This famous island set in a Virginian sea": Ireland in the British Empire, 1690–1801'; *Vol. III,* David Fitzpatrick, 'Ireland and the Empire'; *Vol. IV,* Deirdre McMahon, 'Ireland and the Empire-Commonwealth, 1900–1948'; and *Vol. V,* David Harkness, 'Ireland'.

properly speaking, a British 'colony', or that it was at best unique, bafflingly anomalous, or, more vaguely, 'semi-colonial'. The contrary position asserts that Ireland was always and self-evidently nothing other than a British colony. Neither position is of much use to the historian. Both posit some ideal colonial form against which the Irish case can be judged as either adequate or deficient, but no such form existed in historical practice. As Joe Cleary puts it, the British Empire 'comprised a heterogeneous collection of trade colonies, Protectorates, Crown colonies, settlement colonies, administrative colonies, Mandates, trade ports, naval bases, Dominions, and dependencies'.[2] The relations of these constituent parts to the metropolis varied considerably across space and time and they followed divergent paths towards independence.

Ireland's relationship to the British Empire has been the subject of much confusion and controversy. 'Most historians would concur that the history of modern Ireland has been intimately associated with that of the British Empire', Stephen Howe observes; but beyond that basic agreement, 'there is wide, often deep, sometimes bitter dispute'.[3] Geography alone has dictated that this should be so: Ireland was too near England to be left alone, but this very proximity helps explain why the country's status within the Empire has been so frequently ignored, questioned, or at best defensively asserted. The term 'colony' brings to mind far-flung 'exotic' possessions, often marked by extreme racial subjugation. Although the Irish were frequently cast as racially inferior, they lacked the requisite quality of distance.

The peculiarities of Ireland's constitutional position muddied the waters still further. From 1541 onwards Ireland enjoyed the formal status of a kingdom. In the eighteenth century it had its own Parliament (though this body met infrequently and had little autonomy except briefly in the 1780s and 1790s). Under the Act of Union, from 1801 to 1921, Ireland was ostensibly an equal partner in the United Kingdom. When these constitutional considerations are combined with geographical and cultural proximity, it becomes less surprising that the great theorists of empire—Hobson, Lenin, and Bukharin among them—all excluded Ireland from their accounts. Ironically, the ubiquity of the English language in modern Ireland may also have lent support to this exclusion, even though it had been partly achieved through the eradication of Gaelic culture.

---

[2] See below, p. 253.   [3] See below, p. 220.

Ambiguous, anomalous, complex, exceptional, unique, or even para-doxical: these are the words most commonly used to describe Ireland's historical relationship with the British Empire. Yet the past is often am-biguous and always complex. Categories of this sort cannot take us very far in historical inquiry. It is hard to see how history could ever actually be paradoxical (false, absurd, contrary to known laws) even if it often appears contradictory. And claims to exceptionalism—the basis of all nationally bounded histories—carry less and less weight in an age when historians are busily transcending the nation-state and framing their narratives in broader transnational, comparative, or global contexts.

Assertions that Ireland's place in the Empire was unique or anomalous merely reiterate the shopworn theme of exceptionalism. Such claims are no more or less true of Ireland than of any other part of the Empire. Each of Britain's many possessions was distinctive; none was anomalous. All of them shared a common history as parts of a larger entity, the British Empire. Ireland's defining peculiarity was that it stood at the world's metropolitan centre; but it was no less a British possession for that. If, in the nineteenth and twentieth centuries, India represented one form of colony, Nigeria a second, and Australia a third, then Ireland represented yet another, combining some aspects of these three with highly particular characteristics of it own.

Within this larger, unifying context, historical inquiry reveals structures and patterns, not just contingency, complexity, and ambiguity. Historians can therefore ask practical—some might say old-fashioned—questions concerning historical causation and influence. Why did the English (and later the British) state so badly need to conquer Ireland? Why and how did Britain retain control of Ireland for several centuries through the modern era? How is this form of control to be described, how did it change over time, and where does it fit into the larger pattern of British imperial history? Historians can also ask (and they excel at answering) particular, temporally specific questions that require extensive and detailed empirical inquiry. What was the relationship between Ireland, Britain, and the Empire at a given point in time, whether 1641, 1801, 1886, or 1922? How did this relationship develop historically? Finally, how do the answers to all these questions help us understand both Irish history and the history of the British Empire? The following eight chapters of this volume, arranged in broad chronological sequence, pursue these questions in various ways. Together they constitute not just a collection of essays that happen to deal with Ireland and the British Empire, but a sustained and cohesive historical interpretation of the subject.

Ireland was an imperial possession of a particular sort, and the purpose of this book is to determine what sort of possession it was in order to establish and explain its position in the British Empire, and how that position changed over time. In addressing these problems the authors adopt a dual strategy. First, they subject concepts such as empire, imperialism, and colonialism to critical scrutiny rather than treating them as givens, so that the concepts become objects, and not just tools, of historical inquiry. If such concepts are to be used in Irish history, they cannot be deployed as though their meaning were timeless and self-evident. They derive their plausibility only from historical inquiry and cannot be used as a priori analytical categories. 'The very terminology involved—colonialism, imperialism, postcoloniality, neo-colonialism and so on—is intensely, complexly contested in global as well as in specifically Irish debates', Howe remarks. 'These terms, moreover, are often used in loosely allusive or even metaphorical ways'.[4] This book attempts to give the terms historical meaning.

A second aspect of Ireland's imperial history is the role of Irish men and women, not simply as imperial subjects, but also as players in the Empire at large: as migrants and settlers, merchants and adventurers, soldiers and administrators, doctors and missionaries. Several of the contributors pursue this theme. As Alvin Jackson puts it, 'Irish people who might be constrained at home also had free access to the Empire and to the social and economic opportunities it provided. For Ireland, therefore, the Empire was simultaneously a chain and a key: it was a source both of constraint and of liberation'.[5] Opponents of the notion that Ireland was ever a 'real' colony are liable to take Irish imperial participation as grist to their mill; proponents of colonial models, on the contrary, sometimes find this participation deeply troubling. Neither position makes sense historically: participation of this sort has always been a standard feature of imperial history and in itself has no bearing on Ireland's colonial status. Throughout history colonized people have fought and died on behalf of the empires that ruled them.[6]

---

[4] See below, p. 221.
[5] See below, p. 136.
[6] See below, pp. 92–95, 104–112.

Not the least dilemma in writing history is where to begin. In the case of Ireland and the British Empire, should one start, for example, in the 1570s when, in Jane Ohlmeyer's words, 'plantation became an instrument of royal policy and private enterprise was put to work for the purposes of the state'?[7] The early plantations were not successful, though by the opening decades of the seventeenth century the more extensive and enduring plantation of Ulster was getting underway. Given these precarious beginnings, perhaps the Cromwellian conquest or even the settlement of 1691 would provide a better starting point? Or should one go back in time, to the early Tudors or, ultimately, the Norman conquest? There are some obvious objections to starting so far back as the twelfth century. The Norman conquest certainly involved colonization and it would be a useful exercise to compare it with the latter settlements under Elizabeth, James I, Cromwell, and William of Orange. Giraldus Cambrensis (Gerald of Wales) penned his prototypical denunciations of Irish barbarity in his *Topographia Hibernica* as early as 1185. Thus, when Edmund Spenser and others followed suit in the sixteenth century, they were drawing on precedents long since established. But early modern England, as Ohlmeyer observes, differed from medieval England in ways that were critical to the onset of colonial expansion: a more powerful centralized state, the availability of aggressive commercial capital, the militant providentialism of Reformation Protestantism, and on the basis of these, a commitment to large-scale permanent settlement of expropriated territory.

Most historians would agree that the British Empire, in the familiar sense of overseas expansion, conquest, and settlement, came into existence only in the late sixteenth or early seventeenth century. There was no British Empire, either in terminology or in fact, before then.[8] Although early usage of the term 'empire' can be traced back to the 1570s, the term 'British' did not enter into common currency until the accession of James I in 1603, and the two terms merged in their modern connotation later still. As David Armitage notes, 'no lasting colonies were planted before 1603 (in fact, none could be said to be permanent until the late 1620s),

---

[7] See below, p. 38.

[8] Consequently, Jane Ohlmeyer favours the term 'English Empire' in her chapter, whereas 'British Empire' is used elsewhere throughout this volume. See David Armitage, *Ideological Origins of the British Empire* (Cambridge, 2000), especially pp. 1–60; Nicholas Canny, 'Introduction', in Canny, ed., *OHBE. Vol. I. The Origins of Empire: British Overseas Enterprise to the Close of the Seventeenth Century* (Oxford, 1998), pp. 1–2.

privateering was only a euphemism for piracy, and the horizons of most Elizabethans remained firmly fixed on the Three Kingdoms and their problems rather than the wider world'.[9] Until at least the mid-seventeenth century, English conceptions of empire rarely extended beyond the North Atlantic archipelago (the present-day United Kingdom and Irish Republic), notwithstanding the establishment of numerous settler colonies in the Americas. Asserting an unbroken continuity between the Norman colonization of Ireland and Britain's early modern imperial Atlantic adventures is therefore implausible and all the more so because so many descendants of the Norman colonists became Gaelicised 'Old English' who would resist the 'New English' expansion into Ireland in the sixteenth and seventeenth centuries.

If the twelfth century is too early a starting point, what then of the fifteenth century, with the incursions of Henry VII? Poynings' Law, passed in 1494, declared that the Irish Parliament could meet only with the King's permission and that it could not pass laws unless they were previously approved by the King and his English Council. English involvement in Ireland at this time had little to do with imperialism in its high Victorian sense and was instead chiefly a matter of domestic dynastic struggles. Such internal struggles for mastery, however, were precisely what 'empire' or *imperium* meant in this early period. European colonialism originated as an internal rather than an external process; only when dominion had been established did overseas empires gradually emerge.[10] And there was one damningly simple reason why Ireland had to be conquered: strategic necessity. To the extent that England, and later Britain, counted Spain and France as antagonists, Ireland's fate was sealed: no backdoor for an invasion could possibly be left open. As Tom Bartlett puts it: 'even if Ireland had been barren rock, its proximity to both continental Europe and to England meant that it constituted in English eyes an all-too-convenient base for foreign enemies and a likely haven for domestic rebels and malcontents'.[11] Control over Ireland in turn provided the security whereby England could embark on its wider imperial adventures in the Atlantic world.

The full-scale colonization of Ireland got underway in the late sixteenth and early seventeenth century. Ohlmeyer examines a wide range of English

---

[9] David Armitage, 'Literature and Empire', in Canny, ed., *OHBE. Vol. I*, p. 101.
[10] Armitage, *Ideological Origins*.   [11] See below, p. 61.

policies and practices in Ireland—military, political, administrative, legal, religious, and cultural—and concludes that together 'these strategies, though often couched in the rhetoric of civility, effectively amounted to a form of imperialism that sought to exploit Ireland for England's political and economic advantage and to Anglicize the native population'.[12] Perhaps the most powerful strategy, she finds, was the introduction of English law, which allowed for the confiscation and redistribution of land, ranging from the adjustment of titles to mass expropriation and the plantation of settlers, all of which helped destroy 'the economic foundations of the old Gaelic order'.[13] This process of Irish colonization was not some anomalous sideshow to Empire: it was at the very heart of British imperial expansion. The settlements on both sides of the Atlantic, as is well known, featured the same types of corporate structures and commercial enterprise, the same sorts of migrants, and in several prominent cases—Humphrey Gilbert, for example, or Walter Ralegh—the same people. Strategically, economically, and culturally, English colonialism achieved its earliest triumphs in Ireland, establishing a model for other ventures further afield.

As in most examples of colonial history, the Irish case involved the co-option, or co-operation, of local élites, and presented significant advantages to certain sectors of the native society. 'As a result, rather than being seen as passive victims', Ohlmeyer observes, 'many Irish Catholics proved reactive and responsive to imperial schemes'. Disempowered and dispossessed Catholics were certainly 'victims of English imperialism', but many Irish people, Catholic as well as Protestant, took advantage of their imperial setting to set up as traders and merchants.[14] During the 1650s and 1660s, Ireland was probably the main source of white migration to the West Indies, in the form of indentured servants and to a lesser extent convicts and prisoners of war. The islands were also populated by a small but powerful group of Irish merchants and planters, typically the younger sons of prominent Catholic families. The economic benefits of Empire to an enterprising few would be a constant theme in Irish history thereafter.

If Ireland's history was entirely bound up with the origins of the British Empire in the early modern era, how are we to characterize its imperial

---

[12] See below, pp. 28–29.
[13] See below, p. 51.
[14] See below, pp. 29, 57.

status thereafter? Ireland's constitutional status in the eighteenth century, as a formal kingdom with its own nominal Parliament, distinguished it from the contemporary American colonies and from subsequent colonies of the British Empire. Some historians have argued that eighteenth-century Ireland cannot therefore be described in colonial terms but was instead more akin to an early modern *ancien régime*. As Bartlett points out, however, there is no reason why features of both types of society could not co-exist within the same polity: nominal status as a dependent kingdom only poorly concealed what was clearly a state of colonial subjection. If Ireland, from the perspective of the Protestant Ascendancy, was ostensibly a 'sister kingdom' to England and Scotland, English politicians nonetheless dismissed it 'as variously a depending kingdom, a foreign country or a child-colony: in no case was equality, much less joint sovereignty, on offer'.[15]

Irish history, to be sure, was complicated by the tripartite religious division between Anglicans, Dissenters, and Catholics. The Irish élite in the eighteenth and nineteenth centuries was of English Protestant extraction and had arrived in the country only recently. The members of this Ascendancy class belonged to the established Anglican Church; Ireland's Presbyterians, by definition, did not, and consequently they suffered a variety of legal and cultural disabilities. Yet, although the Irish Anglican élite belonged to the British social and imperial ruling classes, they never did so on equal terms. They were, in the end, Irishmen of a particular sort. Accordingly, the more politically minded among them, ranging from Jonathan Swift to William Molyneux, began to assert their rights—'as freeborn Englishmen'—against metropolitan condescension. The result was a distinctively Irish form of 'colonial' or 'settler' nationalism, which Bartlett describes as 'a potent mixture of triumphalism, anxiety, and wounded *amour-propre*'.[16]

Deeply attached, like colonial settlers in many other places, to the land where they settled, these Irish Protestants strongly resented several aspects of English rule. Irish political leaders fought against restraints on trade, against the bestowal of Irish peerages on English outsiders, and against discrimination in appointments to the judiciary, the armed forces, and the Established Church. Despite British fears, however, they did not seek

---

[15] See below, p. 68.
[16] See below, p. 70.

independence for Ireland, let alone a breach with the Empire. The more radical threat came from Ulster Presbyterians, descendants of the Scottish planters who had settled the northern province in the seventeenth century. By the mid-eighteenth century, these Irish Presbyterians occupied a precarious middle ground between zones of perceived 'civilization' and 'barbarism' on both sides of the Atlantic ocean. They served as an economic, military, and cultural buffer between Catholics and Anglicans in Ulster and between colonial governments and frontier Indians in North America. But, as Protestants of the wrong sort, they could never belong to the élites whose interests they protected. Their dissatisfaction at the religious, political, and cultural disabilities they endured would culminate in the United Irishmen's rebellion of 1798.

Because of Ireland's distinctive religious history, then, its eighteenth-century nationalist movements were led not by Catholics, as one might expect, but by Protestants. Matters came to a head with the American Revolution, which inspired Irish Protestant patriots to push, successfully, for free access to colonial trade and the repeal of Poynings' law, culminating in a newly empowered national Parliament in 1782. Yet, as Bartlett demonstrates, the success of the American and then the French Revolution, while inspirational to Irish patriots and republicans, may actually have sounded the death-knell for Irish autonomy (not to mention independence). Each of the colonies in America had some sort of legislature of its own; their removal from the Empire made Ireland's legislative autonomy appear irregular and threatening. At the same time, America's secession and the threat of republican France heightened concerns about unity and stability at the heart of the Empire. With popular Catholic nationalism on the rise by the 1790s, the threat was considerable. Catholic and Presbyterian discontent would culminate at the end of the decade in the greatest insurrection in Irish history.[17]

As soon as the insurrection was suppressed militarily, the London government moved to abolish the autonomous Dublin Parliament. Under the Act of Union, Ireland was formally assimilated into the British constitutional structure. In Jackson's words, 'William Pitt's Union of 1801 was an effort to integrate Britain's oldest colony into the metropolitan core of the Empire. It was an effort to provide a stable constitutional foundation for the Empire at a particular moment of both European and domestic

---

[17] See below, pp. 74–82.

military crisis, and in the context of an ongoing process of administrative centralization'.[18] Supporters of the new arrangement saw an autonomous Irish Parliament as a serious threat to imperial unity. They argued that a constitutional union, with a single imperial legislature at its heart, would strengthen Britain and the Empire and Ireland too. The debates on the Act of Union, Bartlett observes, 'revealed clearly how far notions of Empire had permeated Irish political discourse'.[19]

Designed to solve a problem at the heart of the Empire, the constitutional arrangement under the Union was peculiar and unstable from the beginning. 'The formal Union of the kingdoms of Ireland and Great Britain (1801–1922)', as David Fitzpatrick noted in volume III of the *Oxford History of the British Empire*, 'masked a hybrid administration with manifest colonial elements, allowing variant interpretations of the character of Ireland's dependency. Was Ireland an integral part of the United Kingdom, a peripheral, backward, sub-region, or a colony in all but name?'[20] That was a matter of contentious opinion: if Unionists celebrated Ireland's equality with the rest of Britain, Home Rulers hoped that legislative autonomy in Dublin might revitalize the country (without denying it the benefits of Empire), while separatists—always a minority, but prepared to use violence if necessary—saw Ireland as a colony that could be redeemed only by a complete break with Britain and the Empire in the form of an independent republic.[21] This variety of irreconcilable positions suggests the dilemma of any historian who would try to characterize nineteenth-century Ireland by a single category.

The fact that Ireland was directly integrated into the United Kingdom in 1801 might be construed as a form of equality, once again rendering colonial models implausible. Given that this integration was clearly not a union of equals, however, one might argue that it intensified rather than diminished imperial control over Ireland. Direct incorporation into the metropolis, after all, suggests a formidable degree of political control. Ireland in this respect stands at the opposite extreme to Gallagher and Robinson's thesis of 'informal empire'.[22] One hundred Irish MPs sat in

---

[18] See below, p. 124.   [19] See below, p. 82.

[20] David Fitzpatrick, 'Ireland and the Empire', in Andrew Porter, ed., *OHBE. Vol. III. The Nineteenth Century* (Oxford, 1999), p. 494.

[21] Ibid.

[22] Ibid., p. 510; John Gallagher and Ronald Robinson, 'The Imperialism of Free Trade', *Economic History Review*, Second Series, VI (1953), pp. 1–15.

Westminster, including some Catholics after 1829; yet this Irish participation in metropolitan governance had emerged only through the abolition of a separate Dublin Parliament by the Act of Union. And, even if Ireland was not officially ruled as a colony, its administration had distinctly colonial elements, including a separate executive in Dublin Castle with a Chief Secretary and a Lord-Lieutenant. This arrangement existed nowhere else in the United Kingdom but would provide a model for British rule in India. The *style* of British rule in Ireland also resembled that in other colonies. 'English officials billeted in Ireland', as Jackson observes, 'developed the same attitudes of mixed bemusement, condescension, complacency, affection, and eagerness to help which characterized their counterparts in India or elsewhere'.[23]

Did Britain gain or lose economically by its possession of Ireland? And did Ireland suffer or prosper by the imperial connection? Questions of this sort are notoriously difficult to answer. What measurements does one take and what sort of evidence is available? The answers can only ever be partial and they tend toward vague assertion rather than demonstrated argument; even those economic historians equipped for the task can produce only tentative accounts. Examining the Empire as a whole for the period 1846–1914, one historian has concluded that the costs of Empire to the British economy significantly outweighed the benefits. The Empire did not provide a major outlet for British overseas investment, most of which went to other foreign locations, where yields were higher. Britain was not heavily dependent on imperial trade, and British emigration went mainly to the United States rather than the colonies: in neither case did the economy benefit significantly from its imperial possessions. Maintaining the Empire, moreover, placed a very high and predictably regressive tax burden on the people of the United Kingdom. Why, then, did Britain build and retain such a vast imperial enterprise? One tentative answer is that government officials overestimated the strategic benefits of Empire while focusing their attention on the tax revenue it produced, to the exclusion of wider economic questions. Clearly the subject is in need of more investigation.[24]

[23] See below, p. 126.
[24] Patrick O'Brien, 'The Costs and Benefits of British Imperialism, 1846–1914', *Past and Present*, 120 (Aug. 1988), pp. 163–200.

How does the Irish case appear in this light? Like India, but unlike the white Dominions, Ireland was required to pay for its own defence through taxation. Local revenue paid for the upkeep of the constabulary, military, and Navy as well as servicing the National Debt. Canada, Australia, New Zealand, and South Africa, by contrast, regulated their own taxation and had relatively low defence budgets as they benefited from imperial military services paid for by British and Irish taxes. In fiscal terms, Ireland would have been better off under Dominion rule than under formal integration. But if integration and direct taxation made Ireland less expensive to govern than it might otherwise have been, this arrangement scarcely enriched the British exchequer. Certain British corporations, employers, entrepreneurs, landlords, or individuals made money out of Ireland, of course, but it is hard to see much benefit to the wider British economy over time. From the government's perspective, strategic concerns always clearly predominated.

Did Ireland gain or lose from the imperial connection? The answer depends on which Irish people are considered. Between one-quarter and one-third of Ireland's residents were Protestant in the two centuries after 1700. Land held by Catholics had been expropriated throughout the early modern era, and this pattern of inequality was written into the penal laws of the late seventeenth and early eighteenth centuries. By 1774 only 5 per cent of Ireland's land was owned by Catholics. British Protestant settlers and their descendants, however, had developed their own Irish identities over time, so that Anglicans and Dissenters as well as Catholics must be included in any analysis of economic costs and benefits. Some individuals and groups from all three backgrounds sought to profit from the country's colonization, its involvement in the Empire, or both.

Ireland, however, was never the most propitious place for this purpose. The colonization of seventeenth-century Ireland was organized by private corporations in pursuit of profit. The Scots Presbyterians who settled Ulster may not have achieved the independence and land-ownership they hoped for, but they settled permanently and were generally much better off than tenants elsewhere in Ireland. The Anglican Church of Ireland sustained itself off tithes extracted from both Catholics and Protestant Dissenters. Ascendancy landlords in the eighteenth century lived on grand estates carved out of expropriated native lands, though by the nineteenth century many were impoverished or bankrupt. A small number of Catholic as well as Protestant Irish merchants and traders benefited from their involvement in colonial trade. Younger sons of Protestant gentry and wealthier Catholic families found careers in the imperial army or civil service; and the Irish poor, both Protestant and Catholic, made a living by enlisting in the British Army. All of these might count as economic benefits to particular groups or individuals, though scarcely to the Irish economy as a whole.[25]

Whatever limited benefits may have accrued to Ireland in the eighteenth century, most of the country descended into poverty, squalor, and social breakdown thereafter. To what extent can this decline be attributed to British economic policies? Much Irish capital had been transferred to London with the Union, weakening the financial and commercial infrastructure. The abolition of protective tariffs in 1824 meant that Irish industry had no chance of competing with British. By sustaining the agricultural basis of the Irish economy, Britain benefited from imports of Irish foodstuffs while guaranteeing a ready market for its own manufactured goods. Would an independent or autonomous Ireland have fared better in the face of massive population growth, British competition, and the contraction of a once widespread domestic textile industry into northeast Ulster? Counterfactual questions of this sort permit no historical answer.

What is certain, however, is that the catastrophe of the 1840s raised big questions about Ireland's place in the Union and the Empire. In 1860, John Mitchel wrote, notoriously, from his exile in the United States, that a million Irish 'men, women and children, were carefully, prudently, and peacefully *slain* by the English government. They died of hunger in the midst of abundance, which their own hands created'. The starvation, he insisted, was the product not of Providence, as the British would have it, but of deliberate intent. 'The British account of the matter', Mitchel concluded, in his most-quoted passage, 'is first, a fraud—second, a blasphemy. The almighty, indeed, sent the potato blight, but the English created the famine'. Yet, despite the catastrophe, Ireland's desire for independence would remain intact 'so long as our island refuses to become, like Scotland, a contented province of her enemy'. For Mitchel, Ireland's 'passionate aspiration for nationhood' would 'outlive the British Empire'.[26] No professional historian today would agree with Mitchel's

---

[25] See below, pp. 63–64.

[26] John Mitchel, *The Last Conquest of Ireland (Perhaps)*, quoted in Peter Gray, *The Irish Famine* (New York, 1995), pp. 178–79.

claims of genocide. Those who do tend towards Mitchel's position, without embracing it, have produced strong arguments on British culpability, but the specifically colonial or imperialist dimension of British policy is generally taken for granted rather than demonstrated.[27] Many of the emigrants who went to America during the famine era, however, do appear to have shared something similar to Mitchel's view: a sense that they had been deliberately banished by the British as government indifference killed their countrymen. Even if historians disagree with such conceptions they must be taken seriously.[28]

Many moderate Irish nationalists who distanced themselves from Mitchel's extremism also interpreted the events of the 1840s as a crisis of both Union and Empire. Isaac Butt, an Irish Conservative and the progenitor of the Home Rule movement (the two roles were not mutually exclusive) is a good example. Denouncing the idea that famine relief should be supported solely out of Irish funds, Butt argued that the British response was in danger of exposing the Union as a sham. 'If the Union be not a mockery', he argued, 'there exists no such thing as an English treasury. The exchequer is the exchequer of the United Kingdom'. He then posed the perennial question: 'If Cornwall had been visited with the scenes that have desolated Cork, would similar arguments [have] been used?' For Butt, the Irish famine was not ultimately a local problem: 'All our measures are based upon the principle that this calamity ought to be regarded as an imperial one, and borne by the empire at large'. The rational Irishman had no choice 'but to feel that the united parliament has abdicated the functions of government for Ireland, and to demand for his country that separate legislative existence'.[29] Whether a Dublin Parliament could or would have responded better to the Irish famine has, again, been the subject of much counterfactual speculation. In the end, whatever one's political perspective, it is difficult to reconcile the events of the 1840s with the notion that Ireland was an integrated and equal member of the United Kingdom.

---

[27] For a brief account, see the historical documents and historiographical excerpts in Gray's *Irish Famine*, pp. 130–83.

[28] Kerby Miller's *Emigrants and Exiles: Ireland and the Irish Exodus to North America* (New York, 1985) is the definitive account.

[29] Isaac Butt, 'The Famine in the Land', *Dublin University Magazine*, XXIX (April 1847), quoted in Gray, *Irish Famine*, pp. 156–57.

An estimated ten million people have emigrated from Ireland to all destinations (Britain and the United States as well as the Dominions) since 1600, whereas only slightly more than five million live on the island today. Ireland's population fell by one-third because of the famine: one million people died and two million more emigrated. Mass migration is one of the defining characteristics of modern Irish history: to what extent can it be explained in imperial terms? And what does this migration, along with Irish military, civil, and missionary work in the Empire, tell us about Irish and imperial history?

The connection between Irish emigration and colonialism has not yet been explored in any sustained fashion. The poverty and uprooting of the rural masses in nineteenth-century Ireland had long-term colonial origins, but it also resulted from massive population growth and internal class antagonism that pitted Irish against Irish. No historian has systematically examined how ongoing British colonial rule of Ireland determined or affected the Catholic exodus in the critical century after 1820. Mass emigration arose in the context of intense population pressure, competition for access to land, the commercialization of agriculture, and the relative absence of urban industrial employment. In most historical explanations, however, colonialism provides background context at most. It should also be noted that, contrary to expedient nationalist interpretations at the time and subsequently, mass emigration produced many economic benefits, not only to those who materially improved their lives abroad, but also to those who stayed behind, by reducing social tensions and competition for scarce resources, enriching commercial farmers and allowing them to consolidate their holdings, creating international trade and family networks, and ensuring a steady inward flow of funds from abroad. An investigation of Irish emigration in colonial or imperial terms would bear these considerations in mind, while also examining the eight million migrants who left before and after, rather than during, the famine era.

Migration is considered in this book not so much for its domestic impact as for its importance in the conquest and settlement of the British Empire. In the seventeenth century, as Ohlmeyer demonstrates, Irish Catholics actively participated in the colonization of the West Indies. In the eighteenth century, emigrants from Ireland to the American colonies outnumbered English and Scots combined. Most of them were Ulster Presbyterians, many of whom settled along the colonial frontier, where they provided the first line of imperial defence against French and Indian attack. In the century after 1820, Irish migration was predominantly Catholic; in addition to the five million Irish people who left for the United States between 1820 and 1920, at least one and a half million went to Britain and another million migrated to the white settler colonies of Canada, Australia, and New Zealand (and to a much lesser extent South Africa) where, as Deirdre McMahon shows, they played an important part in both national and imperial politics.

Emigration was but one aspect of Ireland's involvement in the affairs of the wider British Empire. As well as belonging to a colony at the heart of the Empire, Irish people helped conquer, govern, and evangelize imperial possessions overseas. Ireland contributed a greatly disproportionate number of enlisted men (most of them Catholics from fairly poor backgrounds) and especially officers (most of them from the Ascendancy class) to the British Army throughout the nineteenth century. Like the Scots, the Irish were also represented in large numbers in the Indian Civil Service and other branches of the imperial administration, while Irish missionaries played an important role in disseminating both Catholicism and the English language in Africa, chiefly through their commitment to education.[30]

With the exception of missionaries, these occupations were reserved exclusively for men. The story of Ireland and the British Empire is in many ways resolutely male. Women's history was, by definition, peripheral to one of the central themes of imperial history: war, conquest, and the exercise of military, administrative, or political power thereafter. Nonetheless, as Philippa Levine notes in another volume in this series, British imperialism was by nature a gendered process. 'The British Empire always seems a very masculine enterprise, a series of far-flung sites, dominated by white men dressed stiffly in sporting and hunting clothes, or ornate official regalia', Levine observes. 'The Empire was, in many ways, a deeply masculine space of this sort, but acknowledging that reality tells only a fraction of the story'.[31] At the most basic level, the Empire, while it was run mostly by men, was obviously composed of men and women in roughly equal proportion. More significantly, all forms of social and cultural practice, including imperialism, are encoded with masculine and

---

[30] See below, pp. 90–121.
[31] Philippa Levine, ed., *OHBE Companion Series: Gender and Empire* (Oxford, 2004), p. 1.

feminine meanings. To give the most obvious examples, soldiering, adventuring, and administrative service were taken to be naturally masculine, while child-rearing and domestic decorum were construed not simply as feminine, but as women's distinctive contribution to national and imperial well-being.

Gender was a pervasive component of all forms of imperialist representation. 'Throughout the nineteenth century', Cleary notes, 'the Irish, like other colonized peoples, had been dually constructed, both as a virile, military race, exercising its natural martial qualities in the wars and adventures of Empire, and as an essentially emotional, irrational, and feminized people incapable of self-government'.[32] This much is true; yet as a discursive category gender is nothing if not inconstant, its malleability depending on the purposes for which it is deployed. Whereas the imperial ruler and the Irish soldier were necessarily male, the colonial subject could be cast not only as feminine and weak but also, at times, as aggressively masculine—as worker or dispossessed tenant, simianized subaltern or simpleton, agrarian rebel or nationalist agitator—the difference being that masculinity in this case signified bestiality and an innate capacity for violence. By contrast, imperialist perceptions tended to exclude colonized women, sometimes to the point of invisibility, other than as undifferentiated peasants, servants, slatterns, or prostitutes. Those élite or upper-middle-class Irish women who did achieve prominence as nationalist leaders—Maud Gonne, for example, or Countess Markiewicz—violated prevailing norms of femininity by their militancy or martial prowess but were also liable to be dismissed as hysterical.

Gender is also central to any understanding of Irish literature, as Vera Kreilkamp demonstrates. Not only were women prominent among Irish writers, Irish novels in the nineteenth century, whether by females or males, frequently dealt with romantic love and marriage, both literally and as a metaphor for constitutional union and its shortcomings. The promise and limitations of the Union, Kreilkamp shows, are central to Irish fiction, from Maria Edgeworth's *Castle Rackrent* (1800) and the 'national tale' inaugurated by Sydney Owenson's *The Wild Irish Girl* (1806), to the Big House novels of Ascendancy decay in the early twentieth century. These Irish novels also feature a recurrent trope of male corruption and decline. In the Big House genre especially, Kreilkamp notes,

---

[32] See below, p. 261.

Ascendancy decay is represented through the declining virility and eroded authority of landlords and patriarchs. Masculinity, the prerogative of the imperial ruler, ebbs away. Mothers, in turn, become monstrous as a dying colonial order turns inward on itself.[33]

The late nineteenth and early twentieth centuries witnessed an upsurge of Irish nationalism, culminating in an armed struggle for independence that shook the Empire. 'Ireland was simultaneously a bulwark of the Empire, and a mine within its walls', as Jackson notes. 'Irish people were simultaneously major participants in Empire, and a significant source of subversion. For the Irish, the Empire was both an agent of liberation and of oppression: it provided both the path to social advancement and the shackles of incarceration'.[34] Most Irish nationalists did not wish to sever the positive bonds with the Empire, merely to weaken the negative ones. There was, however, always a hardline republican minority, and in time its viewpoint would prevail.

When William Gladstone came out in favour of Home Rule for Ireland in 1885, his opponents protested that the Empire itself was under threat. The Irish crisis occurred at a time of unrest in South Africa, Egypt, and Afghanistan. This imperial context, McMahon observes, 'explains why the Home Rule debates of 1886 are so revealing of English fears about the potential effect of Irish Home Rule on the body politic of England, Ireland, and the Empire. The debates provoked profound soul-searching about ideology, race, national character, religion, the constitution, and history'.[35] Not surprisingly, during the Home Rule debates in Parliament, Gladstone's critics generally used the terms 'United Kingdom' and 'Empire' interchangeably, notwithstanding the Home Rulers' insistence that they had no desire to break with either. Home Rule, in any case, could not be passed until the Lords' veto over the Commons was abolished, which occurred only in 1911.

By then, the war in South Africa had helped transform the face of Irish nationalism. The Irish Parliamentary Party was reunited under John Redmond's leadership in January 1900, and Irish republican separatism was reinvigorated. Two Transvaal Irish Brigades were formed to fight on

---

[33] See below, pp. 174–79.
[34] See below, p. 123.
[35] See below, p. 184.

behalf of the Boers, attracting a small number of volunteers from Ireland and more from the United States and South Africa. Serving on the opposing side, McMahon notes, were about 28,000 Irish soldiers in the British Army; and, if pro-Boer activism inspired the Irish republican movement, imperial service against the Boers became an important component of Ulster Unionist identity. The pro-Boer Irish Transvaal Committee, founded in 1899, included figures such as Arthur Griffith, Maud Gonne, John McBride, W. B. Yeats, James Connolly, and Thomas Clarke. The analogy between Irish and Boer nationalism conveniently ignored the latter's treatment of black Africans, but the pro-Boer movement 'greatly contributed to the growth of radical nationalism in Ireland in the critical decade-and-a-half before 1914'.[36] This new generation of radical nationalists increasingly came to see participation in Westminster politics as pointless and irrelevant.

At the heart of early twentieth-century Irish nationalism, as Cleary notes, was a powerful cultural resurgence. The well-known Literary Revival of this period is most closely associated with figures such as W. B. Yeats, J. M. Synge, and Augusta Gregory. There was, in addition, a related Gaelic Revival, stimulated in part by Douglas Hyde, whose seminal lecture of 1892, 'The Necessity for De-Anglicising Ireland', inspired the foundation of the Gaelic League the following year. While Hyde and some other leading figures in the Gaelic Revival came from the same Ascendancy élite as Yeats and Gregory, the membership were mainly Catholic and middle class. Writers and critics of the subsequent, post-independence generation, as Cleary shows, bitterly criticized the Literary Revival for what they saw as its insular romanticism and anti-democratic tendencies, and castigated the Gaelic Revival for instilling a spirit of joy-less sexual puritanism into the new nation. But it was through the revivalist movement—in both the English and the Irish languages—that nationalism at the turn of the century assumed much of its form, content, and power.

Irish nationalism emerged triumphant in the period 1912–21, commencing with the introduction of the third Home Rule Bill and concluding with the creation of the Free State. When the Home Rule Bill was introduced in April 1912, Ireland came close to civil war. Two paramilitary forces, the Ulster Volunteer Force in the north and the Irish Volunteers in

---

[36] See below, p. 193.

the south, were ready for battle; a third, heavily Irish force, the British
Army, stood by. With the Lords' veto reduced to a three-year moratorium,
the Bill passed into law in September 1914; one month earlier war had
broken out in Europe, and the measure was suspended for the duration of
the conflict. Redmond, seeing a chance to demonstrate the compatibility
of Home Rule with Irish loyalty and imperial unity, urged Irishmen to
enlist and fight on the British side. He believed, mistakenly, 'that British
public opinion would be so grateful for Irish support that after the war it
would rally round Home Rule; and that the war might dissolve the sectarian tensions between Protestant and Catholic, nationalist and Unionist'.[37]
Although an estimated 200,000 men from all parts of Ireland enlisted
during the war, a small but powerful anti-war movement emerged; it
included three veterans of the Transvaal Committee—Connolly, McBride,
and Clarke—who would be executed for their role in the Easter 1916
insurrection. We should be wary, however, of assuming that service in the
British Army necessarily excluded radical nationalism. 'Taking the Queen's
shilling', Jackson points out, 'certainly did not automatically induce loyalism: there has been an intriguing overlap between service in the British
Army and revolutionary activism from at least the eighteenth century,
through to the recent "Troubles"'.[38]

The 1916 rebellion came at time of mounting crisis in the Empire,
from South Africa to Nigeria and from Egypt to India. It also enflamed
anti-British sentiment in the Dominions, to the consternation of local
administrators, and especially in the United States. In Ireland, radical
nationalism won the day: in the 1918 general election Sinn Féin won
seventy-three seats and Redmond's Irish Party was destroyed. In January
1919, Sinn Féiners gathered in Dublin to set up their own assembly, *Dáil
Éireann*. In the ensuing armed struggle, British officials repeatedly expressed their fear that losing Ireland would irreparably harm or even
destroy the Empire. Despite or because of these fears, many British
officials also suggested that the whole affair was caused by a few violent
trouble-makers who had intimidated the moderate majority. If
these trouble-makers were taken care of, by whatever degree of force
necessary, the matter would quickly be solved. Thinking of this sort, as
McMahon notes, 'was to be an enduring theme in later colonial wars'.[39]

---

[37] See below, p. 200.
[38] See below, p. 142.
[39] See below, p. 205.

When a truce was declared in July 1921, the most important consider-ations for the British government were that the southern portion of Ireland should remain in the Empire, stay loyal to the monarch, and make certain defence concessions. Sovereignty was the critical issue, not partition. The Government of Ireland Act, passed in December 1920, had already provided for separate devolved Parliaments in Dublin and Belfast. The outcome of the Anglo-Irish treaty is well known: Dominion status, followed by civil war and the eventual consolidation of an Irish Free State. 'By the wave of a constitutional wand reminiscent of the first Home Rule debates in 1886', McMahon writes, 'Ireland was given the same constitu-tional status as Canada. . . . The Canadian analogy, however, was based on a profound misconception: Ireland, unlike Canada, was a Dominion by revolution not evolution'.[40] Canada was distant and huge, Ireland adjacent and small. There was nothing Britain could do to prevent Canada from leaving the Empire whenever it wished; Ireland had no such flexibility. Lumping Ireland and Canada into the same category made little practical sense. 'The Dominion settlement', McMahon concludes, 'suffered from fatal flaws: as a concept Dominion status was still in the process of evolution; the Irish had never asked for it; it came too late; it was imposed; and it was accompanied by partition and civil war. The surprise is that it lasted as long as it did'.[41]

Over the next two decades, Ireland moved steadily away from Britain and the Empire. Dominion status finally received coherent definition in the Balfour Report of 1926, but by then Commonwealth membership for Ireland 'resembled the chafing of an ill-fitting shoe'.[42] The Irish consti-tution of 1937 amounted to a republic in all but name. Ireland, alone among the Commonwealth nations, remained neutral during the Second World War. Finally, on 7 September 1948, the Irish *Taoiseach* John A. Costello declared that Ireland would become a republic and leave the Commonwealth, even as newly independent India and Pakistan were de-ciding to stay in. Given Ireland's proximity to Britain, this strategy was perhaps the only way to secure meaningful independence, but it was not without its critics at the time and subsequently. Northern Ireland, of

[40] See below, p. 210.
[41] See below, ibid.
[42] See below, p. 211.

course, remained part of the United Kingdom. For the rest of the island, three centuries of involvement with the British Empire had formally come to an end. Independence, however, did not remove Ireland from Britain's powerful economic, political, and cultural orbit. Life in the Free State and the Republic was moulded by ongoing interaction with Britain and by a variety of postcolonial legacies built into the structure of the new nation state.

The term 'postcolonial' refers not simply to a time-period but also to a form of cultural and political criticism, derived from the experience of former colonies around the world, that seeks to illuminate colonial history both before and after independence. Given the fundamental disagreements over Ireland's place in the Empire, and the suspicions of many historians about cultural theory, readings of this sort are inevitably controversial. In Ireland, as Cleary observes, the response to postcolonial criticism has taken contrary forms: some have welcomed it as invigorating; others have condemned it for 'politicizing' literary and aesthetic criticism; others still have dismissed it as a covert return to nationalist orthodoxy. Howe's chapter also examines some of the criticisms of Irish postcolonial theory, including charges that 'its command of non-Irish historical evidence and indeed of empirical data on Ireland was questionable, its conception of colonialism itself unduly homogenizing and ahistorical, its view of historians' method unduly dismissive'.[43]

Cleary's resolutely historical analysis of Irish culture helps bridge the divide. Most objections to the use of postcolonial theory in an Irish context, he points out, rest on the familiar fallacy that there exists a definitive colonial form against which Ireland can be judged. Given the diversity of the former British colonies, searching for a single form of post-coloniality would be fallacious. None the less, the various ex-colonies had belonged to the same Empire and consequently exhibited some broad similarities, for example partition—in Ireland, Palestine, India, and Cyprus—as an imperial solution to ethnic antagonisms. Another dilemma all the former colonies faced was how to reconstruct or invent a national culture, a task rendered more difficult in many places, including Ireland, by the need to integrate an indigenous language into the new polity while balancing the needs of cultural authenticity and modern nation-building. Many former colonies also had to accommodate the substantial presence

---

[43] See below, p. 245.

of disempowered settler-colonist élites. In Ireland's case, the dilemma of the beleaguered southern Unionist class is memorably captured in the Big House fiction of Elizabeth Bowen, Edith Somerville, and Molly Keane. 'The central architectural motif of these novels', Kreilkamp notes, 'is a decaying mansion isolated from a countryside of native hovels, but regularly sharing characteristics with them'.[44]

Many former colonies, including Ireland, also had to grapple with legacies of gender inequality bequeathed in part by their nationalist movements. Most Irish nationalist groups at the turn of the century, including the Irish Republican Brotherhood and the Home Rule Party, had excluded women and opposed female suffrage. Irish feminists, however, had the capacity not just to augment but to subvert nationalism: they belonged to an international movement and they welcomed Protestants as well as Catholics, Unionists as well as nationalists. How was this cosmopolitanism to be reconciled with the masculine ethos of the nationalist movement? If 1916 had promised gender equality, the dominant ideology of the Free State did not. Females were exempted from jury service and married women were excluded from teaching. De Valera's 1937 constitution accorded a 'special position' to the Catholic Church and especially its teachings on the family and divorce. While Ireland had much in common with inter-war Britain, the United States, and other countries where feminism was in retreat and stagnating economies curtailed opportunities for women, critics have traced some of the repressive sexual atmosphere and gender inequalities of the Free State to the masculinist heroics and myopia of early twentieth-century Irish nationalism.

A more enduring and violent colonial legacy came to the fore in the 1960s, with the outbreak of the 'Troubles'. All sides to the conflict in Northern Ireland invoked colonial and imperial history in one form or another. Hardline republicans saw the conflict as a struggle to unite and liberate England's last remaining colony, thereby bringing to an end a 'British' occupation of Ireland that stretched back eight centuries. Extremists at the other end of the spectrum agreed that the conflict was a colonial one, but celebrated the fact: their historical duty was to uphold the accomplishments of their ancestors during the Siege of Derry (1688–89), the South African War (1899–1902), or the First World War. Both sides also drew analogies from colonial or postcolonial struggles in Africa, with

---

[44] See below, p. 175.

some republicans identifying with black liberation movements in South Africa and some loyalists finding solace in the struggle of white Rhodesians against devolution. Those who sought a more moderate solution to the conflict, whether they were based in Belfast, Dublin, or London, also tended inevitably to think along lines laid down during the Union of 1801–1921, with some form of power-sharing and Home Rule as the most plausible option.

The conflict in Northern Ireland exhibited many of the old bedevilling ironies typical of Ireland's historical relationship with the British Empire. Ulster Unionists who took pride in their Britishness encountered anti-Irish prejudice when they travelled elsewhere in the United Kingdom. The Northern Ireland administration, during the half-century after partition, resembled the old Dublin administration under the Union more than it did the remainder of the contemporary United Kingdom. The imperial trappings surrounding the Northern Ireland administration, with its Governor at Hillsborough representing the Crown, were obviously a source of pride to many; but they were also increasingly anachronistic. By the 1960s the Empire was everywhere in decline or decay. To the extent that Ulster Unionism rested on a discourse of empire, its relevance and influence outside its local setting had been eroding steadily since the onset of decolonization. In the Irish Republic, meanwhile, many people sympathized with the plight of northern Catholics, but most were at best vaguely committed to the idea of thirty-two county national unification, and hostile to the suggestion that it was worth pursuing through force.

If the conflict in Northern Ireland had colonial origins, there could no longer be an imperial solution. The settlement arrived at in the late 1990s, actively involving Dublin as well as London, reintroduced a form of Home Rule based on the principle of majority consent. Longer-term solutions may well lie in the realm of European integration, leaving behind some of the restrictive legacies of colonialism. Ever since Ireland abruptly quit the Commonwealth in 1949, there has been intermittent behind-the-scenes discussion of its rejoining. By the 1990s, however, an unprecedented economic boom, fuelled by intelligent deployment of European Union funds, appeared to have rendered this prospect moot. By the turn of the twenty-first century, Dublin's enthusiasm for European integration was matched only by London's scepticism. And so, putting its colonial legacies as far as possible to one side, the Irish Republic leapfrogged its British neighbours into an enthusiastic embrace of Europe.

Select Bibliography

DONALD HARMAN AKENSON, *The Irish Diaspora: A Primer* (Belfast, 1996).

DAVID ARMITAGE, *Ideological Origins of the British Empire* (Cambridge, 2000).

ANDY BIELENBERG, ed., *The Irish Diaspora* (London, 2000).

DAVID CAIRNS and SHAUN RICHARDS, *Writing Ireland: Colonialism, Nationalism and Culture* (Manchester, 1988).

NICHOLAS CANNY, *The Elizabethan Conquest of Ireland: A Pattern Established, 1565–1576* (New York, 1976).

—— *Making Ireland British, 1580–1650* (Oxford, 2001).

—— 'The Origins of Empire: An Introduction', in Canny, ed., *The Oxford History of the British Empire. Vol. I. British Overseas Enterprise to the Close of the Seventeenth Century* (Oxford, 1998), pp. 1–33.

JOE CLEARY, *Literature, Partition and the Nation State: Culture and Conflict in Ireland, Israel and Palestine* (Cambridge, 2002).

SCOTT B. COOK, 'The Irish Raj: Social Origins and Careers of Irishmen in the Indian Civil Service, 1855–1919', *Journal of Social History*, 20 (Spring 1987), pp. 507–29.

SEAMUS DEANE, *Strange Country: Modernity and Nationhood in Irish Writing Since 1790* (Oxford, 1997).

DAVID FITZPATRICK, 'Ireland and the Empire', in Andrew Porter, ed., *The Oxford History of the British Empire. Vol. III. The Nineteenth Century.* (Oxford, 1999), pp. 494–521.

RAYMOND GILLESPIE, *Colonial Ulster: The Settlement of East Ulster, 1600–1641* (Cork, 1985).

DAVID HARKNESS, *The Restless Dominion: The Irish Free State and the British Commonwealth of Nations, 1921–31* (London, 1969).

MICHAEL and DENIS HOLMES, eds., *Ireland and India* (Dublin, 1997).

STEPHEN HOWE, *Ireland and Empire: Colonial Legacies in Irish History and Culture* (Oxford, 2000).

KEITH JEFFERY, ed., *'An Irish Empire'? Aspects of Ireland and the British Empire* (Manchester, 1996).

DECLAN KIBERD, *Inventing Ireland: The Literature of the Modern Nation* (London, 1995).

DAVID LLOYD, *Anomalous States: Irish Writing and the Post-Colonial Moment* (Dublin, 1993).

NICHOLAS MANSERGH, *The Unresolved Question: The Anglo-Irish Settlement and its Undoing, 1912–72* (London, 1991).

PHILIP ROBINSON, *The Plantation of Ulster* (New York, 1984).

2

A Laboratory for Empire?: Early Modern Ireland and English Imperialism

JANE H. OHLMEYER

'Ireland is another India for the English, a more profitable India for them than ever the Indies were to the Spaniards.'[1] This statement, attributed to the Earl of Thomond by the Old English historian John Lynch in the early 1660s, recaptures the reality of Ireland's colonial position for much of the early modern period. Yet it is also ironic since Ireland, after 1541, enjoyed the constitutional status of a kingdom. Moreover, the Old English, as the descendants of the Anglo-Norman conquerors were known, perceived themselves as subjects of the English Crown, rather than victims or perpetrators of imperialism. The ambiguity inherent in Ireland's constitutional position confounded the Old English and, after 1603, many native Irishmen, as they struggled to reconcile their sense of loyalty to the monarch with the realities of English imperialism and colonization.

This conundrum has also bedevilled later historians as they have attempted to disentangle the extent to which early modern Ireland was a kingdom, a colony, or a unique combination of both. Even such terms as civilization and imperialism, and other associated phrases like Anglicization and colonization, defy easy categorization in the context of early modern Ireland. 'Empire', as one historian has recently noted, 'was always

At the request of Professor Kenny, I have substantially revised my original contribution '"Civilizinge of those rude partes": Colonization within Britain and Ireland, 1580s–1640s', in Nicholas Canny, ed., *The Oxford History of the British Empire* (hereafter *OHBE*). *Vol. I. The Origins of Empire: British Overseas Enterprise to the Close of the Seventeenth Century* (Oxford, 1998), pp. 124–47. I am very grateful to David Ditchburn, Andrew MacKillop, Micheál Ó Siochrú, and Geoffrey Parker for their constructive and insightful comments on an earlier draft of this chapter. I am also indebted to the Leverhulme Trust for funding leave which enabled me to undertake some of the research that informs this chapter.

[1] John Lynch, *Cambrensis Eversus*, trans. Mathew Kelly, 3 vols. (Dublin, 1851–52), III, p. 75.

a language of power'.[2] Certainly, English imperialism in Ireland was driven by military, political, and, increasingly, religious and economic concerns, and by the determination to colonize the island with English, Welsh, and Scottish settlers. The definition of civilization is much more ambiguous. The desire to civilize and to Anglicize the Irish spawned discussions about how unruly subjects could be reformed, how overmighty lords could be tamed, how thuggery and feuding could be replaced with law and order, how labour could be channelled into production rather than destruction, and how Irish culture and customs could be replaced with English ones. While some Irish Catholics, wedded as they were to the island's juridical status as a kingdom, may have shared a desire to civilize and even to anglicize Ireland, by the early decades of the seventeenth century most rejected more militaristic manifestations of imperialism at home. Yet these qualms did not impede colonizing endeavours abroad nor hinder the ability of Irish Catholics to act as effective imperialists elsewhere in the English-speaking Empire. Indeed, their experiences of 'internal colonization' at home may well have prepared them particularly well for frontier life abroad.

Just as Ireland's constitutional status proved fraught with tensions and contradictions, so too were the policies of those who ruled the country. Did the early modern state favour the annihilation of the native people followed by the wholesale colonization of the island? Or was the assimilation of the resident population to the culture and religion of the metropole and the introduction of English political, legal, and economic processes sufficient? Edmund Spenser, in *A View of the Present State of Ireland* (1596), favoured the use of aggressive imperialism over that of assimilation. He called for the destruction of the existing Gaelic order and the systematic colonization of Ireland with English settlers who were to be made responsible for the erection of the political, economic, and social framework that was considered the necessary support of a civil life and the Protestant faith. Thomas Wentworth, later Earl of Strafford, who sponsored the publication of Spenser's *View* in 1633, clearly shared this vision. He became the greatest seventeenth-century exponent of imperialism through conformity with the Church of Ireland and, above all, plantation. Wentworth believed that the settlement of English (but not Scottish) colonists remained the best means of enriching the English government and

[2] David Armitage, *The Ideological Origins of the British Empire* (Cambridge, 2000), p. 29.

for 'civilising...this people, or securing this kingdom under the dominion of your imperial Crown'. He considered that 'plantations must be the
only means under God and your majesty to reform this subject as well in
religion as manners'.[3]

Whether aggressively pursued or not, there was nothing new in these
calls for the civilization of Ireland, which dated back to the twelfth century. What distinguished the early modern state from its medieval predecessor was its ability to drive forward an imperial agenda in Ireland in a
way not hitherto possible. Yet even during the early modern period, the
personalities of the monarchs and their ministers, a chronic lack of financial resources, and changing priorities tempered metropolitan policies and
attitudes towards Ireland.[4] As a result, state-sponsored imperialism, which
promoted military conquest, plantation, and active colonization, was pursued throughout the sixteenth and seventeenth centuries alongside more
reforming assimilationist policies. Crudely stated, during these years, the
metropole first intended to complete the military conquest of Ireland;
then, having pacified the island, the state aimed to establish—at the national, provincial, and local levels—political, administrative, and legal
control over all elements of Irish society, and especially over the semi-
autonomous Irish lords. Closely linked to this was the determination to
secure, wherever possible, religious conformity with the Church of Ireland. Alongside political subjugation and conversion to Protestantism
stood cultural assimilation and the need to reform 'uncivil' natives and to
anglicize their apparently barbarous customs, practices, and culture.
Finally, a combination of reform initiatives in the 1540s, 1570s, and 1580s,
together with official plantation and unregulated colonization, transformed the legal basis on which land was held in Ireland and thereby
reconfigured Ireland's economic and tenurial infrastructure in accordance
with English commercial models and patterns of landowning. Collectively
these strategies, though often couched in the rhetoric of civility, effectively
amounted to a form of imperialism that sought to exploit Ireland for

---

[3] W. Knowler, ed., *The Earl of Strafforde's Letters and Despatches with an Essay towards his
Life by Sir George Radcliffe....* 2 vols. (London, 1739), I, p. 450. See also, Nicholas Canny,
'The Attempted Anglicisation of Ireland in the Seventeenth Century', in J. F. Merritt, ed., *The
Political World of Thomas Wentworth, Earl of Strafford, 1621–1641* (Cambridge, 1996), pp. 157–86.

[4] For example, Buckingham, as Victor Treadwell has demonstrated, was a major agent of
'Britishisation' in Ireland between 1616 and 1628. Victor Treadwell, *Buckingham and Ireland,
1616–1628: A Study in Anglo-Irish Politics* (Dublin, 1998), p. 299.

England's political and economic advantage and to Anglicize the native population.

The burden of implementing these policies in Ireland fell to a range of 'sub-imperialists'. These individuals included Lord Deputies such as Arthur Chichester (1605–15), Thomas Wentworth, later Earl of Strafford (1633–40), and James Butler, later Duke of Ormond (1643–49, 1662–69, 1677–85); but also government officials, Church of Ireland clergy, lawyers, and local lords. The majority of these imperial agents were Protestant newcomers or Irish converts. Given the scale of the enterprise and the lack of central funds, however, Irish Catholics, especially members of the traditional social and ruling élite, were also encouraged to serve as exemplars of civility and, whether wittingly or not, they collectively facilitated the implementation of civilizing and imperial policies throughout the island. Yet their involvement in these processes afforded them an opportunity to negotiate compromises that best suited their personal circumstances and political ambitions. As a result, rather than being seen as passive victims, many Irish Catholics proved reactive and responsive to imperial schemes. Moreover, the fact that English imperialism in Ireland lacked any overriding, coherent, and consistent framework allowed some Catholics, especially members of the élite, together with many Protestant planters, not only to co-opt the colonial processes to strengthen their regional power bases but even to subvert the original imperial agenda. As a result, multiple colonizations, occurring at a variety of levels, took place at different times and with varying degrees of intensity during this era. Hardly surprisingly, then, no neat imperial or civilizing model can be easily applied to early modern Ireland.

The fact that the political, social, cultural, and economic practices of much of Irish society did not coincide with the 'norms' of Lowland England prompted scorn among Englishmen. The Irish were compared with the ancient Britons (whom the Romans had civilized) or with the Amerindians of the New World. Giraldus Cambrensis had consistently referred to the Irish as 'a barbarous people', 'a rude people' with 'primitive habits', 'living themselves like beasts'.[5] In his description 'of the character, customs, and habits of this people', published in The Topography of Ireland

[5] Andrew Hadfield and John McVeagh, eds., Strangers to that Land: British Perceptions of Ireland from the Reformation to the Famine (Gerrards Cross, Buckinghamshire, 1994), p. 27.

(1188–89), he argued that Ireland's geographical isolation from the 'civilized nations' ensured that 'they learn nothing, and practice nothing but the barbarism in which they are born and bred, and which sticks to them like a second nature'.[6] Later observers simply appropriated this twelfth-century rhetoric. They included members of the Old English community, who had traditionally viewed themselves as the protectors and promoters of the English interest in Ireland against the degenerate native, Gaelic-speaking population. As late as 1614, David Rothe, Bishop of Ossory, implored the Catholic synod 'to eliminate barbarous customs, abolish bestial rites and convert the detestable intercourse of savages into polite manners and a care for the commonwealth'.[7]

As the Reformation in Ireland gathered pace, Protestant commentators also adopted this discourse of civility, but manipulated it for their own political purposes. Fynes Moryson, secretary to Lord Mountjoy, travelled throughout Europe, North Africa, the Middle East, and Turkey but saved his greatest scorn for the 'meere Irish' whom he regarded as filthy, rude, barbaric, wild beasts. Their women were drunken sluts. Other writers even failed to make a distinction between the Old English and the native or 'meere' Irish: both groups were equally uncivil. In *A Discovery of the True Causes why Ireland was never entirely subdued* (1612), the legal imperialist, Sir John Davies, portrayed the Irish as barbarians, murderers, and villains who behaved 'little better than Canniballes, who doe hunt one another, and hee that hath most strength and swiftnes doth eate and devoures all his fellowes'.[8] Thus, contemporaries clearly regarded segments of the Irish population as savages and barbarians who had failed to progress, to farm for their food, or to inhabit an ordered polity regulated by the law and Christian morality.[9] Where, of course, Catholic and Protestant writers disagreed was how a civilizing agenda might best be implemented.

Given that these contemporary perceptions of the Irish as uncivil and barbaric were consistently used to justify imperial initiatives, how accurate were they? Even by the mid-sixteenth century, Ireland remained sparsely populated, with widely dispersed settlements, few towns, and difficult internal communications. Pastoralism, especially cattle farming, formed the mainstay of the local economy, with herds moved to high pastures

---

[6] Ibid., p. 28.   [7] Cited in Treadwell, *Buckingham*, p. 30.

[8] Hadfield and McVeagh, eds., *Strangers to that Land*, p. 47.

[9] Anthony Pagden, *The Fall of Natural Man: The American Indian and the Origins of Comparative Ethnology* (Cambridge, 1982), p. 26.

during the summer months, a practice known as transhumance or 'booley-ing'. From the perspective of Lowland England, this consumption-oriented, redistributive economy remained relatively unsophisticated. Trade was limited to the exchange of raw materials. Nevertheless, the rudimentary economy played a critical role in sustaining the social and political infrastructure of late medieval Ireland. A fragmentary patchwork of patri-archal septs (clans) ruled the country. A small number of powerful Gaelic Irish and Old English overlords not only controlled their own territories but also collected tribute (in the form of military service, food, lodgings, and agricultural labour) and demanded submission from previously inde-pendent regions, thereby extending their political control and enhancing their standing within their own lordship.

Since military might determined dynamic lordship, maintaining and sustaining an effective army became a priority for any Irish lord. It also underpinned the social order, for a lord's followers were not only obliged to feed and house soldiers but to offer military service themselves in return for his protection. This elaborate system of extortion, intimidation, and protection was known to the Old English as 'coign and livery' and enabled individual lords to field substantial private forces. For instance, the rebellious Earl of Tyrone and his Ulster allies allegedly mustered 2,000 *buannachts* (or native mercenary soldiers) in 1594, and between 4,000 and 6,000 ordinary swordsmen regularly enlisted for service during the later stages of the Nine Years War (1594–1603).[10] Scottish mercenaries had long since supplemented these native soldiers and between the 1560s and the 1590s some 25,000 Scottish mercenaries found employment in militarised Ulster.[11] These mercenary troops received part of their payment in cattle. Since livestock, especially cows, constituted an important form of wealth, cattle raiding, particularly in the long winter evenings, formed an integral part of the local, redistributive economy. Moreover, a successful cattle-raid resulted in the submission of a territory, which enhanced the military and political standing of those who led the raids, bringing increased riches in the form of tribute. As a result, 'the chief inclination of these people', as one Spanish traveller noted in the late 1580s 'is to be robbers, and

[10] For further details see Ciaran Brady, 'The Captains' Games: Army and Society in Elizabethan Ireland', in Thomas Bartlett and Keith Jeffery, eds., *A Military History of Ireland* (Cambridge, 1996), pp. 144–47.

[11] Allan I. Macinnes, 'Crown, Clan and Fine: The 'civilising' of Scottish Gaeldom, 1587–1638', *Northern Scotland*, XIII (1993), p. 33.

to plunder each other; so that no day passes without a call to arms among them'.[12]

Of course, military might also underpinned English imperialism in Ireland. The endemic revolts and rebellions of the sixteenth century required the Tudor state to maintain thousands of English soldiers in Ireland. Between 1594 and 1599, 20,000 troops served against the forces loyal to the Earl of Tyrone; between 1649 and 1651 the English Parliament dispatched 55,000 men to serve in Ireland; and at the Battle of the Boyne (1690) King William of Orange commanded a force numbering 36,000. Each English victory, especially in 1603, 1653, and 1691, brought with it a fresh wave of expropriation and colonial activity as the metropole exercised its military and political dominance.[13]

If 'fighting' served as one central pillar on which late medieval Irish society rested, 'feasting' was another. The importance of guesting (demanding hospitality from followers) and feasting as a public display of a lord's power over his followers cannot be overstated. The description of a mighty banquet given by Brian O'Rourke, a County Leitrim chieftain, which was later translated from Irish and popularized by Jonathan Swift, captured the extravagance of such occasions: after devouring 140 cows and drinking 100 pails of whiskey, the guests danced, brawled, and then collapsed in a stupor on the floor.[14] Though 'coshering' and providing victuals for these lavish feasts placed enormous burdens on followers, especially during times of dearth, these traditions enhanced a lord's standing and status within his lordship in much the same way that maintaining a large household of swordsmen, brehons (or lawyers), hereditary physicians, harpists, bards, minstrels, ballad singers, and storytellers (*seanchaidhthe*) did. In return for rent-free farms and other privileges, they entertained and glorified local lords and their followers.

The removal of these Irish-speaking 'tympanours, poets, story-tellers, babblers, rymours, harpers, or any other Irish minstrels', who served as symbols of the 'feasting and fighting' culture, became a priority for

---

[12] C. Maxwell, ed., *Irish History from Contemporary Sources (1509–1610)* (London, 1923), p. 319.

[13] Scott Wheeler, 'The Logistics of Conquest', in P. Lenihan, ed., *Conquest and Resistance: War in Seventeenth-Century Ireland* (Leiden, 2001), pp. 177–207.

[14] Seamus Deane, ed., *The Field Day Anthology of Irish Writing*, 3 vols. (Derry, 1991), I, pp. 399–400.

monarchs and their ministers as they set out to civilize 'those rude parts'.[15] The promotion of the English language was another. From the later Middle Ages the English language had served, and was perceived, as an important instrument of Empire.[16] An Act of 1537 aimed to introduce 'a conformitie, concordance, and familiarity in language, tongue, in manners, order and apparel' and to cast aside 'the diversitie that is betwixt them [the English and Irish] in tongue, language, order and habite'.[17] Yet, by the turn of the seventeenth century, only a minority of the population spoke English.[18] To change this and to foster cultural assimilation, many advocated the establishment of parochial and grammar schools, thereby breeding 'in the rudest of our people resolute English hearts', as the Old English writer Richard Stanihurst put it, and making them 'good members of this commonwealth'.[19] According to Sir John Davies, only education could guarantee 'that the next generation will in tongue and heart, and every way else, become English; so that there will be no difference or distinction, but the Irish sea betwixt us'.[20]

By the mid-sixteenth century Protestantism had became a further and key index of civilization. After 1603, James VI and I set out both to revitalize and to reform the Church of Ireland with a view to persuading, rather than coercing, the Catholic population to conform. As the Elizabethan prelates died out he replaced them with able English and Scottish prelates and by 1625 only three out of twenty-five bishops were of Irish provenance. Since the desire to convert the Irish to the Established Church often drove colonial impulses, Protestant clergymen increasingly spearheaded imperial initiatives.[21] Andrew Knox, Bishop of the Isles, who

[15] Edmund Curtis and R. B. McDowell, eds., *Irish Historical Documents, 1172–1922* (London, 1943), p. 55.

[16] P. Hulme, *Colonial Encounters: Europe and the Native Caribbean, 1492–1797* (London, 1986), p. 1.

[17] *The Statutes at Large Passed in the Parliaments held in Ireland (1310–1800)*, 20 vols. (Dublin, 1786–1801), I, p. 120.

[18] Patricia Palmer, *Language and Conquest in Early Modern Ireland: English Renaissance Literature and Elizabethan Imperial Expansion* (Cambridge, 2001) examines 'linguistic imperialism' and suggests how language shaped colonial ideology and identity.

[19] Quoted in Raymond Gillespie, 'Church, State and Education in Early Modern Ireland', in Maurice O'Connell, ed., *Education, Church and State* (Dublin, 1992), p. 44.

[20] John Davies, *A Discovery of the True Causes why Ireland was never entirely subdued* (1612; London, 1968), p. 272.

[21] John McCavitt, *Sir Arthur Chichester, Lord Deputy of Ireland, 1605–16* (Belfast, 1998), pp. 109, 111.

had played a central role in tackling problems in the Highlands and Islands, arrived in Donegal in 1611, as Bishop of Raphoe, to tame the 'wild Irish' there. Wentworth's unpopular patriarch, John Bramhall, Bishop of Derry, behaved as an 'episcopal ogre' as he enforced canonical norms and recovered ecclesiastical patrimony in a bid to anglicize the Church of Ireland.[22]

The Church and state also focused their efforts on educating Catholic youths or, at least, preventing them from being instructed abroad, 'where they may have been infected with poperie and other ill qualities, and so become evill subietts...'.[23] The Court of Wards insisted that the underage sons of leading Catholic landowners, mercantile, and civic figures attend Trinity College, Dublin (founded in 1592) so 'that the ward shall be brought up...in English habit and religion'.[24] Determined to Anglicize and to protestantize the social élite, the King also tried to pressure prominent Irish peers to send their sons to be educated in England. In the instances where a lord died leaving a minor, the Crown enjoyed even greater control. In hopes of minimizing the authority of his Catholic relatives and to prevent him from marrying a 'papist', the young 16th Earl of Kildare, heir to Ireland's premier aristocratic lineage, was dispatched to Oxford.[25] As it turned out, Kildare conformed with enthusiasm, as did his successors. During the early decades of the seventeenth century the premature deaths of their fathers meant that the heirs to the houses of Ormond, Inchiquin, Mayo, and Castleconnell all converted to Protestantism and became political and cultural pawns of the state. Lord Deputy Wentworth maintained that if Ormond had been raised 'under the wing of his own parents' he would have been Catholic like his brothers and sisters. 'Whereas now he is a firm Protestant, like to prove a great and able servant to the crowne, and a great assistant...in the civill government; it

---

[22] John McCafferty, 'John Bramhall and the Church of Ireland in the 1630s', in A. Ford, J. McGuire and K. Milne, eds., *As by Law Established: The Church of Ireland since the Reformation* (Dublin, 1995), p. 104.

[23] Timothy Cochran, *Studies in the History of Classical Teaching* (Dublin, 1911), p. 56.

[24] Ibid., p. 63; H. F. Berry, 'Probable Early Students of Trinity College, Dublin (being wards of the Crown), 1599–1616', *Hermathena*, XVI (1911), pp. 19–39; H. F. Kearney, 'The Court of Wards and Liveries in Ireland, 1622–1641', *Proceedings of the Royal Irish Antiquaries*, LVIII, Section C (1955–6), pp. 29–68.

[25] *Calendar of State Papers relating to Ireland, 1625–32* (hereafter *CSPI*) (London, 1900), p. 490; Treadwell, *Buckingham*, p 120; C. W. FitzGerald, *The Earls of Kildare and their Ancestors, 1057 to 1773* (Dublin, 1858).

being most certaine that no people under the sunne are more apte to be of the same religion with their great lords as the Irish be'.[26]

Yet not all of the converts shared Ormond's zeal. Despite spending a year at Trinity, under Wentworth's watchful eye, and having a Protestant mother, William Bourke, 5th Baron of Castleconnell, married a Catholic and took an active role in the 1641 rebellion.[27] Similarly, under the pressures of war and rebellion, Miles Bourke, 2nd Viscount Mayo, and his heir, who had been reared a Protestant and had also wed one, reverted to Catholicism.[28] Interestingly, the state later recognized the general problems inherent in this conversion and education strategy. Writing in 1661, Roger Boyle, Earl of Orrery, noted how the Court of Wards had not only failed in its mission but how potential converts had subverted the very process that sought to civilize them. 'We cannot find six instances in the memory of man of any converted to the Protestant religion by the education of the Court of Wards', he wrote, adding ominously that 'an English education and an Irish religion is much more dangerous than if both were Irish'.[29] Perhaps Orrery had in mind the likes of Sir Phelim O'Neill. Despite being educated at the Inns of Court and briefly conforming to Protestantism, O'Neill led the Ulster rebellion of October 1641 which plunged all of Ireland into a decade of bitter and bloody civil war and threatened the very survival of the English and Scottish colonies there.

Important though education and conversion were to contemporaries, it was the introduction of English law throughout the island that became the critical prerequisite for the civilization of Ireland and served as the platform from which imperial initiatives could be launched.[30] This was nothing new. From the twelfth century the English kings had attempted to impose the English legal system on Ireland and had introduced a court structure modelled on that of England. In practice, however, 'a very

---

[26] Thomas Carte, *The Life of James Duke of Ormond....* 6 vols. (Oxford, 1851), VI, p. 214. A zealous convert, Ormond later adopted similar tactics. For instance, after recovering the estates of his kinsman, Lord Dunboyne, he promised to restore them to the impoverished baron on the condition that 'he lets me have the breeding of his sonne, a youth of about 13 years old': Historical Manuscripts Commission, *Report 11. Appendix 5* (London, 1887), p. 14.

[27] Knowler, ed., *The Earl of Strafforde's Letters and Despatches*, II, p. 342.

[28] Mary Hickson, ed., *Ireland in the Seventeenth Century*, 2 vols. (London, 1884), I, p. 380.

[29] *CSPI, 1660–1662* (London, 1905), p. 415.

[30] For further details see Ciaran Brady, *The Chief Governors: The Rise and Fall of Reform Government in Tudor Ireland, 1536–1588* (Cambridge, 1994), p. xi.

unusual kind of judicial dualism existed' that effectively excluded the native Irish.[31] From the mid-sixteenth century the state set out with renewed vigour to assert law and order by attacking the military systems on which lordly power rested and by pressuring lords, Old English and native Irish alike, to accept royal authority. Thus, as Sir William Gerard, a lawyer and briefly Lord Chancellor, argued, 'sharpe lawes muste woorke the reform'. And, in a report of 1576, he asked 'can the sword teache theim to speake Englishe, to use Englishe apparell, to restrayne theim from Irish axactions and extotions, and to shonne all the manners and orders of the Irishe. Noe it is the rodd of justice that must scower out those blottes.'[32] Accordingly, legislation proscribed the collection of tribute, cattle-raiding, and the maintenance of armed retainers, and mandated that all law suits be settled by English common law, in an attempt to bring the people to 'the obedience of English law and the English empire'.[33]

Thanks in part to the revitalization of central government and the introduction (by Lord Deputy Chichester) of a national system of assize courts, the use of English law quickly spread throughout Ireland.[34] On the eve of the 1641 rebellion the Lords Justice noted ever-optimistically how 'the great Irish lords, who for so many ages so grievously infested this kingdom, are either taken away or so levelled with others in point of subjection as all now submit to the rule of law, and many of them live in good order'.[35] Despite complaints about the cumbersome nature of the judicial system and gripes about the corruptness of individual lawyers, judges, and juries, levels of litigation appear to have increased significantly.[36] This suggests that the population enjoyed a level of confidence in the legal system and especially in the central courts. Analysis of 415 individual Dublin Chancery Recognizances dating from 1627 to 1634 reveals

---

[31] R. Bartlett, *The Making of Europe: Conquest, Colonization and Cultural Change, 950–1350* (London, 1994), p. 214.

[32] Hadfield and McVeagh, eds., *Strangers to that Land*, p. 40.

[33] *CSPI, 1625–32*, p. 58; Steven Ellis, *Reform and Revival: English Government in Ireland, 1470–1534* (London, 1986), esp. chap. 4; J. G. Crawford, *Anglicizing the Government of Ireland: The Irish Privy Council and the Expansion of Tudor Rule, 1556–1578* (Dublin, 1993).

[34] John McCavitt, '"Good Planets in their Several Spheares"—The Establishment of the Assize Circuits in Early Seventeenth Century Ireland', *Irish Jurist*, XXIV (1989), pp. 248–78; and McCavitt, *Sir Arthur Chichester*, pp. 97, 99, 103.

[35] *CSPI, 1633–47* (London, 1901), pp. 275–6.

[36] T. C. Barnard, 'Lawyers and the Law in Later Seventeenth-Century Ireland', *Irish Historical Studies* (hereafter *IHS*), XXVIII (1993), pp. 256–82.

that litigants embraced every ethnic and religious group living in early modern Ireland.[37] The fact that a disproportionately large number of Catholic Gaels appear in these legal records is particularly significant and indicates that Chancery also acted as a forum whereby suits arising from English common law and Gaelic customary law could be mediated. Moreover Catholic lawyers, themselves trained at the English Inns of Court, acted as particularly effective mediators, negotiating local settlements that, at the very least, protected Catholic interests and, where possible, exploited the English legal system to the advantage of their native clients.

A significant proportion of seventeenth-century legal cases concerned suits over land. Whether as contested mortgages, landlord-tenant disputes, remedies for defective transfer, failure to pay rents, to improve or build property, these cases highlight the centrality of land to the political, economic, and social fabric of early modern Ireland. The ability to meddle in Irish landholding or to confiscate and then distribute Irish acres to the loyal not only empowered the Crown but also underpinned imperialist expansion and colonization. Tenurial imperialism took on a variety of forms, ranging from interference in an individual's title to land to expropriation and plantation.

A series of reforming policies characterized the sixteenth century. From the 1540s the Crown negotiated 'surrender and regrant' agreements with leading Gaelic chieftains. Land held by a non-English title was surrendered to the Crown and regranted to its holder with title and tenure good in English law. In return, the lord agreed to renounce his Gaelic title for an English one, to recognize the King's writ and courts, and to Anglicize his territories. Over time, these arrangements became increasingly sophisticated. Throughout the 1570s and 1580s, the state pressured leading powerbrokers to accept 'composition' agreements which sought to demilitarize the local magnates by appealing directly to their principal followers and enhancing the power of the state in the process. Thus, the 'Composition of Connacht' (1585) promoted Anglicization in the lordships of Clanricarde and Thomond and paved the way for moderate reform. Ultimately, however, it weakened rather than strengthened the position of the lesser landowners and enshrined in English law the 'essential

---

[37] Jane Ohlmeyer, 'Records of the Irish Court of Chancery: A Preliminary Report for 1627–1634', in Desmond Greer and Norma Dawson, eds., *Mysteries and Solutions in Irish Legal History* (Dublin, 2001), pp. 15–49; Mary O'Dowd, 'Women and the Irish Chancery Court in the Late Sixteenth and Early Seventeenth Centuries', *IHS*, XXXI (1999), pp. 470–87.

characteristics of the traditional lordships'.[38] Thus, these reforming arrangements not only protected, at least in the short-term, the estates of
leading lords from confiscation but also represented an effective form of
'unconscious colonization'.

While demands for the expropriation of native lands dated from the
later Middle Ages, only after the Desmond rebellion of the 1570s did
wholesale plantation win widespread acceptance. Further rebellions, especially the Nine Years War and the Confederate Wars (1641–52), focused
further attention on the 'treachery' of the Irish and facilitated further
waves of colonization. There are European parallels here. Wide-scale revolt
among the Morisco population of Granada between 1568 and 1570
prompted the Habsburg government to transplant the bulk of this un-
assimilated racial minority to Castile and to introduce 50,000 Old Christian settlers from Galicia, Asturias, and León. Sir John Davies later drew
on the transplantation of the Moors and of the Grahams from the Anglo-
Scottish Borders in his justification of the Ulster plantation.[39]

In Ireland, early attempts at plantation, on the lands belonging to the
O'Connors, O'Mores, and O'Dempseys in Laois and Offaly, or at Newry,
failed. Similarly, in Ulster efforts in 1571–72 by Sir Thomas Smith (in the
Ards) and the Earl of Essex (in Clandeboye) to establish private military
settlements, which would provide bulwarks against the destabilizing
influences exerted by the MacDonnells, ended in disaster.[40] After the outbreak of the Desmond rebellion, however, plantation became an instrument of royal policy and private enterprise was put to work for the
purposes of the state. In 1585, shortly after the first abortive English
attempt to colonize the New World, the government announced an ambitious scheme which aimed to recreate the world of south-east England on
the confiscated Munster estates of the Earl of Desmond. Grants of land,
ranging from 4,000 to 12,000 acres, were awarded to thirty-five English

[38] Bernadette Cunningham, 'Political and Social Change in the Lordships of Clanricard and
Thomond, 1596–1641' (unpublished MA thesis, NUI, University College Galway, 1979), p. 168
and 'The Composition of Connacht in the Lordships of Clanricard and Thomond, 1577–1641',
IHS, XXIV (1984), pp. 1–14. Also see Bernadette Cunningham, 'Theobald Dillon, A Newcomer
in Sixteenth-Century Mayo', *Cathair na Mart: Journal of the Westport Historical Society*, VI
(1986), pp. 24–32.

[39] Sir John Davies, *Historical Tracts*, ed. George Chalmers (Dublin, 1787), p. 283.

[40] Hiram Morgan, 'The Colonial Venture of Sir Thomas Smith in Ulster, 1571–5', *Historical
Journal*, XXVIII (1987), pp. 261–78; R. Dunlop, 'The Plantation of Leix and Offaly, 1556–1622',
English Historical Review (hereafter *EHR*), VI (1891), pp. 61–96.

landlords who vowed to introduce English colonists and to practice English-style agriculture based on the cultivation of grain. By the end of the sixteenth century roughly 12,000 settlers were actively engaged in this type of farming, and estimates suggest that by 1641 Munster had attracted 22,000 Protestant planters and, after 1660, 30,000. Certainly, on the eve of the Irish rebellion, as one recent historian has noted, 'The English visitor to Munster in 1640 would...have been faced with many familiar objects. As he moved about the province, using the passable roads, he would notice the number of enclosures, stone buildings and the occasional large house, surrounded by gardens and orchards'. Many inhabitants now wore shoes (rather than brogues), and English caps, stockings, breeches, and jerkins, while an ever-increasing number of people spoke English.[41]

Following English victory in the Nine Years War, Ulster met a similar fate to that of Munster. As King of Scotland, James VI had attempted to tame the Western Isles by planting, as he noted in *Basilikon Doron*, 'colonies among them of answerable inland subjects, that within short time may reform and civilise the best inclined among them: rooting out or transporting the barbarous and stubborn sort, and planting civility in their rooms'.[42] His plans came to nothing in Scotland but, instead, reached fruition in Ireland. The unexpected flight of leading Irish lords to the continent in 1607 and the revolt of Sir Cahir O'Dogherty in 1608, enabled the state to confiscate vast tracts of Ulster (encompassing the present-day Counties Armagh, Tyrone, Fermanagh, Londonderry, Cavan, and Donegal). Influenced by the Munster experience and by his attempts to plant Harris and Lewis, the King allocated land in relatively small parcels (ranging from 1,000 to 2,000 acres) to 100 Scottish and English 'undertakers' and about 50 'servitors' (largely English army officers who had settled at the end of the war) in the hope that they would create a Lowland type of rural society. In addition, he set aside other acres to endow those key civilizing institutions, the church, towns, schools, and

---

[41] Michael MacCarthy-Morrogh, 'The English Presence in Early Seventeenth Century Munster', in Ciaran Brady and Raymond Gillespie, eds., *Natives and Newcomers: The Making of Irish Colonial Society, 1534–1641* (Dublin, 1986), p. 188.

[42] W. C. Dickinson and G. Donaldson, eds., *A Source Book of Scottish History*, 3 vols. (Edinburgh, 1961), III, p. 261. Local hostility to the venture frustrated three attempts (1595–1602, 1605, 1609) to settle the forfeited Isles of Lewis and Harris with adventurers from Fife. In stark contrast, the informal colonization of Orkney and Shetland by planters from Fife resulted in the successful—albeit unregulated—extension of Lowland practices to the Northern Isles.

Trinity College, Dublin. He also obliged the City of London to take on the entire county of Londonderry in an effort to bring capital and economic prosperity to a commercial backwater. Finally, in the hope of creating a vested interest in the settlement, and of civilizing the native population, James allocated land to 300 'deserving' Irishmen.[43]

While significant numbers of Scottish and English settlers (roughly 12,000 by 1622) were attracted to the escheated counties, the reality of the scheme failed to match the King's intentions. Many settler landlords did not construct the required number of buildings, and exploited their holdings for a quick return. Colonists such as John Rowley, initially chief agent for the Londoners, and Tristram Beresford, Mayor of Coleraine, illegally exported timber and illicitly felled trees for pipe-staves which they then sold. They set up breweries, mills, and tanneries without license, alienated church lands, and rented holdings at extortionate rates to native Irish tenants. More importantly, from the government's perspective, the settlement did not generate substantial revenue, and during the reign of Charles I the wranglings over how the plantation in County Londonderry should be administered alienated members of the London business community at a time when the King desperately needed their support in his struggle against his increasingly belligerent English Parliament.[44]

Ironically, the unofficial and unregulated plantation of the non-escheated counties of Down and Antrim proved to be much more successful and by 1630 had attracted roughly 7,000 migrants, mostly of Scottish provenance. In 1605 Sir Hugh Montgomery, 6th laird of Braidstone in Ayrshire, and another Scottish favourite of the King, James Hamilton, carved up the estates of Conn O'Neill, lord of Upper Clandeboye and the Great Ards. In a tripartite agreement with O'Neill they attracted a significant number of settlers to the region. In County Antrim, Sir Randal MacDonnell, later 1st Earl of Antrim, introduced many Scottish, Protestant settlers to his vast patrimony and on numerous occasions the King thanked this Catholic lord for 'his services in improving those barren and uncultivated parts of the country, and planting a colony there'.[45] Randal would have been familiar with this concept because he had been fostered on the Scottish island of Arran (hence his name Randal Arranach) and

---

    [43] Jane H. Ohlmeyer, 'Strafford, the "Londonderry Business" and the "New British History"', in Merritt, ed., *The Political World*, pp. 209–29.
    [44] Ibid.   [45] Maxwell, ed., *Irish History*, p. 301.

thus exposed to James's unsuccessful attempts to 'plant' the troublesome Highlands with Scottish Lowlanders. One scholar has suggested that Randal formed an important human link between the Irish and Scottish plantations.[46]

In addition to promoting plantation in Ulster, James VI and I established in 1606 the Commission for the Remedy of Defective titles which, on pain of fine or forfeiture, required all Irish landowners to prove their title to their holdings. Many failed. This resulted, especially between 1610 and 1620, in the redistribution of land in Counties Wexford, Leitrim, Longford and other areas in the Midlands to Protestant officials and Crown favourites.[47] After 1635, Wentworth attempted, by interfering in land titles, to plant English colonists in parts of Clare, Connacht, and the lordship of Ormond. Ultimately, local vested interests, the tenacity of the Galway lawyers, and the courtly contacts of the local Catholic lord not only frustrated his plans but thoroughly alienated large sections of the Catholic population, and thereby contributed to the outbreak of rebellion in October 1641. The rising, which during its early stages probably claimed the lives of 4,000 settlers, was not simply a response to plantation and tenurial insecurity. Other 'long-term' causes directly linked to English imperial initiatives in Ireland, especially a desire to have the Catholic Church restored to its pre-Reformation status and the native response to commercialization, together with short-term political factors, triggered the onset of a decade of bitter and bloody civil war.

Closely linked to colonization, in whatever form it took, was the need to commercialize and urbanize Ireland. Again, the medieval parallels are striking. Writing in the twelfth century, William of Malmesbury compared the 'ragged mob of rustic Irishmen' to the French and English, 'with their more civilised way of life in towns'.[48] Contemporaries in the early modern period also perceived towns, especially corporate towns on the English model, as key features of the civilizing and commercializing process. Towns, according to one historian, 'provided a focus for the diverse elements of rural society by means of regional gatherings, such as assizes

---

[46] Maurice Lee, *Great Britain's Solomon: James VI and I in his Three Kingdoms* (Urbana, Ill., 1990), p. 212.

[47] Kevin Whelan, ed., *Wexford: History and Society. Interdisciplinary Essays on the History of an Irish County* (Dublin, 1987), esp. chaps. 5 and 6.

[48] *Gesta Regum Anglorum*, eds. R. A. B. Maynous, R. M. Thomson, and M. Winter-Bottom (Oxford, 1988–99), I, pp. 739–41.

and quarter sessions, and acted as engines of economic growth, centres of trade, and points from which new ideas and technology could be diffused'.[49] Between 1600 and 1640, the Crown issued patents for 560 markets and 680 fairs throughout Ireland. In Ulster alone 153 patents for markets and eighty-five for fairs were handed out. In 1612 and 1613, James VI and I also created forty parliamentary boroughs out of the newly founded plantation towns, which enabled him to pack the Irish House of Commons with Protestant MPs. Yet these early seventeenth-century urban initiatives did not always achieve the effects that the King had originally envisaged. While many of these towns permanently transformed the Irish landscape and stand as a permanent legacy of the Jacobean plantations, the Irish urban network never developed as fully as its English or Scottish counterparts.[50] By 1670, of the twenty-eight corporate towns that had been established in Ulster, only four—the medieval town of Carrickfergus and the planter towns of Belfast, Coleraine, and Derry—enjoyed adult populations of over 500.[51] Elsewhere more modest settlements of between thirty and 100 adults, comprising mostly tradesmen and artisans, dominated the urban landscape.[52]

Moreover, Irish towns never became fully integrated into the rural economy and often depended for their survival on the activities and connections of local landed grandees. For example, during the early decades of the seventeenth century, the Scottish planter, Andrew Stewart, Lord Ochiltree (later Baron Castlestewart), oversaw the growth of Stewartstown, County Tyrone, into a proto-industrial settlement of three gentlemen, twenty-four tradesmen—a ditcher, shoemaker, tailor, carpenter, butcher, malt maker, some weavers—and a schoolmaster.[53] Similarly, evidence from the 1641 Depositions highlights how urban settlement in Queen's County in Leinster depended on the local Protestant élite.[54] The

---

[49] Raymond Gillespie, 'The Origins and Development of an Ulster Urban Network, 1600–41', *IHS*, XXIV (1984), pp. 15–16. See also Robert Hunter, 'Ulster Plantation Towns: 1609–1641', in David Harkness and Mary O'Dowd, eds., *The Town in Ireland* (Belfast, 1991), pp. 55–80.

[50] Discussed at length in Peter Borsay and Lindsay Proudfoot, eds., *Provincial Towns in Early Modern England and Ireland* (Oxford, 2002), pp. 24–25.

[51] Philip Robinson, 'Urbanisation in North-West Ulster, 1609–1670', *Irish Geography*, XV (1982), pp. 35–50.

[52] W. H. Crawford, 'The Creation and Evolution of Small Towns in Ulster in the Seventeeth and Eighteenth Centuries', in Borsay and Proudfoot, eds., *Provincial Towns*, pp. 98–105.

[53] Nicholas Canny, *Making Ireland British, 1580–1650* (Oxford, 2001), p. 231.

[54] Ibid., pp. 373–77.

civil wars of the 1640s shattered these baronial developments and totally disrupted the trade and proto-industry that had grown up around many of the Irish towns. Some never fully recovered from the ravages associated with the conflict; others had to wait until the late 1650s, 1660s, and 1670s before doing so.[55]

The disproportionate influence enjoyed by regional landed powerbrokers over Irish urban development highlights the importance of securing their support for civilizing and imperial initiatives. One way of achieving this was to create a 'service élite' or colonial hierarchy loosely modelled on the English aristocracy.[56] Thus, during the first three decades of the seventeenth century, the Crown (and its agents) bestowed 258 new Irish knighthoods, 'of which just under a third was awarded to men of Old English or Irish name'.[57] Between 1603 and 1640, the resident Irish aristocracy more than doubled, from twenty-nine peers to sixty-nine. The number of Protestant peers increased tenfold over the same period, from three to over thirty-six. Thus, the Crown created a new generation of ambitious and avaricious peers, usually Protestant and largely of English and, to a lesser extent, Scottish extraction who were determined to make their fortunes in Ireland and to secure public reward and social recognition.[58] As a result, the aristocratic hierarchy ceased to be determined simply by the rank held by a peer or by other traditional criteria (such as lineage, regional status, or the number of followers over whom a lord wielded power). Instead, lordship came to reflect a peer's financial prowess, his ability to exploit his landed resources, and his success in securing high office along with his ability to network, especially at court.

Protestant lords, especially those who held senior administrative and legal posts, worked actively as imperial agents, serving as bureaucrats, judges, regional governors, and military commanders. Richard Boyle, the 'upstart' Earl of Cork, serves as an excellent example of this new breed of Irish lord whose rise can be directly attributed to administrative or military service to the Crown. Boyle arrived in Munster virtually penniless but thanks to his administrative and political offices, his entrepreneurial activities, and a series of wily (and often dubious) land deals, he became

---

[55] Raymond Gillespie, 'The Irish Economy at War, 1641–1652', in Jane Ohlmeyer, ed., *Ireland from Independence to Occupation, 1641–1660* (Cambridge, 1995), pp. 160–180.

[56] G. R. Mayes, 'The Early Stuarts and the Irish Peerage', *EHR*, LXXIII (1958), pp. 227–51.

[57] Treadwell, *Buckingham and Ireland*, pp. 105–06.   [58] Ibid., p. 299.

one of the richest men in all three kingdoms. By 1641 his annual income amounted to £18,000. Cork represents a classic example of a sub-imperialist who combined public service with private gain. Writing in 1613, a fellow English planter claimed that 'No subject in 40 years hath done or will do so much in building, enclosing and planting with English and altogether after the English fashion, insomuch that all his lands are English colonies, even in the midst of Irish countries'.[59] Cork, together with other leading planters, also assiduously promoted urban developments at Kinsale, Bandon, Tallow, Dungarvan, and Youghal. As the extant estate records vividly recapture, he attracted considerable numbers of artisans— weavers, fullers, tanners, coopers—together with fishermen, iron and timber workers, shipbuilders, and merchants to his various industrial and commercial enterprises.[60] Moreover, Cork and his Munster neighbours cultivated trading networks with England, Scandinavia, India, South-East Asia, and the West Indies, and thereby helped to lay the foundations for future mercantile links with the English Atlantic Empire and to reinforce imperial developments both at home and abroad.[61]

In addition to promoting newcomers to Irish peerages, the Crown continued to cultivate influential Gaelic-speaking native lords, many of whom had entered into surrender and regrant agreements in the previous century. For instance, Henry VIII had elevated the Gaelic chieftain, Murrough O'Brien, to the earldom of Thomond in 1543, but it was not until the late sixteenth century that his great-grandson, Donough, the 4th Earl (d. 1624), who had been reared at the English court, embraced Protestantism.[62] During the course of his lifetime, the 4th Earl transformed his vast Connacht patrimony. Thomond nurtured urban development (especially at Sixmilebridge, Kilrush, and Ennis) and encouraged English and Dutch tenants to settle on his estates, particularly their more fertile

[59] Alexander B. Grosart, ed., *The Lismore Papers*, Second Series, 5 vols. (printed for private circulation, 1888), I, 156–57; also see I, pp. 148–49; Nicholas Canny, *The Upstart Earl: A Study of the Social and Mental World of Richard Boyle, First Earl of Cork, 1566–1643* (Cambridge, 1982).

[60] Canny, *Making Ireland British*, pp. 308–21.

[61] Paddy O'Sullivan, 'The English East India Company at Dunaniel', *Bandon Historical Journal*, IV (1988), pp. 3–14.

[62] Thomond held numerous public offices: Governor of County Clare and Thomond, member of the Irish Privy Council, Commissioner for the Presidency of Munster and for the Plantation of Ulster, and President of Munster. Brian Ó Dálaigh, 'A Comparative Study of the Wills of the First and Fourth Earls of Thomond', *North Munster Antiquarian Journal*, XXXIV (1992), pp. 48–63.

areas.[63] He improved his lands by promoting tillage; he introduced new breeds of cattle; he promoted the English language, dress, and legal system; he educated his sons at Oxford and attempted to convert his kinsmen to Protestantism by offering to educate them; and he encouraged members of his extended family to intermarry with Protestant planters. Little wonder that his followers held Thomond to be 'more English than Irish'. A senior government official in Ireland paid a further tribute to him: 'In the ordering of his house or governing of his country, his course has always been English, striving to bring in English customs and to beat down all barbarous Irish usages, that he might in time make his country civil, and bring the inhabitants in love with English laws and government'.[64] Another hoped that 'the example of the earl...will within a few years alter the manners of this people and draw them to civility and religion both'.[65]

Yet the 4th Earl retained many of the vestiges of a traditional Irish lord. Like his ancestors before him, he remained a patron to the Gaelic literary classes.[66] In his will, Donough reminded his heir to nurture his native Irish followers, as well as the newcomers: 'Be true, respective and honourably affected towards the gentlemen and inhabitants of Thomond, whom I have ever found as honest and faithful followers to me as any noblemen had and so I assure...they will grow to my children if they be wisely and honourably [treated]...which I enjoin my said sons to do; as also the[y] cherish and favour all the English amongst them'.[67] Significantly, none of his successors shared the 4th Earl's concerns for his native followers. By the 1670s, Henry, the eldest son of the 7th Earl (and great-grandson of the fourth), urged his own heir 'to cherish the English uppon his estate and driue out the Irish, and specially those of them whoe are under the name of gentlemen'.[68] Thus, 130 years after the original surrender and regrant

---

[63] Cunningham, 'Political and Social Change in the Lordships', pp. 217, 219, 222. Canny, *Making Ireland British*, pp. 329–31, suggests that Thomond and Clanricard 'appear to have emulated the earl of Cork's estate management'.

[64] *CSPI, 1606–1608* (London, 1874), p. 65.   [65] Ibid., p. 470.

[66] Thomond remained a patron to Mac Bruaideadha poets until his death in 1624. See Cunningham, 'Political and Social Change in the Lordships', pp. 131–32. See also, Jane Stevenson and Peter Davidson, eds., *Early Modern Women Poets: An Anthology* (Oxford, 2001), pp. 174–77.

[67] Ó Dálaigh, 'A Comparative Study of the Wills of the First and Fourth Earls of Thomond', p. 61.

[68] John Ainsworth, ed., *Inchiquin Manuscripts* (Irish Manuscripts Commission, Dublin, 1961), p. 512.

agreement had been signed, the metropole had finally succeeded in Anglicizing this leading native dynasty.

Eager to expand their territorial empires and to secure royal goodwill, many members of the Catholic élite followed the examples of Cork and Thomond and became enthusiastic exemplars of civility. Predictably, personal agendas, local circumstances, and patronage and kin-links often shaped their civilizing fervour. Richard Bourke, 4th Earl of Clanricarde, attracted English tenants and did his utmost to 'improve' his patrimony by encouraging his tenants to build stone houses, enclose land, plant trees, and adopt 'modern' agricultural techniques. He also maximized profits from his mills (which in itself suggests increased grain production) and developed the natural resources on his estates (particularly ironworks and fishing).[69] Moreover, the 4th (and later the 5th) Earl's prolonged residence at court in London and ties of kinship with leading English courtiers ensured that the Clanricardes exercized considerable political influence both at home and in England despite their staunch Catholicism.[70]

Surviving deeds from the estates of the 1st and 2nd Gaelic, Catholic Earls of Antrim demonstrate their eagerness to become, and be perceived as, 'improving' landlords. Both encouraged English and Scottish Protestant tenants to settle on their lands and by the late 1630s the Antrim estate could boast well over 300 'British' (or Protestant) families, while the town of Dunluce consisted 'of many tenements, after the fashion of the Pale, peopled for the most part with Scotsmen'.[71] In addition, both Earls carved their vast estate into manageable units of one or more townlands and offered long-term leases to men of substance, requiring them to invest time and capital in improving the property and to attract good tenants who were to enclose poor land, mark boundaries, build stone houses, plant trees, and pay their rents in cash rather than kind. The 2nd Earl took

---

[69] Cunningham, 'Political and Social Change in the Lordships', pp. 226, 231, 240. See also, Bernadette Cunningham, 'Clanricard Letters: Letters and Papers, 1605–1673, preserved in the National Library of Ireland manuscript 3111', *Journal of the Galway Archaeological and Historical Society*, 48 (1996), pp. 162–208.

[70] Patrick Little, '"Blood and Friendship": The Earl of Essex's Protection of the Earl of Clanricarde's Interests, 1641–6', *EHR*, CXII (1997), pp. 927–41.

[71] 'A report of the voluntary works done by servitors...within the counties of Downe, Antryme, and Monahan', PRONI, T.811/3, f. 13. See also, Jane H. Ohlmeyer, *Civil War and Restoration in the Three Stuart Kingdoms: The Career of Randal MacDonnell, Marquis of Antrim, 1609–1683* (Cambridge, 1993), pp. 24–26, 39–42.

some pride in reporting his own achievement to the Dublin government in 1637: 'I have compounded my affairs here with my tenants wherein I was not so inward to my [own] profit as to the general good and settlement by binding them to plant [trees] and husband their holdings so near as may be to the manner of England'.[72] This delighted Charles I, just as the 1st Earl's initiatives had prompted James VI and I to laud 'his dutiful behaviour to the state and the example of his civil and orderly life endeavours very much of the reformation and civilizing of those rude parts ... where he dwells'.[73] The Earls of Antrim, like the Clanricardes, may well have won royal acclaim for their 'improving' policies, but they also publicly demonstrated their devotion to Rome by patronizing St Patrick's purgatory at Lough Derg and by encouraging the Franciscans to maintain a friary at Bonamargy, near Ballycastle, which became the headquarters from which they ministered to their tenants and set out on missions to the Western Isles.[74]

Thus, many nobles, including Catholic Gaels, quickly realized that, in order to survive and be considered 'worthy subjects', they had no alternative but to accept the new commercial economic order inherent in the Crown's civilizing and 'improving' initiatives. One scholar has suggested that this 'unconscious colonization' not only represented a viable alternative to formal colonization but actually protected estates that might otherwise have been vulnerable to expropriation.[75] In addition to reorganizing their estates, regional powerbrokers increasingly adopted London fashions and English and Scottish architectural styles. In 1618 the 4th Earl of Clanricarde spent £10,000 he could ill-afford building a grand fortified house, with mullioned bay windows and an ornate interior, at Portumna, on the banks of the Shannon. Though the outer buildings of the Earl of Antrim's principal seat at Dunluce remained defensive in character, the inner great house resembled an English manor house with two-storied bay windows and leaded, diamond-shaped panes of glass. Likewise Antrim's 'pleasant house' at Glenarm was built to impress both his followers and his peers and to demonstrate his 'Englishness'. Without doubt these residences rivalled any of the other planter castles at Belfast, Carrickfergus, Mountjoy, or Donegal and were 'very richly furnished', presumably according to

[72] Antrim to Ormond [?], 2 Aug. 1637, Sheffield City Library, Strafford MSS 17, f. 151.
[73] James I to Chichester, 3 May 1613, British Library (hereafter BL), Add. MSS, 4794, f. 233.
[74] Ohlmeyer, *Civil War and Restoration*, pp. 27, 47, 75.
[75] Cunningham, 'Political and Social Change', p. 285.

the latest London fashions. Even in remote areas such as County Sligo, English fashions, architectural styles, and economic practices became increasingly widespread.[76]

Building, combined with increased conspicuous expenditure (on furniture, clothing, education, legal expenses, living at court, and marriage) resulted in widespread indebtedness, disrupting the traditional redistributive economic order. By the late 1630s the Earl of Antrim's debts hovered around £42,000 and pressure from his creditors for repayment forced him to mortgage nineteen properties on the Strand in London, together with the entire barony of Cary, the lordship of Ballycastle, and Rathlin Island. The majority of his Ulster neighbours, Catholic and Protestant alike, faced a similar predicament, as did other prominent Irish figures, such as the Earls of Ormond, Thomond, and Clanricarde. Indebtedness on the eve of the outbreak of war in 1641 highlights the precariousness of the economic position of the landed élite and particularly the Catholic lords. In the short term, a willingness to adopt the civilizing and colonizing policies of the core often brought immediate political gain and strengthened the regional position of landed powerbrokers. In the longer term, the insidious financial and economic pressures to which these imperial initiatives gave rise, exacerbated by the onset of civil war in 1641 and again after 1688, left the Catholic élite more vulnerable still to more forceful waves of imperialism.

That a handful of prominent Catholic lords embraced the Crown's commercial and civilizing strategies should not suggest that the bulk of the native population shared their enthusiasm. On the contrary, many did not. Extant bardic poetry and vernacular verse helps to recapture their responses to these civilizing processes.[77] Many members of the traditional learned classes, reeling in the wake of political, but not intellectual, collapse, clearly abhorred the changes wrought by colonial processes. Some

---

[76] Mary O'Dowd, *Power, Politics and Land: Early Modern Sligo, 1568–1688* (Belfast, 1991), p. 103.

[77] Interestingly, some poets readily accepted grants of land in the plantation scheme, while bards on both sides of the North Channel modified the traditional themes of their poetry to meet the new circumstances and the changed priorities of their new patron. Bernadette Cunningham and Raymond Gillespie, 'The East Ulster bardic family of Ó Gnímh', *Egise*, XX (1984); B. Ó Buachalla, 'James our True King. The Ideology of Irish Royalism in the Seventeenth Century', in D. George Boyce, Robert Eccleshall, and Vincent Geoghegan, eds., *Political Thought in Ireland since the Seventeenth Century* (London, 1993), p. 10; Canny, *Making Ireland British*, pp. 426–27.

bards criticized the 'new methods of fortification, enclosure, and cultivation that followed the displacement of the native Irish by English and Scottish planters'.[78] Others condemned the workings of the Court of Wards, the central and local courts, or members of the Catholic élite who had converted to Protestantism.[79] Still more vented their spleen against the newcomers, whom they regarded as lowborn thugs and 'English-speaking bastards' drawn, according to John Lynch, 'from the barbers' shops, and highways, and taverns, and stables and hogsties of England'.[80] Fear Flatha Ó Gnímh, whose family had served as the traditional poets to the O'Neills, penned a lament ('Pitiful are the Gaels') which described Ireland as 'a new England in all but name'.[81]

Defeat in the civil wars of the 1640s and further dispossession in the wake of the land settlements of the 1650s and 1660s inflamed the intensity of the anti-colonial rhetoric. Depicting English imperialism as a cultural, as well as a political, force, the poets lambasted those whom they believed had abandoned long-established values and betrayed their traditional leadership roles.[82] Writing after the Restoration, Dáithí Ó Bruadair, in 'How Queer this Mode', ridiculed Ormond for his Anglicized ways: 'With haughty, upstart ostentation lately swollen,/ Though codes of foreign clerks they fondly strive to master,/ They utter nothing but a ghost of strident English'.[83] Nicholas French, the Catholic Bishop of Ferns, also aimed his animus against the Lord-Lieutenant. In the *Unkinde Desertor* (published at Paris in 1676) Ormond, 'a great bramble cruelly scratching and tormenting Ireland', attracts particular scorn.[84] French concluded *Unkinde Desertor* by hoping that posterity would censure Ormond's

---

[78] Brian Ó Cuiv, 'The Irish Language in the Early Modern Period', in T. W. Moody, F. X. Martin, and F. J. Byrne, eds., *New History of Ireland. III. Early Modern Ireland, 1534–1691* (Oxford, 1978), p. 526.

[79] Nicholas Canny, *Making Ireland British*, pp. 428–31.

[80] Lynch, *Cambrensis Eversus*, III, p. 75.

[81] Cunningham and Gillespie, 'The East Ulster Bardic Family of Ó Gnímh'; Bernadette Cunningham, 'Native Culture and Political Change in Ireland, 1580–1640', in Brady and Gillespie, eds., *Natives and Newcomers*, pp. 148–70.

[82] Michelle Ó Riordan, '"Political" Poems in the Mid-Seventeenth-Century Crisis', in Ohlmeyer, ed., *Ireland*, pp. 112–27.

[83] J. C. MacErlean, ed., *The Poems of Dáithí Ó Bruadair*, 2 vols. (Irish Texts Society, London, 1910), I, p. 19. See also, 'Thou Sage of Inanity', in ibid., I, pp. 195–207.

[84] Nicholas French, *The Unkinde Desertor of Loyall Men and True Frinds* ([Paris], 1676) reprinted in S. H. Bindon, ed., *The Historical Works of... now for the First Time Collected* (Dublin, 1846), p. 15.

betrayal of the Catholics, which 'had made the noble house of Ormond an infamous den and couch of rapine whose whelps are made fat by the prey and booty made upon their neighbours'.[85]

The concerns articulated in these contemporary writings were very real. Military defeat after 1649, followed by English reconquest, exposed Irish Catholics to yet another round of expropriation and English imperialism on a scale that not even Spenser or Wentworth would have imagined possible. The settlement of the 1650s, which represented the most ambitious attempt to plant Ireland at any point in the island's history, reduced many to landless penury. Others—prisoners of war, petty criminals, vagrants, orphans and priests—were forced into exile in Europe, the American colonies, and the West Indies where they either served as cannon fodder or helped to satiate the demand for forced labour. The Adventurers' Act (March 1642) began the process of expropriation by offering Protestant speculators 2,500,000 acres belonging to Irish delinquents. Legislation the following year allotted parliamentary soldiers serving in Ireland land in lieu of their pay on the same terms as the adventurers. In order to recompense these soldiers and adventurers the English Parliament stipulated in the Act of Settlement (August 1652) that virtually all land held by Catholics should be confiscated and that many of the dispossessed should be transplanted to Connacht. Implementation of the Cromwellian land settlement proved problematic and 'a projected influx of 36,000' dwindled to 8,000 (7,500 of whom were soldiers and 500 civilians).[86]

In any event, the restoration of Charles II in 1660 overtook attempts to redistribute land. It then fell to the Lord-Lieutenant, the Duke of Ormond, to oversee the Restoration land settlement. Unable and, in some instances, unwilling to turn the clock back to 1641, Ormond nevertheless tempered the extremes of the earlier measures and restored numerous 'loyal' Catholics to their estates.[87] Despite this, the revolution in Irish landholding, which began with the plantations of the early seventeenth century and culminated with the Cromwellian and Restoration land

---

[85] Ibid., p. 194.

[86] T. C. Barnard, 'New Opportunities for British Settlement: Ireland, 1650–1700', in Canny, ed., *OHBE. Vol. I*, p. 311.

[87] L. J. Arnold, 'The Irish Court of Claims of 1663', *IHS*, XXIV (1985), pp. 417–30.

settlements, reduced the Catholic share of land from 59 per cent in 1641 to 22 per cent in 1688.[88] This tenurial upheaval may have moved forward the process of creating more commercially viable estates; but it also resulted in a reconfiguration of Irish society. The destruction of the economic foundations of the old Gaelic order was accelerated and the rise of a native Protestant ascendancy, determined to protect its landed and political position, had been facilitated.

The 1640s and 1650s marked a watershed in other important respects. With the emergence of political economy as a distinctive discourse and with trade increasingly determining the thinking and actions of the English government, Ireland's colonial status became more apparent still during the later seventeenth century. From the mid-seventeenth century the English Parliament exercised strict legal control over the economic activities of colonies, whether in Ireland, the Atlantic, or the East.[89] In short, priorities shifted from conquest, colonization, and civilization to commerce and economic protectionism and these years witnessed the emergence of a new concept of Empire, one firmly grounded on English economic and political domination.[90]

This transformation manifested itself in England's need to regulate Ireland's burgeoning economy with restrictive statutes, such as the Navigation Acts and Cattle Acts or legislation controlling the woollen industry. While contemporaries, especially leading Protestant colonists, complained bitterly against this legislation, it did stimulate domestic innovation. After 1661, the Irish Parliament established a Standing Committee for Trade and Lord-Lieutenant Ormond took a more direct interest in nurturing the nation's economic development. For instance, Ormond set out to improve the manufacture of Irish textiles, especially on his own estates in Counties Tipperary and Dublin. In 1671, the Duke instructed Colonel Richard Lawrence to develop the linen industry at Chapelizod, County Dublin, and imported craftsmen from Brabant, La Rochelle, and the Isle of Rhé.[91] Many Irish towns and ports also prospered and from the

---

[88] Moody, Martin, and Byrne, eds., *New History of Ireland. III*, p. 428.

[89] Carla Gardina Pestana, *The English Atlantic in an Age of Revolution, 1640–1661* (Cambridge, Mass., 2004).

[90] Nicholas Canny, 'The Origins of Empire', in Canny, ed., *OHBE. Vol. I*, pp. 22–23.

[91] Toby Barnard and Jane Fenlon, eds., *The Dukes Of Ormonde, 1610–1745* (Woodbridge, 2000), p. 37; Carmel McAsey, 'Chapelizod, Co. Dublin', *Dublin Historical Record*, XVII (1962),

late seventeenth-century Dublin became the second largest city in the English Empire, with a population of 62,000 by 1706. Yet, despite the development of textile manufacturing and the growth of Dublin, Ireland became economically (as well as politically) more reliant on England. This dependence also defined Ireland's commercial relationship with other imperial dominions and offered enterprising Irishmen, particularly those resident in London, enhanced access to later Stuart imperial ventures. These men included Catholic merchants and influential entrepreneurs such as Arthur Annesley, Earl of Anglesey.[92] Annesley was not only England's Lord Treasurer but also one of the key political figures in Restoration Ireland. He was the eldest son of Francis Annesley, Lord Mountnorris, who had used his government office and his close relationship with Lord Deputy Chichester to acquire extensive estates throughout Ireland during the early part of the century.[93] As entries in Annesley's diary record, whilst in London he regularly attended meetings of the 'Gambia Company' and the Committee of Trade and Plantations, or with Commissioners from New England and Tangiers, and entertained other entrepreneurs who shared his imperial business interests. His dining companions included Lords Baltimore, Inchiquin, and Longford, who, like Annesley, all enjoyed close Irish links.[94]

Anecdotal as they are, the reports of their colonial activities highlight the diverse experiences of the Irish as imperialists in the English Atlantic and Eastern empires. Despite his Catholicism, Baltimore's father, George Calvert, had been a favourite of the Duke of Buckingham and had acquired over 9,000 Irish acres together with an Irish peerage in the early seventeenth century. In 1628, keen to promote plantations 'in those remote parts of the world', he transferred his interests from Ireland to the New World, first to Newfoundland (he had obtained a charter to found a colony in 1623) and later to Maryland (the charter was issued shortly after

---

p. 42. Little wonder then that Lawrence, writing in 1682, dedicated his *The Interest of Ireland in its Trade and Wealth* (two vols. in one, Dublin, 1682), to Ormond's grandson and heir, James, Earl of Ossory.

[92] Louis M. Cullen, 'Merchant Communities, the Navigation Acts and the Irish and Scottish Responses', in L. M. Cullen and T. C. Smout, eds., *Comparative Aspects of Scottish and Irish Social History* (Edinburgh, 1977), pp. 165–76.

[93] Treadwell, *Buckingham and Ireland*, pp. 54–56; McCavitt, *Sir Arthur Chichester*, pp. 53–79.

[94] Annesley's diary, 1671–1675, BL Add. MSS, 40860 and Annesley's diary, 1675–1684, Add. MSS, 18730.

he died in 1632).[95] In the event, his eldest son, Cecil, and 200 English Catholic migrants founded the Maryland colony which his younger son, Leonard, later governed.[96] Though Baltimore abandoned one colony on the 'near periphery' of the transoceanic English Empire for another on the 'outer periphery', both enjoyed a number of similarities. As in Ireland, principles of improvement and civilization guided the colonization of Maryland and neighbouring Virginia. 'Agents in both plantations', one historian recently noted, 'were given detailed and almost identical instructions on the erection of houses and churches'.[97] Contemporaries made frequent comparisons. Lord Deputy Chichester noted in 1610 that 'I had rather labour with my hands in the plantation of Ulster, than dance or play in that of Virginia'.[98] Many colonists shared Chichester's preference for Ireland and, certainly, the colonization of Ireland during the early seventeenth century progressed at a faster pace than the settlement of North America. It has been estimated that prior to 1641, 100,000 people migrated to Ireland from Britain (30,000 Scots, largely to Ulster, and 70,000 Welsh or English migrants), which helps account for the probable rise in the Irish population.[99] By 1640 Virginia had attracted only about 12,000, of whom 8,000 survived. Equally important, those colonists who settled in Ireland during the period were more skilled and fared better than those who migrated across the Atlantic.[100]

The numbers of Irish migrants crossing the Atlantic remained relatively small and probably averaged 200 migrants *per annum* during the first half of the seventeenth century and 400 *per annum* during the second.[101] For the most part, these migrants went as indentured servants and labourers and settled in Virginia, Maryland, and the Carolinas (and, by the later

---

[95] Treadwell, *Buckingham and Ireland*, p. 305.

[96] James Horn, 'Tobacco Colonies: The Shaping of English Society in the Seventeenth-Century Chesapeake', in Canny, ed., *OHBE. Vol. I*, pp. 178, 186.

[97] Canny, 'The Origins of Empire', in Canny, ed., *OHBE. Vol. I*, p. 10.

[98] *CSPI, 1608–10* (London, 1874), p. 520.

[99] The Irish population rose from an estimated c.1.4 million in 1600 to 2.1 million in 1641 (a growth of 1 per cent per annum). T. C. Smout, N. C. Landsman, and T. M. Devine, 'Scottish Emigration in the Seventeenth and Eighteenth Centuries', in Nicholas Canny, ed., *Europeans on the Move* (Oxford, 1994), p. 79.

[100] Nicholas Canny, 'English Migration into and across the Atlantic during the Seventeenth and Eighteenth centuries', in Canny, ed., *Europeans on the Move*, pp. 64–75.

[101] L. M. Cullen, 'The Irish Diaspora of the Seventeenth and Eighteenth Centuries', in Canny, ed., *Europeans on the Move*, pp. 126–27, 139.

1680s, New England) and the West Indies.[102] It was only in the middle and later decades of the eighteenth century that the Irish, especially Protestants from Ulster who were largely of Scottish provenance, went to North America and the Caribbean in substantial numbers. Whenever they left or whatever their geographic origins, these transatlantic settlers took with them direct experiences of colonization and plantation. For example, historians have shown how English expansionists—including Sir Walter Ralegh, Humphrey Gilbert, and William Penn—used their Irish experiences to confirm their assumptions of savagism, paganism, and barbarism and applied these 'to the indigenous population of the New World'.[103]

From the perspective of Ireland, the West Indies—the 'hub' of the Atlantic trading system—was more significant than the mainland colonies both as a destination for traders and transportees and in economic terms.[104] From the early seventeenth century remarkable numbers of Irish people migrated (often as indentured servants and labourers) to the Caribbean, especially to Barbados and the Leeward Islands (Nevis, Antigua, St Kitts, and Montserrat, the latter known as the 'Irish island'). By the mid-seventeenth century leading Irish merchant families had established themselves on Barbados and the Leeward Islands, where Irish capital funded the lucrative tobacco trade.[105] A recent case study of the tiny island of Montserrat shows that the Irish—'schooled in early English

---

[102] For a detailed case study of one Irish Catholic, Charles Carroll, who travelled to Maryland in 1688 as the Attorney General, see Ronald Hoffman, *Princes of Ireland, Planters of Maryland: A Carroll Saga, 1500–1782* (Chapel Hill, NC, 2000).

[103] Nicholas P. Canny, *The Elizabethan Conquest of Ireland: A Pattern Established, 1565–1576* (New York, 1976), p. 160; Howard Mumford Jones, 'Origins of the Colonial Idea in England', *Proceedings of the American Philosophical Society*, LXXXV, 5 (1942), pp. 448–65; D. B. Quinn, 'Ireland and Sixteenth Century European Expansion', in T. D. Williams, ed., *Historical Studies* (London, 1958), pp. 20–32. See also Rolf Loeber, 'Preliminaries to the Massachusetts Bay Colony: The Irish Ventures of Emanuel Downing and John Winthrop Sr', in Toby Barnard, Dáibhí Ó Cróinín, and Katharine Simms, eds., *'A Miracle of Learning': Studies in Manuscripts and Irish Learning* (Aldershot, 1998), pp. 164–200; Patricia Coughlan, 'Counter-Currents in Colonial Discourse: The Political Thought of Vincent and Daniel Gookin', in Jane Ohlmeyer, ed., *Political Thought in Seventeenth Century Ireland* (Cambridge, 2000), pp. 56–82.

[104] Hilary D. Beckles, 'The "Hub of Empire": The Carribean and Britain in the Seventeenth Century', in Canny, ed., *OHBE. Vol. I*, pp. 218–39.

[105] Martin J. Blake, ed., *Blake Family Records, 1600 to 1700* (London, 1905), pp. 106–13 and A. Gwynn, 'Documents relating to the Irish in the West Indies', *Analecta Hibernica*, IV (1932), pp. 139–286.

imperialism (sometimes quite unpleasantly)'—became aggressive and expert imperialists themselves.[106] By the mid-seventeenth century, the population of Montserrat consisted of roughly 1,000 families, the majority of whom were of Irish Catholic provenance, including both Old English and native Irish. Numbers increased significantly with the Cromwellian transportations of the 1650s, when as many as 10,000 Catholics were shipped to the West Indies. By the late seventeenth century nearly 70 per cent of Montserrat's white population was Irish. Thus, Montserrat 'registered the highest concentration of persons of Irish ethnicity of any colony in the history of both the first and second English empires'.[107] These Irish settlers not only prospered but 'became more economically powerful' than their Scottish and English counterparts, largely because 'they well knew how to be hard and efficient slave masters'.[108]

Annesley's other dinner guest, William O'Brien, 2nd Earl of Inchiquin and Governor of Jamaica, presumably fell into this category. England had acquired Jamaica from Spain in 1655 (as part of Oliver Cromwell's 'Western Design') and had quickly colonized the island, developing it as a sugar and slavery colony. By 1670, of 717 property owners, at least 10 per cent were of Irish extraction. This percentage, however, only represented a small proportion of the number of Irish settlers over whom Inchiquin ruled after being dispatched to the island by William III in 1690. Formerly a commander of Charles II's forces in Africa and a Governor of Tangiers, Inchiquin spent only sixteen months in Jamaica as he died prematurely in 1692. The Earl's will, however, reflects both his Irish interests and his imperial priorities.[109] His extensive ancestral patrimony in Connacht, which his Catholic father, Murrough (1614–1674),[110] had managed to cling on to after the Restoration, passed to his eldest son, William. The second Earl's younger son, James, who had accompanied him to the West Indies,

---

[106] Donald Harman Akenson, *If the Irish Ran the World: Montserrat, 1630–1730* (Liverpool, 1997), pp. 7, 174.

[107] Ibid., p. 107.   [108] Ibid., p. 117.

[109] PROB 11/414/66, will undated but enrolled 13 Jan. 1691/2.

[110] Though born a Catholic, O'Brien converted to Protestantism around the time of his marriage to the daughter of Sir William St Leger, Lord President of Munster. During the civil war of the 1640s he initially served the King; but in 1644, when Charles I failed to make him Lord President of Munster, he joined the English Parliamentarians and fought with great brutality against the Catholics (hence his Irish nickname 'Murrough of the Burnings'). However, in 1648 he changed sides once again, serving the Stuart kings first in Ireland and then in their exile on the continent, where during the mid-1650s he reverted to Catholicism.

received an annuity of £250 (from the manor of O'Brien's Bridge in Ireland), his father's estate in County Cavan, 'all money and other effects and revenues in the Assiento and all other his estate in America', together with the Earl's interest in a ship called the *Adventure* (and her cargo).[111] Inchiquin's secretary, George Reeve, inherited the Earl's share in 'the sloope *Queene Mary*' and became the manager of the *Adventure*. Given the economic importance of the West Indies (driven in large part by Irish demand for tobacco and sugar) and the fact that prior to 1690 'Ireland dominated the provisioning trade' to the Caribbean, Inchiquin's involvement in commerce is entirely understandable and it undoubtedly contributed to the family's fortunes in Ireland.[112]

Ireland's mercantile links were not limited to the English Atlantic Empire. They extended to the East Indies too. Trade with Asia underpinned the development of the East India Company, which by the later seventeenth century made the bulk of its profits from importing cheap Indian calicoes to England. Jealously guarded by a narrow circle of London merchants and entrepreneurs, the East India Company, initially at least, offered few openings to Irishmen.[113] There were, however, exceptions, especially for those with connections to London's financial community. Another Irish associate of Annesley's was Francis Aungier, 3rd Baron and 1st Earl of Longford, whose brother, Gerald, enjoyed a prominent career with the East India Company. Gerald's grandfather, Francis, Lord Longford, had served as Master of the Rolls in Ireland and had played an active role in the plantations of Ulster, Wexford, Leitrim, and Longford. Ultimately, however, it was Gerald's family links with Sir Thomas Roe that secured his introduction to the directors of the East India Company. In 1669 Gerald became Governor of Bombay, which the Portuguese had ceded to England as part of Charles II's marriage settlement. He was the first to recognize Bombay's potential. During his eight-year tenure of office Aungier oversaw the draining of the swamps, the building of the first Protestant church, the establishment of a judiciary and police force, and the construction of new-style fortifications around Bombay castle. He also reformed the revenue system.[114] Writing after his death, one colleague

---

[111] James died shortly after his father and bequeathed all of his estate to his elder brother, William. Ainsworth, ed., *Inchiquin Manuscripts*, p. 517.

[112] Thomas M. Truxes, *Irish-American Trade, 1660–1783* (Cambridge, 1988), p. 14.

[113] P. J. Marshall, 'The English in Asia to 1700', in Canny, ed., *OHBE. Vol. I*, pp. 264–85.

[114] Holden Furber, *Rival Empires of Trade in the Orient, 1500–1800* (Oxford, 1976), pp. 92–93.

noted how Aungier transformed Bombay 'from a dunghill to what it now is'.[115] From Bombay, he became President of Surat, the chief English factory in India and the principal centre for the calico trade, where he died a childless widower in 1677. Like the Earl of Inchiquin, he left a considerable fortune, which enriched his equally ambitious elder brother, Francis, Earl of Longford, who, like so many Irish peers before him, held a variety of important political and administrative offices in Ireland.[116] The precise ways in which their Irish experiences shaped the mindsets and initiatives of Baltimore, Inchiquin, and Aungier remain to be unravelled. It is likely that Ireland served, to some degree or other, as a laboratory for Empire for them, as it had for other earlier English adventurers.

During the early modern period, segments of the Irish population, especially the disempowered and dispossessed Catholics, can be viewed as victims of English imperialism. Many were excluded from or overtly rejected colonial initiatives; others failed to adapt to the new economic and commercial order that colonization introduced to Ireland. Yet, other Irishmen, including Catholics, often proved effective and enterprising colonizers at home and abroad, where they contributed not only to the development of an English Empire but to the growth of the Portuguese, Spanish, Austrian, and French global empires. Irish social and political leaders were strikingly receptive to internal 'civilizing' and colonial processes, incorporating them to strengthen their own regional power bases. This also helps to explain their successful colonizing endeavours overseas and their effectiveness as imperialists elsewhere. Thus, in Amazonia Irish adventurers worked, during the early decades of the seventeenth century, in partnership with the English and Dutch and attempted to court the Portuguese; from the 1650s, Galway entrepreneurs contributed to the economic growth of the English Atlantic Empire by providing capital for the lucrative West Indian tobacco trade; and, in the early eighteenth century,

[115] Charles Fawcett, *The English Factories in India*, 4 vols. (Oxford, 1936–1955), I, p. 173; see also, I, pp. vii–viii, 134–35 and III, p. 57.

[116] Anonymous, 'Gerald Aungier of the East India Company: The Story of a Younger Son', *Notes and Queries*, 146 (Jan–June 1924), pp. 147–51, 165–68, 185–87, 204–08. Historical Manuscripts Commission, *Calendar of the Manuscripts of the Marquess of Ormonde*, New Series, 8 vols. (London, 1908–20), V, pp. 51, 133, 165. In 1679 Lord Longford expected to receive £4,000 from his brother's will.

Irish merchants, based at St Malo, involved themselves in French colonial trade, especially the traffic in slaves.[117] Ireland's position within and contribution to the English-speaking Empire has been the focus of this chapter, but this should neither obscure nor diminish the role that the Irish played in the overseas expansion of other European powers, in both the Atlantic and the East.

If Catholic Ireland's close links with these continental powers represented a potential threat to England, Ireland's ambiguous constitutional position—as both a kingdom and a colony—further complicated Anglo-Irish relations. Thus, for many of the ministers and minions in London, early modern Ireland was perceived as an irritating distraction for England, attracting large numbers of English, Welsh, and Scottish migrants and speculators and, especially at times of military crisis, draining state coffers. As Nicholas Canny has noted, this human and financial investment in Ireland probably delayed overseas colonization and economic investment elsewhere in the English Empire.[118] Yet, given Ireland's geographic proximity to England and the strategic threat that it represented throughout the early modern period, how could things have been otherwise? Just as the elimination of the 'Moorish problem' facilitated Spanish overseas expansion, the elimination of the 'Irish problem' formed the *sine qua non* for English expansion. And by the end of the seventeenth century England had finally—after two centuries of trying—conquered and colonized Ireland. English legal, political, and administrative institutions and procedures prevailed and all landed and commercial transactions were now recognizably English. In the process Ireland had indeed become 'another India for the English'.[119] This story of Empire in Ireland, however, was complex, full of contradictions, and in several respects unique.

---

[117] Joyce Lorimer, ed., *English and Irish Settlement on the River Amazon, 1550–1646* (London, 1989); L. M. Cullen, 'Galway Merchants in the Outside World, 1650–1800', in Diarmuid Cearbhaill, ed., *Galway: Town and Gown, 1484–1984* (Dublin, 1984), pp. 63–89; Mary Ann Lyons, 'The Emergence of an Irish Community in Saint-Malo, 1550–1710', in Thomas O'Connor, ed., *The Irish in Europe, 1580–1815* (Dublin, 2001), pp. 24, 107. Jan Parmentier's research on the Irish merchant community in Ostend and Bruges in the late seventeenth and eighteenth centuries highlights how merchants, dispossessed during the 1640s, relocated to the southern Netherlands and enjoyed very close links with the Ostend East India Company.

[118] Canny, 'The Origins of Empire', pp. 8, 9, 12.

[119] See n. 1 above.

Select Bibliography

DONALD HARMAN AKENSON, *If the Irish Ran the World: Montserrat, 1630–1730* (Liverpool, 1997).

K. R. ANDREWS, N. P. CANNY, and P. E. H. HAIR, eds., *The Westward Enterprise: English Activities in Ireland, the Atlantic and America, 1480–1650* (Liverpool, 1978).

DAVID ARMITAGE, *The Ideological Origins of the British Empire* (Cambridge, 2000).

CIARAN BRADY and RAYMOND GILLESPIE, eds., *Natives and Newcomers: Essays on the Making of Irish Colonial Society, 1534–1641* (Dublin, 1986).

NICHOLAS CANNY, *Making Ireland British, 1580–1650* (Oxford, 2001).

—— ed., *The Oxford History of the British Empire. Vol. I. The Origins of Empire. British Overseas Enterprise to the Close of the Seventeenth Century* (Oxford, 1998).

—— ed., *Europeans on the Move* (Oxford, 1994).

RAYMOND GILLESPIE, *Colonial Ulster: The Settlement of East Ulster, 1600–1641* (Cork, 1985).

—— 'Explorers, Exploiters and Entrepreneurs: Early Modern Ireland and its Context, 1500–1700', in B. J. Graham and L. J. Proudfoot, eds., *An Historical Geography of Ireland* (Dublin, 1993), pp. 122–57.

ANDREW HADFIELD and JOHN McVEAGH, eds., *Strangers to that Land: British Perceptions of Ireland from the Reformation to the Famine* (Gerrards Cross, Buckinghamshire, 1994).

MAURICE LEE, *Great Britain's Solomon: James VI and I in his Three Kingdoms* (Urbana, Ill., 1990).

MICHAEL MACCARTHY MORROGH, *The Munster Plantation: English Migration to Southern Ireland, 1583–1641* (Oxford, 1986).

T. W. MOODY, F. X. MARTIN, and F. J. BYRNE, eds., *New History of Ireland. Vol. III. Early Modern Ireland, 1534–1691* (Oxford, 1978).

B. Ó BUACHALLA, 'James our True King: The Ideology of Irish Royalism in the Seventeenth Century', in D. George Boyce, Robert Eccleshall, and Vincent Geoghegan, eds., *Political Thought in Ireland since the Seventeenth Century* (London, 1993).

JANE OHLMEYER, *Civil War and Restoration in the Three Stuart Kingdoms: The Career of Randal MacDonnell, Marquis of Antrim, 1609–1683* (Cambridge, 1993; reprinted Dublin, 2001).

—— ed., *Ireland from Independence to Occupation, 1641–1660* (Cambridge, 1995), esp. the chaps. by Raymond Gillespie, Kevin McKenny, and Michelle Ó Riordan.

JANE OHLMEYER, 'Seventeenth-century Ireland and the New British and Atlantic Histories', *American Historical Review,* CIV (April 1999), pp. 446–62.

MICHAEL PERCEVAL-MAXWELL, *The Scottish Migration to Ulster in the Reign of James I* (London, 1973).

PHILIP ROBINSON, *The Plantation of Ulster* (Dublin, 1984).

VICTOR TREADWELL, *Buckingham and Ireland, 1616–1628: A Study in Anglo–Irish Politics* (Dublin, 1998).

3

Ireland, Empire, and Union, 1690–1801

THOMAS BARTLETT

'Ireland is too great to be unconnected with us and too near to be dependent on a foreign state and too little to be independent': C. T. Grenville's aphorism of 1784 encapsulated the inherent difficulties in the Anglo-Irish relationship. Ireland's position within the eighteenth-century Empire was even more problematic. The country was, admittedly, 'England's oldest colony', but had been held rather than wholly governed since the twelfth century. Moreover, since 1541 Ireland had also constituted a kingdom in its own right. This regal status, along with the (albeit fitful) existence of a Parliament of undeniable medieval origins consisting of a House of Commons and House of Lords, seemed to mark Ireland off decisively from every colony subsequently acquired by England, for they could only boast of assorted Assemblies, councils, and courts. Furthermore, as an island lying closely off a larger island itself located just off continental Europe, Ireland conspicuously lacked the eighteenth-century colonial stereotypes (extreme temperatures, exotic produce, curious animals, slavery, distance from the mother country). In fact, the country grew nothing that could not be had, at allegedly better quality, in England. True, there was fertile land in abundance, and this was an undoubted attraction. But even if Ireland had been barren rock, its proximity to both continental Europe and to England meant that it constituted in English eyes an all-too-convenient base for foreign enemies and a likely haven for domestic rebels and malcontents. Ireland was simply 'too near', as Grenville remarked, to be left alone by England or other European powers: but proximity and colonial status seemed at odds with one another. To paraphrase V. T. Harlow's question, was there a place for a colony on the

This chapter incorporates new material, especially on the Act of Union, into my original chapter in P. J. Marshall, ed., *The Oxford History of the British Empire* (hereafter *OHBE*). Vol. II. *The Eighteenth Century* (Oxford, 1998), pp. 253–75.

doorstep of the mother country?[1] And if Ireland were not a colony, could two kingdoms, adjacent to one another, and under the one King, co-exist in the one Empire?

A further complication lay in the fact that, unlike other colonies in the Atlantic world, the population of Ireland by the late seventeenth century resolutely resisted simple categorization into colonized and colonizer. Religion, not national origins or even date of arrival, was to be the great divide: but this is not to say that Protestant-Catholic hostility is the key to understanding Irish history in this period. In the early eighteenth century Protestant Ireland was riven by rivalry between the members of the Presbyterian church and the adherents of the Established Church. The latter, called by historians the Anglo-Irish, were not at all disposed to share the fruits of the victories over the Catholic Irish at the Boyne (1690) and Aughrim (1691) with the largely Scottish, anti-episcopal, and socially inferior Dissenters. Accordingly, while the Anglican governing élite in the 1690s brought in penal laws against Catholics, it also legislated against Presbyterians. It did so because the Catholic threat had been seen off, because the Presbyterians seemed to be a new rival for power, and because the Anglo-Irish were confident of English goodwill and support. At an early date, however, it was made clear to the Anglo-Irish that English ministers were by no means disposed to view the Anglo-Irish as partners in the 'Glorious Revolution': certainly there was no question of automatic access for Irish goods into the trade network of the British Empire. In this respect at least, Ireland though at the centre, was still irredeemably peripheral.

By the late seventeenth century, then, Ireland, 'this famous island set in a Virginian sea', resembled not so much a model colony, a *terra Florida* near home, drawn up in conformity with an official blueprint, but rather an unruly palimpsest, on which, though much rewritten and scored out, could be discerned in an untidy jumble: 'kingdom', 'colony', 'dependency', and, faintly, 'nation'.[2] The ambiguities within such designations, and the attempt to resolve the contradictions between them, are fundamental to any assessment of Ireland's developing position within the British Empire during the 'long' eighteenth century.

[1] Vincent T. Harlow, *The Founding of the Second British Empire, 1763–93. Vol. I. Discovery and Revolution* (London, 1952), p. 505.

[2] Fynes Moryson, quoted in Nicholas P. Canny, *Kingdom and Colony: Ireland in the Atlantic World, 1560–1800* (Baltimore, 1988), p. 131.

In 1672, Sir William Petty had forecast a splendid future for Ireland in the expanding commerce of the Atlantic world: the island, he noted, 'lieth Commodiously for the Trade of the new American world: which we see every day to Grow and Flourish'.[3] In the event, just as Ireland's strategic position athwart the main Atlantic trade routes afforded her advantages in the competition for commerce with the West Indies and with British North America, so too her apparently favourable situation could not fail to excite the resentment of competing English interests. 'Forraigne trade', considered to be the primary source of a nation's wealth, had to be jealously protected and zealously policed: colonial trade should uniquely be the preserve of the mother country; Ireland, whether viewed as a depending kingdom, domestic colony, or foreign country, fell awkwardly outside the accepted categories for full participation in the trade of the 'English Empire'.[4] Ireland, fatally, was viewed by important English vested interests as a competitor: indeed, as one pamphleteer noted, 'among the many Rivals to our Trade and Navigation, I have often thought Ireland to be the most Dangerous'.[5] These jealousies and resentments, voiced by various English vested interests, were given shape from the 1660s on by increasingly restrictive legislative pronouncements, usually denominated the Laws of Trade and Navigation.

By an Act of 1696 no goods of any kind could be landed in Ireland from the American plantations. This remained the legal position until 1731, when a new Act, the result of a successful lobbying campaign by West Indian and Irish interests in London, permitted Ireland to import non-enumerated goods from the colonies, a position unchanged until the American Revolution. So far as Asian trade was concerned Irish merchants were also disadvantaged, though they were no worse off than their English counterparts. The East India Company had the sole monopoly and no Irish merchants as of right could take part in Indian trade. It was only in the 1790s that this monopoly was breached by Ireland.

An earlier generation of historians was certain that the Navigation Acts 'had the effect of completely ruining the Irish Plantation trade', but it is now clear from more recent work that Ireland, so far from being excluded from colonial trade throughout the eighteenth century, actually took an

---

[3] Quoted in Thomas M. Truxes, *Irish-American Trade, 1660–1783* (Cambridge, 1988), p. 6.
[4] Joshua Gee, *The Navigation of Great Britain Considered* (London, 1730), p. 65.
[5] Quoted in Truxes, *Irish-American Trade*, p. 12.

active role in it. The evidence for this, both qualitative and quantitative, is decisive.[6] Yet colonial trade was always a minor segment of Irish overseas trade throughout the eighteenth century. Irish trade in this period meant in fact Anglo-Irish trade; England took over 45 per cent of the value of Irish exports in 1700, rising to 85 per cent in 1800, while some 54 per cent of Irish imports derived from England in 1700, rising to near 79 per cent in 1800.[7] A large proportion of these imports, between 50 per cent and 60 per cent, were in fact re-exports of colonial products—especially sugar and tobacco—which by law had to be landed first in Britain before going on to their final destination. Direct Irish colonial trade was substantial enough, running at between 9 per cent and 12 per cent of the value of Irish exports, though rarely reaching 8 per cent of imports in the period 1731–75.[8]

Irish exports to the West Indies and to the British colonies in North America centred on three items: provisions (salted beef, pork, and butter), linen (usually the cheaper, coarser cloth), and people (passengers, convicts, and indentured servants).[9] Especially in the early eighteenth century, Irish barrels of salted beef, butter, pork, and cheese found a ready market in the West Indies, where the planter population retained the diet of the mother country. As the eighteenth century wore on, however, and as the white population of the islands decreased while competition in foodstuffs from North America grew, Irish provisions exports to the Caribbean declined. The growth in exports of salted fish from Ireland to feed the slaves in the West Indies compensated for this downturn, but in any case demand for Irish salted provisions remained buoyant in the mainland colonies. By the 1760s Irish beef, pork, and butter accounted for well over 50 per cent of all direct Irish exports to the British colonies in North America. And during the American War of Independence, Irish provisions fed both the British and the Continental Armies.

The balance of Irish exports to the colonies was largely made up by linen. Although this article could legally (since 1705) be exported direct from Ireland, in fact, because of the provision of a bounty on its re-export

---

[6] R. C. Nash, 'Irish Atlantic Trade in the Seventeenth and Eighteenth Centuries', *William & Mary Quarterly*, Third Series, XLIII (July 1985), pp. 329–56.

[7] L. M. Cullen, *Anglo-Irish Trade in the Eighteenth Century* (Manchester, 1968), p. 44.

[8] Truxes, *Irish-American Trade*, p. 37.

[9] My discussion of Ireland's trade with the British colonies in North America is based on Truxes, *Irish-American Trade*.

instituted in the early 1740s, the vast bulk of linen (perhaps 90 per cent) destined for North America went through England. After Britain, America was Ireland's largest customer for linen and constituted the most important market for the coarser linens that clothed the slaves (among others) and were soon known in the trade simply as 'Irish'.[10]

In a separate category of 'export' lay the direct trade in Irish emigrants. A thriving and lucrative colonial trade with Ireland was superimposed on the mechanisms by which large numbers of Irish people were transferred to the West Indies or to the mainland colonies. For this reason then, emigration—voluntary or otherwise—should be treated as a branch of commerce. And just as statistics of trade are relatively imprecise, so too the numbers of those moving from Ireland to the West Indies and the mainland colonies must always remain problematic: voluntary emigrants may have been in the region of 65,000. To this number should be added the generally accepted figure of 10,000 convicts from Ireland, along with the figure of around 40,000 emigrants (mostly indentured servants) who went to the West Indies, though most of these came in the late seventeenth and early eighteenth centuries. In total, the net migration from Ireland to British North America, including the West Indies, for the period 1630–1775 was around 165,000, with anything up to 100,000 making the journey between 1700 and 1775, and perhaps as many more in the period up to 1800.[11]

Convicts cost around £5 per head to transport but their work contracts were scheduled to last between seven and fourteen years and could be sold for anything up to £20. Similarly, indentured servants—those who entered voluntarily into an agreement to work in return for passage to the New World—were a valuable commodity even though their service would typically only last for four years. Taking out indentures could involve opportunity as well as bondage: these servants were indeed 'bound for America' but, as Truxes comments, 'for the ambitious and energetic poor, [indentured service] was the only practical means of removing to the colonies'.[12]

[10] For the wider ramifications of the Irish linen trade in the imperial economy, see Jacob. M. Price, 'The Imperial Economy, 1700–1776', in Marshall, ed., *OHBE. Vol. II*, pp. 87–88.

[11] James Horn, 'British Diaspora: Emigration from Britain, 1680–1815', in Marshall, ed., *OHBE. Vol. II*, esp pp. 31–32, 46–49.

[12] Truxes, *Irish-American Trade*, p. 128.

What did Ireland take from the colonies in return for these exports? Inevitably, sugar and tobacco, landed first in England or Scotland and then re-shipped for Ireland, were by far the most valuable imports from the West Indies and from the mainland colonies: at no time in the eighteenth century did Ireland's import of non-enumerated goods match the import of sugar and tobacco from Great Britain. Direct imports from North America were dominated by flax-seed, which was paid for by Irish exports of cheap linen and by salted provisions: some 85 per cent of Irish flax-seed originated in North America. Rum distilled in the West Indies but shipped to Ireland both from the islands and from the mainland colonies was an important component in Ireland's list of colonial imports. Other direct imports were timber and lumber products, potash (enumerated in 1764 but 'non-enumerated' in 1770), and wheat and flour which supplemented imports from Great Britain in years of scarcity.

Any final assessment of Ireland's overall trading position within the Atlantic Empire is rendered difficult not only by the relative weight to be accorded direct and indirect exports and imports but also by the existence of two largely distinct markets, the West Indies and the mainland colonies. In composite (direct and indirect combined) trade with the mainland American colonies up to the 1760s, Ireland sustained a healthy surplus. After enjoying a modestly favourable balance of payments in her composite trade with the West Indies in the middle decades of the century, as imports of sugar and rum grew, Ireland moved decisively into the red on this account. Between 1736 and 1776, the value of composite imports from the British plantations in America totalled around £12,185,000 while composite exports amounted to just over £12,612,000, thus allowing a very modest trade surplus in Ireland's favour of about £500,000 over these forty years.[13]

These figures prove that Ireland was never 'excluded' from colonial trade and that as often as not it enjoyed a surplus in its dealings with 'our plantations in America' (as the Irish customs officials termed them). Operating under the protective carapace of imperial regulations, Ireland did rather well in the eighteenth-century commercial Empire. Yet these conclusions in their turn, so far from resolving the question of Ireland's trading position within the Empire once and for all, must prompt a rather larger question: given that Ireland had access to an expanding colonial

---

[13] Totals from Truxes, *Irish-American Trade*, App. II, pp. 260–61, 282–83.

trade, that it enjoyed overall a modest surplus in this trade, and that Irish producers and manufacturers—and the Irish economy—benefited from this commerce, then how was it that the prosperity associated with these trades proved so brittle and ephemeral?

A brief comparison with Scotland may be instructive here.[14] Both Ireland and Scotland had an undistinguished economic base in the later seventeenth century, though on balance Ireland appeared to offer the better prospects for the future. At any rate, tens of thousands of Scots thought so, for they flocked to Ireland in the late seventeenth and early eighteenth centuries. However, by the later eighteenth century, Scotland had moved decisively ahead, and throughout the nineteenth century, it left Ireland behind both in manufacturing industry and agricultural output. The sources of this Scottish 'success' story may be debated, but of prime importance was the Anglo-Scottish Act of Union of 1707 which allowed Scotland unrestricted access to the trade of the Empire. Ireland was not on nearly so favourable a footing, and hence while Scottish merchants revelled in the opportunities offered by the expanding re-export trade in tobacco and, to a lesser extent, in sugar, Irish merchants were firmly excluded. Tobacco profits partly funded the expansion of Scottish linen and underpinned improvements in Scottish agriculture. Moreover, a substantial re-export trade in tobacco centred on Glasgow promoted the growth of sophisticated financial services and institutions: lacking any re-export trade, Ireland signally failed to develop a similar infrastructure in the eighteenth century. The bounty on linen meant that the vast bulk of Irish linen was exported through England, and the Irish provisions trade was largely managed by the London sugar interest. While individual Irish merchants, and small houses, were to be found throughout the chief trading ports of the Empire, the Irish colonial trade was dominated by English merchant houses, English intermediaries, and English capital. If Ireland had had unrestricted access to the trade of the colonies, could it have profited? Glasgow's success with tobacco re-exports may have had as much to do with the fact that there was a large presence of Scottish merchants in the southern mainland colonies who were able to direct the trade to that city. Certainly when Ireland gained full access to the trade of the American colonies after 1780, the pattern of her colonial trade did not

---

[14] See L. M. Cullen and T. C. Smout, eds., *Comparative Aspects of Scottish and Irish Economic and Social History, 1600–1900* (Edinburgh, 1977).

significantly change, though perhaps the trade networks were by that date too entrenched to be easily altered.

Without doubt, Ireland benefited from the imperial connection in the eighteenth century. Irish linen could never have found such a lucrative market outside the protected walls of the British Empire, and the Munster provisions industry centred on Cork City took full advantage of ready access to imperial markets. Where else could the region's agricultural surplus have gone but to the British North American colonies? Yet Irish gains from transatlantic trade did not enter deep enough into the Irish economy to foster self-sustaining development. What is not clear, however, is whether unrestricted access to all colonial trade throughout the eighteenth century would have produced that happy result: Ireland's poor economic performance in the nineteenth century may more legitimately be attributed to those insidious colonial legacies of cultural conflict, religious disharmony, and political division, than to the effects of the Laws of Trade and Navigation.

Throughout the eighteenth century, restrictions on Irish colonial commerce were regularly denounced as evidence both of England's resolve to keep 'poor Ireland poor' and of her determination to do down a prospective rival. Imperial trade regulations found few defenders in Ireland, while the insensitive action of the English Parliament in restricting Irish trade, colonial or foreign, wounded Irish pride. Instead of being welcomed as partners in the Glorious Revolution (and ushered to a seat at the table of Empire), Irish Protestants were dismayed to find themselves cast as colonists, with their Parliament derided as a subaltern assembly. Ireland, a sister kingdom to England in their eyes, was contemptuously dismissed by English politicians as variously a depending kingdom, a foreign country, or a child-colony: in no case was equality, much less joint sovereignty, on offer. In self-defence, Irish Protestants formulated a conception of their rights as the English-born-in-Ireland, which they pitted against metropolitan condescension, its oppressive agents, and their colonial theory. English imperialism was combatted by 'Protestant' or 'colonial' nationalism.

This proprietary nationalism of the Protestant governing élite had diverse origins.[15] Like colonial élites everywhere, Irish Protestants slowly

---

[15] Thomas Bartlett, '"A People Made rather for Copies than Originals": The Anglo-Irish, 1760–1800', *International History Review*, XII, 1.1 (1990), pp. 11–25.

developed a deep affection for their adopted land and a keen appreciation of its distinctive beauties. Joined to this local affection was a profound consciousness of the historic Protestant mission in Ireland. In particular, a collective historical experience stemming from the terrifying ebbs and flows of seventeenth-century Irish history had moulded the Protestant nation of eighteenth-century Ireland in the most emphatic way. A Providential reading of the rebellion of 1641, the advent of Cromwell, the threat offered by James II, and the deliverance vouchsafed by William of Orange, led inescapably to the conclusion that the Protestants of Ireland were under God's special protection, that they were His chosen people in Ireland.

Protestant confidence that they constituted the 'Whole People of Ireland' (Jonathan Swift's term) was closely allied to Protestant resentment that they were 'never thanked for venturing our lives and fortunes at the Revolution; for making so brave a stand at Londonderry and Iniskilling'.[16] Denied the fruits of a victory so dearly bought by them, Irish Protestants had further cause for resentment at the curbs on Irish colonial trade. Moreover, Irish Protestants soon felt that there was a settled policy of discrimination against them where the more prestigious appointments in the Irish law, armed forces, and the Established Church were concerned. Further outrage was provoked by the flagrant abuse of the Irish pension list to pay off English jobs, and by the humiliating way that Irish peerages were bestowed on Englishmen or others who had no connection with Ireland.

Paradoxically, Protestant confidence and Protestant resentment were accompanied by residual Protestant anxiety. Irish Catholics remained a large majority on the island, maintaining close connections with the Jacobite court in France. Could the penal laws bring about that reconfiguration of the confessional landscape of Ireland without which Irish Protestants could not know permanent security? Irish Presbyterians, already numerically greater and expanding rapidly, caused huge concern. Fiercely anti-Catholic, they were equally aggressively anti-episcopal and showed no regard for the sensitivities of churchmen. Could the penal laws against them curb their pretensions and restrain their ambitions? Lastly, Irish Protestants had assumed the permanence of English goodwill

---

[16] Anon., *Some Remarks on the Parliament of England as Far as it Relates to the Woollen Manufacture* (Dublin, 1731), pp. 12–13.

in the aftermath of the Glorious Revolution. This assumption had proved groundless: to their dismay, Irish Protestants found themselves regarded more as a subject people than as fellow subjects after 1690.

This 'nationalism' of Irish Protestants, a potent mixture of triumphalism, anxiety, and wounded *amour-propre*, despite what English opinion might fear, never constituted a plea for Irish secession, nor was it suspicious of Empire. Rather, those who, like William Molyneux, argued Ireland's 'Case', sought an Irish partnership in the *imperium*, demanded access to imperial trade, and maintained that in the great wheel of Empire, Ireland's natural position should be at the hub not on the rim. In seeking recognition for their achievements and sacrifices, and in attempting to discharge their Providential burden, Irish Protestants served notice on English ministers that they would not allow them to define unilaterally the Anglo-Irish relationship as simply Irish colonial subordination to imperial England. In particular, Irish Protestants vigorously resisted the notion that Ireland was on the same footing as one of England's 'colonies of outcasts in America'.[17] Ireland's 'Case', wrote William Molyneux in his celebrated pamphlet, had to be separated from the other colonies in the Atlantic world. Ireland, he argued, was not a colony at all but a sister kingdom.

Molyneux's arguments were grounded on 500 years of Irish history and the whole was painstakingly researched. His critics' scornful and abusive replies fully revealed the chasm that lay between the English and Irish perceptions of the imperial connection. To the English, Ireland was a troublesome child-colony to whom mother-England owed protection but whose primary purpose was to benefit that country. English writers professed to disbelieve that anyone could think otherwise.[18]

Given these opposing viewpoints, occasions of conflict were in fact surprisingly limited in the years up to 1750. Apart from the Woods' Halfpence dispute of the 1720s, in which Swift memorably opposed Wood's patent to coin halfpennies, relations between London and Dublin ran quite smoothly. The consolidation of the Hanoverian dynasty and the absence of political upheaval in England after 1714 were partly responsible for this relative calm in Ireland. Equally, the firm political

---

[17] Jonathan Swift, quoted by F. G. James, *Ireland in the Empire* (Cambridge, Mass., 1973), p. 140.

[18] Thomas Bartlett, *The Fall and Rise of the Irish Nation: The Catholic Question, 1690–1830* (Dublin, 1992), p. 36.

control maintained by the Irish political magnates, the so-called 'Under-takers', allied to a general desire to avoid provocation, left Irish politics in a relatively somnolent state. Although the Declaratory Act of 1720 had expressly confirmed the Irish Parliament's subordinate status by maintain-ing that the British Parliament could pass laws to bind Ireland, no attempt was made to implement this claim. In the end, the importance of this undoubtedly contentious Act remained largely exemplary.

The enactment of the Declaratory Act, the persistent restrictions on Irish legislation imposed by Poynings' Law (1494), and the informal con-trol exercised by the London-appointed Irish government, could all be taken as proof that the Irish Parliament, notwithstanding its hereditary House of Lords, its relative antiquity, and its mimetic pageantry, was merely just another colonial Assembly in the Atlantic world. Certainly, British ministers appreciated the worth of Poynings' Law and on occasion toyed with the idea of extending it to other colonial Assemblies; and when a ringing assertion of British legislative supremacy was required at the time of the repeal of the Stamp Act (1766), it was the Irish enactment of 1720 that was dusted down and adapted to fit the new circumstances. Furthermore, instructive comparisons have been found between the Irish Parliament and other local legislatures especially in the mainland colonies of North America. In some respects the Irish Parliament was less powerful than most colonial Assemblies, but in the years up to 1750, like colonial legislatures everywhere, it assumed increasing control over finances. The Irish legislature and the other colonial Assemblies together raised that 'question of ultimate sovereignty' which was to be the rock on which the first British Empire foundered.[19] J. P. Greene has described the Irish contribution to an emerging 'imperial constitution', separate from the British one and yet distinct from the written charters of the various colonies. Increasingly, the British Parliament, whose own imperial respon-sibilities were not so much defined as assumed, found itself struggling against the growing assertiveness of hitherto subordinate legislative bodies within the Empire, including Ireland.[20]

Ireland and the Irish Parliament fitted uneasily into the imperial para-digm of mother and child, metropolitan legislature and local Assembly,

[19] James, *Ireland in the Empire*, p. 252.
[20] Jack P. Greene, *Peripheries and Centers: Constitutional Development in the Extended Polities of the British Empire and the United States, 1607–1788* (Athens, Ga., 1987), esp. chap. 6.

imperial core and colonial periphery. Indeed, so impressive is Ireland's awkwardness in these matters that some historians have discarded the entire colonial nexus as a way of understanding eighteenth-century Ireland.[21] S. J. Connolly has argued that Ireland can be best viewed as a typical *ancien régime* society rather than as a colony; and that the Irish Parliament has more in common with the Parlement of Bordeaux than with the Virginia House of Burgesses. However, 'colonial' society and *ancien régime* facets could co-exist within the same polity, and the period chosen by Connolly within which to situate his thesis is peculiarly apposite for his purposes. After the Seven Years War (1756–63) the colonial dimension to Irish history re-asserted itself in an unmistakeable way, and Ireland, until the end of the century, was engulfed in the crisis of Empire.

Before the Seven Years War, Empire meant above all trade: after 1763, it signified dominion as well. However, the acquisition of a new Empire— 'this vast empire on which the sun never sets and whose bounds nature has not yet ascertained'—brought with it knotty problems of defence, finance, and administration.[22] Following the war, British ministers and imperial administrators agreed that the legislative supremacy of the British Parliament had to be made explicit, that the bonds of Empire had to be tightened up, and that the colonies had to pay their way. The case of Ireland would not be excluded from this re-appraisal of the purpose of Empire.

During the Townshend Viceroyalty (1767–72), the parliamentary control of the Irish political magnates—the 'Undertakers'—was broken: Lords-Lieutenant for the future would reside constantly in Ireland; Poynings' Law received a ringing endorsement; and a significant attempt was made to increase the King's hereditary revenue in Ireland so as to diminish the executive's dependence on the bi-annual supply voted by the Irish Parliament.[23] These initiatives were all taken at the prompting of Townshend rather than of the London government; but they should be viewed in an imperial context, for Townshend, like his younger brother, Charles, was

---

[21] S. J. Connolly, *Religion, Law and Power: The Making of Protestant Ireland, 1660–1760* (Oxford, 1992), pp. 2–3.

[22] Sir George Macartney, *An Account of Ireland in 1773 by a late Chief Secretary of that Kingdom* (London, 1773), p. 55.

[23] Thomas Bartlett, 'The Townshend Viceroyalty', in Thomas Bartlett and D. H. Hayton, eds., *Penal Era and Golden Age: Essays in Irish History, 1690–1800* (Belfast, 1979), pp. 88–112.

firmly in favour of asserting imperial authority. 'Ireland', he wrote, 'hath not yet caught the American or English distemper', but there could be no room for complacency, and preventative measures were needed.[24]

On coming to Ireland in 1767, Townshend's primary objective had been to obtain the Irish Parliament's agreement to augment the number of troops paid for by Ireland from 12,000 to 15,325.[25] Though sometimes seen as 'the Irish counterpart to the Stamp Act', it was in fact the administrative demands of the new regimental rotation system that lay behind the proposed augmentation of the Army.[26] Since 1763 Irish regiments had been reduced in size compared to British regiments (c.280 officers and men in an Irish regiment, c.500 in a British one) and as these regiments, by the new rules, were henceforth to rotate throughout the Empire, it was necessary to have regiments everywhere of a similar strength.

That said, the proposal to augment the Army in Ireland had a clear imperial dimension. Since 1763 the problems of garrisoning a far-flung Empire had exercised the minds of British ministers. Ireland's share of the imperial defence burden had hitherto been largely limited to supplying soldiers; and in 1767 an increase in recruits was sought by British ministers. The difficulties that Townshend encountered in his efforts to win the Irish Parliament's agreement to this proposal persuaded him that indirect rule through Irish 'Undertakers' had to be abandoned and replaced by a new system of direct rule by a resident Chief Governor supported in the Irish Parliament by a 'Castle party' of 'Lord Lieutenant's friends'. In this respect, the new system of regimental rotation, in itself devised in response to vastly increased military responsibilities after 1763, ultimately triggered a profound change in the method of governing Ireland.

The unfolding of events during the Townshend Viceroyalty clearly showed how imperial defence issues could disturb Irish domestic politics; and such military questions—notably that concerning the recruitment of Irish Catholic recruits—continued to have an impact long after Townshend's departure.[27] By law, only Protestants could serve either as officers

[24] Townshend to Lord Weymouth, 4 Aug. 1770. Townshend letterbook, ii., W. L. Clements Library, University of Michigan, Ann Arbor, Michigan.

[25] Thomas Bartlett, 'The Augmentation of the Army in Ireland, 1769–72', *English Historical Review*, XCVI (July 1981), pp. 540–59.

[26] R. G. Coupland, *The American Revolution and the British Empire*, rev. edn. (New York, 1965), pp. 97, 100–01.

[27] Bartlett, *Fall and Rise of the Irish Nation*, pp. 82–86.

or in the ranks of the armed forces of the Crown, but the expansion of
Empire, the provision of more garrisons (and the greater size of armies
generally), meant that more and more soldiers were needed for imperial
service. The military reservoir of Irish Protestants, however, soon ran low,
and British politicians and generals began to gaze longingly at that
'weapon of war yet untried': the Irish Catholic. Already by the 1770s covert
enlistment of Irish Catholics was underway, and soon large numbers were
being taken into the Marines and especially into the East India Company's
army. When war broke out in the late 1770s with the American colonists
and then with their French and Spanish allies, the government of Lord
North, desperate for more soldiers, supported a policy of concessions to
Irish Catholics in return for Irish Catholic recruits. By then, however, war
in America had re-opened more than the Catholic Question, for the whole
constitutional relationship between Ireland and England was now openly
disputed.

The worsening relations between Britain and its colonies in America had
not gone unnoticed in Ireland. Tens of thousands of emigrants had left
Ireland during the eighteenth century. Disproportionately Presbyterian,
they maintained close personal and commercial links with the home
country. Irish Presbyterians in the New World may not have been united
in their support for the colonial cause, but in Ireland Dissent aligned itself
firmly in opposition to 'the unnatural, impolitic and unprincipled war in
America'.[28]

Colonial leaders such as Benjamin Franklin were well aware of Irish
sympathies and took steps to detach Ireland from England in the contest.
During the Stamp Act controversy of the mid-1760s, Irish goods were
specifically excluded from the colonial non-importation agreements, and
there was a similar exemption for Ireland in the colonial resistance to the
Townshend duties of the late 1760s. However, as the troubles deepened
between mother country and colonies in the early 1770s, attitudes in the
colonies hardened and Ireland was no longer so favoured. When a trade
war broke out following the passing of the 'Coercive Acts' in 1774, Ireland
found itself, despite the best efforts of Franklin, denied the privilege of
shipping linens and provisions direct to the colonies. Irish anger at this

---

[28] Quoted in R. B. McDowell, *Ireland in the Age of Imperialism and Revolution, 1760–1800*
(Oxford, 1979), p. 244.

turn of events, however, was directed more at British ineptness than at the resistance of the colonists; and that indignation was further fuelled in February 1776 by Dublin Castle's imposition of a total embargo on the export of Irish provisions to the colonies.[29] This wartime embargo aroused a storm of protest partly because it was blamed—unreasonably—for bringing on an economic recession, but especially because it confirmed the thoughtless way Irish commercial interests were handled by England. The latent Irish resentment against English restrictions on Irish trade was thus re-awakened.

Moreover, because these restrictions were viewed as an inevitable product of Ireland's constitutional subordination to England, a potent fusion of commercial with constitutional grievances was effected. Constitutional issues were in the air, for the war between Mother Country and colonies had been accompanied by furious debate on the respective obligations of each to the other, on the rights of the imperial Parliament over the colonies, and on the location of sovereignty in the Empire.[30] These issues were argued in a plethora of pamphlets, letters, and printed speeches, which were produced in Ireland: not surprisingly, appropriate lessons were drawn. It was claimed that if the British government succeeded in taxing the colonists without their consent, then Ireland would surely be next on the list for such oppressive treatment. Evidently, the cause of America, as Franklin and others never ceased to point out, was ultimately the cause of Ireland. Irish opinion quickly recognized that what the colonists were struggling to defend—essentially the right to legislate for themselves—Ireland did not even possess.

The British defeat at Saratoga in October 1777, followed by the entry of France into the war in early 1778, ushered in a period of near continual crisis in Anglo-Irish relations that ended only with the signing of the Peace of Paris in 1783. By the war's end, Irish patriot politicians had taken the opportunity afforded them by the imperial crisis to win 'A Free Trade' and to adjust the constitutional relationship between Ireland and England.

Central to the great changes in these years was the formation of the Volunteers, a defence force that at its peak numbered around 60,000. These part-time soldiers were independent of Dublin Castle and had sprung up ostensibly to defend Ireland from French incursion or from raids by American privateers such as John Paul Jones. However, the

---

[29] Truxes, *Irish-American Trade*, pp. 235–45.   [30] See Greene, *Peripheries and Centers*.

Volunteers, predominantly Presbyterian in Ulster where they were strongest, but with significant Anglican support both there and elsewhere, and with some tacit Catholic approval, soon realized that there was little danger of a French invasion. They quickly turned their attention to Ireland's grievances and demanded redress. Irish public opinion, hitherto inchoate, had now found a focus.

The Volunteers first addressed the restrictions on Irish overseas' commerce and demanded 'A Free Trade'. Throughout 1778 and 1779, pressure mounted on North's government to yield to Irish demands. Reports from Dublin spoke of civilian and paramilitary demonstrations, an Irish House of Commons out of control, and the widespread defection of erstwhile supporters. In November 1779 Lord North, faced with failure in America and opposition in Britain, chose to avoid confrontation in Ireland and announced sweeping concessions. Save for that portion controlled by the East India Company, Ireland was to be allowed direct access to colonial trade, 'upon equal conditions with Great Britain'. It was further promised that all the securities, allowances and restrictions by which Anglo-Irish trade would be regularized 'should, so far as they respect Ireland, be imposed by the Irish parliament'. Lastly, Irish subjects were to be admitted into the Turkey Company and Irish ports were to be opened to the trade of the Levant.[31]

If North thought that these concessions would solve the Irish Question, he was to be speedily undeceived. Behind the merits or otherwise of Britain's restrictions on Irish trade there had always lain, as Buckinghamshire, the Lord-Lieutenant, put it, 'the constitutional question of the legislative power of Great Britain to restrain the commerce of Ireland', and indeed the power generally of the British Parliament to pass laws to bind Ireland.[32] It was naïve to expect these issues to fade away with the announcement of the trade concessions. By the end of February 1780 the future of Poynings' Law, the absence of an Irish Habeas Corpus Act, the tenure of Irish judges, and the need for an Irish Mutiny Act—all humiliating badges of Ireland's resented colonial status—had been raised in the Irish House of Commons, and it was evident that there would be further discussion of these issues in the months to come.

[31] Heron to Shannon, 15 Jan. 1780, PRONI, Shannon MSS, D2707/A2/2/66.
[32] Buckinghamshire to Hillsborough, 14 Dec. 1779, London, NA, PRO, SP63/467, pp. 247–49.

Events in America ultimately broke the deadlock in Ireland. The war there had taken a more favourable turn from Britain's point of view in 1780 and 1781, but in November 1781 came news of Cornwallis's surrender at Yorktown. North's government was mortally wounded and by March 1782 his parliamentary majority had crumbled. His ministry was suc-ceeded by that headed by Lord Rockingham and the Earl of Shelburne, a change taken by the Opposition in Ireland to herald concessions for Ireland. When the Irish Parliament reconvened following the Easter recess on 16 April 1782, Henry Grattan's motion calling for Irish legislative independence met with little resistance; the new Lord-Lieutenant and Chief-Secretary, the Duke of Portland and Richard Fitzpatrick respectively, considered 'the question as carried', and saw no point in further opposition.[33]

On 18 May, 1782 Shelburne informed Portland that the British Parlia-ment had decided 'to meet the wishes of the Irish people'. The Declaratory Act was to be repealed by the British Parliament, an Irish biennial Mutiny Act allowed, and severe modifications to Poynings' Law conceded. From now on, formally rather than as heretofore informally, the Irish Parlia-ment would have the initiative where legislation was concerned. In addition, Irish judges were to hold office with the same terms of tenure as their English brother judges and the appellate jurisdiction of the Irish House of Lords was restored. For the first time in the Empire, the consti-tution of a colony would approximate that of the mother country. By the 'Constitution of 1782' Ireland had been accorded something akin to 'Dominion status': it had, it seemed, achieved legislative independence, and had done so within the Empire and without recourse to war. Not altogether mischievously, the American Peace Commissioner, Henry Lau-rens, challenged the chief British negotiator, Lord Shelburne, with having made those timely concessions to Ireland which had been peremptorily denied the American colonies—and which if granted might have pre-vented them seceding from the Empire.[34]

The winning of the 'Constitution of 1782' was undoubtedly the high point of Protestant nationalism in Ireland; but amidst the euphoric cele-bration and reverential invocations of the shades of Molyneux and Swift, there were those who sounded a note of caution. The opportunistic

---

[33] Bartlett, *Fall and Rise*, p. 97.

[34] A. P. W. Malcomson, 'The Treaty of Paris and Ireland', in Prosser Gifford, ed., *The Treaty of Paris (1783) in a Changing States System* (Lanham, Md., 1985), p. 75.

manner in which the gains had been achieved and the paramilitary agency by which they had been won gave cause for concern. The sudden eruption of the Volunteers on to the political scene, claiming the right to speak for the 'people' and threatening violence if their demands were not met, was hardly reassuring—especially as this extra-parliamentary armed body, its victory gained, showed no disposition to retire gracefully from the political arena. The Volunteers had successfully imported the gun into Irish politics: it might prove difficult to remove it. Moreover, Ireland had clearly taken advantage of England's difficulties in America to win those important concessions of 1782 (and 1779) and such opportunism held an obvious corollary for the future. An Irish crisis might provide the opportunity for the Empire to strike back; Ireland's difficulty could yet be England's opportunity. Lastly, it was ominous for the future that British ministers were uneasy at what had been yielded to Ireland. Irish legislative independence was considered a threat to imperial unity, for the constitutional concessions had starkly revealed Ireland's awkward role in the Empire. Accordingly, at the end of 1782 Shelburne called for 'the fixing by a sort of treaty, a commercial system between the two countries and a proportionable contribution to be paid by Ireland for the general protection of the Empire'.[35] Few doubted that 'a final adjustment' was needed or that it would come in time. 'It seems to me', Edmund Burke noted, 'that this affair [the Constitution of 1782] so far from ended, is but just begun. A new order of things is commencing. The old link is snapped asunder. What Ireland will substitute in the place of it to keep us together, I know not'.[36]

In the event, nothing was done, for the times were unpropitious. Grattan denounced in advance any attempt to make Ireland pay for its independence, and suggested to those British politicians anxious that 'some solid and permanent connection should be established' that they should rather rely for future harmony on 'the ties of common interest, equal trade and equal liberty'. Having just lost a humiliating war and shed a valuable portion of the Empire, and now confronting a hostile world, British ministers were understandably reluctant to put much weight on those 'dear ties of mutual love and mutual affection' which Irish patriots offered

[35] See James Kelly, *Prelude to Union: Anglo-Irish Politics in the 1780s* (Cork, 1992), chap. 2 for a full discussion.

[36] Burke to Duke of Portland, 25 May 1782, in Thomas W. Copeland and others, eds., *The Correspondence of Edmund Burke*, 10 vols. (Cambridge, 1958–70), IV, p. 455.

as a substitute for Poynings' Law and the Declaratory Act.[37] Such 'dear ties' had snapped recently, and the so-called 'Renunciation crisis' of 1783, when British ministers were forced to yield yet another constitutional point to Ireland, revealed these sentiments to be altogether absent. Nor were they evident in 1785, when a calculated attempt to define precisely Ireland's position in the Empire foundered in the face of Irish pride and English insensitivity. The rejection of the Anglo-Irish commerce-defence pact of that year meant that the relationship between England and Ireland would remain unreformed, that the much sought-after 'final adjustment' would prove elusive, and that Ireland's position within the Empire would continue to be ambiguous. True, the King still had a veto over Irish legislation, but ministers were well aware that this blunt weapon was unlikely to forge imperial unity. The lofty link of a shared monarch hardly seemed to affect day-to-day policy. In fact the frailty of this bond of a shared monarch was revealed in 1788 during the Regency crisis provoked by George III's madness. Unilateral action by the Irish Parliament raised the question: could there be a King of Ireland who was not King of England?

Finally, the legislative independence won by Ireland in 1782 was not the sole problem for the future, nor was it the vague nature of the post-1782 imperial connection that caused difficulties. The 'Constitution of 1782' was merely of symbolic importance and Ireland's role in the Empire had ever been indistinct and contested: what exacerbated matters was the departure of thirteen colonies from the Empire and, with them, thirteen legislatures of varying origins, nomenclature, power, and prestige. So long as the old Empire had existed with its crazy-paving of legislatures, the anomalous position of the Irish Parliament had not been unique (nor of course was it unique after 1783, for there were still representative institutions in the West Indies and in the Maritime Provinces of British Canada); but there had undoubtedly been a comforting shared ambiguity within the pre-revolutionary Empire that had offered the Irish Parliament some safety-in-numbers. Shorn of its sheltering sister-institutions in the American colonies, the Irish Parliament's anomalous position after 1783 was laid bare and—despite all its new powers and enhanced prestige—a huge question mark had been placed against its future. Viewed in this light, is it so surprising that the quest for that 'final adjustment' to the

---

[37] Kelly, *Prelude to Union*, p. 38.

'Constitution of 1782' should have concluded with the legislative Union of 1801?

During the 1790s, a decade of war and revolution, Ireland's hitherto abstract position as the weak link of the Empire was all too clearly revealed. The outbreak of war with revolutionary France in 1793 set the stage for yet another assault on the integrity of the British Empire, similar to that which had proved successful in the American war of independence. Just as the American rebels had sought independence with the aid of the French, so too disaffected groups in Ireland planned secession with French help. Moreover, as in America, Dissent provided the backbone of the independence movement in Ireland, for the Presbyterians of the north of Ireland, who had begun the Society of United Irishmen in 1791, saw their opportunity to break free of Anglican rule. Irish Catholics too had no reason to love the Established Church and many were prepared to play a role in the revolutionary movement of the 1790s. Dissident elements within (or just outside) the Protestant governing élite—Arthur O'Connor, Lord Edward Fitzgerald, Theobald Wolfe Tone—were prepared to help and take a lead. Admittedly, the movement for independence in America had been made possible by the removal of the Catholic—or French— threat in 1763; and the drive to secede from the Empire had been fuelled by colonial fears that the British government ever since had sought to re-institute the French Catholic menace in Canada, and elsewhere.

The comparison with Ireland breaks down at this point: Irish Catholics indisputably remained a large majority in Ireland, and if anything, Catholic assertiveness had increased in the 1790s. Given the religious furies—a legacy of the seventeenth century—that lurked just below the still surface of Irish life, surely disaffected Irish Presbyterians and their dissident Anglican colleagues ought to have trodden cautiously in the tumultuous 1790s rather than seeking to emulate their American cousins? In fact, both Presbyterian and Anglican subversives were confident that they could control the coming revolution in Ireland. Presbyterians drew encouragement from the civic virtue exhibited by those French Catholics who had deposed their king and bade defiance to the Pope: perhaps Irish Catholics were not wholly lost to the cause of liberty? Disaffected members of the Protestant Ascendancy firmly believed that they would maintain their position as the natural leaders of the country after the revolution. In any case, for both Presbyterian and Anglican radicals, the presence of a substantial French military force in Ireland would provide further reassurance that their Catholic allies would be kept under a firm military discipline.

The 1798 rebellion bore some comparison to the American War of Independence. Both were Dissenter-led secessionist movements within the Empire; both faced ferocious opposition from loyalists; and both relied for ultimate success on French intervention. In the American case, French intervention tilted the balance in favour of the colonists. With hindsight, the Irish failure can be attributed to the failure of the French to invade in force. If the 14,000 soldiers commanded by Hoche had effected a landing at Bantry Bay in December 1796, they might have proved as decisive to the outcome of the Irish struggle as the military and naval forces led by Lafayette and Rochambeau had been in the American War. Certainly, the 1,000-odd French soldiers under the command of Humbert that waded ashore in Sligo in September 1798 created alarm out of all proportion to their numbers; and even though Cornwallis's army outnumbered Humbert's men many times over, he treated them with consummate caution. Having once been out-manœuvred by the French at Yorktown (with the consequent loss of the American colonies), Cornwallis was determined that a similar fate should not befall him in Ireland.

In the end, the Irish and American contests, for all their superficial similarities, were really quite distinct. The Americans went to war and then drew in the French: the United Irishmen sought to take advantage of a war already begun. There was nothing comparable in Ireland to the Continental Congress, and there was no unified rebel military command. Almost certainly, loyalism was much stronger in Ireland than in the American colonies. The decisive difference, however, lay in the fact that Ireland was perceived as vital to Britain in a way that the American colonies were not. When the French had intervened on the American side, Britain's primary concern had been for the safety of the Sugar Islands, not the mainland colonies: hence the despatch of the British fleet to the Caribbean, which in turn cleared the way for the French navy to trap Cornwallis at Yorktown. With Ireland, however, it was all radically different. The French threat to Ireland in the late 1790s forced Britain to embark on a swift military build-up on the island: by 1798 there were nearly 100,000 soldiers of various descriptions there and, as an added precaution, British naval squadrons were stationed off the Irish coasts. Ireland would never be given up to an enemy nor, unlike the American colonies, could it be allowed to go its own way. Indeed, as a result of the departure of the American colonies, Ireland may have become even more strategically important to Britain. Certainly, it was central to British plans for an assault on the French West Indies in the 1790s.

In the event, immediately on learning of the Irish rebellion, Pitt had determined that the moment had now arrived to put through a legislative union, and that trusted imperial trouble-shooter, Cornwallis, was chosen to go to Ireland to carry out this policy. Given Cornwallis's previous experience in America and India, the choice was entirely appropriate, for the proposed Union was designed to consolidate the Empire and to scotch once and for all secessionist tendencies in Ireland.

Edmund Burke would surely have approved of this concentration on Empire. For him, the only true union between Ireland and England was an imperial one, and throughout his career he had looked to an Empire governed upon 'a prudent and enlarged policy'. By the time of his death in 1797, however, he had despaired of seeing this. Protestant Ascendancy in Ireland, 'Indianism' in Asia, and Jacobinism in Europe—the three great evils of the 1790s in his view—were in effect cut from the same cloth. Their thrust was to persuade 'the many' that they had no connection with 'the few', so to sever the bonds of civil society, and ultimately usher in bloody chaos. As an Irish-born English statesman of Catholic descent, Burke was uniquely placed to contemplate the blighted promise of the Old Empire, and surely he would have applauded the fresh start the Union offered.[38]

The Union debates of 1799 to 1800 in the British and Irish Parliaments revealed clearly how far notions of Empire had permeated Irish political discourse. This was a recent development. Previously, Empire whether as term or concept, had scarcely entered into the lexicon of those in favour of Union. In 1751, Lord Hillsborough's *A Proposal for Uniting the Kingdoms of Great Britain* had merely stressed the general utility of a Union, and claimed that it would pluck Ireland out of the obscurity in which it then languished: 'At present, Ireland hath no character, nor even a name in the

---

[38] Edmund Burke to Sir Hercules Langrishe, 26 May 1795, in Copeland, ed., *Correspondence of Edmund Burke*, VIII, p. 254; Conor Cruise O'Brien, *The Great Melody: A Thematic Biography of Edmund Burke* (London, 1992); Terry Eagleton, *Heathcliff and the Great Hunger: Studies in Irish Culture* (London, 1995), pp. 35–53.

affairs of Europe'. There was no explicit mention of imperial benefits.[39] By contrast, in 1799 the prospect of a strengthened Empire, the notion of an imperial partnership, and the idea of 'an Union for Empire' were key elements in the Unionist arguments. For Lord Cornwallis, the essential backdrop to Union was 'the general cause, which engages the empire' and the compelling need to strengthen the Empire in the face of French aggression.[40] For Castlereagh, too, a Union would 'consolidate the strength and glory of the Empire', though he rather went on to spoil matters by tactlessly raising the question of Ireland's 'Imperial contribution', and claiming that Ireland's colonial trade was a matter 'not of right but of favour', both touchy subjects with Irish MPs.[41] Other Irish pro-Unionists took up this theme of a Union for Empire, though here the emphasis was on the threat posed by an independent Irish Parliament to imperial unity. Thomas Connolly, for example, pointed out that 'two independent legislatures in one Empire [were] as absurd and monstrous as two heads on one pair of shoulders'; while the young lawyer William Smith argued that only a legislative Union could ensure 'that ONE Empire shall no longer be exposed to the risque of wavering languidly and inertly between the dissentient systems of two parliaments'.[42]

It was, however, William Pitt, in the British Parliament, who spelled out in detail what might be called the imperial argument. For Pitt, the ongoing war with France was 'the most important and momentous conflict that ever occurred in the history of the world'; the fate of the British Empire hung in the balance. Union with Ireland (that 'mighty limb of the Empire') would increase 'the general power of the Empire...to a very great extent by a consolidation of the strength of the two kingdoms'. Especially, Pitt held out the exciting prospect of the creation of an entirely

---

[39] Lord Hillsborough, *A Proposal for Uniting the Kingdoms of Great Britain* (Dublin, 1751; reprinted, 1800). An earlier pro-Union pamphlet, *The Queen an Empress and Her Three Kingdoms an Empire* (London and Dublin, 1706) had proposed the integration of the three kingdoms into a 'British Empire', but on examination this work delivers much less than its title suggests and David Hayton has dismissed it as 'hardly a serious contribution to the public debate on Union'. D. W. Hayton, 'Ideas of Union in Anglo-Irish Political Discourse, 1692–1720', in D. G. Boyce, Robert Eccleshall, and Vincent Geoghegan, eds., *Political Discourse in Seventeenth and Eighteenth-Century Ireland* (London, 2001), p. 154.

[40] *A report of the Debate in the House of Commons of Ireland...22 and 23 January 1799 on the subject of an Union* (Dublin, 1799), p. 2.

[41] Ibid., p. 44.

[42] Ibid., p. 14; *The substance of Mr. William Smith's speech on the subject of a legislative union...delivered in the House of Commons on Thursday 24 January 1799* (Dublin, 1799), p. 3.

new Assembly, one that would be neither British nor Irish but instead would be a 'General Imperial Legislature', an institution which, 'free alike from terror and from resentment, removed from danger and agitation, and uninflamed by the prejudices and passions of that distracted country', would adjudicate impartially and disinterestedly on those vicious issues that had riven Ireland for years and had left her so exposed to French intrigues.[43]

Pitt's remarks were echoed by his colleagues. Henry Dundas, Minister at War, identified the prevalence in Ireland of 'new doctrines, so dangerous to the existence of all regular governments, consequently so dangerous to that of the Empire', as making a Union necessary, and he forecast that after Union 'the voice of Irishmen... would be heard, not only in Europe but in Asia, Africa and America'.[44] The former Irish Chief Secretary, Sylvester Douglas, a Scot, dismissed the argument that post-Union Ireland would suffer a loss of constitutional status by arguing that 'Ireland, by an Union, no more becomes a *province* in any offensive sense of the word, than Great Britain: they both become provinces, or component parts of one whole and integrated Empire'. And, unconsciously echoing Wolfe Tone, Douglas pointed out that currently 'Ireland cannot either plant a colony or establish a foreign settlement'.[45] He and Dundas agreed that Union would give Ireland both a new role and a new voice in the Empire.

Another Scot, Lord Minto, made the conventional point that a Union with Ireland would afford 'an occasion of real and efficient force to our present Empire, as a navel [sic] and military power', but he then went on to consider the wider imperial dimension. The only connection Ireland had with England was an imperial one and it was this 'imperial connexion which makes Ireland a member of the noblest Empire of the globe'. In his view, the proposed Union was simply building on that foundation. 'For what, after all', he asked rhetorically, 'is this imperial connexion in the necessity of which we are all agreed? If it be anything more than a name and if it afford any substantial advantage, does it not consist in securing a conformity or rather a perfect uniformity and unity in the counsels of the

---

[43] *Speech of the Rt. Hon. William Pitt... Thursday 31 January 1799* (London, 1799), pp. 31, 34, 43.

[44] *Substance of the speech of the Rt. Hon. Henry Dundas... Thursday 7 February 1799* (London, 1799), p. 17.

[45] Edward Cooke, *Pro and Con: being an impartial abstract of the principal publications on the subject of a legislative union...* (Dublin, 1800), pp. 6, 10 [Cooke quoting Douglas].

two countries on affairs of imperial concern?' And, again in terms that recalled Tone's strictures on Ireland's poor imperial performance, Minto depicted the harsh reality of Ireland's current imperial role. 'Ireland', he wrote, 'cannot by the utmost success of the war acquire an acre of new territory to the Irish dominion. Every acquisition made by the forces of the Empire, however great her share may have been in the danger or exertion accrues to the crown of Great Britain'. Thus, he continued, 'If an island were taken by regiments raised in Ireland and composed wholly of Irishmen and by ships manned altogether by Irish seamen, that island is a British conquest, not an Irish one'. Minto promised that all this would change following Union. For Tone, Ireland's inability to acquire overseas dominions was an argument in favour of separatism; for Minto, it was a key attraction of Union. After Union, he concluded, 'Ireland is still Ireland, while a new scope is given to the pride, and a larger field opened to the patriotism, of every Irishman'.[46]

Beyond the walls of the Irish and British Parliaments, pro-Union pamphlet writers took up and elaborated this theme of a Union for Empire. Archibald Redfoord wrote of the 'powerful tendency [of Union] to give the British Empire strength and stability', and he reassured doubtful Protestants that it would be a 'Protestant Empire', one which would have an overwhelming majority of Protestants within 'the Imperial state'.[47] Or, as another writer had it: 'By an Union, the majority of the Empire will be Protestant and they have the right and the power to fix the national religion'.[48] The improbably named 'An Orangeman' stressed the career opportunities at the heart of the Empire that would open after Union: 'Is not Irish genius equal to the task of Imperial government?' he asked, before going on to point to the glittering examples of Burke, Sheridan, and Barré, imperial statesmen all: 'Where would we have heard of them, had they remained at home to wrangle in the little infantine squabbles of a local legislature?'[49] In short, declared an anonymous author, '[Union] is pregnant with immense, unequivocal and permanent Imperial advantages'

[46] *The speech of Lord Minto in the House of Peers, 11 April 1799 ... respecting an Union* (London, 1799), pp. 50, 109, 113–14, 117.

[47] Archibald Redfoord, *Union necessary to security, addressed to the loyal inhabitants of Ireland* (Dublin, 1800), pp. 34, 67, 69.

[48] Anon., *The necessity of an incorporate union between Great Britain and Ireland proved from the situation of both kingdoms* (Dublin, 1799), p. 54.

[49] An Orangeman (pseud.), *Union or Not?* (Dublin, 1799), p. 37.

and it was only the 'reformists, republicans, and separatists of this town' who refused to support it.[50]

So common—and, it appears, so attractive—was this theme of Empire in the general Union debate, that those opposed to Union were forced to make an attempt to rebut it. They did so in two ways. First, anti-Unionist writers stated that English prejudice against the Irish was both inveterate and deep-rooted. At a basic level, anxieties were expressed that Irish orators would be unable to gain a hearing for themselves in the London legislature. An Irish gentleman, wrote 'Molyneux', 'smell[ing] of the turf of boggy Ireland...would be ashamed to exhibit the Irish brogue in the British Senate'.[51] In this regard, the cautionary example of Henry Flood, was cited: an Irish Demosthenes when speaking in the Irish Parliament, yet at Westminster, whither he had removed himself in the 1780s, he suffered the humiliation of concluding 'a very able and eloquent speech amidst the yawns and coughs of an English Senate'.[52] More substantially, English antipathy towards the Irish, it was claimed, was simply too great to be overcome: 'We are a savage, immoral, ill-mannered race...I well know such are the sentiments', wrote one pamphleteer, 'which the low and the vulgar of your country entertain of the people of Ireland'.[53] 'I am well aware of the rooted prejudices, I had almost said hatred', wrote another, 'that lodges in the breast of some Englishmen towards Ireland'.[54] The English 'have been taught to hate and despise [us] from their infancy', argued Denis Taafe, so much so that even the 'very liberal' Englishman cannot but consider the Irish as 'semi-barbarous, destitute of industry, punctuality, and honesty'.[55] Such naked prejudice on its own, it was pointed out, would stop Irishmen taking up the promised role in imperial direction.

[50] Anon., *Verbum Sapienti: or a few reasons for thinking that it is imprudent to oppose and difficult to prevent the projected Union* (Dublin, 1799), pp. 7, 8, 14.

[51] Anon., *A reply to the memoire of Theobald McKenna Esq. on some questions touching the projected Union of Great Britain and Ireland* (Dublin, 1799), p. 18.

[52] Anon., *A reply to the gentleman who has published a pamphlet entitled 'Arguments for and against an Union'* (Dublin, 1799), p. 18; see also, for Flood's fate, *An Answer to a pamphlet entitled the speech of the Earl of Clare on the subject of a legislative Union* (Dublin, 1800), p. 34.

[53] Charles Ball, *An Union neither necessary nor expedient for Ireland* (Dublin, 1798), p. 7.

[54] Anon., *A reply to the gentleman who has published a pamphlet entitled 'Arguments for and against an Union'*, p. 18.

[55] The Rev. Denis Taafe, *The probability, causes, and consequences of an Union between Great Britain and Ireland discussed* (Dublin, 1798), p. 29.

Second, and in a more sophisticated way, some anti-Unionist politicians and writers claimed that Union would ultimately prove fatal for Empire. Admittedly, John Foster, the principal opponent of Union in the Irish Parliament, would base his arguments against Union on the grounds that it would prove a bad deal for the Irish economy, and he would deny that any British Parliament could be trusted to defend the interests of Irish Protestants. But even Foster was forced to confront the 'imperialists': contrary to what was promised, post-Union Ireland will not be at the heart of Empire, he maintained, but instead, 'we shall become a colony on the worst of terms'. And there was a further threat: 'exclusive of all its injuries to Ireland, [Union] is big with danger to the old fabric of the British constitution, and if it falls, the Empire goes with it, and they and we and all of us fall down'.[56] Foster was concerned that the 100 Irish MPs who would go to Westminster would overset the balance of the constitution because they would be little more than ministerial cannon fodder. Others forecast disaster for the British Empire, for Irish anger at this 'provocation' (Union) might turn the people towards France. 'Would not, might not the measure of Union drive the people of Ireland (which God avert) to seek protection from our natural enemies, even under a republican form of government?'[57] Another author claimed that Union could never solve Ireland's religious problems but 'on the contrary [would] prove the means of final separation'.[58] Taking the longer view, Charles Ball found the outcome of Union easily predictable: '[it] would ultimately involve this country in the next greatest calamity that could befall it—a total separation from England'; and this in turn would lead to the break up of the Empire.[59]

Notwithstanding arguments such as these, the anti-Unionists lost the debate, and the Union was passed. Many factors help explain the passing of the Irish Act of Union, and these have been well canvassed in the two hundred years since its enactment. What may be said is that, when linked to Empire, the Unionist case was certainly an impressive one; the offer of 'an Union for Empire' struck a chord with the politically involved classes,

---

[56] *Speech of the Rt. Hon. John Foster, speaker... delivered in committee, 17 February 1800* (Dublin, 1800), pp. 38, 42.

[57] Mathew Weld, *No Union, being an appeal to Irishmen* (Dublin, 1798), p. 18.

[58] Anon., *A reply to the memoire of Theobald McKenna Esq.*, p. 35.

[59] Charles Ball, *An Union neither necessary nor expedient for Ireland* (Dublin, 1798), p. 53.

and to an extent forced anti-Unionists on to the defensive. Grattan's famous peroration against the proposed Anglo-Irish trade-defence treaty of 1785—'perish the Empire but live the constitution'—could not be dusted down and re-deployed in 1799; surely a sign that Empire was held in much higher regard in 1800 than it had been even fifteen years earlier?[60]

In the event, while few of the promises held out by Unionists were realized in the hundred years after 1800, the Union did in fact prove to be a gateway to Empire. Throughout the nineteenth century, and beyond, Irishmen and Irishwomen entered enthusiastically into the business of Empire, whether as merchants, soldiers, settlers, missionaries, doctors, or administrators. The Empire was religiously blind, at least where Irish Protestants and Irish Catholics were concerned, and both would quickly become eager imperialists, the latter group taking especial pride in the heroic deeds of Irish soldiers and the heroic self-sacrifice of Irish priests and nuns. Throughout the nineteenth century, the Empire offered career opportunities—male and female, clerical and lay—that were simply not available in Ireland. Indeed, from the 1830s on, what was called the 'colonial patronage' was explicitly drawn on to meet the career aspirations of the Irish Catholic middle classes who clamoured for tangible benefits from emancipation.[61] Inevitably, the Catholic Irish nation would have major problems with the Protestant British State in the nineteenth century; but an appreciation of the benefits of Empire meant that Irish protests tended to be circumspect. Both the Repeal movement and the Home Rule movement explicitly denied any intention of disrupting the Empire. We may surmise that throughout the nineteenth century, the bond of Empire was at all times stronger than that of Union.[62]

---

[60] George Knox, member for Phillipstown, King's County, recalled Grattan's peroration but it was not followed up: See *A report of the debate in the House of Commons of Ireland . . . 22 and 23 Jan. 1799*, p. 44.

[61] A. T. Singleton to Maurice Fitzgerald, 13 April 1830, PRONI, T3075/13/47; S. B. Cook, '"The Irish Raj": Social Origins and Careers of Irishmen in the Indian Civil Service, 1855–1914', *Journal of Social History*, XX (Spring 1987), pp. 507–29.

[62] In this essay, I have drawn on my 'Britishness, Irishness and the Act of Union', in Dáire Keogh and Kevin Whelan, eds., *Acts of Union* (Dublin, 2001), pp. 243–58, and on '"An Union for Empire": The Anglo-Irish Union as an Imperial Project', in Michael Brown, Patrick M. Geoghegan, and James Kelly, eds., *The Irish Act of Union: Bicentennial Essays* (Dublin, 2003), pp. 50–57.

Select Bibliography

THOMAS BARTLETT, ' "A People Made rather for Copies than Originals": The Anglo Irish, 1760–1800', *International History Review*, XII (1990), pp. 11–25.

—— 'The Augmentation of the Army in Ireland, 1769–72', *English Historical Review*, XCVI (1981), pp. 540–59.

—— *The Fall and Rise of the Irish Nation: The Catholic Question, 1690–1830* (Dublin, 1992).

NICHOLAS P. CANNY, *Kingdom and Colony: Ireland in the Atlantic World, 1560–1800* (Baltimore, 1988).

S. J. CONNOLLY, *Religion, Law and Power: The Making of Protestant Ireland, 1660–1760* (Oxford, 1992).

R. G. COUPLAND, *The American Revolution and the British Empire* (1930; New York, 1965).

L. M. CULLEN, *Anglo-Irish Trade in the Eighteenth Century* (Manchester, 1968).

—— and T. C. SMOUT, eds., *Comparative Aspects of Scottish and Irish Economic and Social History, 1600–1900* (Edinburgh, 1977).

DAVID DICKSON, *New Foundations: Ireland, 1660–1800* (Dublin, 1987).

MARIANNE ELLIOTT, *Wolfe Tone: Prophet of Irish Independence* (New Haven, 1989).

JACK P. GREENE, *Peripheries and Centers: Constitutional Development in the Extended Politics of the British Empire and the United States, 1607–1788* (Athens, Ga., 1987).

VINCENT T. HARLOW, *The Founding of the Second British Empire, 1763–93. Vol. I. Discovery and Revolution* (London, 1952).

F. G. JAMES, *Ireland in the Empire* (Cambridge, Mass., 1973).

JAMES KELLY, *Prelude to Union: Anglo-Irish Politics in the 1780s* (Cork, 1992).

R. B. McDOWELL, *Ireland in the Age of Imperialism and Revolution, 1760–1800* (Oxford, 1979).

KERBY A. MILLER, *Emigrants and Exiles: Ireland and the Irish Exodus to North America* (Oxford, 1985).

T. W. MOODY and W. E. VAUGHAN, eds., *A New History of Ireland. Vol. IV. Eighteenth-Century Ireland, 1690–1801* (Oxford, 1985).

R. C. NASH, 'Irish Atlantic Trade in the Seventeenth and Eighteenth Centuries', *William and Mary Quarterly*, Third Series, XLIII (1985), pp. 329–56.

PETER ROEBUCK, ed., *Macartney of Lissanoure: Essays in Biography* (Belfast, 1983).

THOMAS M. TRUXES, *Irish-American Trade, 1660–1783* (Cambridge, 1988).

4

The Irish in the Empire

KEVIN KENNY

On 13 April 1919 a crowd of some 20,000 people gathered in Amritsar on a piece of waste ground called the Jallianwala Bagh. Defying a recent ban on such assemblies, they had come together to protest the arrest and imprisonment of two local nationalist leaders. The arrests had been followed by several days of rioting in Amritsar, and now Brigadier-General Reginald Dyer approached the Bagh with two armoured cars bearing mounted machine guns. Unable to get the cars through any of the narrow entrances to the field, he led a troop of some fifty soldiers up an alleyway and, without any warning or order to disperse, commanded them to open fire. They continued to fire for about ten minutes. According to official sources, 379 people were killed; other estimates run as high as 600. About 1,200 were injured. Many of the casualties were women and children. 'Such was Amritsar, the single event which by common consent did most to undo British rule in India'.[1]

Like so many aspects of British imperial rule, this episode was not a straightforward matter of Englishmen versus 'natives'. The riflemen were Sikhs and Gurkhas. Reginald Dyer had been born in the Punjab in 1864, the son of an Irish brewer, and was educated at Midleton College in County Cork and the Royal Military College in Simla. Commissioned in the Queen's Royal Regiment in 1885 and transferred to the Indian Army, he commanded British operations in south-east Persia during the First World War. The Lieutenant-Governor of the Punjab at the time of the Amritsar massacre was Michael O'Dwyer, an Irish Catholic from County Tipperary

---

Particular thanks to Thomas Bartlett, Joe Cleary, Kathleen Costello-Sullivan, Elizabeth Butler Cullingford, Stephen Howe, Marjorie Howes, Niamh Lynch, Prasannan Parthasarathi, Paige Reynolds, Robert Savage, James Smith, and Peter Weiler.

[1] Sir Michael O'Dwyer, *India as I Knew It, 1885–1925* (London, 1925), esp. pp. 263–329; Derek Sayer, 'British Reaction to the Amritsar Massacre, 1919–1920', *Past and Present*, 131 (Feb. 1991), pp. 130–64 (quotation at p. 131).

who had joined the Indian Civil Service in 1882. O'Dwyer quickly made known his approval of Dyer's actions. The unrest in the Punjab was followed by courts martial, public floggings, ritual humiliations, executions, and even aerial bombardment. In British India, and among some circles at home, Dyer was lauded as the 'Saviour of the Punjab'.[2]

The ensuing investigation by the Hunter Committee of the House of Commons is rich with historical insights about British imperial rule and the role of the Irish therein. The Committee censured Dyer and invited him to resign from the Army, but without further punishment or prosecution. In June 1920 Michael O'Dwyer joined Rudyard Kipling and others in contributing to an 'Appeal to Patriots' launched by the *Post* on Dyer's behalf. When the case was debated in the House of Commons in July, Winston Churchill, then Secretary of State for War, denounced Dyer's actions and endorsed his censure. But the Ulster Unionist leader, Sir Edward Carson, having been briefed by Michael O'Dwyer, argued that Dyer was being denied due process. Coalition Unionists, with Ulster MPs to the fore, voted heavily against the government and in favour of Dyer. Their sentiment was neither altruistic nor unthinkingly imperialist. Instead, 'the whole Dyer controversy was a thinly coded discussion of Ireland, then in open revolt'.[3]

At stake was how the British Empire should be ruled, and there was substantial support in Ireland, Britain, and especially India, for Dyer's approach to that question. Parts of Ireland, Egypt, and India were in, or close to, rebellion. Mohandas K. Gandhi had been arrested early in April 1919, just before the massacre, while trying to enter the Punjab to join the nationalist protests there. Dyer insisted that the fate of the Empire was in the balance at Amritsar, and that he had done his moral duty by sending a message to India as a whole. In his proclamation of martial law in the Punjab on 15 April 1919, O'Dwyer had said precisely the same thing. A small but powerful sector of the British establishment could not help but agree. Among them was the Longford-born Chief of the Imperial General Staff, Field-Marshal Sir Henry Wilson, a vocal supporter of Dyer in the summer of 1920, who would declare in March 1921: 'If we lose Ireland we have lost the Empire.'[4]

[2] O'Dwyer, *India as I Knew It*, pp. 283–87, 298–304; Sayer, 'British Reaction', p. 130.

[3] Sayer, 'British Reaction', p. 153.

[4] Wilson to Arnold Robertson, 30 March 1921, in Keith Jeffery, ed., *The Military Correspondence of Field-Marshal Sir Henry Wilson, 1918–22* (London, 1985), p. 250.

Reginald Dyer was retired on half-pay, died of natural causes on 23 July 1927, and received a military funeral. Michael O'Dwyer, who had left the Punjab in the wake of Amritsar, was subsequently knighted for his service to the Empire. In his memoir, *India as I Knew It*, published in 1925, he offered a strenuous defence of his administration and rejected all analogies between Irish and Indian autonomy. Proposals for democratic reform in India, he insisted, were 'based on the false premise that the Indian masses have the desire and capacity for representative institutions which British people have. The results of pouring the new heady wine of the West into the ancient wine-skins of the East', he concluded, 'have been so far disastrous'.[5] On 13 March 1940 O'Dwyer gave a lecture at a meeting of the East India Association, at Caxton Hall in London, on the contemporary Afghan crisis. In the audience was Udham Singh, a Sikh, who had spent most of his childhood in Amritsar's Central Orphanage and may have been in the Jallianwala Bagh in April 1919. He had spent time in Africa and the United States before moving to England in 1932. At the end of the lecture Singh called out O'Dwyer's name, O'Dwyer turned, and Singh shot him dead with a revolver. Singh was swiftly hanged at Pentonville. How, one wonders, did he see the Irish—whether Reginald Dyer, Michael O'Dwyer, or Edward Carson? Not, presumably, as the oppressed members of a colonized people. Perhaps he did not see the Irish soldiers and administrators who ruled him as Irish at all but simply as agents and instruments of Empire. Whatever questions may have applied to Irish racial identity in the Atlantic world, the colonized of India and Africa could scarcely have doubted that the Irish were white.[6]

As well as belonging to a colony at the heart of the British Empire, Irish people helped conquer, populate, and govern the colonies overseas. Some historians have seen this ambiguous position *vis-à-vis* the Empire as a contradiction or even a paradox. 'Far from empathizing with indigenous peoples overseas', one writes, 'the Irish, whatever their experience at home, were as brutal as any other white colonisers. Not surprisingly, this paradoxical involvement in British imperialism has yielded an ambivalent heritage'.[7] Seeking to explain the 'paradoxes to be found in the relation-

---

[5] O'Dwyer, *India as I Knew It*, p. 449.

[6] See David R. Roediger, *The Wages of Whiteness: Race and the Making of the American Working Class* (New York, 1991); Noel Ignatiev, *How the Irish Became White* (New York, 1995).

[7] Hiram Morgan, 'An Unwelcome Heritage: Ireland's Role in British Empire Building', *History of European Ideas*, 19 (July 1994), pp. 619–25 (quotation at p. 619).

ship of Irish people with India', another scholar comments that, '[o]n the one hand, Irish people participated in imperialism, and were instrumental in establishing and maintaining British rule in India. On the other, they also have a significant anti-colonialist reputation arising from the achievements of Irish nationalism and independence'.[8] A third historian notes that, while 'Engels described Ireland as England's first colony' and critics today 'frequently characterise it as having a post-colonial society', Ireland 'was also a part of the metropolitan core of Empire and supplied many of its soldiers, settlers, and administrators'. This dual status results in 'the paradox that Ireland was both "imperial" and "colonial"'.[9]

Where is the paradox? There is nothing anomalous in members of one colonized people helping to govern their homeland, or to conquer and govern another country elsewhere in the same Empire. Indians helped govern India, and they served in huge numbers in the British Army both at home and throughout Asia, the Middle East, and Africa. Colonial subjects of the French Empire did similar service.[10] Irishmen helped conquer and govern both Ireland itself and the British colonies overseas, and took full advantage of the military, career, and commercial opportunities presented by their situation at the heart of the largest Empire in history. They were to be found at all times in every part of the Empire: as migrants and settlers in North America, Australia, and New Zealand; as soldiers and administrators in India and the Dominions; and as missionaries in Asia and, especially, Africa. The historian's task is to make sense of this activity and what it means for Irish history.

From the beginnings of the British Empire in the sixteenth century to its demise in the twentieth, the Irish were both subjects and agents of imperialism. The term 'agency' can cover a wide range of activities, some of them actively imperialist and others at best passively so, simply by dint of their taking place within the bounds of the Empire. Thus, while Anglo-Irish military officers were among the most vehement of all proponents and enforcers of British imperialism, the Irish Catholic soldiers they commanded typically enlisted in the British Army for economic rather than

---

[8] Michael Holmes, 'The Irish in India: Imperialism, Nationalism and Internationalism', in Andy Bielenberg, ed., *The Irish Diaspora* (London, 2000), p. 235.

[9] Keith Jeffery, ed., *'An Irish Empire'? Aspects of Ireland and the British Empire* (Manchester, 1996), front matter, n. p.

[10] V. G. Kiernan, *Colonial Empires and Armies*, rev. edn. (Montreal and Kingston, 1998); Keith Jeffery, *The British Army and the Crisis of Empire, 1918–22* (Manchester, 1984), p. 1.

jingoistic reasons and sometimes served as mere cannon fodder. But they enlisted none the less, in massive numbers, and they played a critical role in ruling the Empire. Irishmen and women, likewise, populated the Empire in their hundreds of thousands, some dispossessing and slaughtering indigenous populations and others joining well-established settler societies; and Irish missionaries brought to their work a combination of egalitarianism and cultural imperialism. On all of these different levels, Ireland was both a component part of the Empire and a significant player in its adventures overseas. Those who subscribe to the view that Ireland was never, properly speaking, a colony of the British Empire may initially find solace in the evidence presented here. Those subscribing to the opposite, and equally simplistic view, that Ireland was always and self-evidently nothing other than a British colony, will not. But that is not the issue here. Both positions assume that Ireland's colonial status somehow stands or falls on the extent to which Irishmen were actively involved in the affairs of the Empire. Yet the fact of imperial service, in itself, neither negates nor supports claims about colonial status. Instead it challenges us to think anew about Irish national history.

In an age when historians all over the world are busily placing national histories in non-national contexts, the story that follows suggests one such context for modern Irish history. Historians of medieval and early modern Ireland have long since moved their subject from its insular setting into wider contexts, whether Catholic, continental, Atlantic, 'archipelagic', or 'new British'. Irish historiography on the modern era is noticeably less cosmopolitan, in large part because the primacy of the nation-state is one of the defining characteristics of this period. But nation-states existed in larger contexts, attaining much of their legitimacy by suppressing this fact. Colonialism and imperialism have long been central themes in Irish national history, but mainly as forces inflicted on Ireland from the outside. They take on a new, expanded meaning if Ireland is restored to its historical place at the heart of the British Empire. Certainly, the great Irish national histories—by Beckett, Lyons, Foster, and Jackson, for example—have not taken this wider imperial context to be an essential framework for interpreting the Irish past. Doing so helps provide a richer understanding of the conditions in which Ireland came to constitute and define itself as a nation-state in the modern era. Colonized by their more powerful neighbour, the Irish lived at the heart of the world's greatest Empire; most Irish people saw themselves as part of that Empire in some way;

many participated, at a variety of levels, in its workings overseas. There is no contradiction here, merely a fact of imperial history.[11]

The beginnings of Irish overseas expansion in the modern era coincided with the ongoing conquest and colonization of Ireland and hence with the emergence of the Empire itself. Migration into and out of Ireland was part of a larger process of imperial expansion that gave rise to the first, largely Atlantic, British Empire (c.1570s to 1780s), encompassing England and Wales, Scotland, Ireland, Newfoundland, Nova Scotia, mainland North America, and the West Indies as well as parts of India. British migration into Ireland and across the Atlantic were roughly equivalent in the seventeenth century: some 350,000 English and a few thousand Scots settled in the Caribbean and mainland colonies, while an estimated 200,000 English and 100,000 Scottish crossed the Irish Sea. The settlement of Ireland and the transatlantic colonies featured the same types of corporate structures, the same types of people, and sometimes even the same individuals. Figures such as Humphrey Gilbert, Walter Ralegh, and Edmund Spenser have received much attention in this respect, and the emerging ideology of British imperialism in the late sixteenth and early seventeenth centuries certainly embraced both Ireland and America. Equally significant connections between Ireland and the other Atlantic colonies can be found at the more mundane levels of indentured servitude, chain migration, and trade networks.[12]

The seventeenth-century Caribbean is a good example. During the 1650s and 1660s, Ireland was probably the chief source of white migration to the West Indies, mainly in the form of indentured servants and to a lesser extent convicts and prisoners of war. The islands, however, were not simply a Cromwellian dumping ground for unwanted Irishmen. The most visible Irishmen there were younger sons of prominent Catholic families who, lacking opportunity at home, set up as merchants and planters in the West Indies. That many of these Irishmen owned African slaves, while some of their poorer countrymen were brought to the Caribbean in

[11] J. C. Beckett, *The Making of Modern Ireland, 1603–1923* (New York, 1966); F. S. L. Lyons, *Ireland Since the Famine* (London, 1973); R. F. Foster, *Modern Ireland, 1600–1972* (London, 1988); Alvin Jackson, *Ireland, 1798–1998: Politics and War* (Oxford, 1999).

[12] Nicholas Canny, 'English Migration Into and Across the Atlantic During the Seventeenth and Eighteenth Centuries', in Nicholas Canny, ed., *Europeans on the Move: Studies in European Migration, 1500–1800* (Oxford, 1994), pp. 61–62.

various states of bondage, points to significant class divisions within white Caribbean society. Given Ireland's very turbulent history in the seventeenth century, the authorities evidently took seriously the prospect of an alliance between the Irish poor and African slaves, possibly with French encouragement.[13]

In the eighteenth century, men and women from Ireland played a fundamental role in peopling the Atlantic Empire, outnumbering the English and the Scots combined. The great age of English migration was over: only 30,000 people left England for the American colonies in the eighteenth century, compared with ten times that number in the previous century. An estimated 75,000 Scots crossed the Atlantic in the century after 1700s. The figure for Ireland, by contrast, may have been as high as 250,000.[14] Historians estimate that people of Irish origin accounted for between 14 and 17 per cent of the white population of the United States at the time of the first federal census in 1790, though all such figures (being based on surname analysis) are necessarily imprecise. Alongside the Germans and Africans, the Irish were the largest group of migrants to the American colonies in this era.[15]

The pattern of Irish transatlantic migration in the eighteenth century was determined directly by the conquest and colonization of Ireland in the previous century. Those parts of the country that had received most English and Scottish immigrants (Ulster and the Southeast) produced most outward migration thereafter. Perhaps one-quarter of the migrants were Catholic, but the great majority were Ulster Presbyterians whose forebears had only recently come to Ireland from Scotland. Overseas migration was as important in eighteenth-century Ulster as it would be in

---

[13] Louis M. Cullen, 'The Irish Diaspora of the Seventeenth and Eighteenth Centuries', in Canny, ed., *Europeans on the Move*, p. 126; Morgan, 'An Unwelcome Heritage', p. 619.

[14] If the most conservative estimate of Irish Protestant migration across the Atlantic for the period before the American Revolution is accepted (66,000), one would still need to add somewhere in the region of 42,000 Catholics in the pre-Revolutionary era, along with perhaps 100,000 to 150,000 of both denominations in the period 1783–1800, leaving a total of between 200,000 and 250,000 for the eighteenth century as a whole. James Horn, 'British Diaspora: Emigration from Britain, 1680–1815', in P. J. Marshall, ed., *OHBE. Vol. II. The Eighteenth Century* (Oxford, 1998), p. 31; Cullen, 'Irish Diaspora', p. 128; Canny, 'English Migration Into and Across the Atlantic', pp. 61–62; T. C. Smout, N. C. Landsman, and T. M. Devine, 'Scottish Emigration in the Seventeenth and Eighteenth Centuries', in Canny, ed., *Europeans on the Move*, p. 97.

[15] David Noel Doyle, 'The Irish in North America, 1776–1845', in W. E. Vaughan, ed., *A New History of Ireland. Vol. V. Ireland Under the Union, I, 1801–70* (Oxford, 1989), p. 692.

Ireland as a whole from the 1820s onward; although the numbers were smaller the proportions of the population departing were much the same. Those who left Ireland in the eighteenth century were very consciously moving within a single Atlantic Empire. The authorities, too, conceived of the matter in imperial terms, fearing that the departure of so many Presbyterians might endanger both the prosperity and the security of Ulster. In the end, these fears proved groundless. Migration provided opportunities for younger sons, acted as a safety-valve for broader social tensions, opened up extensive new trade and commercial networks, and thereby stabilized social and economic structures at home. Even those who left the country as indentured servants—perhaps half of all Ulster migrants between 1720 and 1770—clearly found opportunity in the Empire and tended to depart from Ireland on the basis of well-calculated choice rather than compulsion or despair. Nor did Ireland's population diminish in line with mass migration; unbeknownst to contemporaries, the country had entered a phase of massive population growth that would endure for the better part of a century.[16]

Placed in its Atlantic imperial context, the history of Ulster's Presbyterians displays a striking pattern from one side of the ocean to the other. In both Ireland and the American colonies, Presbyterians occupied a middle ground between the zones of perceived 'civilization' and 'barbarism'. In Ulster most of them were tenant farmers, some substantial and others precarious; very few of them penetrated to the largely Anglican landowning class. They were, none the less, considerably better off than the dispossessed Catholic population surrounding them, whose land they now occupied. As Dissenters, they faced religious penalties in Ireland; but, while they were excluded from some of the political prerogatives pertaining to membership in the Established Church, they faced considerably fewer disabilities than the Catholic majority. This intermediate status between Anglican and Catholic had its counterpart in matters of security. Despite their social and political disadvantages, Ulster Presbyterians were expected to defend the Anglican élite from potential Catholic rebellion, especially in the seventeenth century.

Irish Presbyterians carried their ambiguous status to America. They left Ulster for America in search of land and opportunity, and in hopes that

[16] Maldwyn A. Jones, 'The Scotch-Irish in British America', in Bernard Bailyn and Philip D. Morgan, eds., *Strangers Within the Realm: Cultural Margins of the First British Empire* (Chapel Hill, NC, 1991); Cullen, 'Irish Diaspora', pp. 131–37, 141.

they might be left alone to practice their religion as they liked. On both counts they were to be disappointed. Facing considerable religious hostility from the eastern tidewater élites—whether Anglican, Quaker, or Puritan—they moved westward and southward in a great internal migration that would take them all the way from Pennsylvania to Georgia and out to Kentucky and Tennessee. Widely despised for their manners and their poverty as well as their religion, they populated the colonial frontier in large numbers, where they squatted on 'empty' land, disregarded treaties previously signed with Native Americans, and gained a gruesome reputation as Indian fighters. Excluded from political power, they none the less protected the eastern élites against combined Indian and French attack (a source of particular grievance in Pennsylvania where the Quaker oligarchy was pacifist). The story of these embattled people, situated on the cultural and geographical margins of the Atlantic Empire but playing a role critical to its survival, has yet to be told.[17]

Irish migration from the 1820s onward was predominantly Catholic and directed mainly to a former British colony, the United States. But, in addition to the 5 million Irish who went to the United States between 1820 and 1920, at least 1.5 million went to Britain and another 1 million migrated to Canada, Australia, and New Zealand. Although the American numbers exceeded those for all other destinations combined, the Irish-born made up a greater proportion of the populations of Scotland, Canada, New Zealand, and the Australian provinces in 1870 than they did in the United States. Like most early European migrants to Australia, the Irish came as convicts, accounting for about one-quarter of the 160,000 transported to Australia between 1788 and 1867. Scots, by contrast, made up only 5 per cent. By the mid-nineteenth century, the Irish ethnic group may have accounted for as much as half the European population of Australia. Migration to the nineteenth-century United States was overwhelmingly Catholic, but in Canada and South Africa (like colonial America), Protestants accounted for a majority of the Irish population, while in Britain, Australia, and New Zealand they formed a minority greater than that in the United States.[18]

[17] See Patrick Griffin, *The People with No Name: Ireland's Ulster Scots, America's Scots Irish, and the Creation of a British Atlantic World, 1689–1764* (Princeton, 2001).

[18] Alan O'Day, 'Revising the Diaspora', in D. George Boyce and Alan O'Day, eds., *The Making of Modern Irish History: Revisionism and the Revisionist Controversy* (London, 1996), p. 189; David Fitzpatrick, 'Ireland and Empire', in Andrew Porter, ed., *OHBE. Vol. III. The*

Virtually all Irish overseas migrants settled in Anglophone colonies, former colonies, or Dominions of the British Empire, which shared an entrenched tradition of anti-Catholicism. This tradition, indeed, helped define the nature of Britishness both at home and abroad. The overseas Irish found themselves on both sides of the religious divide: while Irishmen of Catholic origin faced considerable prejudice, those of Protestant extraction were often in the vanguard of anti-Catholic movements. The Orange Order became a militant forum for the expression of anti-Catholicism wherever Irish Protestants settled, and by the late 1870s there were an estimated 5,000 lodges throughout the British Empire.[19] Orangeism, however, was but one small aspect of yet another Irish imperial story that has yet to be told. 'The religious history of Irish settlement', as one historian puts it, 'ought to be more than a catalogue of catholic pietism, protestant anti-popery, and broken heads'.[20] Given the close identification of Britishness with Protestantism and of Irishness with Catholicism, the dynamic between these two religious cultures played a significant role in the national development of the heavily Irish Dominion states. The leading historian of the Irish in Australia, for example, places the interplay between Protestantism and Irish immigrant Catholicism at the heart of Australian national development, a claim that has some merits given the size of the Irish population there in the nineteenth century.[21]

Irish-Australians displayed considerable ambivalence at times regarding their position, and that of Ireland, in the Empire. For the most part they 'accepted, indeed took pride in, belonging to Australia and the empire', readily incorporating 'God Save the King' into their annual St Patrick's Day festivities,[22] but like their American counterparts, if to a lesser extent, they also lent support to nationalist movements in Ireland. In its Home Rule variety, Irish nationalism was rarely anti-imperialist, searching instead for a secure and profitable niche within the Empire. Supporting this

---

Nineteenth Century (Oxford, 1999), pp. 512–14; Andy Bielenberg, 'Irish Emigration to the British Empire', in Bielenberg, ed., *Irish Diaspora*, p. 220; Marjory Harper, 'British Migration and the Peopling of Empire', in Porter, ed., *OHBE. Vol. III*, pp. 78–82.

[19] Bielenberg, 'Irish Emigration to the British Empire', p. 228.

[20] David Fitzpatrick, '"A Peculiar Tramping People": The Irish in Britain, 1801–70', in Vaughan, ed., *New History of Ireland. Vol. V*, p. 630.

[21] Patrick O'Farrell, *The Irish in Australia* (Kensington, NSW, 1986).

[22] Patrick O'Farrell, 'The Irish in Australia and New Zealand, 1870–1990', in W.E. Vaughan, ed., *New History of Ireland. Vol. VI. Ireland under the Union, II, 1870–1921* (Oxford, 1996), p. 708.

moderate form of nationalism therefore presented few problems in terms of imperial loyalty. Irish nationalism throughout the diaspora grew more extreme, however, after the events of 1916. In both Australia and New Zealand, as in Ireland and the United States, the ensuing conflicts were bound up with the national and imperial emergencies of the First World War.[23]

While the Irish global presence thereby intersected uncomfortably with questions of pressing imperial concern—whether military conscription in Australia or anti-British wartime sentiment in Irish America—the subject of migration also demands consideration in terms of its domestic origins and impact. Most pressingly, what is the connection between British control of Ireland and the massive depopulation of the country since 1800? About 10 million people have emigrated from Ireland to all destinations, including Britain, almost twice the number living on the island today. No European country other than Portugal lost so high a proportion of its population to emigration in the modern era. Two out of every five Irish-born people were living overseas at the end of the nineteenth century. Yet, while popular memory at home and abroad appears to have sustained a pervasive sense of emigration as British-imposed exile, there was sometimes an element of expediency in the invocation of this theme. Those who stayed behind in Ireland clearly benefited from mass emigration in all sorts of ways, even as they blamed it on British iniquity. Post-Famine Ireland was noticeably more prosperous and less violent than pre-Famine Ireland had been. Strong commercial farmers not only benefited from this new stability in general terms, they received massive financial remittances from their families abroad; and they contributed directly to mass emigration themselves by evicting their subtenants, consolidating their landholdings, and converting their farms from tillage to pasture. The existence of this protracted internal class struggle in no way precludes an explanation of Irish migration history in terms of British colonialism; the point, however, is that the colonial (or postcolonial) framework, to the extent that migration scholars have found it desirable or appropriate, has so far been largely taken for granted rather than demonstrated historically. Approaching this question from an economic standpoint would make obvious sense. In the meantime, whatever the causal link between colonialism and migration may have been, historians

---

[23] O'Farrell, 'The Irish in Australia and New Zealand, 1870–1990', pp. 712–22.

need to take seriously the very widespread sense among the migrants, especially in the mid-nineteenth century, that they had been banished from their native land.[24]

Sir Michael O'Dwyer, whom we have already encountered at Amritsar, was one of fourteen children. Born in 1864, he recalled a childhood of 'green pastures, luxurious crops, fine cattle and well-bred horses' where 'the atmosphere..., though essentially Irish, showed no signs of racial or religious feeling'. His father owned 'four or five hundred acres' of prime pasture land, a sizeable property by Irish standards, and had high ambitions for his children. The sons were sent first to the Jesuits and then to Trinity College, Dublin, to study law and medicine; two of them joined the Jesuit order and others took up medicine, business, or farming. With an elder brother already in the Indian Medical Service, Michael O'Dwyer passed the examination for the Indian Civil Service (ICS) in 1882 and entered Balliol College, Oxford as a Probationer. He was just completing his training for the ICS examination when word arrived from Dublin of one of the most notorious acts of Irish political violence in the nineteenth century, the assassination in Phoenix Park of the new Chief Secretary, Lord Frederick Cavendish, and his Under-Secretary, T. H. Burke. In his memoirs, O'Dwyer recalled how he 'for the first time felt ashamed of being an Irishman'. With 'the legitimate movement for Home Rule' now 'under the control of unscrupulous men who exploited it for seditious and even revolutionary purposes', the family farmstead became a target; threatening letters were received and a plot to maim the cattle discovered, shots were fired into the house, and Michael O'Dwyer came back from Oxford to find his home under police protection. He recalled this experience of violent agitation, and the prominent role of informers in the Phoenix Park case, as formative influences on his subsequent policies in the Punjab, where he served as Lieutenant-Governor from 1913 to 1919, earning a reputation for tyrannical rule.[25]

Michael O'Dwyer was no ordinary Irishman. He came from an unusual family, was very well educated, and given his relatively modest

[24] Kerby Miller, *Emigrants and Exiles: Ireland and the Irish Exodus to North America* (New York, 1985); Jim MacLaughlin, 'Changing Attitudes to "New Wave" Emigration?: Structuralism versus Voluntarism in the Study of Irish Emigration', in Bielenberg, ed., *Irish Diaspora*, pp. 317–30.

[25] O'Dwyer, *India as I Knew It*, pp. 1–7.

Irish Catholic background he insinuated himself into the British imperial élite with considerable ease. Yet his religious background in itself was by no means atypical. Throughout the Empire, Irish Catholics served as soldiers and administrators, or worked as policemen, doctors, engineers, lawyers, journalists, or businessmen. India was the principal venue. An estimated 20 per cent of the British population there in 1817 was Irish, declining to 13 per cent in the closing decades of the century and falling to 10 per cent in 1911. The Scots, though more renowned for their imperial service, were slightly less numerous in India than the Irish. The two principal occupations for Irishmen in the Empire abroad were administration and soldiering. And the great majority of Irishmen who entered these two branches of imperial service were Catholics.[26]

Although soldiering was easily the most important of the two, the imperial civil service offered another way to avail oneself of the opportunities presented by the Empire, especially for younger sons of relatively prosperous Catholics. Especially important in the nineteenth century was the Indian Civil Service. Until mid-century, ICS officers were recruited via Haileybury College in a patronage system controlled by the East India Company. Then in 1855, with the support of Sir Charles Trevelyan and Thomas Babington Macaulay, Sir Charles Wood (the Secretary of State for India) oversaw the abolition of the patronage system, the closure of the East India Company's training school at Haileybury, and the introduction of competitive examinations designed to shift the basis of recruitment in favour of merit, character, and intelligence. The result, though Wood had not intended it that way, was a surge in Irish recruitment. Whereas only 5 per cent of the Haileybury appointees between 1809 and 1850 had been Irish-born, fully 24 per cent of recruits between 1855 and 1863 came from Irish universities. In the latter period, the figure for Scottish recruits fell from 13 to 10 per cent, and that for English from 54 to 51 per cent (with the remainder coming from outside the United Kingdom, mainly from India).[27]

---

[26] Ibid., pp. 1–8, 17–21; Scott B. Cook, 'The Irish Raj: Social Origins and Careers of Irishmen in the Indian Civil Service, 1855–1919', *Journal of Social History*, 20 (Spring 1987), p. 509. Scotsmen accounted for about 8 per cent of India's British-born population during the last quarter of the nineteenth century while their share of the British population as a whole remained stable at 11 per cent.

[27] Cook, 'Irish Raj', p. 510.

The Irish universities had responded quickly to the new system, Trinity College establishing chairs in Sanskrit and Arabic and the new Queen's Colleges in Belfast, Cork, and Galway offering courses in Indian languages, history, geography, and law. Thus, in the year 1857, when Ireland made up roughly 20 per cent of the UK population, 33 per cent of all ICS recruits were Irish. Alarmed by this influx of Irishmen, Wood and his successor, Lord Salisbury, arranged the redistribution of points allotted to certain subjects and lowered the maximum testing age in such a way as to tilt the balance away from London and the Irish universities and towards Oxford and Cambridge. Sharing the conviction that 'English gentlemen were the best conceivable imperial guardians', Wood and Salisbury had grave doubts about 'the ability of the Irish either to rule themselves or govern others'.[28] Most of these Irish imperial 'governors', of course, were Catholic. In the period 1886–1914, one historian finds, only 13 per cent of ICS recruits came from the Irish peerage or landed gentry, and fully 80 per cent from the Catholic middle class of professional, mercantile, business, or commercial farming background. Recruitment was weighted disproportionately towards the Dublin area and the North-east, with the provinces of Munster and Connacht lagging far behind.[29] Service in the Indian administration reached its peak in the mid-1880s, when 15 per cent of all ICS officers were from Ireland. In the same decade, two Anglo-Irishmen (Lords Dufferin and Lansdowne) served as Viceroy, while in the 1890s seven of the eight Indian provinces, including Burma, had Irish-born Governors.[30]

Military rather than administrative service, however, remained the chief form of Irish activity in India throughout this period. Just as in the case of migration, the beginnings of Irish imperial service were closely linked to the colonization of Ireland. The Munster plantations of the late sixteenth century, the decisive defeat at Kinsale in 1601, and the settlement of 1691, all led to significant departures of Irish soldiers, chiefly to Spain and France, in whose armies they formed their own regiments. The impoverished Catholic gentry, especially in the south and west of Ireland, used their kinship networks in France, Spain, and Austria to secure military careers for their younger sons. In the aftermath of the Glorious Revolution, these continental Irish Brigades were strongly Jacobite, supporting a plan to invade Britain in 1692 and plans for several Jacobite risings in

---

[28] Ibid., p. 514.   [29] Ibid., p. 508.   [30] Ibid., pp. 512–22.

Britain thereafter. Ireland's colonial subjugation rested on fears of a Spanish or French invasion, a strategic consideration that surely outweighed all other arguments in favour of colonization. Irish service in the armies of Catholic Europe was thus of particular concern to the imperial authorities. In the 1690s, for example, over 1,000 Irish exiles in French military service were charged, in their absence, with treason. And, in an irony that could scarcely have escaped contemporaries, the French forces at the Battle of Wandewash in India in 1760 were led by Galway-born Count Lally-Tollendal and the British by Limerick-born Eyre Coote; and Irish soldiers fought on both sides. Irish regiments were involved in various French plans to invade Ireland from the 1750s through the 1790s, though the United Irish leader Wolfe Tone was surprised to learn that French strategy in this respect still seemed to be based on the idea of a Stuart restoration.[31]

From the mid-eighteenth century onward, Irish Catholic soldiers typically served the British Empire rather than its enemies. Following the Glorious Revolution (1688), Irish Catholics were prohibited from enlisting as soldiers; even Irish Protestants were excluded from the ranks, though they were still permitted to serve as officers (and they provided about one-third of the British officer corps by the mid-1770s).[32] During the Seven Years War (1756–63) the British turned a blind eye toward Catholic recruitment; Catholics were recruited on a widespread basis from the early 1770s onward and were openly admitted after 1793. By the early nineteenth century Ireland was supplying a disproportionate share of the Army's soldiers. In 1830, for example, when Ireland's share of the United Kingdom population was just under one-third, 42 per cent of British Army soldiers were Irish-born (more than were born in England).[33] The disparity was even greater in the army of the East India Company, which set up four recruiting offices in Ireland in 1813 and recruited as much as 50 per cent of its intake from the country between then and 1857. By the time of the Indian Mutiny, half of the Company's 14,000 soldiers, and perhaps 40 per

[31] Herman Murtagh, 'Irish Soldiers Abroad', in Thomas Bartlett and Keith Jeffery, eds., *A Military History of Ireland* (Cambridge, 1996), pp. 294–308; Thomas Bartlett, 'The Irish Soldier in India, 1750–1947', in Michael Holmes and Denis Holmes, eds., *Ireland and India: Connections, Comparisons, Contrasts* (Dublin, 1997).

[32] Alan J. Guy, 'The Irish Military Establishment, 1660–1776', in Bartlett and Jeffery, eds., *Military History of Ireland*, pp. 217–19.

[33] Peter Karsten, 'Irish Soldiers in the British Army, 1792–1922: Suborned or Subordinate?', *Journal of Social History*, XVII (Fall 1983), p. 36.

cent of the 26,000 regular British troops in India, were Irish. Most were Catholics of low income, who enlisted for reasons of economic necessity rather than imperial patriotism. As one historian puts it: 'without Irishmen, the rampant growth of Britain's Empire at this stage would scarcely have been possible'.[34]

The rebellion of Indian troops (*sepoys*) in the infamous 'mutiny' of 1857 revealed the extent of the Irish military and administrative presence in the sub-continent. Six Irish regiments were involved in putting down the rebellion, along with many Irish enlistees in both the regular British Army and that of the Company. Ulstermen were very prominent in both the military and the civil service. The three Lawrence brothers, all of them educated in Derry, held high office at the time, George in Rajputana, and John and Henry as Chief Commissioners respectively of the Punjab and Oudh (Auadh), a recently annexed region of present-day Uttar Pradesh. It was under Henry Lawrence that the siege of Lucknow commenced. Mortally wounded, he is said to have instructed the garrison, drawing his inspiration from the Siege of Derry in 1689: 'No surrender! Let every man die at his post, but never make terms!'[35] John Lawrence disarmed and disbanded native regiments of the Bengal Army that he saw as potentially mutinous, formed alliances against the rebels with a number of Indian princes, and directed the military offensive to recapture Delhi. Irish officers and soldiers developed an enduring reputation for brutality; one such was John Nicholson (his birthplace is disputed and may have been either Lisburn or Derry) who became notorious for blowing mutineers from the mouths of cannons. 'He hated India and Indians', writes the historian of British imperial military history, 'and seems to have suffered from morbidities, characteristic perhaps of classes imperialist by nurture'.[36]

With responsibility for India transferred from the Company to the Crown after 1857, a new military structure was put in place. Henceforth the Army would be manned largely by Indians (mainly Punjabi) serving under British or Anglo-Irish officers, and supported by British Army

[34] Bartlett, 'The Irish Soldier in India', pp. 12–17; Karsten, 'Irish Soldiers in the British Army', p. 37; Linda Colley, *Captives* (New York, 2002), quotation at p. 310.

[35] Bartlett, 'Irish Soldier in India', p. 19.

[36] Kiernan, *Colonial Empires and Armies*, pp. 21 (quote), 47–48; Bartlett, 'Irish Soldier in India', pp. 18–19. See also Charles Allen, *Soldier Sahibs: The Men Who Made the North-West Frontier* (London, 2000).

regulars. While conditions for enlistees in the British forces overseas improved gradually over time, they remained bleak and harsh throughout the nineteenth century: those serving in India enlisted for very long stretches, had little hope of marrying or settling while in service, were subject to brutal discipline, and were outnumbered five-to-one by their *sepoy* counterparts. British officers were generally contemptuous of all lower-class men, but surely the lowest of these 'captives in uniform' were the Irish. The Irish proportion of the British Army diminished steadily from the 1870s onward, though in large part this decline occurred because Ireland's proportion of the British population as a whole fell dramatically, in line with the massive emigration of the nineteenth century. On the eve of the Great Famine, when some 40 to 50 per cent of all British enlisted men were Irish, Ireland accounted for about one-third of the total population of the United Kingdom. By 1910, only 9 per cent of British soldiers were Irishmen, but Ireland's share of the UK population had fallen accordingly, to 10 per cent. While Irish service in the British Army declined steeply in numerical terms, then, it remained constant in proportional terms until the First World War.[37]

Unlike their Catholic countrymen, the Anglo-Irish officer class continued to play a highly disproportionate role in the British Army. Throughout the second half of the nineteenth century, they accounted for an estimated 17 per cent of officers in the British Army, and perhaps as many as 30 per cent of those serving in India. Nearly all were Protestant rather than Catholic. As in previous centuries, military service in India offered numerous opportunities to younger sons of the gentry: commissions in the regular Army were expensive and offered nowhere near the same opportunities for plunder and booty. Anglo-Irish imperial service was based strongly on family tradition. Lacking the means to sustain themselves as officers in the British Army, less prosperous Anglo-Irishmen gravitated toward the Indian regiments. Among them were two of the best-known Indian Field Marshals, Lord Roberts of Kandahar and Sir Claude Auchinleck. 'India', as one historian mordantly remarks, 'offered a career, field sports (bandits, polo and tiger-hunting), and a possible transfer to a regiment in the regular Army. In addition, service in India pro-

---

[37] Bartlett, 'The Irish Soldier in India', pp. 20–21; Keith Jeffery, 'The Irish Military Tradition and the British Empire,' in Jeffery, ed., 'An Irish Empire'?, p. 94; Linda Colley, 'Captives in Uniform' in Colley, ed., *Captives*, chap. 10.

vided a down-at-heel gentry with a theatre in which to strut its pretensions to being a master race, in a way that would not be condoned "at
home".[38]

While most regular Irish soldiers were Catholics, nearly all the officers
were Protestants, members of an Anglo-Irish Ascendancy class that
formed an integral, if not always equal, part of a larger British élite. They
came, by and large, from neither the Irish Catholic nor the Protestant
Unionist sectors of Irish society, representing instead a small, genteel, and
often impoverished class sitting precariously on top of the Irish social and
political order. While many of these Anglo-Irishmen had firm roots in
Ireland, and placed equal emphasis on each side of their hyphenated
identity, others were Irish simply by accident of birth and were in every
other respect 'British' or, more properly, 'English'. Thus, in many cases:
'Irish birth was incidental or even embarrassing to the heroes of Britain's
colonial wars'.[39] Among the more prominent were the Duke of Wellington,
Lords Canning, Mayo, Dufferin, Lansdowne, and Kitchener, and Sir
Henry Wilson.

Can Anglo-Irish military service really be counted as an 'Irish' contribution to the Empire? The career of Sir Henry Wilson offers a test case.
Wilson was born in 1864 on the family estate of Currygrane, in County
Longford, to 'a middling family of Protestant Irish landlords who traced
their ancestry back to a man reputed to have landed at Carrickfergus,
County Antrim, in the suite of King William III in 1690'.[40] As the second
of four sons in a family of minor Irish gentry, he was a prime candidate
for an imperial military career. At age thirteen, Wilson was sent to Marl-
borough; a poor student, he left the school and twice failed to pass the
Army entrance exam, instead gaining a commission in the Longford militia in 1882, the same year Sir Michael O'Dwyer went to Balliol. Wilson
joined the Royal Irish Regiment and the Rifle Brigade in 1884, and was
posted to India the following year. A protégé of Henry (later General
Lord) Rawlinson and then of Lord Roberts, he served in Burma and
Natal. He was very active during the Irish Home Rule crisis of 1913–14,
supporting the Curragh mutineers (those British officers who threatened
to disobey any order to move against the Unionist 'rebels' in Ulster) and

---

[38] Fitzpatrick, 'Ireland and Empire', p. 511; T. G. Fraser, 'Ireland and India,' in Jeffery, ed.,
'An Irish Empire'?, p. 78; Bartlett, 'Irish Soldier in India', quotation at pp. 21–22.

[39] Fitzpatrick, 'Ireland and Empire', p. 511.

[40] Jeffery, 'Introduction', Jeffery, ed., Military Correspondence, p. 1.

lobbying hard for the Irish Unionist cause. In February 1918 he was appointed Chief of the Imperial General Staff, serving in that capacity for
four years. An outspoken advocate of a full-scale military assault on the
Irish Republican Army (IRA) in the period 1916–21, he none the less
referred to Ireland in this period as 'my unfortunate country' and expressed to James Craig, the first Prime Minister of Northern Ireland, his
'unlimited belief in our corner of Ireland' (the reference, despite Wilson's
Longford origins, being to the north-east). Words like these betray a clear
sense of Irish identity, one that was part of, but also quite distinct from,
the larger British and imperial identity to which Wilson subscribed. To
count men like Wilson, without qualification, as 'Irish' agents of Empire
would be misleading at best; but to simply exclude the Anglo-Irish from
true Irishness altogether hardly solves the problem. The Anglo-Irish represented one of Ireland's several and often antagonistic cultures. Their imperial military service was, in its own way, as much a part of Irish history
as Fenianism or the Home Rule movement, and it cannot be written out
of the historical record.[41]

By the turn of the twentieth century the age of Irish imperial service
was drawing to a close. The First World War and its complicated aftermath proved to be the watershed. Irishmen made up about 10 per cent of
British Army recruits in 1913, compared to 20 per cent in 1870. When war
broke out the following year, most Irish Catholics, led by John Redmond
and his Irish Parliamentary Party, enthusiastically supported the British
effort. So too did Ulster Unionists, despite their recent threats to use
armed force to block Home Rule. Both sides proposed transferring their
existing Volunteer forces, complete with officers, into the regular British
Army. While the War Office rejected Redmond's idea for a new Irish
Brigade along these lines, the 36th (Ulster) Division was created largely out
of the Ulster Volunteer Force as 'an unambiguously unionist and Protestant formation'.[42] About 140,000 Irishmen, northern and southern, enlisted
during the war (not counting those of Irish extraction who enlisted in
Britain, Australia, New Zealand, and Canada); perhaps 30,000 were killed.
As ever, economic motives for enlisting were paramount; some 70 to
80 per cent of those who enlisted were unskilled labourers and Dublin,

---

[41] Ibid., quotation at p. 1; see also pp. 2–9; Wilson to Lieutenant-General Sir Walter
Congreve, 26 April 1920 and Wilson to Craig, 16 June 1921, in ibid., pp. 167, 273.

[42] Keith Jeffery, *Ireland and the Great* War (Cambridge, 2000), p. 39.

because of its high unemployment, was a better recruiting ground than Belfast. But there were other reasons to sign up: at least at the outset of the conflict, war was widely perceived as a positive good; and people all over Ireland evidently retained considerable loyalty to Britain and the Empire in a time of need. The service of the 'sons of Ulster' was commemorated as early as 18 November 1921, when Field-Marshal Sir Henry Wilson dedicated a monument to their memory at Thiepval, on the Somme. It would be another twenty years before the official Irish war memorial was dedicated at Islandbridge in Dublin, the protracted delay testifying to a bitter and ambivalent imperial heritage.[43]

The Empire had come close to operating militarily as a single entity during the war. 'Australians had fought alongside Indians, Nigerians by South Africans, Canadians by Irishmen', as one historian observes. 'Nearly one million white troops from the dominions had rallied to the flag during the war along with 1,400,000 Indian recruits'.[44] Overall, however, the war marked a sharp reversal of Ireland's traditionally disproportionate contribution to the British Army. In the Dominions, enlistment during the war varied from 13 to 19 per cent of the white male population; for Ireland the figure was only 6 per cent. Irish recruitment declined after the events of Easter 1916 and in light of mounting casualties on the continent, picked up briefly toward the end of the war, and then fell off sharply after 1921, when most of the Irish infantry regiments of the British Army were disbanded. Even so, the new Irish Free State continued to provide significant numbers of men to the surviving Irish regiments. An estimated 43,000 residents of southern Ireland joined the British Army during the Second World War, compared to 38,000 from Northern Ireland. The bonds of Empire were not yet severed, even if those bonds were forged mainly of necessity rather than imperial patriotism.[45]

One curious outgrowth of the nationalist ferment in Ireland during and after the Great War was the 'mutiny' of the Connaught Rangers in the Punjab in 1920. The Rangers had been formed in 1793 and had served at different times throughout the British Empire, especially in India. Their

[43] Jeffery, 'Irish Military Tradition', pp. 95–98; Thomas P. Dooley, *Irishmen or English Soldiers? The Times and World of a Southern Catholic Irish Man (1876–1916) Enlisting in the British Army during the First World War* (Liverpool, 1995), pp. 1, 4–5, 214; Jeffery, *Ireland and the Great War*, pp. 107–43.

[44] Jeffery, *British Army and the Crisis of Empire*, p. 1.

[45] Jeffery, 'Irish Military Tradition', pp. 97–102.

revolt, such as it was, began in Jullunder, in the Punjab, on 27 June 1920, when a group of Rangers protested against the conduct of British troops in Ireland by grounding arms and ignoring orders. They were quickly joined by several hundred of their colleagues. The protestors declared that they would not return to duty until all British soldiers had left Ireland, and proceeded to hoist the new Irish tricolour. Emissaries were then sent to the Ranger companies at Jutogh and Solon. The men at Jutogh remained loyal; those at Solon grounded arms, agreeing however to lock away their weapons for fear that Indians might seize them. When a group of the Solon Rangers led by Private James Daly, a native of Mullingar whose brother was among the protestors at Jullunder, attempted to seize the munitions store, two men were killed; within a few days, the 'mutiny' was crushed. Because of its explicitly Irish character, it drew harsh retribution from the authorities. Sixty-one Rangers were convicted by courts-martial of mutiny; fourteen were sentenced to death, the rest to terms in prison. Most of the sentences were reduced on appeal but James Daly was executed, on 2 November 1920.[46]

The 'mutiny' of the Connaught Rangers certainly had an element of Irish nationalism at its heart, symbolized by the Irish tricolour raised at Jullunder. The rebels explicitly protested against the brutal tactics of the 'Black and Tans' in Ireland. Yet, the Rangers had themselves employed brutal tactics in India; like many Irish soldiers abroad, they seem to have responded to British condescension with overt displays of virility and violence, and had become 'notorious, not only for fighting and general indiscipline but also for their attitude toward the Indian population'.[47] On the other hand, descriptions of this sort were notoriously part of British contempt for the Irish. The Rangers' reputation for brutality may simply have reflected the wider tendency of lower-class enlistees of all backgrounds to deflect their anger against the aristocrats and gentry who commanded them by, as one recent historian puts it, striking out 'physically, verbally, or only in their minds at those they presumed to call "natives"'.[48] This helps explain the otherwise curious fact that some Englishmen appear among the rebels. Viewed from the perspective of the British authorities, moreover, the events of June 1920 represented a

---

[46] Bartlett, 'Irish Soldier in India', pp. 22–25; Karsten, 'Irish Soldiers in the British Army,' pp. 49–51.

[47] Bartlett, 'Irish Soldier in India', p. 22.   [48] Colley, *Captives*, p. 344.

significant threat to both military and imperial authority. With memories of 1857 still running deep, the Rangers had carefully avoided the word 'mutiny'; but Ireland was in rebellion, India and Egypt were dangerously unstable, and the actions at Solon and Jullunder set a very bad example that could not go unpunished. On the other hand, after 1916 executing Irishmen had become somewhat risky; and so just one man, James Daly, bore the brunt. In the end, he 'had to die, not for Ireland, but for India'.[49]

Within a year of the 'Connaught mutiny' twenty-six Irish counties had secured independence, or at least a close approximation. Field-Marshal Sir Henry Wilson, sounding a long-familiar theme, predicted that this would be disastrous for the British Empire. Feuding with Winston Churchill in June 1920, he insisted that IRA depredations would 'continue until the Government realize that they are at war with the Sinn Fein and say so and *act* on the fact'. What this might mean in practice became clear at Croke Park, Dublin, on 21 November 1920, when British 'Black and Tans' fired into a football crowd to avenge a series of IRA assassinations that morning; though this first 'Bloody Sunday' killed only twelve people, the resemblance with Amritsar was clear. Writing in December to Lord Rawlinson, the British Commander-in-Chief in India from 1920 to 1925, Wilson recommended the imposition of martial law in Ireland to 'knock out the murder gang', assuring him that 'the vast bulk of the people in Ireland are sick to death of this murder campaign and will thank God when we have shot or hung the last of the filthy brutes'. In July 1921 he confided in Rawlinson that 'we are in a fair way to lose Ireland first, then Egypt, and then India'. 'The Palestine problem', he told Rawlinson, 'is exactly the same as the Irish—two different sets of people living in a small area, each hating the other for the love of God'. Even after the Anglo-Irish treaty, Wilson refused to accept Ireland's new autonomy, gloomily viewing it as the death knell for the Empire at large. In his last letter as Chief of Staff, he informed Rawlinson that there was no 'way out of it except by the loss of Ireland and the proclaiming of a republic there, in which case we lose our Empire, or by the reconquest of the whole place'. Three months later, this most prominent of Irish imperialists met his death at the hands of two of his countrymen. His assassins, Joseph O'Sullivan and Reggie Dunne, had served on the Western Front before joining the IRA. They

[49] Bartlett, 'Irish Soldier in India', pp. 23–26 (quotation at p. 25).

met him on the steps of his house in Eaton Square, carrying British Army service revolvers and ammunition.[50]

The dominant form of Irish activity in British overseas territory in the twentieth century was significantly different from what had come before. Most Irish migrants now went to Britain rather than to the Dominions or the United States. The Irish poor continued to enlist in the British Army, but in greatly reduced numbers. And, although Ireland remained part of the Commonwealth until 1949, the events of 1916–21 had constituted an irrevocable break. Yet Irish activity in the Empire, far from dying out, entered a new and vibrant phase featuring a remarkable outgrowth of missionary activity in the Asian and, most significantly, the African colonies. The contours of this 'spiritual empire', whose origins can be traced back to the nineteenth century, were 'roughly coterminous with the British Empire'.[51] Catholic mission work assumed considerable prominence in Ireland's self-definition as a postcolonial society from the 1920s onward. But how is this new phase of activity to be included in the general story of 'the Irish in the Empire'?

Like the history of migration, Irish religious endeavours in the Empire had at first been largely Protestant rather than Catholic. Ulster Presbyterians played a significant role in the expansion of education in the American colonies. With individual Bible-reading as a defining characteristic of reformed religion, basic literacy was a requirement. Wherever they settled in America, the Ulster Irish set up elementary schools to teach reading, writing, arithmetic, catechism, and the Bible. Training adequate numbers of clergy was a big problem, however, as Presbyterians demanded remarkably high standards of their clergy, requiring Latin, Greek, and Hebrew as well as theology. At first, most of the Scottish and Ulster Presbyterian ministers in America continued to be graduates of Glasgow and Edinburgh, but as early as 1726 Gilbert Tennent founded his Log College in Pennsylvania to train ministers, and in 1746 he joined a group of Presbyterian ministers from Scotland and Ulster to found the College of New Jersey, later renamed Princeton University. In all these ways,

---

[50] Wilson to Churchill, 24 June, 28 June, 1920; Churchill to Wilson, 25 June, 2 July, 1920; Wilson to Arnold Robertson, 30 March 1921; Wilson to Rawlinson, 18 May 1921, 14 June 1921, in Jeffery, ed., *Military Correspondence*, pp. 167, 181, 182, 184, 213, 273, 275, 276, 277, 286, 309, 323, 336, 338–39; Jeffery, *British Army and the Crisis of Empire*, p. 94.

[51] Thomas Bartlett, ' "This famous island set in a Virginian sea": Ireland in the British Empire, 1690–1801', in Marshall, ed., *OHBE. Vol. II*, p. 273.

Ulstermen advanced the Presbyterian tradition of education in the Atlantic Empire.[52]

Irish Protestants also played a significant role in missionary work within the Empire in the nineteenth century. Once again, this aspect of Irish imperial history is inseparable from British control of Ireland; for, just as the British settlement of Ulster soon stimulated mass emigration to North America, so too Protestant evangelical work in Ulster in the eighteenth and nineteenth centuries—especially by Methodists and Presbyterians—gave rise to missionary work in the Empire at large. The turn of the nineteenth century was a period of evangelical awakening on both sides of the Atlantic, and in this context British missionaries extended their efforts beyond the Atlantic world, especially to India. The major new English evangelical societies, such as the Church Missionary Society, the London Missionary Society, and the British and Foreign Bible Society, worked extensively in Ireland, both to spread the gospel there and to recruit Irish Protestants for mission work overseas. In 1812 the Ulster Synod formally lent its support to foreign missionary endeavours and in 1833, following the lead of the Church of Scotland seven years earlier, Ulster Presbyterians set up their first missions in India.[53]

Ireland's 'spiritual empire', however, was largely a Catholic rather than a Protestant undertaking. It can be considered under two principal headings: the institutional expansion of the Catholic Church under Irish domination in North America, Australia, and New Zealand, and the extensive activities of Irish Catholic missionaries and educators in India and Africa. Despite formidable obstacles, including the hostility not only of Protestant churches and secular governments but also that of the existing Catholic hierarchies in the countries where they settled, the Irish quickly won control of the Church. They divided the nations of settlement into parishes, dioceses, and archdioceses, building churches, parochial schools, colleges, and seminaries, and thereby providing the institutional and emotional centre of Irish life throughout the world.[54] In this way, Catholicism became virtually synonymous with 'Irishness', abroad just as at home, giving rise to 'an international consciousness, as the pride in

[52] Daniel Murphy, *A History of Irish Emigrant and Missionary Education* (Dublin, 2000), pp. 170–82.

[53] David Hempton and Myrtle Hill, *Evangelical Protestantism in Ulster Society, 1740–1890* (London, 1992), pp. 29–39, 47–50.

[54] Murphy, *History of Irish Emigrant and Missionary Education*, pp. 169–434.

religion and nationality at home was reinforced by an awareness of a new empire of common faith and purpose beyond the seas'.[55]

The expansion of the Catholic Church in Australia, New Zealand, and Canada was largely driven by Irish migrants and clergymen. All Hallows College was founded in Dublin in 1842 to train priests to serve the Irish community abroad; about 45 per cent of these priests went to the United States over the next half-century, with 30 per cent going to Australia and New Zealand, and 12 per cent to England and Scotland, but fewer than 4 per cent to India and Africa combined. Numerous female and male religious orders also served the Irish diaspora in the Anglophone Empire, including the Sisters of Mercy, who opened convents in Newfoundland, Auckland, Perth, Brisbane, Adelaide, and Buenos Aires, as well as Belize, Jamaica, and South Africa, in the period 1842–97. Irish Dominican Sisters from the Sion Hill convent in Dublin settled in Australia and New Zealand in the 1860s, as did Irish Christian Brothers in the 1860s and 1870s. In Britain, Canada, and the antipodes the Irish-dominated Catholic Church built an extensive network of parochial schools, followed by colleges and universities, designed to preserve Catholicism in a hostile Protestant environment.[56]

The first attempt to move beyond the Anglophone Empire came with the short-lived Maynooth Mission to India, based in Calcutta and Madras, cities that had a combined Catholic population estimated at 25,000 by the early 1830s (most of them descendants of early Portuguese colonists, but including an increasing number of East India Company employees and their dependents, of whom the majority were Irish). In the 1840s Dr Patrick Carew of Maynooth worked with Irish Presentation Sisters in both Madras and Calcutta to set up schools and an orphanage for Catholic children. As in the Anglophone colonies, the initial intention of this first Irish mission in India was to minister to an existing Catholic population rather than evangelize non-Christians. Although the mission soon failed, the community of Presentation Sisters that remained eventually expanded its efforts to native-born as well as European children, as did several other Irish missionary teaching orders in the second half of the nineteenth century. Among the most prominent were the Patrician Brothers, the De La

---

[55] Sheridan Gilley, 'The Roman Catholic Church and the Nineteenth-Century Diaspora', *Journal of Ecclesiastical History*, 35 (April 1984), p. 197.

[56] E. M. Hogan, *The Irish Missionary Movement: A Historical Survey, 1830–1980* (Dublin, 1990), p. 20.

Salle Brothers (who had come to Ireland from France in 1882), the Sisters of the Good Shepherd and the Sisters of St Joseph of Cluny (both also of French origin), the Loreto Sisters, and the Presentation Sisters. Carew had also invited the Irish Christian Brothers to Calcutta, and after their arrival in 1848 they became the leading Irish teaching order in India, establishing six schools in Bengal by the end of nineteenth century (catering to some 1,300 students), and running a total of seventeen schools in India by the 1940s, with an enrolment of about 9,000 students.[57]

Africa, however, was the main field of Irish missionary endeavour. In sharp contrast to India, European evangelism—Protestant as well as Catholic—exercised an enormous influence on African religious life. 'In India by 1947 less than 2 per cent of the population had converted to Christianity', one historian notes, 'but in Africa by the end of the colonial era Christianity rivalled Islam as the major religion of the continent'.[58] Like other Christian missionaries, those from Catholic Ireland left a lasting impact on African culture, especially in the realms of healthcare, education, politics, and the dissemination of the English language. Permeated by the spirit of romantic adventure characteristic of Christian mission work more generally, the work of Irish Catholic missionaries in Africa also helped define postcolonial Ireland's sense of itself and its role in the twentieth-century world. The *Missionary Annals* of the C. S. Sp. (Holy Ghost Fathers) and the *African Missionary*, published by the Society for African Missions, were filled with stories of heroic missionaries, surrounded by danger and suffused with religious courage, bringing Christianity to the 'Dark Continent', 'benighted Africa', and other exotic parts of the world. While these are stock images of romantic racialism, they also invoked the prevailing language of heroism and self-sacrifice in Irish political life, especially in the wake of Easter 1916. The Irish missionary was portrayed very much as a man of his time, willing to die for his faith; and missionaries helped resuscitate the idea of Ireland's historical mission as a 'land of saints and scholars', incorporating this idea into the new sense of Irish national identity articulated by the generation of 1916.[59]

[57] Hogan, *Irish Missionary Movement*, pp. 17, 27–28; Kenneth Ballhatchet, 'Missionaries, Empire and Society: The Jesuit Mission in Calcutta, 1834–1846', *Journal of Imperial and Commonwealth History*, VII (Oct. 1978), pp. 18–34.

[58] Wm. Roger Louis, 'Introduction', in Judith M. Brown and Wm. Roger Louis, eds., *OHBE. Vol. IV. The Twentieth Century* (Oxford, 1999), p. 18.

[59] Hempton and Hill, *Evangelical Protestantism in Ulster Society*, p. 51; Hogan, *Irish Emigrant and Missionary Education*, pp. 56, 60, 146–58, 162–63.

In British East Africa, Irish efforts were based in Kenya and Uganda. Among the most prominent of the missionaries there was Mother Kevin (b. Teresa Keaney in County Wicklow), who established several clinics, dispensaries, and a hospital after settling in Uganda in 1902. 'From *nothing*, in a single year, she has built her convent, her dispensary, her entire equipment for launching a native Community, and the greater part of her substantial chapel; all these buildings are of brick, and permanent', observed the Indian-based Irish missionary T. Gavan Duffy while touring Africa in 1927. Mother Kevin, he noted, was also training sixty-five local women for the Little Sisters of Saint Francis, a congregation of native sisters she had set up as an outgrowth of the Franciscan Missionary Sisters for Africa (the Dundalk-based order she founded and headed).[60] Also especially active in East Africa was Edel Quinn of the Legion of Mary, a lay organization founded in Dublin in 1921. With the support of Bishop John William Heffernan, Vicar Apostolic of Zanzibar (actually based in Nairobi), Quinn established branches of the Legion in Kenya, Uganda, Tanzania, and Zanzibar. In southern Africa, Irish missions catered initially to the small Irish and British Catholic population, especially on the Cape, branching out in the course of the nineteenth century to provide mission schools for the local population, both in present-day South Africa and in Zimbabwe, Swaziland, and Zambia.[61]

West Africa was the centre of Irish missionary activity. Catholic missionaries from Ireland were active in Liberia and Sierra Leone, but it was in Nigeria that they achieved their greatest influence. At the heart of this enterprise was the Irish branch of the C. S. Sp., or Holy Ghost Fathers. The C. S. Sp. had originated in France in 1703 and was active in African missionary work throughout the nineteenth century. Members of the order established a foothold in Ireland in 1859, hoping to raise support for mission work. Ironically, their recruiting efforts were initially hampered by the excellence of the schools they founded, starting with Blackrock College in 1860, as so many of the priests they trained were required to stay in Ireland as teachers rather than going to the African missions as originally envisioned. The French Holy Ghost Fathers first came to Nigeria in 1885,

[60] T. Gavan Duffy, *Mission Tours—Africa. Or, For Short, Let's Go* (Boston, 1928), pp. 111–12.

[61] Murphy, *Irish Emigrant and Missionary Education*, pp. 442–86; Bishop Leon-Joseph Suenens, *Edel Quinn: Envoy of the Legion of Mary to Africa* (Dublin, 1953). A Kenyan group called the 'Legio Maria' broke away from the Roman Catholic Church in the early 1960s, went on to appoint its own bishops, cardinals, and Pope, and remains active today.

competing directly with British Protestant missionaries. A few Irish members of the order had joined their French brethren by the end of the century, and thereafter southern Nigeria became the principal field of Irish missionary endeavour, with the charismatic figure of Bishop Joseph Shanahan as the commanding presence.

Born to a farm labourer's family in County Tipperary in 1871, Joseph Shanahan was the third of ten children. The household included a beloved uncle, Pat Walsh, who left for France in 1875 to join the Holy Ghost Fathers. In 1886, four years after Michael O'Dwyer entered Balliol College and Henry Wilson gained his commission in the Longford militia, Joseph Shanahan followed his uncle to France and, like him, in due course joined the C. S. Sp. Ordained in 1900, he set sail two years later for Nigeria, fulfilling a lifelong dream. He was appointed Prefect Apostolic of the Lower Niger (south-east Nigeria) in 1905 and spent the next quarter-century as leader of the Onitsha mission, founding two additional missions, and overseeing the foundation of a third. Much respected by the population of southern Nigeria for his ability to translate his Catholic message into the medium of local religious beliefs and practices, Shanahan built a vast network of schools and recruited locally for missionary priests, brothers, sisters, and lay persons, before retiring in 1932. In 1955, twelve years after his death, the Igbo accorded him the singular honour of disinterment and reburial at the Onitsha cathedral.[62]

Irish Catholic missionaries, especially female religious, tended to the sick as part of their African ministry, opening dispensaries, visiting homes, and sometimes sacrificing their lives during epidemics. Catholic efforts were hampered, however, by canon law prohibiting missionaries from assisting at childbirth and, under a sweeping provision of 1917, from involvement in medicine or surgery without a dispensation from Rome.[63] Mother Kevin of Uganda, despite her outspoken opposition, was among those denied a dispensation to train midwives. The prohibition against midwifery was lifted only in 1936, at which time dispensations for surgery and general medicine were also made more readily available. Several Irish female religious orders were formed in response, while older institutes, such as the Sisters of the Holy Rosary, expanded their work into the

[62] John P. Jordan, *Bishop Shanahan of Nigeria* (Dublin, 1949); Gavan Duffy, *Let's Go*, pp. 336–38, 407–12; Hogan, *Irish Missionary Movement*, pp. 98–105.

[63] Hogan, *Irish Missionary Movement*, pp. 106–13; Murphy, *Irish Emigrant and Missionary Education*, p. 470; Gavan Duffy, *Let's Go*, pp. 111–12.

medical field. Mother Mary Martin, a veteran of the Irish missions in Nigeria, founded the Medical Missionaries of Mary in Drogheda in 1937. As well as running several local institutions, the sisters opened an International Mission Training Hospital in 1957 to train midwives, nurses, and doctors for the missions in east and west Africa. The International Hospital also became the leading Irish centre for the treatment of tropical diseases. Julius Nyerere, the first president of Tanzania, was an honoured guest of the hospital when he visited Ireland in 1979.[64]

Easily the most important form of Irish missionary activity was in the realm of education. Drawing an analogy with St Patrick, who had encountered in early Ireland 'a country peopled by a wild pagan tribe', Bishop Shanahan quickly came to see children and their education as the key to all Catholic efforts in Nigeria: 'baptised in the schools, they would go back to their pagan homes, full of the Life of God', suffused with the desire 'to see their fathers with them in Heaven'.[65] Mission schools, both Irish and French, soon became the primary means of Catholic evangelism in Africa; but they also provided a range of practical, cultural, and political advantages and, by the time of independence, had helped equip much of British Africa with the makings of a national infrastructure. Among the most important functions of the schools during the colonial era, indeed, had been their education of an emerging nationalist élite. Julius Nyerere, for example, taught at a Catholic mission school in Tabora, adopting the name 'Mwalimu' (teacher). During his twenty-five-year presidency of Tanzania, he remained in contact with Irish orders such as the Medical Missionaries of Mary and gave high priority to an educational system based on the mission school and combining Christian, socialist, and indigenous religious elements. Kwame Nkrumah, the founding father of Ghana, attended a Roman Catholic primary school; like Nyerere, he became a Catholic school teacher; and he spent time in a Catholic seminary before pursuing further education in the United States and England. Robert Mugabe, who also served as a teacher before turning to politics and becoming his country's first postcolonial President, was raised and educated at the Kutama Catholic mission in north-western Rhodesia. Some historians have suggested that the Christian colonial

---

[64] Hogan, *Irish Missionary Movement*, pp. 119–20; Sister M. Anastasia Taggart and Sister Isabelle Smyth, *The Medical Missionaries of Mary in Drogheda, 1939–1999* (Drogheda, 1999).

[65] Jordan provides no documentation and appears to be quoting from memory.

education of the nationalist élite may have served to perpetuate rather than undermine repressive forms of government, though it is hard to see how this influence could be measured.[66]

If, as might be expected, Irish Catholic missionary work was shot through with cultural condescension, can it therefore be dismissed as an inherently imperialist endeavour? Recent historians of Christian mission work more generally have qualified the assumption that missionaries merely represented the spiritual arm of a European campaign to eradicate African cultures. To be sure, missionaries often depended on colonial élites for their survival and in turn served to buttress authority and promote social stability. Yet, while often critical and condescending toward non-Christian cultures, missionaries could sometimes offer 'powerful stimuli for local resistance and opposition to colonial rule' and 'a means of expressing social and political aspirations based on biblical concepts of history as progress, revolt, and millenarian expectation'.[67] Missionary thinking could also be 'profoundly egalitarian: "race" was immaterial, humans everywhere corrupt yet equally open to conversion and redemption'.[68]

Where does Irish Catholic missionary work fit into this picture? The argument that Ireland's own colonial status somehow exempted it from imposing colonialism on others carries little weight historically.[69] Yet Irish Catholic missionaries played no part in the nexus of Christianity, commerce, and military force that had helped build the Empire in the eighteenth and nineteenth centuries, arriving in Africa only as the great age of conquest and colonization was drawing to a close. And, even in the face of considerable racism and cultural condescension, few Africans were averse to the benefits of healthcare and education per se. Bishop Shanahan based his evangelical efforts on a clear realization of this fact.[70] In general, the schools were much valued in the postcolonial era: most of them survived independence, some were invited to establish themselves thereafter, and

---

[66] Murphy, *Irish Emigrant and Missionary Education*, pp. 460–61, 486, 488, 527; Andrew Porter, 'Religion, Missionary Enthusiasm, and Empire', in Porter ed., *OHBE. Vol. III*, pp. 222–45.

[67] Louis, Introduction to Brown and Louis, eds., *OHBE. Vol. IV*, p. 17.

[68] Porter, 'Religion, Missionary Enthusiasm, and Empire', p. 229.

[69] Cf. Murphy, *Irish Emigrant and Missionary Education*, p. 526.

[70] P. B. Clarke, 'The Methods and Ideology of the Holy Ghost Fathers in Eastern Nigeria, 1885–1905', in O. U. Kalu, *The History of Christianity in West Africa* (London, 1980), p. 54.

many continue to operate today, for example in Nigeria, Ghana, Tanzania, Kenya, Uganda, Zambia, and South Africa.[71]

At the heart of Catholic evangelical work in Africa lay an uneasy tension between liberation and cultural imperialism. The character of mission work in Nigeria, once again, reveals the contradictions. As members of an Irish Catholic order of French origin, Shanahan's Holy Ghost Fathers were inevitably suspect in the eyes of British colonial administrators; yet they co-operated closely with the administration in building their network of schools, receiving grants-in-aid to do so. Was this co-operation a matter of imperialism, pragmatics, or both? The alliance was clearly symbiotic, carrying benefits to both parties: the British had little enthusiasm for building schools before the 1930s, while the Irish missionaries always regarded co-operation with the government as a means to their higher goal of evangelization.[72] At the same time, the schools met a heavy Igbo demand for education, a prerequisite for advancement in the new world Europeans were building in Africa. The schools, moreover, were free and they were open to all children: if this violated existing norms of ethnicity, class, and gender, it did so in the name of a Christian egalitarianism that was soon readily embraced by many Africans. More broadly, while Irish and French Catholic missionaries shared much of the prevailing imperialist contempt for 'native' and 'pagan' customs and beliefs, explicitly targeting social and cultural practices that impeded Christianity, in so doing they undermined not only idolatry but slavery and even human sacrifice. And some Irish Catholic missionaries broke through the framework of imperialist perception, most notably Shanahan, who in converting the Igbo 'sought to transform, not to destroy, to appreciate and not to despise indigenous habits and ways of life'. Shanahan's biographer and fellow C. S. Sp. missionary John P. Jordan, on the other hand, displayed a more ambivalent mixture of love and condescension toward the Nigerian people.[73]

In the story of Ireland's African missionaries, Nigeria provides an end as well as a beginning. 'Nigeria was the showpiece of Ireland's "religious empire"', one historian notes. 'Of that country's 850 Catholic priests [in 1967], more than 500 were Irish; the Irish Church ran 2,419 primary

---

[71] Murphy, *Irish Emigrant and Missionary Education*, p. 529.

[72] Gavan Duffy, *Let's Go*, pp. 336, 413–46.

[73] Clarke, 'Methods and Ideology of the Holy Ghost Fathers', pp. 36–62 (quotation at p. 58); Jordan, *Bishop Shanahan*.

schools catering for 561,318 pupils, twice as many as in the remainder of Africa.[74] Nigeria had achieved full independence within the Commonwealth in 1960. Irish missionaries were heavily concentrated in the eastern region of the country, which in 1967 sought its independence from the largely non-Christian majority of the country. Local Irish priests—most of them Holy Ghost fathers—played a role that embarrassed the Irish government. Many of them outspokenly supported the secessionists, seeing in the struggle a familiar pattern: 'David against Goliath, the little Christian island, the Muslim threat, British betrayal'.[75] The subsequent suffering and starvation in Biafra struck a deep chord in Ireland, where consciousness of famine and religious persecution, combined with a sense of Catholic mission, were among the central ingredients of postcolonial national identity. There was another reason why Biafra became so important to Ireland. The role of Irish priests in supporting the secessionists provoked not just a reaction against Nigerian Christians, but a move for Africanization within the Catholic Church. When secession failed, the Irish missionaries were rounded up and expelled from Nigeria, bringing to an end one cycle of Irish imperial history.[76]

By that time the Empire too was gone. Over the previous four centuries, Ireland's history had been forged in the British imperial crucible. The story of how Ireland was conquered, colonized, and ruled by its more powerful neighbour—a neighbour that soon came to dominate much of the world—is a familiar one. Less well understood is the extent to which Ireland, simply by virtue of its location and subordination, participated in the affairs of the Empire at large, and how this participation influenced Ireland's national history. Ireland helped populate, govern, and evangelize the Empire, and Irishmen fought and died for the Empire in large numbers. Just as British historians have recently begun to reconsider the impact of the Empire on Britain, they may also begin to examine how the Irish presence—especially the Catholic one—affected the texture of everyday life among British imperialists abroad. Comparative work with the Scots, as ever, presents a fruitful ground for research. Above all, historians of Ireland may now wish to examine in greater depth how imperial belonging shaped the course of Irish history.

---

[74] Irish religious also ran 47 hospitals serving over 700,000 patients. Enda Staunton, 'The Case of Biafra: Ireland and the Nigerian Civil War', *Irish Historical Studies*, XXXI (1999), p. 512.

[75] Adrian Hastings, *A History of African Christianity, 1950–1975* (Cambridge, 1979), pp. 198–99.

[76] Staunton, 'Case of Biafra', pp. 519–21, 527–28.

Select Bibliography

DONALD HARMAN AKENSON, *The Irish Diaspora: A Primer* (Belfast, 1996).

THOMAS BARTLETT, 'The Irish Soldier in India', in Michael and Denis Holmes, eds., *Ireland and India: Connections, Comparisons, Contrasts* (Dublin, 1997), pp. 12–28.

THOMAS BARTLETT and KEITH JEFFERY, eds., *A Military History of Ireland* (Cambridge, 1996).

ANDY BIELENBERG, ed., *The Irish Diaspora* (London, 2000).

NICHOLAS CANNY, ed., *Europeans on the Move: Studies in European Migration, 1500–1800* (Oxford, 1994).

SCOTT B. COOK, 'The Irish Raj: Social Origins and Careers of Irishmen in the Indian Civil Service, 1855–1919', *Journal of Social History*, 20 (Spring 1987), pp. 507–29.

LOUIS M. CULLEN, 'The Irish Diaspora of the Seventeenth and Eighteenth Centuries', in Nicholas Canny, ed., *Europeans on the Move: Studies in European Migration, 1500–1800* (Oxford, 1994), pp. 113–49.

SHERIDAN GILLEY, 'The Roman Catholic Church and the Nineteenth-Century Irish Diaspora', *Journal of Ecclesiastical History*, 35 (April 1984), pp. 188–207.

E. M. HOGAN, *The Irish Missionary Movement: A Historical Survey, 1830–1980* (Dublin, 1990).

MICHAEL and DENIS HOLMES, eds., *Ireland and India* (Dublin, 1997).

KEITH JEFFERY, ed., *'An Irish Empire'? Aspects of Ireland and the British Empire* (Manchester, 1996).

PETER KARSTEN, 'Irish Soldiers in the British Army, 1792–1922: Suborned or Subordinate?' *Journal of Social History*, XVII (no. 1, 1983), pp. 31–64.

V. G. KIERNAN, *Colonial Empires and Armies*, rev. ed. (Montreal and Kingston, 1998).

R. B. McDOWELL, 'Ireland in the Eighteenth-Century British Empire', *Historical Studies*, IX (1974): pp. 49–63.

HIRAM MORGAN, 'An Unwelcome Heritage: Ireland's Role in British Empire Building', *History of European Ideas*, 19 (July 1994), pp. 619–25.

DANIEL MURPHY, *A History of Irish Emigrant and Missionary Education* (Dublin, 2000).

PATRICK O'FARRELL, *The Irish in Australia* (Kensington, NSW, 1986).

DEREK SAYER, 'British Reaction to the Amritsar Massacre, 1919–1920', *Past and Present*, 131 (Feb. 1991), pp. 130–64.

5

Ireland, the Union, and the Empire, 1800–1960

ALVIN JACKSON

If, as Andrew Porter has argued, the British Empire of the nineteenth century was a fundamentally ambiguous enterprise, then Ireland under the Union epitomized its elusiveness, its contradictions, and its paradoxes. Ireland was simultaneously a bulwark of the Empire, and a mine within its walls. Irish people were simultaneously major participants in Empire, and a significant source of subversion. For the Irish the Empire was both an agent of liberation and of oppression: it provided both the path to social advancement and the shackles of incarceration. By the end of the nineteenth century the Empire harnessed much Irish talent, and colonial statesmen were often actively sympathetic to Irish national aspirations. Yet many Irish people saw the Empire (which their kinsmen had helped to shape) as alien and menacing; and they viewed colonial administrations (which were often supportive of Irish patriotic aspirations) as lackies of the Saxon foe.[1]

This chapter seeks to unravel these complexities, and to identify some of the defining features of the relationship between Ireland and Empire during the years of the Union settlement. It is divided into three main sections: it examines the broad impact of the Empire upon Ireland, and then (conversely) aspects of the Irish contribution to Empire, and it pursues the theme of Empire into the history of Northern Ireland, again both in terms of impact and contribution. The chapter ranges from a consideration of political élites through to popular and material political culture. It examines constitutional and economic issues, the monarchy, the Army and the honours system, but also delves into individual histories as well as the physical impact of Empire within Ireland. At root, Empire was

[1] Andrew Porter, 'Introduction: Britain and the Empire in the Nineteenth Century', in Porter, ed., *The Oxford History of the British Empire* (hereafter *OHBE*). Vol. III. *The Nineteenth Century* (Oxford, 1999), p. 27.

never simply a secondary theme, an after-thought, in the history of Ireland under the Union. A consideration of Ireland and the British Empire involves, not merely the footnotes of Irish history, but rather an unveiling of some of the fundamental features of the island's political culture. If this essay has any particular contributions to make, then these lie in emphasising the symmetry between political institutions and political culture, and in underlining the diversity of the British imperial presence in Ireland.

The explanation for the complex relationship between Ireland and Empire rests partly with the ambiguous nature of the island's constitutional position in the nineteenth century. Some of the contradictions were rooted in the incomplete nature of the Union between Great Britain and Ireland, and in the substantial but incomplete degree of British political and cultural influence in Ireland. William Pitt's Union of 1801 was an effort to integrate Britain's oldest colony into the metropolitan core of the Empire. It was an effort to provide a stable constitutional foundation for the Empire at a particular moment of both European and domestic military crisis, and in the context of an ongoing process of administrative centralization. But Pitt's vision of an inclusive Union was only partially enacted; while Irish people were included in a united Parliament, Catholics remained excluded from the British political nation until 'emancipation' in 1829. To the extent that the Union (and indeed British identity) only very slowly accommodated Irish Catholic political and economic needs in the 1830s and after, then for most of the nineteenth century it served in fact as a distraction from Empire, and often indeed as a threat to the imperial enterprise. On the other hand, in so far as Catholic social mobility was thwarted in Ireland under the Union, then a spur was provided for Irish Catholic participation in the less constricted political and administrative imperial environment. In this way the Union was simultaneously a challenge and a support to the Empire.

Ireland was ruled partly in colonial and partly in metropolitan terms, and was partly assimilated within a British cultural context. The compromised and half-hearted nature of British political and cultural supremacy in Ireland was reflected in the ambiguities of popular Irish attitudes towards Empire. Ireland was nominally an integral element of the new United Kingdom, and sent representatives to the House of Commons and House of Lords at Westminster. Irish people, or those of Irish descent (such as George Canning in the 1820s or Bonar Law during the Great War), came to occupy high office in successive British governments. This pre-eminence was particularly evident in the last quarter of the nineteenth century when a succession of Irishmen—the Tories, Earl Cairns and Edward Gibson (Lord Ashbourne), and Catholic Liberals such as Lord O'Hagan and Lord Russell of Killowen—held senior ministerial or judicial rank.

Complementing and contradicting these metropolitan trappings was some colonial political architecture. Ireland possessed a Lord-Lieutenant, or Viceroy, and the remnants of a separate executive centring on the Chief Secretary. As David Cannadine has observed, 'the regime established in Dublin provided the proconsular prototype for what would later evolve on the imperial periphery, in India, in the dominions of settlement, and eventually in the dependent Empire'. The Indian viceroyalty, established under the Imperial Titles Act of 1876, followed 'the precedent and example of the Irish viceroyalty in Dublin'.[2] The elaborate protocol of the viceregal court, its intricate hierarchy, and the ambitions, resentments, intrigue, and snobbery which it generated, were broadly familiar features of Calcutta and New Delhi, and dozens of other, more minor, gubernatorial establishments throughout the Empire.

The civil service in Ireland conformed to this pattern of metropolitan and colonial elements, being divided between separate local boards and departments, and the bureaucratic outposts of Whitehall. The gaggle of interlayered and overlapping offices has been understandably described (by David Fitzpatrick) as a 'mess'.[3] As late as 1899, Ireland was newly endowed with a separate Department of Agriculture and Technical Instruction. The administration of numerous matters, including (after 1831) education and (after 1836) the police, tended to be highly centralized, conforming to colonial rather than metropolitan norms. There was, in addition, a separate legal establishment, headed by the Lord Chancellor of Ireland. Given the proximity of the two islands, however, Dublin-trained barristers such as the politician-lawyers James Campbell (Lord Glenavy), Edward Carson, Tim Healy, and Charles Russell, were able to practice successfully at the English bar. For men such as these, the House of Commons provided a useful forum within which forensic and intellectual ability might be advertised to a much wider audience. But, as the career of R. A. McCall (Treasurer of the Middle Temple in 1918, among many other legal honours and appointments) demonstrated, Parliament

---

[2] David Cannadine, *Ornamentalism: How the British Saw their Empire* (London, 2001), pp. 15, 45.

[3] David Fitzpatrick, 'Ireland and the Empire', in Porter, ed., *OHBE. Vol. III*, p. 496.

was by no means a necessary feature of every Irishman's success at the English bar.

If the structures of government blended colonial and metropolitan elements, the culture and attitudes of those in power reflected these same disparate influences. On the one hand, Irish leaders (such as Daniel O'Connell, Charles Stewart Parnell, and John Redmond) were able to wield considerable influence within the institutions at the very heart of the Union. On the other hand, there are parallels between the culture and preoccupations of the British administration in Ireland and elsewhere in the Empire. The Victorian bureaucratic obsession with the acquisition of statistical information was reflected fully in Ireland, and through the wide range of information-gathering undertaken (for example) by the officers of the Royal Irish Constabulary, and fed through its district and county structure to Dublin Castle. The establishment of the Ordnance Survey in Ireland (1824) was a critical development in terms of detailed British control over the island, and scholars have placed a similar emphasis on the political resonance of the work of the Great Trigonometrical Survey in India (1818) and the Geological Survey of India (1851).[4] English officials billeted in Ireland developed the same attitudes of mixed bemusement, condescension, complacency, affection, and eagerness to help which characterized their counterparts in India or elsewhere. The memoirs of Sir Henry Robinson, of the Local Government Board, or Maurice Headlam, a Treasury official exiled in Edwardian Ireland, chime with those of officials in further-flung corners of the Empire.[5]

British imperial influence in Ireland was exercised not just through the formal mechanisms of government, or of economic management, but also through informal means. As in other parts of the Empire, British rule was sustained in Ireland partly through the deployment of the monarchy and through honours and titles, but also through a spectrum of cultural influences from sporting activity to the stage and cinema. More work needs to be done on the possible transmission of British and imperial values through Irish theatres and the nascent cinema business of the early twentieth century. Some research has been undertaken by Alan Bairner,

---

[4] For the Ordnance Survey in Ireland see J. H. Andrews, *A Paper Landscape: The Ordnance Survey in Nineteenth Century Ireland* (Oxford, 1975). See also, Robert Stafford, 'Scientific Exploration and Empire', in Porter, ed., *OHBE. Vol. III*, p. 305.

[5] Sir Henry Robinson, *Memories: Wise and Otherwise* (London, 1923); Maurice Headlam, *Irish Reminiscences* (London, 1947).

W. F. Mandle, Neil Garnham, and others on the issue of sport and imperial values within nineteenth-century Ireland. Bairner has argued, for example, that 'the threat of British sporting hegemony in Ireland was, by the last quarter of the nineteenth century, very real'.[6] It seems clear that sporting and other types of informal imperialism were important influences in Ireland, as in other British territories.

Numerous scholars have begun to explore the importance of the Crown in nineteenth and early twentieth-century Ireland.[7] On the whole the British royal family was more popular in nineteenth-century Ireland than was British imperial rule. Royal visits to Ireland (as to India and elsewhere) were one way in which ties with the imperial government and the existing social and political hierarchy were sustained. These visits tended to be successful. The unlovely George IV was greeted by rapturous Irish crowds in 1821, while Victoria was received with equal warmth during her occasional visits (the last of which was in 1900). The sybaritic Edward VII was successfully marketed as an accessible and ecumenical monarch, and was hailed as such when he visited Dublin in 1903. Even the relatively colourless George V was warmly received when he paid his coronation visit to Ireland in 1911, on the eve of the Home Rule and revolutionary era. Just as there was an ongoing imperial debate about the useful employment of junior royals as Governors of (especially) the four Dominions, so in late nineteenth-century Ireland there were frequent discussions about a permanent royal residence in Ireland, to be occupied on a regular basis by, perhaps, the Prince of Wales. In neither case, however, was a lasting conclusion reached. Canadian winters, Australian heat, and Irish mists never quite held the same attraction for the royals as the fleshpots of London and the home counties.

The link between the royal family and the proliferation of imperial honours and titles has been readily identified; and it seems that Irish people were as susceptible to titles and baubles as their counterparts elsewhere in the Empire. Here, as elsewhere, Ireland conforms partly to the broader imperial experience, and partly to that of metropolitan Britain.

---

[6] Alan Bairner, 'Ireland, Sport and Empire', in Keith Jeffery, ed., *An Irish Empire?: Aspects of Ireland and the British Empire* (London, 1996), p. 64.

[7] See, for example, James H. Murphy, *Abject Loyalty: Nationalism and Monarchy in Ireland during the Reign of Queen Victoria* (Washington, 2001) and Senia Paseta, 'Nationalist Responses to Two Royal Visits to Ireland, 1900 and 1903', *Irish Historical Studies* (hereafter *IHS*), XXXI, 124 (Nov. 1999), pp. 488–504.

On the one hand, the establishment of the Order of Saint Patrick in 1783, after the winning of legislative autonomy, helped to bind senior figures within the Irish aristocracy to the Crown at a time when the possibility of drift was very real. Membership of the Order was greatly valued throughout the nineteenth century until Irish independence; and indeed there were periodic discussions about its revival after 1921 for the benefit of the luminaries of Northern Ireland, particularly with the profusion of Second World War military commanders who had Ulster connections of one kind or another. The Order of Saint Patrick may be seen as a forerunner of the senior ranks of the Order of the Star of India, established in 1861, which was awarded, amongst others, to the princely families of the sub-continent.[8]

There were, however, differences between Ireland and the imperial experience here, as elsewhere. Peerages, baronetcies, and knighthoods probably fell more readily within the reach of the greatest Irish magnates than among their counterparts elsewhere in the Empire. This may be simply another way of saying that access to the British metropolitan élite was much easier for the most elevated ranks of Irish society than for their colonial equivalents. On the other hand, given that the Order of Saint Patrick was indeed so very exclusive, there were relatively few honours and awards which were accessible to a broader range of Irish society. In India, the junior ranks of the Order of the Indian Empire (founded in 1878) served to reward comparatively lowly figures within both Anglo-Indian and Indian society. Elsewhere in the Empire, the Order of Saint Michael and Saint George fulfilled a broadly similar function. The creation of the more populist Order of the British Empire in 1917 came much too late to be of use in binding Irish people within the embrace of the honours system and, in any event, its blatantly imperial designation made life difficult for nationally minded recipients at the time and ever since.

Competition in late nineteenth-century Ireland occurred, not so much over honours of this kind, as over magistracies, appointments as justice of the peace, or, at a more elevated level, Deputy-Lieutenant. With the establishment of relatively democratic local government in Ireland in 1898, the rank of county councillor or urban or rural district councillor provided a dangerous elected alternative to the royal system of honours and rewards.

---

[8] Cannadine, *Ornamentalism*, pp. 88–90. See also, Peter Galloway, *The Most Illustrious Order: The Order of Saint Patrick and its Knights* (London, 1999).

It is a moot point whether the creation in the early or mid-nineteenth century of a popular Irish order along the lines of the junior ranks of the Order of the Indian Empire might have served to bind a wide, and perhaps critical, section to the British and imperial connection. But it would certainly be ironic if one of the minor explanations for the ultimate collapse of British rule in Ireland was the failure to invest at the right time in the production and bestowal of a few crucial baubles.[9]

Aside from the honours system, there were also distinctions between the physical presence of imperial government in Ireland and in India and other colonies. It is unquestionably the case that the expansion of British government in Victorian Ireland brought with it the ever-impinging presence of official buildings and symbolism. The growth of the Royal Irish Constabulary, the Post Office, and other agencies of government brought barracks and offices, and even (at a more modest level) the construction of post-boxes, all adorned with the monogram of the reigning monarch. Street names in Belfast and Dublin proclaimed royal and imperial connections, as the work of Yvonne Whelan has demonstrated. In Ireland, as in India, the threat of self-government seems to have stimulated the imperial authorities into an architectural response. New Delhi, envisioned in the last decades of the Raj by Sir Edwin Lutyens and Sir Herbert Baker, is scarcely to be compared in terms of scale or ambition with the suite of government buildings erected in the last years of the Union by the British authorities in Merrion Street, in the centre of Dublin. Each might, however, be seen as a defensive, monumental response to the impending collapse of British rule.[10]

As always, however, the qualified nature of colonial rule in Ireland means that it is impossible to push such analogies too far. In India, imperial builders such as Lutyens and Baker exploited a distinctive Indo-Saracenic style of building which strikingly combined indigenous as well as European architectural motifs. In Ireland, it is hard to escape the sense that the physical expression of British rule was always more remote and forbidding. An overwhelming Gothic or a vigorous classicism were the standard idioms, only occasionally softened by references to the imagery of the Celtic Revival. Again, it is an interesting speculation whether British

---

[9] For a discussion of the importance of commissions of the peace for the residual Ascendancy interest see David Fitzpatrick, *Politics and Irish Life, 1913–21: Provincial Experience of War and Revolution* (Dublin, 1977), p. 55.

[10] See Philip Davies, *Spendours of the Raj: British Architecture in India, 1660–1947* (London, 1985).

rule in Ireland might have been rendered more accessible, with the adoption of a Celtic aesthetic and a gaelicized face.

The strategies of British government in Ireland resembled their colonial counterparts in many ways. In particular, the British dependence upon, and exploitation of, local allies in Ireland bears comparison with similar strategies in India and elsewhere. The cultivation of these allies might be linked to the policies of division and rule which were often the hallmark of the British colonial presence. The British governed Ireland, as they governed India and much of Africa, in conjunction with local élites. In Ireland, as in India, these alliances might shift; in both places, division and disruption were the effective (if not the intended) outcomes of these arrangements. British India in the nineteenth century rested partly upon the acquiescence of Hindu 'scribal gentries', military élites, and later the great princely families: 'by 1914', Robin Moore has observed, 'governing India required the careful manipulation of cooperative Indians'.[11] In the first decades of the twentieth century, British preferences and courtship seem to have shifted away from the Hindu élites towards the Muslims. The Muslim population of the sub-continent was separately enfranchised; and Lord Curzon's partition of Bengal (which amongst other matters assisted the Muslims of East Bengal) was a foretaste of the partition of India itself.[12]

Shifting alliances and the effective encouragement of local divisions were hallmarks of British rule in nineteenth-century Ireland. Just as maharajahs and nawabs were an important element in the operation of British rule in nineteenth and early twentieth-century India, British government in Ireland was sustained with the co-operation of the Irish Protestant landed classes (or 'Ascendancy'). Ireland before the Union was governed by an effective alliance of the British-controlled executive and the Ascendancy-dominated Irish Parliament (although some British wavering is evident through the Fitzwilliam Episode of 1795 and Pitt's interest in Catholic emancipation). This alliance was sustained in the early years of the Union, with Irish representation in the United Kingdom House of Commons squarely in the hands of Protestant interests.

---

[11] Robin Moore, 'Imperial India, 1858–1914', in Porter, ed., *OHBE. Vol. III*, p. 444.

[12] Ibid., p. 438. For a striking contemporary defence of Curzon's partition scheme see Lovat Fraser, *India under Curzon and After* (London, 1911), pp. 365–96.

The emancipation of Catholics in 1829 saw the beginnings of a shift. The informal alliance of 1835 between O'Connell, his followers, and the Whig government ('the Lichfield House Compact') is interesting as an early experiment in collaboration between a British government and the emergent Catholic élite. Such flirtation is occasionally evident throughout the mid-nineteenth century, but it matured into a more substantial relationship between successive British administrations, particularly Liberal ones, and Catholic Ireland. By the 1880s the British Liberal Party had again formulated an alliance with Catholic Ireland, as represented in the Home Rule movement. Land legislation in the 1880s and 1890s, including Conservative legislation, increasingly favoured the Catholic tenant interest. Indeed, the culmination of these reforms—George Wyndham's land act of 1903—was an ambitious effort to fund a transfer of Irish land from the landlord to the tenant class. It is arguable that this shift from British sponsorship of the old Ascendancy to a more direct engagement with the developing élites of Catholic society was in line with wider patterns of colonial administration. In the Ireland of 1900, as in the formal colonies, British attention was turning to the patronage and cultivation of local indigenous élites.[13]

The hallmark of such British patronage, however, was always its uncertainty and fluidity. The British, in Ireland and elsewhere, were always keen to exploit division, and to transfer their affections and support from one local community to another, depending on their calculation of advantage. In Ireland the divisions within constitutional nationalism which followed the death of Charles Stewart Parnell in October 1891 were discreetly welcomed and encouraged by successive British ministers. Arthur Balfour, as Chief Secretary for Ireland, privately discouraged southern Irish Unionist candidates from standing in elections where there was a fight between Parnellites and anti-Parnellites.[14] By the 1920–21 period these same southern Irish Unionists had outlived their usefulness, and were discarded by British ministers with alacrity. Equally, as will become clear, while British ministers exercised influence in Northern Ireland after 1920 through the agency of the Stormont administration and the Ulster Unionist political

---

[13] For a general history of the development of Home Rule, see Alvin Jackson, *Home Rule: An Irish History* (London, 2003).

[14] Balfour to Goschen, 12 Dec. 1891 (copy), Arthur Balfour Papers, BL. Add. MSS, 49830, f. 428.

establishment, these, too, were sidelined when they became more political bother than they were evidently worth.

In some, more particular, ways the British encouragement of local Irish élites mirrored practice throughout the Empire. The land purchase legislation which was promoted from the Ashbourne Act of 1885 through to the Wyndham Act of 1903 was designed to defuse agrarian unrest, and to create a settled and passive class of small proprietors in the Irish countryside. These, and related, land reform Acts have been seen as providing an inspiration for Indian statutes offering protection to the small cultivator.[15] Land purchase was about disconnecting the land and the national questions; it might also be suggested that it was about separating rural from urban nationalism. To this extent, therefore, land purchase was of a piece with other British strategies of division and rule. It also had rough parallels in the wider Empire, where the challenge of radical urban nationalism in (say) inter-war India, or Malaya in the 1950s or South Arabia in the 1960s, was offset by the deployment of more conservative rural societies. This motif in British policy has been observed in the bonding of Singapore within the Federation of Malaya, the uniting of Aden within the Federation of South Arabia, and—closer to the era of Irish land purchase—the encouragement of the Indian princes as a counterweight to the challenge of urban nationalism on the sub-continent.[16]

Land purchase was part of a reformist and paternalist style of government in Ireland which was sometimes called 'constructive Unionism', and there are parallels between this and some other imperial strategies of rule. It would be wrong to exaggerate the affinities binding Lord Curzon's administration of India (1898–1905) and George Wyndham's Chief Secretaryship in Ireland (1900–1905); but (as one might expect, given their shared personal histories as, for example, fellow Etonians and 'Souls') there are some suggestive parallels. Curzon's combination of paternalist reform and interest in the traditional ruling classes has been wittily described as 'Tory-entalism' by Niall Ferguson.[17] Curzon's reformist zeal was perceptible in the areas of land and higher education, while his sense of the feudal and theatrical was visible in his encouragement of the princely

---

[15] Fitzpatrick, 'Ireland and Empire', p. 517.

[16] The politics of land purchase are discussed in Andrew Gailey, *Ireland and the Death of Kindness: The Experience of Constructive Unionism, 1890–1905* (Cork, 1987). See also Cannadine, *Ornamentalism*, pp. 88–90.

[17] Niall Ferguson, *Empire: How Britain Made the Modern World* (London, 2003), p. 204.

families and in lavishly staged events such as the Delhi Durbar of 1903. Wyndham, for his part, had a similar vein of Tory romanticism, emphasizing some of the traditional elements of Irish society, and ignoring some inconvenient realities about the direction of Irish politics. Like Curzon in India, Wyndham was interested in alleviating the condition of the Irish 'peasant'; like Curzon, he was perhaps most comfortable in the company of the most emollient and Anglophile sections of the traditional landed élite. Each man was interested in medals and honours and ceremonial and, again like Curzon, Wyndham applied a romantic Tory sensibility to the challenge of imperial government. Each had ambitious dreams of winning his charges permanently to the Empire, and a social and cultural vision which fitted certain aspects of their respective domains but was perhaps more directly a response to the condition of Edwardian England than to that of India or Ireland. This vision would soon prove to be an inadequate rendering of a much more complex picture. Both men, therefore, were doomed to disappointment, though Wyndham, who died at the age of fifty in 1913, was at least spared from knowing the extent of his, and the British, failure in Ireland.[18]

The complexities of Ireland's relationship with Empire were nowhere more clearly evident than in the matter of economics. Britain's colonies and dependent territories have often been seen (certainly within Marxist or Leninist readings) as the victims of an imperial economic vampire. Their financial life-blood was, in this analysis, remorselessly drained away, and their whole economic being was subjected to the needs of their imperial master. The economic backwardness of Victorian India was sometimes blamed upon British rule. India's riches were (it was said) siphoned off to Britain through the costs of administration and policing, and through the returns on British capital invested in India. The development and diversification of the Indian economy was constricted because of British policy and influence: the ubiquity of cheap British goods suffocated Indian manufacturing industry, and kept the economy in an undeveloped and pliant condition.[19]

Similar arguments have been applied to other British territories, and not least to Ireland. Here it is sometimes suggested that the Union of 1801

---

[18] See Alvin Jackson, 'George Wyndham (1863–1913)', in *Oxford Dictionary of National Biography* (Oxford, 2004).

[19] Moore, 'Imperial India', pp. 443–44.

served to subvert the Irish industrial and manufacturing economy. Small-scale manufactures and handicrafts were badly hit in the short term by the effective transfer of much Irish spending power from Dublin to the new parliamentary capital, London. By 1824, the protective tariffs applied by the old Irish Parliament were finally abolished, with concomitant damage to (for example) the cotton industry. Parallel to this apparent process of industrial suffocation was a rising demand for Irish agricultural produce, fuelled by the massive military and naval forces either fielded or subvented by the British during the Napoleonic Wars, and by the growing needs of an increasingly urbanized English population. Ireland, in this argument, began to serve as a kind of Sicily or Africa to London's Rome, a necessary breadbasket for the imperial heartland.

A variant of this argument for economic control has been applied to what was by far the greatest disaster of the Union period, the Great Famine of 1845–51. In 1845 the crucial Irish potato crop was attacked by a virulent fungus, causing a partial failure of the harvest. The situation worsened in 1846, and remained dire until at least 1848 or 1849. Estimates vary, but perhaps one million Irish people died as a result of famine-related disease and starvation in the Famine years. Though the origins of the disaster were natural and ecological, the stunted and begrudging relief efforts of the Whig government in London attracted considerable criticism at the time and ever since. In particular, radical nationalists saw British policy in the Famine years as embodying a heartless expression of London's social, political, and economic interests in Ireland. John Mitchel, who supplied a critical link between the era of Young Ireland and that of Parnell, declared famously that 'the Almighty indeed sent the potato blight, but the English created the Famine'. In this and related interpretations the British were not only culpable for the deaths of the million or so famine victims, but cynically exploited this cataclysm in order to engineer an Ireland more in tune with their own needs. This view has resonated into contemporary interpretations of the Famine which sometimes see British relief strategies as being tied to a crude reformist agenda. Once again, it appeared that the British government was brutally prepared to use the Union as a tool of its social and economic strategies.[20]

[20] See, for example, E. Strauss, *Irish Nationalism and British Democracy* (London, 1951). For the Famine, see Christine Kinealy, *This Great Calamity: The Irish Famine, 1845–52* (Dublin, 1994) and *A Death-Dealing Famine: The Great Hunger in Ireland* (London, 1997).

Other interpretations of Ireland's broad economic relationship with Britain, however, are defensible. David Fitzpatrick has assembled the case for supposing that Ireland under the Union was an insignificant, if complicated, asset for Britain, 'whether as a trading partner, a site for capital investment, or even a source of revenue from taxes and duties'.[21] Oliver MacDonagh has argued that if 'economic "exploitation" is conceived of as a necessary element in colonialism, it is difficult to see what Britain gained from her Irish "possession" in the nineteenth century'.[22] Free access to British imperial markets certainly served to stimulate Irish agriculture in the late nineteenth century; but this same access also helped to encourage significant industrial growth in eastern Ulster, with Belfast boasting shipyards, ropeworks, and engineering concerns of international importance. Indeed, it might well be argued that east Ulster was one of the main props of the 'engineering imperialism' which underpinned the infrastructure of the Empire. On the other hand, Britain's balance of trade with Ireland (in so far as figures are available) favoured the Irish; in addition, 'the net flow of capital was undoubtedly from Britain to Ireland'.[23] There is a case for accepting that for a period in the late nineteenth century Ireland was relatively heavily taxed, but that the balance of advantage had shifted in the Irish direction by the Edwardian era and the emergence of a nascent welfare state.

Clearly, no simple model of exploitation can be applied to what was an exceedingly complex economic relationship between the two islands. Ireland's proximity to Britain, and Irish access to British and imperial markets, probably helped to shape parts of its economy in ways that were mutually beneficial. Ireland under the Union was not consistently the victim of a crude, economic imperialism. At particular times, however, and within particular areas of the relationship, the evidence for exploitation is more persuasive.

Turning from the role of Empire within nineteenth-century Ireland to the role of the Irish within the nineteenth-century Empire, it may be argued that the complexities of the island's status were intimately connected with those of its political culture. The defining irony of Ireland's imperial bond

[21] Fitzpatrick, 'Ireland and Empire', p. 503.
[22] Quoted in ibid.
[23] Ibid.

was that the often suffocating colonial elements in Irish life under the Union actually helped to spur its engagement with the Empire. Indeed, it is possible to go further than this: the semi-colonial nature of British rule in Ireland underpinned not only Irish participation in Empire, but also, in some senses, Irish nationalism and the revolt against imperial rule.

Pursuing this point, John Hutchinson's well-known argument about the interconnections between British rule and cultural nationalism may be applied and adapted.[24] Hutchinson saw colonial rule in Ireland as a constraint upon the ambition of educated lower-middle class Catholics, and he argued that these thwarted men and women found an alternative outlet for their aspirations within the cultural revival and the new nationalism of the late nineteenth century. It might further be suggested that the incomplete and half-hearted quality of British colonial rule in Ireland created the space within which a nationalist culture might develop alongside its imperial counterpart. In terms of constraints, oppression, and laxity, British rule helped to forge the conditions within which an anti-colonial movement was able to develop.

The argument may be applied still further. One of Ireland's defining qualities was that it occupied a half-way house between Britain and the Empire. Cultural nationalism supplied one source of redress or compensation for the Irish within this system of rule. But another crucial outlet for those who were thwarted at home was supplied by the very nature of British rule. For Ireland was not only a half-hearted colony, it was also a half-hearted component of the imperial metropolis; and Irish people who might be constrained at home also had access to the Empire and to the social and economic opportunities it provided. For Ireland, therefore, the Empire was simultaneously a chain and a key: it was a source both of constraint and of liberation.

Thus, British imperial rule in nineteenth-century Ireland generated a political culture where families might be divided through their Irish or imperial allegiance. Indeed, the fluidity of Irish politics may be illustrated, not just by divisions within families, but also by the oscillations within individual careers. Imperial cultural hegemony was never fully attained in Ireland, but it made some inroads into the Irish political consciousness. And, as Richard English has demonstrated with the life of Ernie O'Malley,

---

[24] See John Hutchinson, *The Dynamics of Cultural Nationalism: The Gaelic Revival and the Creation of the Irish Nation State* (London, 1987).

even the most ferocious Irish patriots were never entirely free from the influence of Empire.[25]

Irish national politics, Irish families, and Irish individuals were divided by empire throughout the nineteenth and twentieth centuries. Doubtless these tensions can be illuminated through psychological as much as political arguments; but the unusually wide range of options supplied by Ireland's semi-colonial culture must surely be seen as part of the explanation. The main expression of Irish nationalism in the late nineteenth and early twentieth centuries, the Home Rule movement, epitomized the tensions binding Ireland and Empire. Home Rulers fought to break the Union, the link with the imperial motherland, but in many cases they were content that Ireland should participate fully within the structures of the Empire. John Redmond famously defined Home Rule in essentially imperial terms; others, such as Sir Charles Gavan Duffy, the Young Irelander, or Edward Blake (MP for Longford South between 1892 and 1907), combined support for Home Rule with earlier careers as ministers of the Crown in colonial administrations. Home Rulers were often proud of Irish feats within the British Army, but contemptuous of the Army itself. They were often simultaneously critical of the rulers of the Empire, while proud of siblings and children who scrambled up the greasy pole of the Indian or colonial civil service. The desire for social mobility was a counterweight to a hatred for Britain and its works.

Irish families simultaneously upheld and subverted the Empire. Illustrations of this can serve, not so much to clinch the point, as to document the diverse career options open to able middle-class Catholics, and the different ways in which the compromise between patriotism and social mobility might be worked out within a family. Two sons of Mark Garvey MacDonnell, a Catholic gentleman-farmer, of Shragh, County Mayo, were educated at Queen's College Galway, but thereafter went their separate ways. Mark Antony MacDonnell trained as a doctor and was employed as Surgeon to the Liverpool Cancer and Skin Hospital, while his brother, Antony Patrick, joined the Indian Civil Service (ICS) in 1865. In 1892 Mark entered the House of Commons as the anti-Parnellite MP for Queen's County (Leix). By 1893 Antony was Acting Governor of Bengal and had been made a Knight Commander of the Order of the Star of India. In 1895 he was translated to govern the provinces of Agra and

[25] See Richard English, *Ernie O'Malley: IRA Intellectual* (Oxford, 1998).

Oudh, and in 1897 he was awarded the Grand Cross of the Order of the Star of India. In 1902 he returned to Ireland to head up the civil service, and in 1908 he was ennobled as Lord MacDonnell of Swinford.[26]

Even the families of leading separatists were not free from the shadow of the ICS. One of the architects of the 'new' cultural and separatist nationalism of early twentieth-century Ireland was Eoin MacNeill, a co-founder of the Gaelic League (1893) and of the Irish Volunteers (1913). MacNeill was also Professor of Early Irish History at University College Dublin, and would serve between 1923 and 1925 as Minister for Education in the Irish government. His brother James, by contrast, joined the ICS in 1890 and served from then until 1915 in different capacities within the Bengal Presidency and beyond, ending his career as the second (and penultimate) Governor-General of the Irish Free State.

If brothers parted company on the question of Empire, so too did fathers and sons. One of the icons of the late Victorian Empire was Sir George White, the defender of Ladysmith during the South African War. From Broughshane, County Antrim, White was Commander-in-Chief in India from 1893 to 1897, gaining the Grand Cross of the Order of the Indian Empire (1893) and of the Star of India (1898) before being given his command in Natal in 1899. White ended his career as a Field Marshal, festooned with additional honours and awards, including the Grand Cross of the Order of the Bath (1897), the Royal Victorian Order (1900), and the Order of Saint Michael and Saint George (1901). His son, Captain James Robert White, showed similar imperial promise, serving in South Africa with the Gordon Highlanders and winning the Distinguished Service Order at the age of twenty-two. But Captain White developed radical second thoughts and in 1913 helped to found the Irish Citizen Army (which James Connolly would later command). His sympathies shifted towards Sinn Féin, and by the mid-1920s he was lecturing a former British Army comrade, Colonel Wilfrid Spender, on the integrity of the Irish revolutionary cause.[27]

A faint but striking parallel with the divisions in the White family came sixty years later with the Bunting family in Northern Ireland. Major Ronald Bunting was a former regular Army officer who had first served

---

[26] The best source for MacDonnell's career remains his papers, housed in the Bodleian Library, Oxford.

[27] White to Spender, 28 April 1924, PRONI, CAB.9Z/1/1.

the King-Emperor, and who later became a political associate of Dr Ian Paisley. His son, Ronnie Jr., was trained as a schoolmaster but later pursued a rather rougher trade, joining the Irish Republican Socialist Party and the Irish National Liberation Army. Ronnie, who was born into the King's Army, ended up shooting British soldiers. In October 1980 he was himself killed by loyalist paramilitaries.[28]

Individual Irishmen pursued careers which embodied the same tensions and ambiguities. Mention has already been made of the gunman and revolutionary, Ernie O'Malley, and of Edward Blake and Charles Gavan Duffy, colonial statesmen and Irish nationalists. O'Malley was an Irish revolutionary who none the less identified with much in the culture of those whom he fought and killed, and whose brother served as an officer in the British Army during the First World War. There is a wider issue here: many hundreds of nationalists accepted John Redmond's imperial vision of Home Rule, fought in the British Army in the Great War, and later graduated into the ranks of the Irish Republican Army. Other Irish separatists, such as Kevin O'Higgins, fought the Empire only to be accommodated comfortably within its workings in the 1920s. Arthur Lynch, born in Ballarat in Australia, served as a Home Rule MP and was a colonel both in the Boer forces during the South African War and in the British Army in the Great War. Pursuing a diametrically opposed trajectory was Eric Dorman-Smith, who served in the Second World War as a British general, and afterwards actively identified himself with the Irish republican cause.[29]

Personal stories such as these document the complex interrelationship of Irish society with the British Empire. They also illustrate the central role that the Empire played for many Irish people. It provided opportunities for almost every section of Irish society, from the landed gentry and the churches to the middle and professional classes and the urban poor. Irish peers could aspire to be imperial proconsuls, while smaller landowners might dignify more modest colonial governorships. Richard Southwell Bourke, 6th Earl of Mayo, became Viceroy of India in 1869, and was assassinated in 1872, while still in office. Frederick Temple Hamilton-Temple-Blackwood, the first Marquess of Dufferin and Ava, and

---

[28] David McKittrick, Seamus Kelters, Brian Feeney, and Chris Thornton, eds., *Lost Lives: The Stories of the Men, Women and Children who Died as a Result of the Northern Ireland Troubles* (Edinburgh and London, 1999), pp. 840–41.

[29] Keith Jeffery, 'The Irish Military Tradition', in Jeffery, ed., *An Irish Empire?*, p. 108.

a County Down nobleman, served as Governor-General of Canada
(1872–78) and as Viceroy of India (1884–88). Henry Charles Keith Petty-
Fitzmaurice, 5th Marquess of Lansdowne and a Kerry landowner, also
served as Governor of Canada (1883–88) and as Viceroy of India (1888–
94). The Tyrone proprietor, Uchter John Mark Knox, 5th Earl of Ranfurly,
was Governor of New Zealand from 1897 to 1904. Another, more minor,
Tyrone landlord, William Grey Ellison-Macartney, served successively as
Governor of Tasmania (1913–17) and of Western Australia (1917–20).
Beyond the ranks of the successful was a gaggle of often indigent and
desperate gentlemen who looked for relief from local and financial worries
through a gubernatorial career. William Johnston, a bankrupt County
Down proprietor and Orange MP, and Lord Arthur Hill, son of the fourth
Marquis of Downshire, each persistently but unsuccessfully sought escape
in this way.[30]

The Empire was not only a form of outdoor relief for impoverished
Irish gentlemen: it also served as a vehicle for the upward mobility of the
Irish middle classes, both Catholic and Protestant. Mention has been
made of the career of Lord MacDonnell of Swinford, but the Queen's
Colleges (MacDonnell was a Galway graduate) and Trinity College, Dublin
were more generally geared to the demands of the Indian and colonial
civil service examinations. Increasing numbers of Irish Catholics were
winning coveted positions in the ICS by the beginning of the twentieth
century. The proportion of Catholics amongst Irish applicants stood at
around 30 per cent in 1914. Michael Francis O'Dwyer, who—like Antony
MacDonnell—was from a relatively modest Irish Catholic provincial background, entered the ICS in 1885 and rose through its ranks to become in
1913, at the relatively early age of forty-nine, Lieutenant-Governor of the
Punjab. O'Dwyer was appointed a Knight Commander of the Order of
the Star of India in 1913 and a Knight Grand Cross of the Order of the
Indian Empire in 1917. A staunch advocate of British rule in India,
he defended General Dyer's bloody actions at Amritsar in 1919, and was
himself assassinated by an Indian nationalist in 1940.[31]

The Empire provided opportunities for other professionals. Engineers,
lawyers, and doctors from the Irish colleges and universities found

[30] Alvin Jackson, *The Ulster Party: Irish Unionists in the House of Commons, 1884–1911*
(Oxford, 1989), pp. 218–22.

[31] T. G. Fraser, 'Ireland and India', in Jeffery, ed., *An Irish Empire?*, pp. 88–89. See also, chap.
4 of the present vol., pp. 101–103.

employment in Britain's colonies or in those territories where the British exercised informal influence. Robert Hart, from Portadown in County Armagh, graduated in law from Queen's College Belfast in 1853 and embarked upon a career in the Chinese Imperial Maritime Customs. Hart was Inspector General of the Customs (1863–1906) and of the Chinese Imperial Postal Service (1896–1906), and was offered (but declined) the British ambassadorship to Peking. He ended his days as a baronet (1893) and holder of the Grand Cross of the Order of Saint Michael and Saint George (1889). Irish doctors, who might otherwise have been consigned to provincial indigence, found a billet in the Army's Indian Medical Service: in the 1870s, 38 per cent of its recruits were Irish. Some, like David Vincent O'Malley, a graduate in medicine from University College Dublin, were promoted to high rank. O'Malley, who joined the Service during the First World War, became a Major-General, a Companion of the Bath, and an honorary physician to King George VI, before retiring to South Africa.[32]

Taken as a whole, the armies of the British Empire contained a disproportionately Irish presence. This disparity was at its greatest in the early nineteenth century, with Irishmen representing 42 per cent of British soldiers in 1830, at a time when Ireland accounted for one-third of the total population of the United Kingdom. Between 1825 and 1850 no less than 48 per cent of the Bengal Army of the East India Company were Irishmen. One such Company soldier was Corporal Hugh Dundas, who served in the 1st Battalion, Bengal Artillery throughout the Indian Mutiny. Dundas was born in March 1827 in Enniskillen, County Fermanagh, and was originally a farmer. He was enlisted for twelve years' service at Dublin on 15 March 1849, during the Famine years, and subsequently embarked for India. He was present at several of the critical battles of the Mutiny, including Delhi and the relief of Lucknow; he fought at Calpee and was at the Alum Bagh on 11 March 1858. In May 1861 Dundas transferred to the British Army as a Gunner in the Royal Artillery. He was finally discharged in September 1868 on grounds of age and ill-health. The probate registers record that Dundas died on 5 February 1895 at home in Garrison, County Fermanagh.[33]

[32] For Hart, see *inter alia* John K. Fairbank, Katherine F. Bruner, and Elizabeth M. Matheson, eds., *The I. G. in Peking: Letters of Robert Hart, Chinese Maritime Customs, 1868–1907* (Cambridge, Mass., 1975).

[33] See chap. 4 of this volume, pp. 103–112, for a discussion of the Army. Dundas's service papers survive: WO.97/1319.

The full social and political importance of the British Army to Victorian
Ireland is difficult to evaluate, but it should certainly not be oversim-
plified. Recruitment to the Army largely hinged on a variety of social and
economic circumstances, rather than any overt political consideration. It
blossomed in the context of the large and relatively poor population
which characterized pre-Famine Ireland. Taking the Queen's shilling certainly did not automatically induce loyalism. There has been an intriguing
overlap between service in the British Army and revolutionary activism
from the eighteenth century through to the recent 'Troubles'. Revolutionary separatists actively sought support in the ranks of the Army from the
1790s through to the time of the Fenian movement, and beyond. The
recruitment figures, however, suggest that the Army was an intimately
familiar feature of the lives of many Irish families; and this, in turn, is
reflected in the relative popularity which the Army retained in Ireland
throughout the nineteenth century. Even during the Anglo-Irish war recruiting to the British Army continued: Keith Jeffery has identified Clon-
mel, Tipperary, as 'far and away the best recruiting office in Ireland' in
1919–20.[34] Moreover, the importance of the Army in terms of acclimatizing
Irish people to the symbolism and strategies of the British Empire should
also be given due emphasis.

In the end, nothing so much defined Ireland's curious but potent role in
the Empire as the manner of the British departure in 1921. Imperial rule in
Ireland was not ultimately sustained, despite all the agencies, institutions,
and influences tending towards this goal, and in 1921–22, Ireland—
Britain's 'oldest colony'—became Britain's first major ex-colony of the
twentieth century. Indeed, as will become clear, the end of the Union to
some extent defined a type of imperial finale for numerous other British
territories throughout the twentieth century.

The Home Rule movement had stimulated admiration and imitation
elsewhere in the Empire, including India, where members of the Indian
National Congress (established in 1885) watched developments in Ireland
with care. Congress initially saw itself as a kind of loyal opposition, and
pledged its fidelity to the Empire. The debate over Home Rule and the
survival of the Union, which was conducted from the mid-1880s through

---

[34] Jeffery, 'Irish Military Tradition', p. 101.

to the First World War, attracted the interest and involvement of other colonial leaders, who frequently endorsed Irish national aspirations. In the Edwardian period this discussion was widened by some imperialist and federalist ideologues, such as F. S. Oliver, to embrace not just reform of the government of Ireland, but reform of the imperial government itself. Indeed, in different senses the debate about Home Rule was always intrinsically an imperial affair. Its proponents saw Home Rule partly as a means of liberating Westminster from the time-consuming entanglements of Irish business, and thus (at a time of debate on the issue of 'national efficiency') creating a more effective imperial administration. Opponents of Home Rule claimed from the start that its enactment would presage the dissolution of the Empire.[35]

It was not the enactment of Home Rule which foreshadowed the end of Empire, however, but the fact that it was so long delayed. Debate, procrastination, re-negotiation all afflicted the Home Rule cause between 1912 and 1916, creating a crisis of popular expectation in Ireland, and giving credibility and vitality to more militant elements within the nationalist movement. It was not Irish parliamentarians in Dublin who supplied a model to the Empire, however, but rather the actions of Irish gunmen. The guerrilla war by which the Irish Republican Army fought the forces of the Crown from 1919 to 1921 was widely copied by later insurgents struggling to win liberation from the British (whether by the Stern Gang and the Irgun in Palestine, or EOKA in Cyprus). The general pattern of the British response to the challenge of the IRA—counter-attack, intensified repression, the unsettling of liberal opinion at home, secret diplomacy, final accommodation—also supplied a template for later efforts at decolonization, whether in Palestine, Cyprus, or Kenya.

In Ireland in 1920, the British response to local political division involved the application of territorial partition. The Government of Ireland Act of that year provided a model of sorts for Palestine (in 1937–38) and, disastrously, for India at the time of independence (1947–48). The lessons of the Irish experience, however, were not always clear. Looking back in 1972, a former Colonial Office official, J. S. Bennett, claimed that even though there were some suggestive links between the administration of Palestine and Ireland in 1937–38, their relevance was sometimes

---

[35] For the Home Rule question see Jackson, *Home Rule: An Irish History.*

questionable. The senior British military officer in Palestine at this time, General Wauchope, had been transferred to the Middle East after completing a stint as General Officer Commanding (GOC) in Northern Ireland. According to Bennett, the chief influence over the Palestine partition scheme in 1937 was Professor Reginald Coupland, who had recently visited Ireland. But Bennett thought that the significance of these connections was more apparent than real. Coupland, for example, had recommended the partition of Palestine, while (in his *The Empire Today* of 1935) also condemning the division of Ireland.[36]

There is less dispute over the relevance of the Irish precedent to the partition of India in 1947–48. Even Coupland, who had evidently been blind to some of the analogies connecting Palestine and Ireland, saw that 'the old-standing quarrel between Catholics and Protestants in Ulster has certain similar features with the Hindu-Muslim quarrel in India'.[37] Writing in *The Indian Problem, 1833–1935* (1942), Coupland was aware that the Muslim minorities, concentrated in the North-East and North-West of the sub-continent, were now seeking the kind of political separation which had been granted to the Ulster Unionists under the terms of the Government of Ireland Act of 1920. Indeed, the Muslim leader, Muhammad Ali Jinnah, frequently defined his people's claims precisely in terms of the Irish precedent.[38]

If the partition of Ireland had a wider imperial resonance, so too did the settlement embodied in the Anglo-Irish Treaty of December 1921. The Treaty granted Dominion status for the twenty-six counties of the new Irish Free State and provided an exciting, fertile, and ambiguous formula which would be applied elsewhere in the Empire. Moreover, the new Irish Dominion, as David Harkness has documented, was a major influence within the evolution of the Empire and Commonwealth in the 1920s and early 1930s. Ireland's emergence by 1937 as a republic (in all but name) within the Commonwealth provided a precedent for nations such as India which, after independence, swiftly rejected the vestigial trappings of monarchy and embraced republican institutions.[39]

---

[36] Cox to Cairncross, 5 June 1972, covering a memorandum by J. S. Bennett on 'Palestine and Ireland', PRO CJ.4/236.

[37] Fraser, 'Ireland and India', p. 90.   [38] Ibid.

[39] See David Harkness, *The Restless Dominion: The Irish Free State and the British Commonwealth of Nations, 1921–1931* (London, 1969).

In Ireland, as in other former colonies, the departing British distributed titles, medals, and pensions, but otherwise left former allies to their fate. Indeed, the British used much the same lavish bestowal of patronage to facilitate the end of the Union (in the twenty-six counties) as they had applied in 1800 to ease its nativity. Former servants of the regime, some of relatively modest standing, entered retirement laden with honours.

Ireland was also the starting point for a long journey into the imperial twilight taken by some of these servants and pensioners of the old regime. When the British left in 1922, the Royal Irish Constabulary (RIC) was disbanded, and some of its officers moved to the Palestine gendarmerie and other colonial enterprises (in the mid-1920s 483 of the 734 officers and men of this gendarmerie were veterans of the RIC). Many of these men moved across to the Palestine Police when it was created in 1926, though alternative opportunities in the Empire were also available. Sir Joseph Byrne, Inspector General of the RIC between 1916 and 1920, had a markedly more glittering career than his junior officers, but was otherwise not untypical of their imperial aspirations. On leaving Ireland, Byrne embarked upon a series of colonial appointments, which culminated in his installation as Governor of Kenya in 1931.[40]

Many of the disbanded constables (some 1,347 in fact) left the fledgling Irish Free State, migrating to that part of the island where the Union and Empire still prevailed: Northern Ireland. There the governing Ulster Unionist movement maintained a close but ambiguous relationship with British imperialism, exploiting the vision and vocabulary of Empire to divert attention from some of the more miserable realities of life in the new partition state. Empire Day, 24 May, became an official holiday in 1916 in the United Kingdom, and was widely celebrated in the Ulster of the inter-war years. Significantly, Empire Day 1921 was chosen as the poll date for the first elections to the new Northern Ireland Parliament. In the political vocabulary of inter-war Ulster, Westminster became the 'Imperial Parliament' and the United Kingdom civil service was the 'Imperial Civil Service'. Loyalist ex-servicemen banded into the paramilitary 'Imperial Guard' in the first months of the partition state. The Orange Order, the exclusively Protestant fraternity which exercised such a considerable

[40] Kent Fedorowich, 'The Problems of Disbandment: The Royal Irish Constabulary and Imperial Migration, 1919–29', *IHS*, XXX, 117 (May 1996), p. 99.

influence within the Unionist movement, continued to be governed by an 'Imperial Grand Master'. Northern Ireland itself was occasionally dubbed the 'Imperial Province'.[41]

Despite this labelling, the peculiar nature of the earlier Union government and of nineteenth-century Ireland's connection with the Empire, was sustained in Northern Ireland through the redefined Union of 1920–21. Ulster Unionists exploited Empire, but were an integral part of the United Kingdom. Their administrative connection with the British government was through the Home Office rather than the Colonial or Dominions Office, while direct political connections were sustained through the Northern Ireland MPs who continued to sit at Westminster. The devolved Parliament which sat in Belfast between 1921 and 1972 gave Ulster Unionists the semblance of legislative autonomy; but the reality was that their institutions were not those of the great Dominions with whom they sometimes identified. The Irish Free State which emerged from the Treaty of 1921 was by contrast a fully fledged Dominion, and under the *Cumann na nGaedheal* government of 1922–32 it exercised a much more significant role within the Commonwealth and Empire than Northern Ireland did. Unionist Prime Ministers, however, certainly acted as if they were important Commonwealth leaders, none more so than Terence O'Neill, Prime Minister of Northern Ireland between 1963 and 1969.[42]

The Ulster Unionist Party occasionally considered the possibility of seeking Dominion status. James Craig (the first Prime Minister of Northern Ireland) toyed with the notion in the inter-war years, and debate was enlivened after 1945 when the pressure of conforming with Clement Attlee's Labour government created strains within Unionism. Here, as on other occasions, however, the Unionists chose to maintain their connection with Westminster. They were ultimately more concerned with copper-fastening partition than with enlarging their independence. They chose dependence and British standards of welfare provision rather than autonomy and relative impoverishment, preferring to cling to the imperial metropolis rather than to pursue the pattern of

---

[41] The latest discussion of the Orange Order is R. D. Edwards, *The Faithful Tribe: An Intimate Portrait of the Loyal Institutions* (London, 1999). For the Imperial Guard see Michael Farrell, *Northern Ireland: The Orange State* (London, 1975). See also Resolution of the Ulster Imperial Guard, 4 Feb. 1922 (R. Boyd, Honorary Secretary), PRONI, CAB.9Z/1/1.

[42] For O'Neill see Marc Mulholland, *Northern Ireland at the Crossroads: Ulster Unionism in the O'Neill Years, 1960–69* (London, 1999). For a complementary critique see Jackson, *Home Rule*, pp. 232–46.

constitutional development followed elsewhere in the Empire. Ulster Unionists uniformly opted to identify, not with the Empire, but rather with the heartland of the Empire.

Still, the contribution of Unionists and, more widely, Northerners to the waning Empire remained considerable. In Rhodesia, as Donal Lowry has chronicled, the second and third Dukes of Abercorn, from County Tyrone, were an active and influential presence in the early twentieth century, while the Larne-born Sir Robert McIlwaine effectively founded the territory's civil service. Lowry has also identified a number of prominent Rhodesian politicians in the post-war era who had strong Ulster connections.[43] Whether or not the linkages between those of Ulster Unionist descent and Rhodesia were uniquely strong remains open to debate; but it is certainly the case that extreme loyalists often saw an analogy between the 'betrayal' of Ian Smith's Rhodesia by Harold Wilson's Labour government and the apparent betrayal by the British of Ulster Unionism.

The long-standing Irish tradition of military contribution to the Empire was maintained in Northern Ireland. The province supplied at least three infantry regiments to the Empire's army after 1921: the Royal Ulster Rifles, the Royal Irish Fusiliers, and the Royal Inniskilling Fusiliers. These helped to sustain the tradition of Irish engagement with the Crown forces, but here again many of the ambiguities of the nineteenth century were replicated. Just as their predecessors had played a role in the consolidation of Empire, so these Ulster regiments were central to the military aspects of decolonization. The Royal Ulster Rifles served in Palestine both before and (with the ending of the British mandate) after the Second World War. They were also present in strength in Cyprus during the EOKA campaign. The Royal Inniskilling Fusiliers served during the insurgency in Malaya and fought against the Mau-Mau rising in Kenya, where the Royal Irish Fusiliers were also deployed. Again, however, just as service in the armed forces had equipped militant Irish nationalists with a military training, some loyalists took the skills which they had acquired in the ranks and applied them within an Irish context. The co-founder of the modern Ulster Volunteer Force, 'Gusty' Spence, was a veteran of the British campaign in Cyprus. Other loyalist paramilitaries gained military experience in Korea, South Arabia, and Borneo. It has been alleged that William

[43] Donal Lowry, 'Ulster Resistance and Loyalist Rebellion in the Empire', in Jeffery, ed., *An Irish Empire?*, p. 202.

Hanna, who won the Military Medal with the Royal Irish Fusiliers during the Korean War, was implicated in the Dublin and Monaghan bombings of 1974.[44]

If Ulstermen continued to play a role in the Empire at large, imperial developments also had an impact within Northern Ireland. Northern Ireland had its own diminished version of the viceregal establishment, with a Governor representing the Crown, aides-de-camp, and other flunkies, all housed at Hillsborough, County Down. Royal and imperial festivals were an important part of the public ceremonial of the Unionist state. The silver jubilee of George V (1935), the coronation of George VI (1937), and that of Elizabeth II (1953) were all seized upon by Northern Ireland's ministers as a means of simultaneously demonstrating and consolidating loyalty to the Crown and the Empire. Royal visits, particularly after the accession of George VI, tended towards the same end. The North's participation in the Second World War strengthened a sense of engagement with a wider imperial and international struggle against fascism. The celebrations of victory in Europe (May 1945) and Japan (August 1945) were, in this sense, imperial occasions.

The physical landscape of Northern Ireland clearly bore the imprint of Empire. The street-names of Belfast reflected this influence. Monuments in Belfast, Armagh, and elsewhere commemorated the sacrifice of Ulster and the wider Empire in the South African War of 1899–1902. In the aftermath of the Great War many towns and villages in the new Northern Ireland built memorials to those who had sacrificed themselves to the imperial and allied cause. Some communities erected monuments to individual heroes of the imperial struggle. In Belfast, in the grounds of the City Hall, a magnificent statue of Lord Dufferin was erected; in the town centre of Lisburn, County Antrim, a statue of the controversial imperial hero John Nicholson was raised. In Banbridge, County Down—interpreting Empire in a wider sense—a monument to the Arctic explorer Francis Crozier was built. In the straitened circumstances of the inter-war years it was not always possible to articulate the power of government through magnificent and costly public buildings; but Sir Arnold Thornley's Parliament building at Stormont, on the outskirts of Belfast, financed by the imperial government, was a marmoreal expression not just of the authority of the devolved administration, but of the imperial muscle which lay behind it.[45]

    [44] McKittrick, Kelters, Feeney, and Thornton, eds., *Lost Lives*, pp. 554–55.
    [45] Alan Greer, 'Sir James Craig and the Construction of Parliament Buildings at Stormont', *IHS*, XXXI, 123 (May 1999), pp. 373–88.

Decolonization, and the decline of the Empire, also had an impact in the North. It is clear that Ulster Unionists identified, and were unsettled by, certain analogies between themselves and threatened British territories elsewhere. Given that the British withdrawal from the twenty-six counties of the new Irish Free State had been so precipitate, however, and given the effective abandonment of southern loyalists, Ulster Unionists did not have to look to Africa, India, or the Middle East for evidence of the uncertainty of imperial ties. There is, indeed, a danger of exaggerating the significance of decolonization for later twentieth-century Ulster politics. The British withdrawal from India was not a major factor in Northern Irish politics in 1947 and 1948, even though there were certain suggestive connections (created through the imposition of Partition and by the numbers of Irish people bound in with Britain's Indian Empire). Decolonization in Africa, Malaya, and Palestine had, perhaps, a greater resonance. Faced with mounting chaos in the Ulster of the later 1960s and early 1970s, the British were inclined to draw upon those with experience in these areas. The first Chief Constable of the reformed Royal Ulster Constabulary, Sir Arthur Young (1969–70), was a veteran of both the Malaya and Kenya police, while one of his successors, Sir Kenneth Newman (Chief Constable between 1976 and 1979), had served in the Palestine Police in the late 1940s. On the other hand, it is worth noting that the key architect of the successful British campaign against communist insurgency in Malaya was an Armagh-born squire, Sir Gerald Templer.

At a more general level, however, it might be suggested that decolonization fed into the decline of Unionism. Given Unionists' investment in Empire, its disappearance may have diminished their movement. Unionist intellectuals celebrated the northern plantation tradition, depicting this colonization as a foundation for the partition settlement. Unionists justified their political actions in terms of the welfare of the broader Empire. The Unionist leadership emphasized the rhetoric and vocabulary of Empire during the inter-war years. Unionists celebrated their community's contribution to Empire, and to the great military struggles of Empire. Given this engagement, it could be argued that one of the implications of decolonization was the diminution of Ulster Unionism. The crisis of late twentieth-century Unionism was thus, at least in part, a reflection of the preceding crisis of Empire.

British policy towards the Unionist administration in Northern Ireland echoed the official attitude towards other élites throughout the waning

Empire. As always with Ireland, there were complications. The Dominions Office, in charge of relations with the Irish Free State, tended to articulate the interests of the nationalist tradition, while the Home Office (which dealt with Northern Ireland) on the whole reflected Unionist concerns. As ever, Britain's interests overrode those of its colonies and dependencies. In 1940, for example, the new Churchill government was perfectly prepared to sacrifice the Unionist regime and the partition experiment in order to win wider Irish adherence to the apparently floundering Allied war effort. On the whole, however, the British found the Unionist administration a useful and pliant instrument, and there were few moments of confrontation between Westminster and Stormont until the late 1960s.

Only after 1968, when the rapid development of civil rights unrest threatened to destabilize Northern Ireland and mar the international reputation of the United Kingdom, did it become evident that Stormont no longer served British interests. Even then, however, the British were slow to abandon an institution and an élite which had proved so useful. The strength of other forces within Northern Ireland, allied with Unionist division and incapacity, however, ultimately forced the British to reorient their allegiance away from Stormont and its government. Not the least of the many shifts within British policy in Northern Ireland since 1970, has been a move away from support for the Unionist establishment towards the quiet encouragement of internal Unionist division and the identification of other potential allies within the North. Here, again, there are faint echoes of imperial practice in an earlier age.[46]

Looking back over two centuries of history, it might well be argued that the failure of the British to define Ireland either in fully metropolitan or colonial terms helped ultimately to break their hold over the island. Irish people were given a glimpse of full metropolitan status in the nineteenth century, but they were simultaneously subjected to a series of colonial-style impositions. In a sense, this was the worst of all worlds, for both Ireland and indeed the British. This half-way house it served to

---

[46] See, for example, Burke Trend to Edward Heath, 24 Feb. 1972, Prime Minister's Office (PREM) 15/1003. In debating how the British government might deal with the able but difficult Northern Ireland Prime Minister, Brian Faulkner, Trend (the Cabinet Secretary) mused: 'we must also consider how far we might isolate him by political action, i.e. by splitting the Protestants as far as possible. In this connection what use can we make of Paisley; and of the Alliance Party and other moderate elements?'.

preserve some of the most anachronistic and dangerous aspects of Ascendancy rule while being simultaneously an offence to patriotic feeling. The British ruled through the Protestant interest for longer than was politically wise. They failed to address the challenge and opportunity presented by the essentially conservative Irish Catholic élites of the early nineteenth century. Equally, they failed to devise wider strategies which might have harnessed the loyalties of those who were ultimately lost to Irish separatism. In the end, the unwillingness of the British to accommodate Ireland fairly and effectively within the Union, or (alternatively) to permit Irish self-government, was to cost them dearly. The ambiguities of British rule in Ireland encouraged political forces which ultimately overturned the Union and served as a model for those who would later subvert the Empire itself.

The nearest the British came to effectively binding Irish national ambitions to the Empire was through the medium of Home Rule. It is one of the more striking ironies of modern Irish politics that Ulster Unionists, who were for long the chief opponents of this creative notion, were to end up in 1920 accepting a form of Home Rule for the six counties of 'their' Northern Ireland. The irony is the more telling, given that the problems which Unionists predicted would flow from Home Rule (such as the unfair treatment of minorities) actually came to an ugly fruition in the devolved administration which they controlled from 1920 to 1972.

Northern Ireland under the Union has sustained some of the more elusive qualities of British rule over the whole island in the era before 1921. Like Ireland as a whole before 1921, Northern Ireland has been formally an integral part of the United Kingdom: like Ireland before 1921, Northern Ireland has been defined neither in fully metropolitan nor colonial terms. Despite occasional Unionist interest in the concept, Northern Ireland never became a Dominion, unlike the Irish Free State. On the other hand, despite its formal constitutional status as an integral element of the United Kingdom, it was always irremediably different from 'mainland' Britain. Its separate Parliament, party structure, civil service, and policing arrangements, ensured that (whatever the legal niceties) Northern Ireland would always seem an exceptionally odd outpost of the United Kingdom.

Indeed, whether or not contemporary Northern Ireland may meaningfully be seen as a colonial problem, its history exposes the repertoire of

British responses to the administration of its Empire. The Stormont years may be seen as an exemplar of colonial-style 'indirect rule', harnessing local élites to mediate between the people and the metropolitan power. After 1969, burdened by a broken and ineffective Unionist élite, the British sought to divide and rule. They have pursued counter-insurgency strategies with precedents in their earlier experience of decolonization and harnessed the skills of those responsible for policing and administering their departure from other territories. In Northern Ireland, as elsewhere, the British seem less concerned about withdrawal than about ensuring that any settlement—whatever its form—is publicly seen to reflect their planning and their wishes.

The ambiguities of Ireland's constitutional position in the nineteenth century were thus inherited by Northern Ireland in the twentieth century. These helped to foster a diverse, volatile, and unpredictable political culture and to propagate a rich inter-relationship with the Empire. Ireland and Northern Ireland have been both agents and victims of the Empire. They have helped to educate the British in their imperial role, yet they have also been subjected to the British experience of Empire.

It remains to be seen whether any settlement in Northern Ireland will successfully embody the accumulated wisdom of Britain's long imperial reign. It is perhaps suggestive that the most convincing recent prospect for a settlement reflects a European model of consociationalism rather than any direct colonial experience. It may be, therefore, that any imperial legacy will be seen more directly in the presentation of a settlement than in its substance. The safest gamble is surely on the likelihood that (as in British India and Africa) any final deal over British Ireland will be offered to world opinion as a reflection of the strategies and dignity of the imperial government.[47]

Select Bibliography

JUDITH M. BROWN and Wm. ROGER LOUIS, eds., *The Oxford History of the British Empire. Vol. IV: The Twentieth Century* (Oxford, 1999).

DAVID CANNADINE, *Ornamentalism: How the British Saw Their Empire* (London, 2001).

[47] Wm. Roger Louis, 'Introduction' and 'The Dissolution of Empire', in Judith M. Brown and Wm. Roger Louis, eds., *OHBE. Vol. IV. The Twentieth Century* (Oxford, 1999), pp. 34, 329.

SCOTT B. COOK, *Imperial Affinities: Nineteenth Century Analogies and Exchanges between India and Ireland* (New Delhi, 1993).

T. M. DEVINE, *Scotland's Empire, 1600–1815* (London, 2004).

KENT FEDEROWICH, 'The Problems of Disbandment: The Royal Irish Constabulary and Imperial Migration', *Irish Historical Studies*, XXX, 117 (May 1996), pp. 88–110.

T. G. FRASER, *Partition in Ireland, India and Palestine: Theory and Practice* (London, 1984).

DAVID HARKNESS, *The Restless Dominion: The Irish Free State and the British Commonwealth of Nations, 1921–1931* (London, 1969).

MICHAEL AND DENIS HOLMES, eds., *Ireland and India* (Dublin, 1997).

ALVIN JACKSON, *Ireland, 1798–1998: Politics and War* (Oxford, 1999).

—— *Home Rule: An Irish History, 1800–2000* (London, 2003).

KEITH JEFFERY, ed., *An Irish Empire?: Aspects of Ireland and the British Empire* (Manchester, 1996).

JOHN MACKENZIE, *Propaganda and Empire: The Manipulation of British Public Opinion, 1880–1960* (Manchester, 1984).

—— ed., *Imperialism and Popular Culture* (Manchester, 1986).

GILLIAN V. MCINTOSH, *The Force of Culture: Unionist Identities in Twentieth Century Ireland* (Cork, 1999).

DEIRDRE MCMAHON, *Republicans and Imperialists: Anglo-Irish Relations in the 1930s* (New Haven, 1984).

JAMES MURPHY, *Abject Loyalty: Nationalism and Monarchy in Ireland During the Reign of Queen Victoria* (Washington, 2001).

ANDREW PORTER, ed., *The Oxford History of the British Empire. Vol. III: The Nineteenth Century* (Oxford, 1999).

BERNARD PORTER, *The Absent-Minded Imperialists: Empire, Society and Culture in Britain* (Oxford, 2004).

SIMON POTTER, ed., *Newspapers and Empire in Ireland and Britain: Reporting the British Empire, 1857–1921* (Dublin, 2004).

STUART WARD, ed., *British Culture and the End of Empire* (Manchester, 2001).

WENDY WEBSTER, *Englishness and Empire, 1939–65* (Oxford, 2005).

YVONNE WHELAN, *Reinventing Modern Dublin: Streetscape, Iconography and the Politics of Identity* (Dublin, 2003).

6

Fiction and Empire: The Irish Novel

VERA KREILKAMP

Irish fiction has long been embedded in the discourse of Empire. In Ireland's first major novel, *Castle Rackrent* (1800), Maria Edgeworth memorably anticipated a successful Union with Britain; thereafter, a rapid succession of works obsessively circled around the Act of Union's failure to resolve the matter of Ireland's ambiguous colonial status. Commencing with the early 'national tale', this preoccupation with the failure of Union was deflected into the pessimism and ideologically loaded subjectivity of a Protestant Gothic fiction and then, in more sublimated forms, into the domestic sub-genre of the Big House novel. Multi-voiced, often fragmented, composed with shifting ideological stances by Catholic and Protestant, male and female, middle-class and Ascendancy writers alike, this fiction offers no uniform response to Ireland's political instability. The novels variously, and on occasion simultaneously, appear as repositories of British colonial assumptions and expressions of anti-British sentiment; as Orientalist descriptions of an exotic Celtic fringe and as patriotic marketing of a periphery to a metropolitan readership; as recurring interrogations of a troubled past; and, more recently, in John Banville's *Birchwood* (1973) and *The Newton Letter* (1982), as parodic responses to the fictional tropes generated by such historical obsessions. Irish fiction therefore resists easy incorporation into the standard binaries of postcolonial theory.

The nineteenth-century Irish novel's resistance to apolitical aestheticization effectively eliminated it from serious attention during the dominance of formalist criticism and a concomitant interest in revivalist literature in the mid-twentieth century. The destiny of much Irish poetry and drama—by, for example, W. B. Yeats, George Bernard Shaw, or Oscar Wilde—to be annexed into an apolitical canon of English literature, was never at issue for this fiction. The pre-Joycean Irish novel's fractured versions of English realism led to its marginalization, as its insistent representations of a divided society and exposures of failed imperial policies appeared to resist the integrative prescriptions of an Anglo-American literary canon. Even a more recent critic, Terry Eagleton, commenting on Ireland's failure to produce an integrative social novel in the tradition of George Eliot's *Middlemarch*, concludes that 'Irish history is too palpably ruptured, turbulent and discontinuous for the tropes of a sedate English evolutionism to take hold'.[1] Yet, in virtually all of these loose and baggy texts, questions of form cannot be separated from ideology; their fracturing of neo-classical ideals of conciliation, and of the generic conventions of English realism, can be seen as a precursor of twentieth-century modernism in Ireland's literature.

Irish critics of these novels have been no more receptive than their Anglo-American counterparts. In the 1890s, Stephen Gwynn saw the Irish novel as morbidly preoccupied with 'special pleading'; by 1931 Daniel Corkery accused Anglo-Irish authors of writing colonial 'traveller's tales' in non-native 'moulds' about a 'strange country' they were unable to enter imaginatively.[2] Even in 1985, a surviving discomfort with the Ascendancy sources of much of the nation's fiction led to sweeping judgements by one of Ireland's leading critics on 'the poverty of the Irish novelistic tradition'.[3] Only by the 1990s did post-Union fiction begin to garner the degree of attention that had previously been focused almost exclusively on Ireland's drama and poetry or on the modernist fiction of Joyce and Beckett. Critics and literary historians turned to the characteristic that had, seemingly, denied these novels previous attention: the historicity of their concerns and their insistent focus on Irish national identity within an imperial context.

The foundation for such a critical rediscovery had appeared as early as 1959, when Thomas Flanagan introduced his study of nineteenth-century Irish fiction with two summary chapters of colonial history, observing that whereas the English novelist was concerned with 'social choice and personal morality', the Irish writer was necessarily preoccupied with questions of 'race, creed and nationality'.[4] Although Flanagan failed to

---

[1] Terry Eagleton, 'Heathcliff and the Great Hunger', in Eagleton, *Heathcliff and the Great Hunger* (London, 1995), p. 7.

[2] Stephen Gwynn, *Irish Books and Irish People* (Dublin, 1919), p. 8; Daniel Corkery, *Synge and Anglo-Irish Literature* (Cork, 1931), pp. 7–8.

[3] Seamus Deane, 'The Literary Myths of the Revival', in Deane, *Celtic Revivals* (London, 1985), p. 32.

[4] Thomas Flanagan, *The Irish Novelists: 1800–1850* (New York, 1959), p. 35.

acknowledge any formal relationship between these novels and Joycean modernism, denying that this early fiction established lasting conventions for the representation of Irish life, his insistence that they be considered within an explicitly historical context anticipated the direction of future attention.[5] By 1987, Tom Dunne, influenced by Hayden White's work on narrativity, counselled a breakdown of disciplinary barriers, arguing that these novels exemplified 'the value of literature as historical evidence'.[6]

Influenced by postcolonial theory, critics increasingly emphasized the politically unresolved state of Ireland, which was central both to the thematic concerns and the formal characteristics of nineteenth-century fiction. Ireland's anxiously negotiated relationship with Britain and the Empire—as a potentially full but deficiently responsible partner, as a subordinated and inferior associate, or as an oppressed colonial subject—was to have far-reaching effects not only on the content, but on the very shape of these novels. This fiction became interesting as critics began, now unapologetically, to investigate its preoccupation with Ireland's fractious and unstable identity within Empire. Recent work has, for example, explored the novel's 'dizzyingly close-up perspective' to the parliamentary Act of Union, in which the texture of local political dialogue voices itself in fiction.[7] Investigations of the specialized Irish sub-genres arising from Ireland's colonial history—the national tale, Protestant Gothic fiction, the Big House novel and its reinventions—continue to redirect attention from the inadequacies to the innovations of these texts.[8] Significantly, this critical shift is occurring just as Commonwealth authors are undermining the dominance of English-language fiction produced in the home country, suggesting a growing acknowledgement by both an academic and a com-

---

[5] Ibid., p. 334.

[6] Tom Dunne, 'Fiction as "the best history of nations": Lady Morgan's Irish novels', in Dunne, ed., *The Writer as Witness: Literature as Historical Evidence* (Cork, 1987), p. 133.

[7] Claire Connolly, '"Completing the Union?" The Irish Novel and the Moment of the Union', in Michael Brown and Patrick Geoghean, eds., *The Irish Act of Union: Bicentenary Essays* (Dublin, 2003), pp. 157–75, quotation at 157.

[8] Katie Trumpener, *Bardic Nationalism: The Romantic Novel and the British Empire* (Princeton, 1997); M. J. McCormack, 'Irish Gothic and After', in Seamus Deane, ed., *The Field Day Anthology of Irish Writing*, 3 vols. (Derry, 1991), II, pp. 831–54; R. F. Foster, 'Protestant Magic: W. B. Yeats and the Spell of Irish History', in Foster, *Paddy & Mr Punch* (London, 1993), pp. 212–32; Vera Kreilkamp, *The Anglo-Irish Novel and the Big House* (Syracuse, NY, 1998); Otto Rauchbauer, ed., *Ancestral Voices: The Big House in Anglo-Irish Literature* (Dublin, 1992).

mercial publishing establishment of the English novel's indebtedness to Empire voices.[9]

Maria Edgeworth's *Castle Rackrent*, published in the same year as the Act of Union, simultaneously reveals and evades the nature of ongoing colonial misrule in Ireland. The body of the novel, a fast moving mini-epic depicting four generations of a landowning family's decline, is narrated through the voice of an ambivalently devoted Irish house servant, Thady Quirk, presented as a thoroughgoing exotic to British readers. Edgeworth's insistent ambivalence in this novel demonstrates not only an Ascendancy author's intimate, even voyeuristic, knowledge of this exotically conceived peasant narrator, but also her formidable textual strategies to control such subversive knowledge. The ill effects of a colonial Irish land policy, while never so identified, are carefully antedated as the lawless improvidence of a landowning class emphatically not 'of the present age'. By protectively locating the failures and fecklessness of the landowning Rackrents in the past, before the years of the Grattan Parliament and her own absentee family's return to their Irish estate in 1782, Edgeworth dissociates a programme of Enlightenment reform from the improvidence and rapacity that surrounded her in County Longford as she was writing the novel. The social origins of the doomed Rackrent landlords, whose rural pillage masquerades in the guise of a long defunct feudalism, are ambiguous; the family are presented as former O'Shaughlins ('related to the Kings of Ireland'), who, despite the novel's evasiveness on the issue, apparently turned Protestant to protect their property from confiscation during the penal era. The Rackrents thus embody a twofold significance: not only do they signal both native Irish and Ascendancy culpability for the dissolute state of Ireland's affairs, they also neatly deflect responsibility from the sectarian colonial conditions underpinning the relationship between the two islands prior to their anticipated union. Edgeworth's careful antedating of Rackrent improvidence in the full title of her tale—*An Hibernian Tale Taken From Facts, And From The Manners Of The Irish Squires Before The Year 1782*—effectively elides the ongoing friction of colonial land settlements and continuing settler-class neglect of Irish holdings. Her

---

[9] Since 1990, for example, the Booker Prize has been awarded to only five English novelists (one of them writing on the eighteenth-century slave trade), with the other awards going to authors from Australia, Canada, Ireland, India, Scotland, South Africa, and Nigeria.

stratagems, undertaken to assert Ireland's readiness for membership in a new Union, betray her anxious depiction of a society that, despite her professed optimism, would be represented as a semicolonial outpost in much subsequent Irish fiction.

Most provocatively, *Castle Rackrent* deploys difference: between the disorderly Ireland of its central narrative and the Enlightenment values of its intrusive 'editor'. Through the editorial frame, Edgeworth addresses her British readers in order to advance a programme of reconciliation anticipating the end of Irish colonial status and political union among equals. The novel's complex editorial apparatus includes a glossary destabilizing the narrative and a preface optimistically predicting Ireland's good-humoured 'complacency' after she 'loses her identity by an union with Great Britain'.[10] In its too insistent certainties, the preface reveals more than it asserts: not only the author's programmatic commitment to Irish reform under Union, but, given the tale she relates, her anxious doubts about such an Anglicized future. The preface's assertion of Ireland's full partnership in the approaching Union sits uneasily with Edgeworth's depiction of Rackrent collapse before, in Homi Bhabha's term, the 'sly civility' of the underclass retainer Thady Quirk, whose upwardly mobile son emerges as the triumphant native usurper of the landlord's property.[11] Thady's son Jason, a lawyer portrayed as an unscrupulous land-grabber, anticipates the Catholic middle class that would, in two centuries of subsequent fiction, bring down the Big House, the last vestige of imperial presence in the Irish countryside.

Edgeworth's ostensible misreading of Ireland's future in *Castle Rackrent's* editorial apparatus implies, rather, an anxious defusing of the threatening contemporary threat of 'loyal' Thady's narrative. Ireland's role within an alarmingly disordered colonial situation in the 1790s—when professed loyalties were rapidly shifting and the Edgeworth family would be threatened by the violence of 1798—suggests ample sources for the editorial insistence on Rackrent decline as 'tales of other times'.[12] But the editorial intrusions, in the form of the preface, epilogue, and long glossary notes explaining strange Irish customs and locutions to English readers, actually underscore an irreconcilability between two countries.

[10] Maria Edgeworth, *Castle Rackrent* in *Castle Rackrent and Ennui*, ed. Marilyn Butler (London, 1992), p. 63.

[11] Homi Bhabha, *The Location of Culture* (London, 1994), pp. 93–101.

[12] *Castle Rackrent*, p. 63.

This textual map of misreadings and miscognitions constituting colonial relations implicitly prefigures the failure of the Union that the preface optimistically anticipates.

Edgeworth's imaginings of colonial relations in the distant reaches of Empire reflect her strategies for reformed Anglo-Irish landlords at home, a theme amply developed in the three post-*Rackrent* Irish novels, *Ennui* (1809), *The Absentee* (1812), and *Ormond* (1817). In 'The Grateful Negro' (1802), an early short story set in Jamaica, Edgeworth transforms a threatening slave revolt into a moral exemplum: a benevolent West Indies plantation owner, much resembling the ideal landlord of her later Irish fiction, offers his slaves practical inducements to self-improvement.[13] Writing about West Indies society little more than a decade after the bloody slave rebellion in San Domingo and only four years after 1798, Edgeworth optimistically asserts that ruling-class paternalism will thwart irrational stirrings toward rebellion. By the 1830s that optimism had dissipated. '[I]t is impossible to draw Ireland as she now is in a book of fiction', Edgeworth observed in a much-cited passage, 'realities are too strong, party passions too violent to bear to see, or care to look at their faces in the looking-glass. The people would only break the glass, and curse the fool who held the mirror up to nature—distorted nature, in a fever'.[14]

This passage appears in a letter of 1834 to Edgeworth's brother Michael Pakenham Edgeworth, an imperial administrator in India. Commenting on her brother's task of collecting rents and revenues, Edgeworth admires his 'generous indignation against oppression', believing that the disputes he must settle on the subcontinent are related to those facing her at Edgeworthstown, the family seat in County Longford. In subsequently asserting that both of them must, in his words, protect the 'poor peasant with his vile trash' from despotic rule, she implicitly joins her goals at home with those of benevolent, if condescending, imperial administrators elsewhere in the British Empire. By the 1830s, however, Ireland's recalcitrance to imperial policy had moved beyond Edgeworth's comprehension. In *Ennui*, her only novel explicitly to confront the fearful trauma of 1798, she had envisioned a native people as simple, misguided, and

---

[13] Edgeworth's source was Bryan Edwards, *The History, Civil and Commercial, of the British Colonies in the West Indies*, second edn. (London, 1794).

[14] Maria Edgeworth to Michael Pakenham Edgeworth, 19 Feb. 1834, in Augustus J. C. Hare, ed., *The Life and Letters of Maria Edgeworth*, 2 vols. (Boston, 1894), II, p. 550.

easily deterred rebels, wholly unlike the well-disciplined participants in O'Connell's agitation for Catholic Emancipation. Jason Quirk, her earliest and darkest premonition of a native Irish presence that might challenge colonial property settlements, had by 1834 cast his shadow on a rapidly changing landscape Edgeworth had abandoned as material for fiction.

The early nineteenth-century national tale after *Castle Rackrent* intervenes in the discourses surrounding the vexed failures of the post-Union decades, with the fiction of Sydney Owenson and Charles Maturin offering insistent readings of Ireland's savage colonial past that Edgeworth largely elides. Although Dublin was clearly no cultural wasteland after 1800, publishing houses had followed Parliament to London and novels were increasingly directed toward English readerships.[15] In the typical national tale, Ireland is perceived as an insufficiently integrated member of the new partnership; thus the English novel's domestic marriage plot resurfaces in a narrative of successful or failed union between Irish and English or cosmopolitan lovers. Existing as a problem that must be explained and represented for England by a mediating voice between reader and subject, Ireland is alternatively disorderly or exotic, often burdened (for Maria Edgeworth) or enriched (for Sydney Owenson) by its traditional past. Both Owenson and Maturin draw on the trope of the Romantic sublime to explain and justify Ireland's recalcitrance in the face of the Union, a stratagem reinforced in Maturin's case by his deployment of increasingly sensationalist Gothic motifs.

National tales explicitly present themselves as political interventions rather than simply as representations of Irish society. Not only do they, as one critic observes, engage in 'marketing the Celtic fringe to the London reading public', they also make extensive claims for a grievously misunderstood and misgoverned neighbour.[16] Although in its explanatory paratext, *Castle Rackrent* loosely approximates the genre, a full-blown version appears six years later with Owenson's immediately popular *The Wild Irish Girl: A National Tale* (1806). Writing in a period of considerable fear about Napoleonic expansion, Owenson forces her readers to acknowledge

---

[15] Terry Eagleton, 'Form and Ideology in the Anglo-Irish Novel,' in Eagleton, *Heathcliff and the Great Hunger*, p. 201; Joep Leerssen, *Remembrance and Imagination: Patterns in the Historical and Literary Representation of Ireland in the Nineteenth Century* (Cork, 1996), p. 33.

[16] Miranda J. Burgess, 'Violent Translations: Allegory, Gender, and Cultural Nationalism in Ireland, 1796–1806', *Modern Language Quarterly*, 59 (March 1998), p. 34.

Britain's, no less than France's, growing commitment to empire-building. After decades of critical marginalization, this hybrid text of novel, romance, and political propaganda is rapidly attaining canonical status in the Irish literature classroom. Moreover, Owenson's career trajectory from author of Irish national tales to works concerning the struggle for autonomy in Greece and Belgium, as well as India, marks her as an early and geographically expansive anti-imperial novelist.

In *The Wild Irish Girl*, Owenson describes the visit of an absentee landlord from London to his family holding on the far western Celtic periphery, her tale serving as a guide to centuries of British misrule and suppression of Gaelic Ireland. Unlike *Castle Rackrent* or Edgeworth's three subsequent Irish works written in a far more novelistic register, *The Wild Irish Girl* emphasizes rather than suppresses or distances the brutal trauma of a recent colonial history and writes Ireland centrally into the discourse of Empire. Retrospectively, in 1846, Owenson described her early work as an 'account of her country's wrongs' and included evidence for the 'testimony of its truthfulness', implicitly asserting that its representations must be viewed as authentic history, not mere imaginative literature.[17] Significantly, in the year of her death the *Athenaeum* remembered Owenson as 'less a woman of the pen than a patriot and a partizan. Her books were battles'.[18]

Owenson's defence of a noble and victimized Gaelic Ireland, like Edmund Burke's championing of an aristocratic Indian society in the Warren Hastings trial of 1788–95, protests against the wider cultural depredations of empire-building. In the figure of the Irish girl Glorvina, a traditional society that the visiting protagonist's Cromwellian ancestors sought to destroy becomes an object of desire rather than abhorrence, ridicule, or fear. Shifts between the text's romance, novelistic, and propagandistic registers appear most obviously in its supplementarity, whereby a digressive paratext insistently interrupts and augments the narrative with historical data culled from eighteenth-century antiquarianism.

---

[17] Sydney Owenson, Appendix: Prefatory address to the 1946 edition, in her *The Wild Irish Girl: A National Tale*, ed., Claire Connolly and Stephen Copley (London, 2000), pp. 246–48. Owenson also published under the name Lady Morgan.

[18] Review of Lady Morgan's *Passages from My Autobiography*, *Athenaeum*, 15 Jan. 1859, p. 73, quoted in Ina Ferris, 'Writing on the Border: The National Tale, Female Writing, and the Public Sphere', in Tilottama Rajan and Julia M. Wright, eds., *Romanticism, History, and the Possibilities of Genre* (Cambridge, 1998), p. 87.

Unlike *Castle Rackrent*, where ironic versions of Irish cultural traditions are relegated to the notes—or, as in Edgeworth's later Irish novels, generally deflected into peripheral characterizations—*The Wild Irish Girl* is organized around Owenson's championing of Gaelic Ireland through the recuperation of national origins in an antiquarian past. Her politics earned enduring hostility from the post-Union Tory establishment, most notoriously through the sustained attacks of the London-based Irish critic, John Wilson Croker.[19] In her literary interventions into contemporary politics, Owenson anticipates the negotiations of the late-century Literary Revival, which again identified and inverted traditional readings of those cultural markers distinguishing England from its Irish periphery.

The astonishment of the imperial visitor before the supposedly uncivil colony is characteristic of the trans-border national tale. Suddenly the tourist or stranger in Ireland, typically a deracinated absentee, discovers the deficiencies of his metropolitan stereotypes: for example, that the Irish chieftain and his family sat in a state of 'perfect nudity' around their fire, that neo-classical Dublin is a city scenically and architecturally inferior to sprawling London, that the 'barbarous' Irish lack refinement and culture. Through the visitor's transformative experiences, Owenson and subsequent authors of national tales invoke the psychically disorienting power of cultural encounter in novels of Empire.[20] The visiting English protagonist Mortimer, in *The Wild Irish Girl*, learns that that the cordoned-off Irish periphery that he initially dismissed as primitive offers a genuine civility he must acknowledge if the brutality of a past colonial history is to be redressed, if union is to occur in more than name. A process of education, eventually including study of the Irish language and antiquarian history in Mortimer's case, leads the English protagonist of this and other national tales, such as those by Maturin and John Banim, into visions of new identity: 'I raised my eyes to the castle of Inismore,' as Owenson's narrator puts it, 'and sighed and almost wished I had been born the lord of these beautiful ruins...the adored Chieftain of these affectionate and natural people'.[21]

---

[19] Claire Connolly, '"I accuse Miss Owenson": *The Wild Irish Girl* as Media Event', *Colby Quarterly*, 36, 2 (2000), pp. 98–113.

[20] Ina Ferris, 'Narrating Cultural Encounter: Lady Morgan and the Irish National Tale', *Nineteenth-Century Literature*, 51 (Dec. 1996), pp. 287–303.

[21] Owenson, *Wild Irish Girl*, p. 50.

Owenson's national tale simultaneously exoticizes and integrates a Celtic periphery that would, in the explicit Edgeworth programme of reform, be rationally Anglicized into Union. Neither eliding nor sublimating the disruptive claims of that surviving society, the text strives to resituate a seemingly archaic fringe centrally into European culture—most strategically through a series of comparisons between the Celts and the Greeks, but also through a portrayal of Glorvina as at once the embodiment of a remote and exotic heritage and the reader of the most advanced European literature. Such stratagems arise from Owenson's responsiveness to ties between Gaelic and continental culture throughout the seventeenth and eighteenth centuries, not simply to an early nineteenth-century Romanticism's transformation of the 'primitive' into the authentic and original. Thus the Irish colonial subject embodies a bewildering complexity of cultural forms to the visiting Englishman, always invoking Ireland's historical ties to continental Europe, which embraces two centuries of military service and Catholic education for Irish exiles. Owenson's fiction reflects the resulting pressures toward cosmopolitanism: Glorvina's chaplain and erudite instructor, Father John, has studied in France, and the protagonists of subsequent novels, *O'Donnel* and *The O'Briens and the O'Flahertys*, have fought with Irish brigades on the continent.

Owenson's exoticizing of Gaelic Ireland does not simply reflect her orientalizing of a subject people, for any straightforward postcolonial hypothesis about such strategies needs significant complication in view of the island's colonial history. Ireland's exoticism emerges, in part, from Owenson's deployment of theories of Empire concocted by eighteenth-century antiquarianism, the tradition by which Anglo-Ireland's intellectuals first began to build cultural connections with a native Celtic society. In the hermetic modes of that speculative enterprise, operating always in the context of destroyed or missing records, national origin was investigated—and invented—by recourse to ancient systems, most commonly etymological or biblical. Such scholarship led, for example, to the Phoenician model of ancestry favoured by late eighteenth-century Patriots. Antiquarians identified Ireland's prehistory with that of other lost civilizations and particularly with the Carthaginians destroyed by the brutally ascendant Roman Empire, itself the ancient precursor of Britain. The Phoenician hypothesis, identifying Ireland's ancestry with a highly developed culture, reversed the Anglocentric equation of Irish barbarity against English civility. This pseudo-history was cited as late as 1907 when James Joyce claimed Oriental origins for the Irish language.[22] In such a context, Owenson's modes of registering Gaelic society as strangely foreign and always exotic—on occasion through eastern metaphors whereby Glorvina is compared to an Egyptian girl in a passage that gives the Irish woman's veil 'Oriental' sources—represents an argument for an internationalist colonized culture unbound by island geography, and not simply, as much postcolonial criticism would have it, an example of an orientalizing or 'othering' of the periphery.[23]

In the most transparent readings of Owenson's national tale, the concluding marriage between the wild Irish girl and her English lover promises a new legitimacy of rule, now based on fusion of the legal claims of Cromwellian conquest with the traditional legitimacies of an older Gaelic order.[24] Darker possibilities intrude, however, to complicate such reconciling readings, threatening presentiments developed most fully in Charles Maturin's Gothic national tales. Waking into consciousness in *The Wild Irish Girl*, Mortimer momentarily perceives the beautiful Glorvina as a 'horrid spectre', with the head of a 'Gorgon', a suggestive foreboding of a Dracula-like return of the colonial repressed to the imperial British subject postulated by recent critical formulations of a Protestant Gothic tradition in Irish fiction.[25] In Maturin's *The Milesian Chief*, where the terror of cultural clash overwhelms any pressure toward accommodation or reconciliation, a female visitor to Ireland recognizes that the scenes she witnesses are like that of a 'new world' and 'shudder[s] at the idea of being the inhabitant of such a country', even as she feels 'the wild transforming effect of its scenery'.[26]

The sublimity of Owenson's Celtic fringe, turbulent, craggy, and always disorienting to the visitor, underscores the island's exoticism and remoteness from more domesticated English settings. Despite *The Wild Irish Girl*'s seeming resolution in spiritual and romantic union between two

---

[22] Leerssen, *Remembrance and Imagination*, pp. 70–77; James Joyce, 'Ireland, Island of Saints and Sages', in Ellsworth Mason and Richard Ellmann, eds., *The Critical Writings of James Joyce* (New York, 1959), p. 156.

[23] For the major argument on Owenson's 'orientalism', see Joseph W. Lew, 'Sidney Owenson and the Fate of Empire', *Keats-Shelley Journal*, XXXIX (1990), pp. 39–65.

[24] See Robert Tracy, 'Maria Edgeworth and Lady Morgan: Legality versus Legitimacy', in Tracy, *The Unappeasable Host: Studies in Irish Identities* (Dublin, 1998), pp. 25–40.

[25] Owenson, *Wild Irish Girl*, p. 58.

[26] Charles Robert Maturin, *The Milesian Chief*, 4 vols. (New York, 1978), I, p. 55.

countries, its construction of this western landscape, unlike Edgeworth's more typical settings in the midlands, implies the resistance of the periphery to imperial assimilation and control. As a central locale of the Irish national tales by Owenson, Maturin, and Banim, the Atlantic seacoast here appears as a region frozen into a past which defies British modernity. This notion of an ancient and aristocratic Celtic locale, fixed in its traditional values, was revived and variously developed later in the century by writers as disparate as Ernest Renan, Matthew Arnold, John Millington Synge, and W. B. Yeats and by painters such as Paul Henry, Charles Lamb, and Seán Keating in the early decades of the Irish Free State. Although cultural historians generally place the construction of 'the West'—authentic, uncorrupted, and Celtic—in the period of the Literary Revival, early stirrings of such regional iconicization emerge already in the national tale's deployment of sublime scenery and architecture as the agent of personal transformation.[27] Resituated and darker versions of such disorienting spaces were to reappear in later Empire fiction by Rider Haggard and Joseph Conrad or in Bram Stoker's Transylvania, thus becoming a staple of colonial exotica and terror.

For Owenson and Maturin, the western landscape, unlike those oral and written traditions forcibly suppressed by centuries of colonization, endured as emotive text attesting both to imperial depredation and national resistance. Related, certainly, to the mouldering castles, glowering weather, and precipitous cliffs of the Gothic, settings in the national tale can merge a distant Milesian prehistory with the more recent Cromwellian and United Irish past. Like the cultural topography of Rome or Greece, Irish landscape was to become incorporated into late-eighteenth and nineteenth-century travel itineraries, attracting visitors as diverse in their interests as Arthur Young, John Carr, Thomas Carlyle, William Thackeray, or Chevalier de Latocnaye. Influenced by Edmund Burke's *A Philosophical Inquiry into the Origins of Our Ideas on the Sublime and Beautiful* (1757), a major text for eighteenth-century landscape aesthetics, tourists followed well-travelled routes to the spectacular natural settings of Wicklow, Killarney, the Boyne Valley, northern Antrim, and Connemara. They turned as well to ruined castles and abbeys and other markers of decay,

---

[27] See, for example, Catherine Nash, '"Embodying the Nation"—The West of Ireland Landscape and Irish Identity,' in Barbara O'Connor and Michael Cronin, eds., *Tourism in Ireland: A Critical Analysis* (Cork, 1993), pp. 86–112.

thus seemingly drawing Ireland into the generalized decay-of-empire discourse of Romanticism.[28]

Efforts to gather more recent remains—those abbeys and churches transformed into ruins by the Cromwellian invasions or the confiscations following 1798—into Romanticism's pleasurably sublime imagery of human mortality and historical oblivion, however, become complicated in the national tale, where popular ruin discourse is simultaneously deployed and deconstructed.[29] Thus, Constantin François de Volney's anticolonial invocation to past civilizations, *The Ruins, or Meditations on the Revolutions of Empires* (1791), is textually inscribed into novels by both Owenson and Maturin, but in ways that explicitly reposition such Romantic ruin speech into a specific and local political context. In the national tale, abandoned castles, abbeys, and monasteries—as well as the Bank of Ireland, occupying Dublin's former Parliament—are corrosive daily reminders of local and recent loss, and less frequently, occasions for the pleasing melancholy of the Romantic aesthetic, which reads in the ruins of Empire inscriptions of a universal mortality or a more heroic past.

Initially, ruins of lost grandeur can indeed summon forth a historically unspecific but transformative sense of 'pastness', as in the popular Romantic fall-of-empire discourse. Thus, early in his process of transformation, the visitor Mortimer, viewing the ruined castle sheltering the Milesian Prince of Inismore, observes 'I felt like the being of some other sphere newly alight on a distant orb'.[30] In contracting centuries of history into single epiphanic moments, Owenson's text itself approximates the aestheticized ruin landscape which her visitor's ecstasy invokes as agent of evolution from absentee to Irishman. But in Charles Maturin's *The Milesian Chief*, a bloody tale of doomed revolution in the wake of 1798, the dispossessed hero's castle, ancient abbey, and family burial ground emphatically exist for him solely as markers of personal and local loss at the hands of recent imperial depredation. When Armida, the young cosmopolitan visitor to Ireland, invokes such Atlantic coast spectacle as part of a Romantic European ruin culture, her fierce admirer (loyal son of the ancient family

---

[28] P. J. Duffy, 'The Changing Rural Landscape, 1750–1850: Pictorial Evidence', in Raymond Gillespie and Brian P. Kennedy, eds., *Ireland: Art into History* (Dublin, 1994), pp. 30–31.

[29] The fullest discussion of the deployment of ruins in nineteenth-century Irish fiction and Maturin's transformation of the national tale into an Irish Gothic appears in Ina Ferris, *The Romantic National Tale and The Question of Ireland* (Cambridge, 2002), pp. 102–26.

[30] Owenson, *Wild Irish Girl*, p. 49.

her father has dispossessed) resists any aestheticizing of his country's history. Her recitation from Volney's radical address to the nameless ruins of Empire is termed 'melancholy without passion, and without remembrance.... But here is a local genius...I feel who lies below; every step I take awakes the memory of him on whose tomb I tread'.[31]

The national tale's political deployment of terrifyingly sublime settings to invoke specific historical loss under imperialism, and, increasingly with Maturin, the doomed resistance of a dispossessed culture, differs from a more depoliticized landscape tradition in Irish visual art during the same period. The popularity of settings of Killarney or Wicklow in eighteenth and early nineteenth-century Irish painting suggests that the country's artists, generally forced abroad for patronage or commissions, were dependent on London's conventions and painted as Englishmen for patrons and élite customers. Artists such as George Barret or Thomas Roberts created typically Romantic craggy mountains, waterfalls, and cliffs alluding to a Burkean sublime, but without invoking the nationalist resistance that Owenson's and Maturin's fiction identified with the Irish landscape. For example, Barret's famous view of a popular tourist site on a Wicklow demesne—A View of Powerscourt Waterfall (1764)—introduces an early Romantic tradition, to be developed by William Ashford and Thomas Roberts, whereby natural scenes were depicted within the controlled prospects of the Ascendancy demesnes. Such imagery, as well as later nineteenth-century paintings by James Arthur O'Connor or George Petrie's watercolours of medieval ruins informed by his antiquarian background, demonstrate the influence of Romantic conventions on Irish artists, but reveal far less development of any politicized visual tradition in a country with few customers for the nationalist artist.[32] Only rarely, as with O'Connor's provocatively subversive midnight landscape The Poachers (1835) or Daniel Maclise's extraordinary staging of his image The Installation of Captain Rock (1834) in an abbey destroyed by Cromwell, did visual artists gesture toward or explicitly engage with political matter.[33] Painting for élite audiences in a developing market economy, early nineteenth-century Irish artists generally avoided those

[31] Maturin, Milesian Chief, I, pp. 186–87.

[32] Fintan Cullen, Visual Politics: The Representation of Ireland, 1750–1930 (Cork, 1997), p. 41.

[33] Luke Gibbons, '"Between Captain Rock and a Hard Place": Art and Agrarian Insurgency', in Tadhg Foley and Seán Ryder, eds., Ideology and Ireland in the Nineteenth Century (Dublin, 1998), pp. 23–44.

particularized exposures of Empire's depredations that figure so prominently in the national tale.

The absentee landlord, homeless both in Ireland and in the imperial capital, is a persistent figure in Irish fiction. Living off his Irish property yet insisting on an English identity even as he faces marginalization in London society, the colonial absentee remains at the centre of Empire discourse in Irish fiction well into the twentieth century. Writing in the eighteenth century, Jonathan Swift had described this figure as a rapacious parasite: 'But all turn Leasers to that Mongril breed/who from thee sprung, yet on thy Vitals feed;/Who to yon rav'nous Isle thy Treasures bear,/And waste in Luxury thy Harvests there'.[34] The absentee's recurring appearance in Edgeworth's last three Irish novels and persistence in major works by Owenson, Maturin, Banim, William Carleton, Charles Lever, and Charles Kickham—and in more allegorical forms in the Gothic fiction of Sheridan Le Fanu and Bram Stoker—suggest the complex relationships between historical and fictional narratives. In Irish fiction, beginning with Edgeworth's recurring focus on the theme, absenteeism becomes a marker of estrangement, signifying the colonial landlord's rootlessness and his fractured relationship with his tenants. At home neither in England nor in Ireland, he remains an alienated figure, ridiculed in London for his brogue, despised in Ireland for dispossessing ancient Milesian families or for allowing his unscrupulous agent to rackrent the tenancy.

Yet the widespread literary deployment of the absentee suggests how historical situations can be exploited by novelists not simply to register specific contemporary abuse, but also to ward off more radical criticism of a colonial land policy. Unlike the benevolent landlord in English country-house poetry or great house portraiture, the figure of the delinquent absentee dominates Irish fiction, existing as a symbol of distance rather than nurturing propinquity.[35] He searches for ready cash rather than community, living far from a peripheral world that exists for him solely as a source of income for his deracinated metropolitan life. Social historians have established that absenteeism decreased significantly in the eighteenth century, yet cultural representations of the land settlements underlying Irish colonial history are best judged not as a mirror of reality, but as a

---

[34] Jonathan Swift, *Poetical Works*, ed. Herbert Davis (London, 1967), pp. 116–17.
[35] Carole Fabricant, *Swift's Landscape* (Baltimore, 1982), p. 106.

formative intervention into it.[36] Novelists made use of absenteeism as a complex symbolic representation of the historical narrative of colonial land settlements: on occasion, certainly, as criticism of such policy, but just as commonly as a recurring motif deployed by Catholic and Protestant writers alike for thwarting a more revolutionary critique of those very policies. In novels by Edgeworth, Owenson, Banim, and Carleton, the severest hostility is repeatedly displaced from the distant landlord, who is generally depicted as capable of reform, to the nearby bailiff or agent.

Despite the rapidly shifting political landscape of the 1820s and the emergence of major fiction about the Catholic peasant or more prosperous farmer class by writers such as William Carleton and John Banim, the rootless Anglo-Irish figure survived as a marker of fractured identity well into the century. Published on the brink of Catholic emancipation, John Banim's novel *The Anglo-Irish of the Nineteenth Century* (1828) offers a compelling portrait of one such Irishman, a hybrid product of Empire, who despite his Cambridge education and friends in the highest circles of the British government, lives in London under the humiliating shadow of his native roots. Publishing this work anonymously, Banim wrote with corrosive satire about his protagonist Gerald Blount's fear of being identified with his too noisy, contentious, or indecorous fellow countrymen in London. Gerald vows to visit Ireland only when, in the words of one of his guardians, its inhabitants 'cease to be merely Irish, and become, like the only proportion of it who are now respectable, intelligent—ay, or civilized,—"English Irish"'.[37] Later, upon identifying himself in Paris as 'English Irish', however, he is mockingly informed that such a nationality can generate only laughter or contempt: 'Have you a country at all . . . or is your country so unworthy that you grow ashamed of it?'[38]

Banim's portrayal of his fellow countrymen in London—not just his alienated protagonist, but a crew of jingoistic Anglo-Irish hangers-on who surround him and the literary and political émigrés scratching for influence in the metropolis—suggests a London-based novelist's bitter recognition of the dangers confronting Irish artists seeking audiences or patronage abroad. Visual artists and writers such as Oliver Goldsmith, Richard Sheridan, Nathaniel Hone, or James Barry in the eighteenth

[36] L. M. Cullen, *An Economic History of Ireland Since 1660*, second edn. (London, 1987), p. 83.
[37] John Banim, *The Anglo-Irish of the Nineteenth Century*, 3 vols. (New York, 1978), I, p. 23.
[38] Ibid., II, p. 23.

century and James Arthur O'Connor, Gerald Griffin, or Banim himself in
the early nineteenth, exist as representative colonial types, displaced
figures often facing anti-Irish sentiment in London and unemployment
and alienation at home. These outsiders, no less than the displaced native
chiefs that Owenson and Maturin invent as doomed Romantic heroes in
their national tales, suggest early sources for the central theme of psychic
exile in Irish modernism. The portrayal of Gerald Blount's life in London
anticipates the early twentieth-century writer's imagining of rootless Irishmen—for example, Joyce's sardonic rewriting of himself, not just in
Stephen Dedalus, but also in the joint characters of Little Chandler/Galla-
her in *Dubliners*—as internal or external migrants, homeless aliens both in
Dublin and London.[39]

For a Catholic Irish writer such as Banim, however, writing amidst the
clamorous claims of Daniel O'Connell's emancipation campaign, the Irish
question had shifted beyond Ascendancy control. Thus, his controlling
pessimism about colonial relations is improbably tempered by an imposition of the national tale's romance plot of reconciliation on *The Anglo-
Irish of the Nineteenth Century*. Deposited on Ireland's shore in a shipwreck, Gerald is reformed into the category of 'mere Irish'; he marries an
Irishwoman whose father contributes to the process of thrusting him into
a new identity by terming the Union an 'atrocious act' rather than preach-
ing conciliation.[40] In the face of O'Connell's mobilization of hundreds of
thousands of Irish Catholics for emancipation, Ireland's role within
Empire is now unconvincingly represented by the national tale's allegory
of romance between two former enemies. Thus, *The Anglo-Irish of the
Nineteenth Century* works more effectively as an ethnological disquisition
and nationalist assertion than as a convincing romance plot of reconciliation. Its most sympathetic character predicts not reconciliation, but independence for Ireland and the collapse of Union. England's 'unsuccessful
experiment of eight hundred years' must culminate in a genuine freedom
in which Ireland's 'real people' will wrest control from the 'sojourning
strangers'.[41] Anticipating by almost three-quarters of a century Yeats's
description of English settlers as 'strangers in the house' in the iconic
revivalist text 'Cathleen Ni Houlihan', Banim's novel signals the growing

---

[39] For varied perspectives on this Irish figure, see, for example, R. F. Foster, 'Marginal Men
and Micks on the Make: The Uses of Irish Exile', in Foster, *Paddy and Mr Punch*, pp. 281–305;
Terry Eagleton, 'Home and Away', in his *Crazy John and the Bishop* (Cork, 1998), pp. 212–48.
[40] Banim, *Anglo-Irish*, III, p. 112.   [41] Ibid., pp. 120–21.

irrelevance of a literary genre that had, in many of its permutations, adopted metaphors of romance to gesture toward a genuine Union.[42] In post-Famine novels, the growing consequences of Union's failures become the darkening background for Irish life.

Ireland's ambiguous status as a subordinate component of an ostensibly United Kingdom generated a variety of fictional forms throughout the post-Union period in addition to the national tale. These included not only political and explicitly historical novels preoccupied with present and past Empire relations, but also a Gothic subgenre reaching its early dark apogee in the work of Charles Maturin.[43] This turn to the Gothic, apparent in the settings of many national tales and subsequent domestic Big House novels, reflects the fears of an increasingly beleaguered Ascendancy society, trapped in overbuilt but decaying homes, surrounded by a newly resurgent Catholic nationalism, and forced to confront its failure to win native Irish allegiance.[44] Thus, even in his international Gothic tour de force, *Melmoth, the Wanderer* (1820), situated largely in Italy, Spain, India, and the South Seas, Maturin anchors a phantasmagoria of sectarian and sado-masochistic violence in a decaying Irish Protestant Big House. There, a dying landlord cries out in terror of his approaching impoverishment at the hands of his tenants, and an ancestral absentee assumes the role of lurid satanic protagonist. Such a framing strategy underscores how the Protestant Gothic emerges from the declining position of the country's Anglo-Irish élite, which has managed to hold on to much of the island's property until the late-century land Acts but is already obsessed by premonitions of future loss.

The Irish Gothic novel stylistically and thematically encodes the sublimated anxieties of a colonial class preoccupied with the corrupt sources of its power. These novels create a range of demonic protagonists, doomed satanic villains who both exploit and rage against authority; they are explicitly identified as Irish landlords by Maturin, Le Fanu, and Somerville

---

[42] William Butler Yeats, 'Cathleen Ni Houlihan', in Yeats, *Collected Plays* (New York, 1953), p. 53.

[43] For a study of the historical novel, see James M. Cahalan, *Great Hatred, Little Room: The Irish Historical Novel* (Syracuse, NY, 1983).

[44] M. J. McCormack, 'Irish Gothic and After,' in Seamus Deane, ed., *The Field Day Anthology of Irish Writing*, 3 vols. (Derry, 1991), II, pp. 832–54; Foster, 'Protestant Magic', pp. 212–32; Eagleton, 'Form and Ideology', pp. 187–99.

and Ross; even Bram Stoker's *Dracula* has recently been incorporated into that company by Seamus Deane.[45] Maturin's *Melmoth, the Wanderer,* Le Fanu's *Uncle Silas* (1864), Somerville and Ross's *An Irish Cousin* (1889), and Stoker's *Dracula* (1897) deploy traditional Gothic motifs to invoke nineteenth-century Anglo-Ireland's growing obsession with miscegenation, racial pollution, and cultural decline. Examples include settings in decaying or terrifying manor houses, lodges, or castles; sadistic threats against or actual sexual violation of helpless young women; or preoccupations with disinherited heirs and lost wills, the missing documentation of a threatened patrimony.[46]

Far too much has been made of the great silence in Irish literature between the Famine and the Literary Revival. Despite the waning of the national tale, the darkening ideological framing of Anglo-Irish relations in the post-Famine era continued to produce novels preoccupied with Ireland's troubled role within Empire, not only in the rich strain of Gothic fiction—for example, William Carleton's renditions of rural Catholic life—but also in a less frequently discussed body of realistic political fiction by Charles Lever. Lever's late political novels, written like Joyce's fiction from a self-imposed continental exile, envision Ireland as a sort of internal colony, whose Otherness disconcertingly resembles *and* differs from England; thus already exhibiting those ambiguous imperial conditions that Fredric Jameson has identified as the source of Irish modernism in Joyce's Dublin.[47] Although strikingly un-modernist in any formal sense, Lever's multi-volume Victorian novels similarly convey Ireland's simultaneous existence as backwater colony and imperial player beyond its island borders. Settings in these novels incorporate Ascendancy Dublin, London, and cosmopolitan Europe. They depict, as well, rural Ireland's abject tenant poverty and Big House opulence. The wide range of characters captures the same duality: on the one hand, young Ascendancy graduates of Trinity and Oxford, politicians at Dublin Castle, absentee landowners on the continent, and Irishmen destined for imperial service in India; on

---

[45] Deane, *Strange Country,* p. 90 characterizes Dracula, who brings his boxes of native earth with him to London, as an absentee landlord 'running out of soil'.

[46] See, for example, Stephen D. Arata, 'The Occidental Tourist: *Dracula* and the Anxiety of Reverse Colonization', *Victorian Studies,* 33 (Summer 1990), pp. 627–34.

[47] Fredric Jameson, 'Modernism and Imperialism', in Seamus Deane, ed., *Nationalism, Colonialism and Literature* (Minneapolis, 1990), p. 44; Eagleton, 'Form and Ideology', p. 154; Luke Gibbons, *Transformations in Irish Culture* (Cork, 1996), p. 6; Declan Kiberd, *Irish Classics* (Cambridge, Mass., 2001), p. xiii.

the other, starving peasants, middle-class Catholic merchants, dispossessed chieftains in their decaying strongholds, rebels in the mountains, republicans at the barricades in Paris.

Within this ambiguous colonial context, Lever focuses relentlessly on social incoherence and breakdown. In *The O'Donoghue* (1845), a parodic version of Edgeworth's reforming landlord appears as a benevolent returned absentee whose inept attempts to rehabilitate the lives of his impoverished tenants succeed only in undermining the patterns of a traditional culture. In the same novel, a young Irishman converts to Protestantism, marries the daughter of the English owner of his family's bankrupted land, and becomes a colonial judge in India, even as the fall of his improvident Irish family suggests cultural loss and national decline. In Edgeworth's *Ennui*, India had appeared, in Marilyn Butler's phrase, simply as a 'moral trampoline', a place where an admirable young man without a large inheritance could exercise his morality and 'get the kudos of turning a bad old world into a brave new one'.[48] In a novel published almost half a century later, Lever responds far more ambivalently to an Irishman's imperial service abroad. The Anglicized younger O'Donoghue's vocation as a colonial administrator—bringing imperial justice to darker-skinned 'natives' than those at home—reflects the historical role played by members of an Anglo-Irish aristocracy, gentry, and professional middle class in India.[49] Later novels, by Somerville and Ross, for example, note service in the Empire as routine employment for the ironically viewed scions of the Big House, denied purposeful vocation at home,[50] but in *The O'Donoghue*, the young Irishman's choice signals personal ambition and the abandonment of an intractable internal colony by its traditional families.

Deeply conservative in his devotion to the feudal pieties and 'old ties' he envisions as once sustaining Irish society, Lever attacks the breakdown of social coherence in Ireland with a ubiquitously directed moral indignation. In his novels, responsibility for the country's inexorable decline from a Union putatively assuring traditional social bonds, rests equally upon the failures of arrogant Anglo-Irish landlords, self-serving middle-class Catholic upstarts, and conniving Dublin Castle politicians. *The Martins of*

---

[48] Butler, Introduction to *Castle Rackrent and Ennui*, p. 45.
[49] See chap. 4 of this volume, pp. 101–112.
[50] For example, *The Real Charlotte* (1894) or *The Big House of Inver* (1925).

Cro' Martin (1854), charting the collapse of a vast feudal property, improbably finds heroism in a successful Catholic politician who separates himself from O'Connellism and worships the memory of the fading Big House, even as the novel exposes the improvidence and arrogance of that symbol of imperial control. In *Lord Kilgobbin* (1872), Lever's last and darkest novel, a Viceroy is chosen for his post only because he knows nothing about Ireland, and the head of an ancient Celtic family speaks of a visiting Englishman with ironic bemusement: 'He belongs to a sort of men I know as little about as I do of the Choctaw Indians. They have lives and notions and ways all unlike ours. The world is so civil to them that it prepares everything to their taste. If they want to shoot', the patriarch continues, 'the birds are cooped up in a corner, and only let fly when they're ready. When they fish, the salmon are kept prepared to be caught; and if they make love, the young lady is just as ready to rise to the fly, and as willing to be bagged as either. Thank God, my darling, with all our barbarism, we have not come to that in Ireland.'[51] Such language, spoken by a beleaguered Catholic gentry landlord, effectively reverses the meaning of 'civilization' and 'barbarism', the very concepts the visiting stranger must unlearn in *The Wild Irish Girl*.

Depicting the anxieties of an isolated Protestant landowning class sinking into social and political oblivion, Big House novels build on conventions established by Edgeworth in Ireland's first widely recognized novel. This developing subgenre, however, deploys a version of *Castle Rackrent* now perceived against the grain, not as the forward-looking dismissal of a past feudal era that its preface confidently asserts, but as a prescient vision of Anglo-Ireland's downward trajectory in the coming century. The persistence of the Big House novel in contemporary Irish writing is characterized more by lacerating irony directed at an improvident class of social and economic losers, than by end-of-empire nostalgia for a lost Anglophone civilization.

From *Castle Rackrent* to Molly Keane's *Loving and Giving* (1988)—in which the last gentry heir retreats to a second-hand caravan parked near her rotting mansion—the domestic disarray of the Ascendancy house in Big House fiction eerily replicates that of the notoriously slipshod rural cabin which pre-Famine English tourists transformed into a trope of

---

[51] Charles Lever, *Lord Kilgobbin* (1872; Boston, 1899), p. 364.

Ireland's baffling 'Otherness'.[52] The central architectural motif of these novels is a decaying mansion isolated from a countryside of native hovels, but regularly sharing characteristics with them. Big House novels thus negotiate the psychic space between recollections of the rural estate as the power centre of agrarian colonial life and its identity as a shabby object of derision and contempt both to imperial visitors and the surrounding Irish communities. Depictions of the physical collapse of the house invariably signal the genealogical breakdown or mounting eccentricity of its occupants as they confront their alienation from imperial London. The rootless landlord grapples with his growing irrelevance as he finds himself pitted against an aspiring professional Catholic plotting to usurp his property and position. Throughout the nineteenth century, these novels appear in various permutations: as politicized Gothic sensation fiction by Maturin or Le Fanu; as narratives of social and political crisis by Lever; or, late in the century, as texts increasingly created by women writers forging a newly politicized domestic tradition.

Dependent on wide readership rather than élite patronage, especially with the rise of British and Irish literacy in the nineteenth century, novelists were far more willing to depict the minutiae of Ascendancy decline than were Irish artists. In the popular visual tradition of eighteenth and nineteenth-century estate portraiture, the Palladian or Georgian Big House asserts an imperial domestication of a wild Irish countryside and Ascendancy control over a newly disciplined landscape. Nature is subordinated to a civility expressed by the conventions of classical architecture and English landscape design. Increasingly, landscape schemes in both England and Ireland devised visual prospects over lakes, rivers, or bucolic grazing fields to distance the realities of a domestic agrarian capitalism from the landlord's aristocratic pretensions; visual artists co-operated in their arrangements of house and demesne on their canvases. Thus, in a much reproduced example of pre-Famine Irish Big House portraiture by James Arthur O'Connor, the artist foregrounds a graceful riverside pleasure demesne modelled on the English landscape designs of Capability Brown. Meanwhile, the red brick grain mills supporting the lifestyle of an entrepreneurial landlord are clustered around a Georgian Big House relegated to the background of the painting.[53]

---

[52] Ferris, *The Romantic National Tale and the Question of Ireland*, p. 35.

[53] James Arthur O'Connor, *Ballinrobe House* and *The Pleasure Grounds of Ballinrobe* (1818), National Gallery of Ireland, Dublin.

Personal bankruptcy, rather than unsightly rural capitalism is, however, the real threat to the Ascendancy in the Big House novel. Such a focus on decline is, of course, absent from the tradition of commissioned Irish estate portraiture, which disappeared as a major landscape genre in post-Famine Ireland as landlords increasingly faced economic pressures. Even as Anglo-Irish Big House novels situate the crumbling Palladian or Georgian country house in a newly imagined landscape of ruin, they resist the pleasures of Romantic nostalgia with which an English poetic and pictorial tradition evacuated the anxiety of historical decline from its local ruins and instead memorialized the antiquity of the British nation.[54] The relentless decay of the Irish Big House in fiction by Edgeworth, Lever, Edith Somerville, and Molly Keane is grounded, rather, in the ironically conceived domestic detail: small cracks in plaster ceilings, a broken window, a leaking roof, and the endless stratagems by which an improvident and isolated society—Empire's new losers—wards off the reality of its marginalization.

As the anxious site of political negotiation and loss, the decaying house only rarely serves as a locus for nostalgia. This subgenre is, in fact, largely resistant to the Yeatsian idealization of an Ascendancy fictive bloom that Seamus Deane finds undermining much twentieth-century Irish fiction: 'The Big House surrounded by the unruly tenantry, Culture besieged by barbarity, a refined aristocracy beset by a vulgar middle-class—all of these are recurrent images in twentieth-century Irish fiction which draws heavily on Yeats's poetry for them.'[55] In view of the deification of the Ascendancy by one strand of the Revival, Big House novelists made surprisingly modest claims for an Anglo-Irish society now uncoupled from Empire. Unlike Yeats and other Revivalists, these novelists generally failed to appropriate heroic territory or construct alliances with a Celtic peasantry as their authority slipped away. Elizabeth Bowen's nostalgic envisioning of the Irish country estate as a moral bulwark against Nazi betrayals in *The Heat of the Day* (1949) is less characteristic of the subgenre than Aidan Higgins's unsparing portrayal of Anglo-Irish submission to a proto-Fascist seducer in *Langrishe, Go Down* (1966). Georgian mansions signaling high culture to Yeats are more often identified with intellectual vacuity, moral collapse, and self-delusion in this fiction. Molly Keane's savage exposures of a

---

[54] Anne Janowitz, *England's Ruins* (Cambridge, Mass., 1990), pp. 54–91.
[55] Deane, 'Literary Myths', p. 32.

decaying Big House society in *Good Behaviour* (1981), *Time After Time* (1983), or *Loving and Giving* (1988) are closer in spirit to the subversive gaze on the gentry estate of *Castle Rackrent* than to nostalgic invocations of the Big House as a stay against modern disorder.

Major works in these narratives of decline cluster around the era of independence, with the burning of an eighteenth-century Georgian house symbolically encoding the final collapse of imperial ties to rural Ireland. Elizabeth Bowen's *The Last September* (1929), in exploring Anglo-Irish society's snobbish resentment of the British garrison protecting it from the IRA, underscores the beleaguered Big House's growing isolation from London. In Edith Somerville's *The Big House of Inver* (1925), an English-man recently arrived from the West Indies—a hostile rewriting of the national tale's imperial visitor to Ireland—marvels that a convent-educated Irish girl is dressed 'like a white woman'. Somerville's vision of Ascendancy snobbery, Irish hostility, and English vulgarity invoke more *schadenfreude* than nostalgia. The national tale's reconciliation plot resur-faces as a narrative of English greed and Anglo-Irish improvidence as the middle-class visitor attempts to buy up both a local Irish girl and the grand aesthetic monument to shabby Ascendancy values. Bowen's *The Last September* is only somewhat less savage toward an enervated and self-deluding Anglo-Irish culture on the verge of oblivion. Because the Big Houses in these novels are ripe for burning, amidst the shock at the destruction of a beautiful artifact emerges a sense of necessary completion, even fulfilment of a historical narrative.

The racial anxieties of *fin de siècle* Empire society, so evident in *Dracu-la*'s preoccupation with pollution and miscegenation, reflect the sexual politics of late nineteenth-century Irish fiction. Lever and Le Fanu replace the national tale's allegorized versions of union between Gaelic and Eng-lish aristocracies with the threatening aspirations of native Irish suitors to the Big House. The easy fluidity between a more stable middle-class and aristocratic society in Jane Austen's rural English settings is inimical to an isolated Anglo-Ireland increasingly obsessed with its lineage and legitim-acy as its power slips away. As the Catholic antagonist gazes longingly at the gentry estate, the defensive response of the Big House invokes sexual and sectarian dimensions, adding the special racial overtones of Empire fiction to the familiar class narrative of the English novel. Like Keane, Somerville and Ross depict societies that on occasion conflate misalli-ance with miscegenation, reflecting a growing eugenic element in late nineteenth and twentieth-century class dynamics, not unrelated to an Anglo-Irish preoccupation with the breeding of horses and dogs for blood sports. In Molly Keane's *Two Days in Aragon* (1941), for example, the daughter of the Big House realizes that sexual alliance with a local Irish man will appear to his mother 'as wrong...as the love of black and white people seemed to her'.[56]

Although the servicing of Big House landlords by Catholic peasant women represents a less threatening sexual contact between the two Irelands in these novels, Somerville and Ross's *An Irish Cousin* and *The Big House of Inver* and Keane's *Two Days in Aragon* reveal that local versions of the *droit du seigneur* never resulted in the social assimilation of two classes, but solely in the victimization of Irish women. The English mythology of Romantic triumph over class barriers driving Samuel Richardson's *Pamela* (1740) or Charlotte Brontë's *Jane Eyre* (1847) is far rarer in Ireland, where divisions of class are complicated by the bigotry engendered by religion, politics, and national loyalties. Edith Somerville and Molly Keane, rather, create heroic protagonists, bastard daughters of landlords and Irish servants, whose internalization of patriarchal norms leads them to fiercely defend the society which condemns them to domestic service in their fathers' houses.

Throughout these end-of-empire novels, recurring shifts in gender roles accompany the social, political, and economic marginalization of the landlord. Even in a domestic fiction centring on the private world of the country estate, personal maladjustments appear grounded in a conquering class's growing political and social impotence. Beginning with Edgeworth's *Castle Rackrent* and continuing in novels by Lever, Le Fanu, and Somerville and Ross, landlords drink, womanize, and overspend their incomes. As the patriarchal world of the Ascendancy decays, ruthless gentry *chatelaines* move into the roles abdicated by their defeated and increasingly ineffective husbands; without an adequate social and political arena for their ambitions, these women now prey on their children. Molly Keane and Jennifer Johnston's monstrous mothers suggest that with the decline of imperialism, the impotent colonial society redirects the habits of a moribund system inward, turning on itself.[57]

[56] Molly Keane [M. J. Farrell, pseud.], *Two Days in Aragon* (1941; London, 1985), p. 15.
[57] Margo Backus, *The Gothic Family Romance* (Durham, NC, 1999).

The improvident and irresponsible landlord depicted in such fiction violates the sternly patriarchal policies of English colonialism, later transformed into a neo-feudal mythology of landlordism by conservative literary revivalists.[58] Committed to a deeply ironic version of fiction's circumstantial realism, the Big House novel slowly undermines nineteenth-century imperial discourse about, for example, a feminine Celtic subject and masculine British overlord.[59] The landlord in major Somerville and Ross novels is presented as an ambiguously gendered intellectual or a senile invalid accompanied by his keeper (*The Real Charlotte*, 1894), a doomed and pig-headed conservative (*Mount Music*, 1919), or a drunken sot (*The Big House of Inver*, 1925). In Molly Keane's work, fathers and husbands, failing to govern their families, estates, or country, neglect their children and countenance maternal brutality. The final vision of the landlord in *Good Behaviour* graphically embodies the collapse of Big House patriarchy: a paralysed, one-legged old man, incontinent and drooling, lies in thrall to the illicit sexual excitement provided by a female servant, once the recipient of his sexual favours, now his devoted Irish nurse.

Such pitiless depictions of cultural breakdown, even when considered along with renditions of gentler and kinder landlords by Jennifer Johnston and William Trevor, suggest a certain congruity between novelists writing from within the Big House and a new generation writing from without. In a series of post-independence novels and short stories, writers such as Sean O'Faolain, Paidric Colum, Liam O'Flaherty, and Julia O'Faolain depict the declining male authority and potency of the former colonizer, expressing a new nation's continuing contempt of the defeated imperial father. Liam O'Flaherty's *Famine* (1937) invokes the sexual dysfunction of an absentee landlord's surrogate, an agent who has been literally unmanned, apparently by a distant subject people during imperial service in India, a narrative detail that neatly displaces a savage revenge to a more distant and 'heathen' group. Julia O'Faolain's *No Country for Young Men* (1980) describes a dying landlord, long guilty of homosexual exploitation of his caretaker's sons. Blackmailed into turning over his property to his victims' family, he has become prisoner of those he once molested. Yet in

---

[58] See, for example, Standish O'Grady's *Toryism and Tory Government* (London, 1886), p. 213.

[59] Matthew Arnold, *On the Study of Celtic Literature* (1867; London, 1976); David Cairns and Shaun Richards, *Writing Ireland: Colonialism, Nationalism, and Culture* (Manchester, 1988), pp. 42–57.

the context of O'Faolain's attack on the virile republican men whose nationalist mythologies destroy Irish women, the landlord's homosexual inclinations appear no more predatory than those of the hyper-masculine men who have replaced him and created a new ruling class.

Realistic novels of Anglo-Irish decline are parodied and reinvented in the postmodern metafiction of John Banville's *Birchwood* and *The Newton Letter* or in J. G. Farrell's *Troubles* (1970), works that suggest the generative impetus of Irish Empire fiction. Farrell's only novel set in Ireland appears as the first in his 'Empire Trilogy' charting key moments of imperial dissolution: the war of independence in *Troubles*, the Indian Mutiny in *The Siege of Krishnapur* (1973), and the fall of Singapore during the Second World War in *The Singapore Grip* (1978). The protagonist of *Troubles*, a shell-shocked English veteran of the First World War, reads as an updated version of the national tale's clueless visitor to Ireland; but rather than capturing his Irish girl, he pursues the daughter of the Big House who is dying, significantly, of a blood disease. Farrell's novel deploys the central realistic conventions of the subgenre, but now viewed through a bizarre comic sensibility. A mansion is invaded by the tropical vegetation growing in its conservatory; an Anglo-Irish landlord rigidly performs the motions of imperial masculinity as his power ebbs away; a final fiery holocaust rains down skeletons of stray cats which have invaded the already undermined house. Such an intertextual novel, alluding always to Big House conventions, and suspended between bizarre comedy and tragedy, rewrites a decline narrative of Empire for postmodern fiction.

The Big House novel and its postmodern reinventions chart the collapse of an increasingly inward-looking Ascendancy society reacting to abandonment by Britain and isolation from Catholic Ireland. But even in these claustrophobic accounts of social isolates, Anglo-Irish decline can appear in a wider context, juxtaposed with the fall of Europe before Nazi aggression in Aidan Higgins's *Langrishe, Go Down*, or with the battlefields of Flanders in Jennifer Johnston's *How Many Miles to Babylon* (1974). William Trevor's scarred protagonists in *Fools of Fortune* (1983) or *The Story of Lucy Gault* (2002) escape personal and political tragedy through self-exile in Italy; in such fiction England is no longer the alternative homeland for the estranged and homeless Irish landlord. As the straitened conditions of nineteenth and early twentieth-century artists and writers working in an economically and politically depressed former capital increased movement outward, the island's historic ties, not only with London, but also with a continental Catholicism, established France and Italy as fictional settings providing alternative perspectives on British imperialism. Such geographically expansive settings for Empire discourse suggest, once again, how Irish fiction significantly complicates the binary structures of a postcolonial emphasis on metropolitan centre and periphery.

Select Bibliography

MARILYN BUTLER, 'Edgeworth's Ireland: History, Popular Culture, and Secret Codes', *Novel*, 34 (Spring 2001), pp. 267–92.

JOHN CRONIN, *The Anglo-Irish Novel* (Belfast, 1980).

SEAMUS DEANE, *Strange Country: Modernity and Nationhood in Irish Writing Since 1790* (Oxford, 1997).

TERRY EAGLETON, 'Form and Ideology in the Anglo-Irish Novel', in Eagleton, *Heathcliff and the Great Hunger* (London, 1995) pp. 148–225.

INA FERRIS, *The Romantic National Tale and The Question of Ireland* (Cambridge, 2002).

THOMAS FLANAGAN, *The Irish Novelists: 1800–1850* (New York, 1959).

DECLAN KIBERD, *Irish Classics* (Cambridge, Mass., 2001).

VERA KREILKAMP, *The Anglo-Irish Novel and the Big House* (Syracuse, NY, 1998).

JOEP LEERSSEN, *Remembrance and Imagination: Patterns in the Historical and Literary Representation of Ireland in the Nineteenth Century* (Cork, 1996).

DAVID LLOYD, 'Violence and the Constitution of the Novel', in Lloyd, *Anomalous States: Irish Writing and the Post-Colonial Moment* (Durham, NC, 1993), pp. 125–62.

OLIVER MACDONAGH, *The Nineteenth-Century Novel and Irish Social History: Some Aspects* (Dublin, 1970).

JULIAN MOYNAHAN, *Anglo-Irish: The Literary Imagination in a Hyphenated Culture* (Princeton, 1995).

KATIE TRUMPENER, *Bardic Nationalism: The Romantic Novel and the British Empire* (Princeton, 1997).

7

Ireland, the Empire, and the Commonwealth

DEIRDRE McMAHON

This chapter opens in 1886 with the introduction of the first Home Rule Bill and Gladstone's recognition that the Act of Union had failed to win over Irish nationalism to the cause of both Union and Empire. The Home Rule debates over the next thirty years illuminated the anomalies of Ireland's domestic and imperial position and highlighted the differences between Ireland and England. This led to heated discussions about race, nationality, and religion. Gladstone saw no incompatibility between imperial unity and Home Rule, but for Unionists Home Rule for Ireland was the slippery slope to imperial disintegration. The debates also revealed that for many in the British political establishment events in Ireland had ramifications not just for the rest of the United Kingdom but for the Empire. These events included the emergence of an effective Irish parliamentary party, the advent of mass democracy, and a rejuvenated radical nationalism in the 1880s and 1890s.

The leader of the Irish Party from 1900 to 1918, John Redmond, articulated a positive vision of Ireland's role within the Empire and saw Ireland as a co-equal member of the Empire alongside Canada and Australia. The third Home Rule Bill was passed in September 1914, just after the outbreak of the First World War, but was suspended until the end of the war. By then the situation had changed irrevocably: the war had proved unpopular in Ireland; the suppression of the 1916 rising marked a decisive shift in favour of the radical nationalists of Sinn Féin; and the Liberal-Conservative coalition government in Britain was determined to suppress the Sinn Féin movement. The signing of the Anglo-Irish Treaty in December 1921 initiated an uneasy membership of the British Commonwealth, which lasted until 1948. The Irish left the Commonwealth just as the Indians joined it and sought other international roles in organizations such as the United Nations and the European Union.

'We have arrived at a stage in our political transactions with Ireland, where two roads part one from the other, not soon probably to meet again...[The Bill] will, above all, obtain an answer—a clear, we hope, and definite answer—to the question whether or not it is or is not possible to establish good and harmonious relations between Great Britain and Ireland'.[1] With this sombre prophecy, the seventy-six-year-old William Gladstone introduced the first Home Rule Bill in April 1886 in a magnificent speech which lasted for over three hours. There were many reasons why Gladstone's wish for harmonious Anglo-Irish relations was not fulfilled. For opponents of Home Rule, the condition of Ireland in the mid-1880s was reason enough. There was the violence of the Land War, including the shocking murders of the Chief Secretary and Under-Secretary in the Phoenix Park in May 1882. The rise of a newly assertive Irish Party at Westminster, under the charismatic leadership of Charles Stewart Parnell, was an equally disturbing development. The party's power was consolidated after the 1884 Representation of the People Act which more than trebled the Irish electorate and gave flesh to the spectre of mass democracy not just in Ireland but throughout the rest of the United Kingdom. The General Election of 1885 laid bare the fissure between nationalism and Unionism, which was to intensify over the following decades with the Irish Party winning every seat outside of north-east Ulster and Trinity College, Dublin.

The early 1880s was also an unsettling period in the wider imperial sphere. The year 1879 had seen the Zulu victory at Isandhlwana and the massacre of the British mission in Kabul. Anglo-French rivalry was accelerating in Egypt and central Africa. The Transvaal Boers defeated British forces at Majuba Hill in 1881 and regained their independence. It was a minor if irritating reverse until huge gold deposits were discovered in 1885 and turned the poverty-stricken Transvaal into one of the richest states in Africa and an unwelcome threat to British interests in the Cape. The year 1882 saw the establishment of what was promised to be a temporary British Protectorate in Egypt, a promise which failed to reassure the French. In April 1884 a new colonial player entered the field when the German Chancellor, Bismarck, claimed South West Africa as a German protectorate and later that month annexed the Cameroons and Togoland in West Africa for good measure. In that same year, the revolt of the

---

[1] *Hansard*, Third Series, vol. 304, cc. 1037–38, 8 April 1886.

Mahdi against Egyptian rule in the Sudan led to a ten-month siege in Khartoum of British and Egyptian forces culminating, in January 1885, in their defeat and the killing of the British commander, General Charles Gordon. Barely two months later an Afghan army was defeated by the Russians at Penjdeh.

This disturbing conjunction of Irish and imperial unrest explains why the Home Rule debates of 1886 are so revealing of English fears about the potential effect of Irish Home Rule on the body politic of England, Ireland, and the Empire. The debates provoked profound soul-searching about ideology, race, national character, religion, the constitution, and history. These fears had already been articulated by the future Conservative Prime Minister, Lord Salisbury, in the famous article 'Disintegration', published in the *Quarterly Review* in 1883. He described Ireland as 'the worst symptom of our malady...our peculiar punishment, our unique affliction among the family of nations'. In Ireland, Salisbury lamented, 'we seem to have the power of conquest, but not to have the faculty of assimilation'.[2] Salisbury's deep antipathy to Ireland and all things Irish was not based on personal knowledge, as he never once visited the country during his long career. Not that Salisbury was unique in this; the later Victorian Prime Ministers—Gladstone, Disraeli, Salisbury, and Rosebery—had little Irish experience and were generally ignorant of the country, unlike previous Prime Ministers such as Melbourne, Peel, Russell, Palmerston, and Derby. Salisbury accurately reflected the crude prejudices about the Irish which existed widely throughout the Victorian governing classes and especially among the Tory backbenchers, whose power over the party leadership had grown exponentially with the rise of the Primrose League, founded in 1883 as a Conservative grass-roots organization which soon reflected the new voters enfranchised in 1884. Gladstone apparently expected that the Conservatives would agree to a bipartisan Home Rule settlement. Given Salisbury's consistent hostility, this was an extraordinary misconception. Salisbury saw any bipartisan approach as a trap but cannily recognized how the Tories could now move to the high ground as defenders of property, Protestantism, and imperial unity.

The Home Rule debates, both inside and outside Parliament, highlighted the anomalies of Ireland's domestic and imperial position. It was part of the United Kingdom but, as opponents and supporters of Home

---

[2] 'Disintegration', *Quarterly Review*, CLVI (July–Oct. 1883), pp. 559–95.

Rule alike acknowledged, a peculiar and problematical part. No term had yet been coined to describe the inhabitants of the United Kingdom; 'English' was resented by the Scots and 'British' was rejected by the Irish. Wales was usually written out of the picture. The Act of Union had united the two Parliaments but a separate executive was maintained at Dublin Castle with a Chief Secretary and a Lord-Lieutenant, an arrangement that existed in none of the other constituent parts of the United Kingdom, though it became the model for British rule in India. Throughout the nearly three decades of debate on Home Rule between 1886 and 1914 Unionists consistently tried to dismiss Irish nationalist votes in the Commons as being somehow invalid or unconstitutional; during the second Home Rule Bill, Salisbury referred to them as 'eighty foreigners'. This ignored the basic fact that Irish votes were a consequence of the Act of Union and were no less valid because they were Irish. During the Home Rule debates the terms 'United Kingdom' and 'Empire' tended to be used interchangeably. 'The unity of the Empire', declared Sir Henry James, who had resigned as Liberal Attorney General over Home Rule, meant 'the unity of Great Britain and Ireland'.[3] For Sir James Fitzjames Stephen, a distinguished judge, a former member of the Indian Legislative Council, and one of the most prominent intellectual opponents of Home Rule, the word 'Empire' was 'susceptible to many different meanings...either the United Kingdom, the United Kingdom and colonies, or the United Kingdom, India and the colonies', but Home Rule was incompatible with 'any and every sense of the word'.[4]

So was Ireland a nation? What was Irish nationality? Was Ireland a colony? If a colony, what sort of colony? In 1880 Sir George Campbell, the former Lieutenant Governor of Bengal, had written in the *Fortnightly Review* that Ireland 'is a colony which we have only partly colonised, and in which the natives have neither been exterminated nor thoroughly assimilated, and we have the race difficulties in the way of self-governing institutions with which we are familiar in other colonies, but in a more aggravated form'. For Campbell, Ireland was 'in a position more analogous to that of the South African colonies, in which only British authority prevents collision between a colonist minority and a native majority'.[5] Ireland was also seen as

<hr />

[3] *Hansard*, Third Series, vol. 305, c. 915, 13 May 1886.

[4] Quoted in Tom Dunne, '*La trahison des clercs:* British Intellectuals and the First Home Rule Crisis', *Irish Historical Studies* (hereafter *IHS*), XXIII (1982), p. 163, n. 162.

[5] Ibid., p. 159.

an imperial dependency, both by supporters and opponents of Home Rule. James Bryce, a future Liberal Chief Secretary, wrote in 1888 that 'Ireland remained after the union as before, a dependency, with the old evils of dependency government concealed in outward seeming by the admission of Irish members to the British parliament'.[6]

The basic conservatism of Gladstone's Home Rule policy was not appreciated at the time; he was, as Tom Dunne has noted, a social conservative but a liberal imperialist.[7] From the first, Gladstone defended Home Rule on imperial grounds and insisted that there was no incompatibility between imperial unity and a Dublin Parliament.[8] Although analogies were drawn during the debates with Norway and Sweden, Austria-Hungary, and the more contentious one of the northern and southern United States, Canada was the analogy which Gladstone emphasized most positively and which was to echo down the years until its apotheosis in the 1921 Anglo-Irish Treaty.

The Canadian analogy was emphatically rejected by Joseph Chamberlain, who had just resigned from Gladstone's Cabinet because of his opposition to Home Rule: 'Canada is loyal and friendly to this country. Ireland, I am sorry to say, at the present time is not loyal, and cannot be called friendly'. Chamberlain expressed surprise that Gladstone was looking to the colonies as his model: 'The present connection between our Colonies and ourselves is no doubt very strong, owing to the affection which exists between members of the same nation. But it is a sentimental tie, and a sentimental tie only'. Since the bonds of Empire were drawing tighter towards federation, Chamberlain wondered that Parnell could look 'with entire satisfaction upon a proposal which will substitute such a connection as that which exists between Canada and this country'.[9] Lord Hartington, another Liberal defector to the *salon des refusés*, considered that 'the distance which separates our Colonies from us makes any analogy which may be drawn between their case and that of Ireland utterly fallacious'. The connection with Canada was purely voluntary and the practical authority exercised by the Imperial Government in Canadian domestic affairs was 'practically nothing'; if the Canadians wanted to separate, no Parliament or statesman would attempt to prevent that by force.[10]

---

[6] Ibid., p. 158.   [7] Ibid., p. 145.

[8] *Hansard*, Third Series, vol. 304, cc. 1081–82, 8 April 1886; vol. 305, c. 585, 10 May 1886.

[9] *Hansard*, Third Series, vol. 304, cc. 1183, 1204, 9 April 1886.

[10] Ibid., c. 1204, 9 April 1886.

One of the most incendiary speeches came not in Parliament but in St James's Hall in London on 15 May when Salisbury addressed an anti-Home Rule meeting. The words 'trust', 'confidence', 'security', and 'safe' resonated throughout Salisbury's speech. One could not place trust or confidence in the Irish because the Home Rule movement was 'animated by passions of antagonism to England'; Gladstone could not be trusted with Home Rule because the 'disastrous series of measures which he started 16 years ago will end in the disintegration of the Empire'; one could not trust the Irish because Ireland was not a nation but rather 'two deeply divided and antagonistic nations'. The Irish, Salisbury concluded, had 'become habituated to knives and slugs', while Irish Catholicism, 'this tremendous, this grievously misused weapon', would be used against 'our Loyalist friends, who are in the main Protestant'.[11] Capping this entertaining compendium of prejudice was Salisbury's celebrated, if oblique, comparison of the Irish to the Hottentots as undeserving of free representative institutions. Curiously, although the Indians, the Greeks, the Russians, and non-Teutonic races were mentioned in the same passage, nobody seems to have minded Salisbury's dismissive comments about them.

To Gladstone's dismay, India, not Canada, was the most frequent point of comparison with Ireland, a comparison which had been discussed for more than a decade. A common theme of the Irish-Indian analogy was that coercion rather than reform worked best. Another was the racial stereotyping of the Irish and the Indians as unfit for self-government. By 1886 the threat which Home Rule posed to India emerged starkly in the anti-Home Rule arguments. 'If democracy in its present state nearly lets Ireland go, what hope is there of holding India?', asked the constitutional historian Goldwin Smith.[12] The Liberal Viceroy, Lord Dufferin, thought this argument had force. Events in Ireland, he noted, had produced 'a very considerable effect upon the minds of the intelligent and educated section of our own native community...I cannot help asking myself how long an autocratic government like that of India...will be able to stand the strain implied by the importation en bloc from England, or rather from Ireland, of the perfected machinery of modern democratic agitation'.[13]

The Indian National Congress had been founded the year before and Dufferin and many others in the Government of India saw Congress through the prism of Irish nationalism. This contributed to the

[11] *Irish Times*, 19 May 1886.   [12] Dunne, '*La trahison des clercs*', p. 162.   [13] Ibid.

mishandling of what was at this stage an essentially moderate party. The comparison of Ireland with India contributed in no small measure to the fears aroused by Home Rule in 1886 and 'underlined the nature of the imperialism which was fundamental to unionism'.[14] Sir Henry Campbell-Bannerman, the Secretary for War (and briefly Chief Secretary in 1884–85) dismissed these arguments about the effects of Home Rule on the Empire, writing to Lord Wolseley: 'Surely you do not take for gospel all the rubbish that does duty on platforms about the disintegration of the Empire and so forth? That is meant only for the groundlings. No one surely believes that to give the Irish the management of their own affairs will break up the Empire—if so, what a rotten state that venerable structure must be in!'[15]

Ireland and India had long been linked in the minds of British ministers and officials even before the first Home Rule Bill. In the 1870s and 1880s Irish MPs dominated parliamentary debates on India, their interest in Indian affairs in marked contrast to the apathy displayed by most British MPs. Parnell had been a firm critic of Britain's acquisition of Empire but was not an agitator for nationalism outside Ireland. His tactics of parliamentary obstruction were, however, closely watched and discussed by Indian nationalists. Two of the most active Irish MPs on India were Frank Hugh O'Donnell and Michael Davitt. O'Donnell believed that Irishmen were specially qualified to prescribe cures for imperial disorders; that Home Rulers were the natural parliamentary allies of the unenfranchised Empire; and that nationalists in Ireland should form an alliance with nationalists in Asia and Africa to achieve self-government. He was one of the first proponents of the idea to transform the Empire into a Commonwealth of equal partners admitted to membership on the basis of that equality. O'Donnell sensed that when the British came face-to-face with the challenge of extended nationalism, they would surrender gracefully and salvage what they could.

Frank O'Donnell was influential in the setting up of the Congress Party in India in 1885. The rising, urban middle classes who were to join Congress were much influenced by Irish nationalism. One Indian journal declared in 1905: 'We have only to follow the example of the Irish. We want a common object to move us; we want a leader to direct us; we want

[14] Ibid., p. 163.
[15] John Wilson, *CB: A Life of Sir Henry Campbell-Bannerman* (London, 1973), pp. 99–100.

the sinews of war to strengthen us'.[16] O'Donnell's brother Charles was a controversial member of the Indian Civil Service (ICS) who had written two pamphlets highly critical of British policy in India. In one of them, *The Ruin of an Indian Province* (1880), he described the plight of the Indian peasantry in the state of Bihar and attacked the feudal system of land tenure. In this and subsequent writings on India over the next thirty years, he was very aware of parallels with Ireland.

The first Home Rule Bill was defeated in the Commons in June 1886 and in the elections which followed, the Conservatives returned to power under Salisbury. The Liberals returned briefly to office from 1892 to 1895 and were dependent on Irish votes. In his final administration, Gladstone made one last attempt to introduce Home Rule. The new Bill included amended provisions for finance and continued Irish representation at Westminster. The debates were protracted, with eighty-two sittings between April and September; and they were bitter, with physical violence erupting on the floor of the Commons on 27 July 1893. But the result was a foregone conclusion. Although this time the Bill passed the Commons by 43 votes, it was crushed in the House of Lords by 419 votes to 41. The debates, inside and outside Parliament, echoed the preoccupations of 1886 but with a new and ominous emphasis on religious differences and Ulster. Here Joseph Chamberlain played a leading role in defending Ulster Unionist interests, presenting them as a microcosm of the English race, Protestant and Anglo-Saxon, in peril. He played a strong anti-Catholic card when speech-making in Scotland and Wales, although he was more circumspect in Ulster.[17]

The late 1890s witnessed a parallel outpouring of imperialist and nationalist feeling, producing a complex interaction between the two. Indeed, both ideologies were articulated in very similar ways, with ceremony and ritual, pageants, and processions. On the nationalist side there were the celebrations for the centenary of the 1798 rebellion, in which radical Irish nationalism played a leading role. Irish communities in Australia, South

---

[16] Howard Brasted, 'Indian Nationalist Development and the Influence of Irish Home Rule, 1870–1886', *Modern Asian Studies*, 14 (1980), pp. 42–65 and 'Irish Nationalism and the British Empire in the Late Nineteenth Century', in Oliver MacDonagh, W. F. Mandle, and Pauric Travers, eds., *Irish Culture and Nationalism, 1750–1950* (London, 1983), pp. 84–95.

[17] James Loughlin, 'Joseph Chamberlain, English Nationalism and the Ulster Question', *History*, 77 (1992), pp. 202–19.

Africa, and North America were planning various events to commemorate the centenary, with Irish-Americans expecting to play a particularly prominent part. However, the outbreak of the Spanish-American War in February 1898 soon put paid to that. Indeed, Irish-Americans made it clear that the needs of the United States took priority over the homeland. 'The paramount duty of every American citizen', announced the New York centennial organizers, 'is to remain at the disposal of his Government while there may be need of his services'.[18] In the Irish commemorations, the leaders of the various nationalist factions engaged in a rhetorical contest, with John Redmond declaring in uncharacteristically green (i.e., republican) tones in May 1898 that, while 'the constitutional movement may be, and will be, in the future of great value to Ireland, I believe that the salt of the public life of Ireland is to be found in the ideas of '98 (cheers)'.[19]

On the Unionist side, the Diamond Jubilee of Queen Victoria in 1897 forged a link between Empire and monarchy and signalled almost fifteen years of belated royal spectacle in Ireland with the three-week visit of the Duke and Duchess of York in 1897, Victoria's last visit in April 1900, the Coronation visit of Edward VII and Queen Alexandra in 1903, and the Coronation visit of George V and Queen Mary in 1911. As a recent study has noted, the nineteenth-century monarchy was often perceived as a 'golden bridge' or link between Britain and Ireland. However, this meant very different things on either side of the Irish Sea. For many Irish nationalist politicians it was merely a useful symbolic link with Britain which could disguise the degree of autonomy they hoped to gain, but this view of the monarchy began to change in the 1880s to such an extent that insults about the royal family became almost a *sine qua non* for political advancement. By the beginning of the twentieth century, nationalism had set its face against monarchy to the point that individuals could express support for the monarchy 'only at the cost of having their Irishness questioned'.[20]

[18] Timothy J. O'Keefe, 'The 1898 Efforts to Celebrate the United Irishmen: The '98 Centennial', *Éire-Ireland*, 23 (1988), pp. 71–72.

[19] Ibid., p. 81. See also Timothy J. O'Keefe, '"Who Fears to Speak of '98?": The Rhetoric and Rituals of the United Irishmen Centennial, 1898', *Éire-Ireland*, 27 (1992), pp. 67–91.

[20] James Murphy, *Abject Loyalty: Nationalism and Monarchy in Ireland During the Reign of Queen Victoria* (Cork, 2001), pp. xii–xxxiii.

Southern Irish Unionism was a rich and diverse culture, though in time its very diversity germinated the seeds of its decline. Within it attitudes to Empire varied. In his study of the Dublin Protestant working class, Martin Maguire has noted the popularity of organizations such as the Primrose League but considers that evangelical Protestantism provided the strongest communal binding.[21] Among the more exalted levels of southern Union-ism, however, feeling for the monarchy and the Empire was deeply held. It was the Earl of Meath, an Anglo-Irish aristocrat, who was the moving spirit behind the first Empire Day in 1903, which aimed at training British youth in its responsibilities towards the Empire. In Ireland, Empire Day was taken up almost exclusively by the main institutions of southern Unionism: Trinity College, the *Irish Times*, and the Protestant churches—especially the Church of Ireland.[22]

The devotion of the Anglo-Irish to the Empire was the subject of an elegiac but acid commentary entitled 'A Doomed Aristocracy' in the *Westminster Gazette* in January 1909. The author was the novelist and play-wright George Birmingham, alias James Owen Hannay, a Church of Ireland clergyman living in Mayo who, unusually for someone of his background, was also active in the Irish language movement. The Anglo-Irish, he wrote, 'avowed themselves Imperialists as soon as the Imperial idea found itself in literature and political speech. They flung themselves into the new cult with all the bacchante abandon of the crowds which shrieked and rioted during the South African war'. The Anglo-Irish, he continued, accepted 'as new scriptures not to be gainsaid, all that has been shouted by the most flamboyant orators or written by intoxicated roman-cers about the Imperial race and its world-wide mission to humanity'. It was 'one of their class', the Earl of Meath, who established 'Empire Day'. Yet their whole conception was fallacious: 'The Irish gentleman has not understood that an Empire is a quickly passing thing, nailed together by force, varnished by diplomacy, waiting the inevitable dissolution of such structures [by nationalism] . . . Here is the last great mistake of the Irish gentry'. Birmingham's reproaches provoked a dignified response from J. M. Wilson of Currygrane, Co. Longford, an active member of the Irish Unionist Alliance. He pointed out that the 1898 Local Government Act

---

[21] Martin Maguire, 'The Organisation and Activism of Dublin's Protestant Working Class, 1883–1935', *IHS*, XXIX (1994), pp. 65–87.

[22] David H. Hume, 'Empire Day in Ireland, 1896–1962', in Keith Jeffery, ed., *'An Irish Empire?' Aspects of Ireland and the British Empire* (Manchester, 1996), pp. 149–68.

had 'eliminated 95 per cent of those who used to work in their counties from sharing in that work any longer'. It was ungenerous, Wilson argued, for Birmingham to now belittle a class, many of whose members were doing their best 'in very difficult circumstances'.[23]

As Birmingham noted and as Wilson's family history demonstrated, Irish soldiers had contributed significantly to the British Army.[24] Starting with the Boer War, however, nationalists successfully targeted Irish recruitment, a campaign that was to be even more successful during the First World War. The growth of radical nationalism, evident in the 1798 centenary commemorations, was even more apparent during the Boer War. South Africa had attracted nationalist interest as early as 1877, long before the Boer War. Irish MPs, notably Frank Hugh O'Donnell, had obstructed the South African Confederation Bill that year, which led to the annexation of the Transvaal.[25] The radical nationalist Arthur Griffith spent some time in the Transvaal in the late 1890s, just before the outbreak of the war, working as a journalist in Middleburg. He worshipped Kruger. At the time of the Jameson Raid in 1895, a group of Irishmen in Johannesburg had formed an Irish Brigade to resist British aggression. When the war started in 1899, two Transvaal Irish Brigades were formed, one led by Major John MacBride and Colonel John Blake, the other by Arthur Lynch. They attracted a small number of volunteers from Ireland and the United States but it is estimated that they never numbered more than 400 men, compared to the 28,000 Irishmen who were serving on the opposing side in the British Army. The Irish Brigades were ineffective and the Boer leaders greatly preferred the Irish who fought in the ordinary Boer commandos. It was the symbolic aspects of the Irish Brigade, however, which counted and their actions and adventures were described in stirring detail in the nationalist press back home.[26]

The Irish Transvaal Committee was formed in Dublin in October 1899 and was dominated by more radical nationalists such as Griffith, Maud Gonne, the socialist leader James Connolly, and the poet W. B. Yeats.

---

[23] *Westminster Gazette*, 16, 21, 23 Jan. 1909. Wilson's brother was Sir Henry Wilson, later Field Marshal and Chief of the Imperial General Staff, whose assassination by the IRA in June 1922 helped precipitate the Irish civil war, during which Currygrane was burned.

[24] See chap. 4, above, pp. 103–12.

[25] Donal P. McCracken, *The Irish Pro-Boers, 1877–1902* (Johannesburg, 1989), pp. 2–11.

[26] Ibid., pp. 142–49; Keith Jeffery, 'The Irish Military Tradition in the British Empire', in Jeffery, ed., *An Irish Empire?*, pp. 95–96.

Thomas Clarke, who had just been released from prison after serving a fifteen-year sentence for Fenian activities, was also involved in the pro-Boer movement. Maud Gonne, the daughter of a British Army officer, was responsible for drafting the Committee's pamphlet *Enlisting in the English Army is Treason to Ireland*. Apart from Griffith, few of the Transvaal Committee knew anything about South Africa and uncomfortable facts such as the Boer hostility to Catholicism and Boer treatment of the black population were ignored.[27] The visit to Dublin of the Colonial Secretary, Joseph Chamberlain, in December 1899, led to serious disturbances and the catastrophic British defeats of 'Black Week' were greeted deliriously (the novelist George Moore described them as 'the greatest event since Thermopylae').[28] When, in April 1900, Queen Victoria paid the last of her rare visits to Ireland, the Transvaal Committee loudly proclaimed that she had come to provide a fillip for falling Irish recruitment, but the steam was already evaporating from the Transvaal Committee. John MacBride had stood in the South Mayo by-election and was defeated.

How true were the claims of the Transvaal Committee that they had frustrated recruiting? The evidence is inconclusive. The number of those enlisting was sustained fairly well, particularly in Dublin, where the anti-recruiting campaign was most active. But even if the Committee's efforts had scant effect, there is little doubt, Keith Jeffery concludes, that the war in South Africa enabled the Transvaal Committee to exploit a heady combination of Irish nationalist sentiment, sympathy for the Boers, anti-English feeling, and growing antagonism towards the British Army.[29] This led to fears of disaffection among Irish soldiers, as the Unionist *Limerick Chronicle* noted in some alarm: 'Every loyal Irishman should...repudiate with scorn the infamous suggestion that the Irish soldier was capable in the face of danger of deserting the colours and joining the enemy'.[30]

Despite this relative lack of success, there is no doubt that the activities of the Transvaal Committee and other pro-Boers greatly contributed to the growth of radical nationalism in Ireland in the critical decade-and-a-half before 1914. It stimulated a rise in the number of Gaelic League

---

[27] The anti-Catholic sentiments of the Boers were pointed out in a letter in the *Galway Express* on 30 Sept. 1899 by a correspondent resident in South Africa who described himself as an 'Irish Colonist, Roman Catholic, Irishman, and Home Ruler', and accused the Transvaal government of being 'benighted, bigoted, and corrupt'.

[28] McCracken, *Irish Pro-Boers*, pp. 61–67.   [29] Jeffery, 'Irish Military Tradition', p. 97.

[30] *Limerick Chronicle*, 14 Oct. 1899.

branches from 107 in 1899 to 400 in 1902. Conventions of the Gaelic
Athletic Association (GAA) passed many pro-Boer resolutions and all
over the country GAA clubs were renamed in honour of Boer leaders such
as Kruger and de Wet. The Association was also deeply involved in the
anti-recruiting campaign. The new county councils, established just
the year before the war under the Local Government Act, vied with one
another in sending resolutions of support to the Boer leaders. The Boer
War left its mark on those who were only children at the time. In September 1921, Michael Collins wrote to de Wet expressing his admiration for
the way he fought the British. 'Your great fight against the same foe
was the earliest inspiration of the men who have been fighting here...
Everyone—man and woman—in Ireland will be delighted to know you
are on our side. They were all on your side', he told the ageing Boer leader
who died a few months later.[31]

   The Boer War helped to rescue the Irish Party from the doldrums of the
Parnell split. The necessity of presenting a united front against the war
was the major reason for its reunion in January 1900 under the leadership
of John Redmond. Redmond's brother William condemned the war in the
House of Commons as 'disastrous, useless, shameful'. Michael Davitt
made one of the most memorable speeches against the war on 25 October
1899. 'To say that because England goes to war Irishmen must back her or
become traitors is a monstrous proposition... We on these benches know
what our attitude on this war will mean, for the time being, to Home
Rule...', Davitt declared. He concluded with ringing declaration: 'But let
me say this for myself... Had I been offered not Home Rule only, but an
Irish Republic by Her Majesty's Govt on yesterday week in return for one
word or one vote in favour of this war to destroy the independence of the
Republics of the Transvaal, I would speak no such word nor record any
such vote'. He also announced that he 'would not purchase liberty for
Ireland at the base price of voting against liberty in South Africa'. To do so
'would be an infamy and a disgrace which no Home Rule, no freedom,
depending on your promise or word, could ever obliterate or redeem'.[32]
Davitt later resigned his seat in protest against the war and went to South
Africa to write a book about the war, *The Boer Fight for Freedom* (1902).

---

[31] Correspondence between Michael Collins, Christian and J. J. de Wet, Sept. 1921–Feb.
1922, National Library of Ireland, Piaras Béaslaí Papers, MS 33,916(4).
[32] *Hansard*, Fourth Series, vol. 77, cc. 460, 621–22, 20, 25 Oct. 1899.

The Irish Party reunited in 1900 after almost a decade of debilitating divisions, but the party was not reformed and the older group of leaders who had dominated its organization since Parnell were to remain in place until 1918, effectively excluding many of the young men who had come to the fore since the Boer War. The result, as Philip Bull has observed, was that 'the party lacked the necessary imaginative and represenative capacities to respond to a rapidly changing social, cultural and political context within which Irish nationalism had now to develop'.[33] The new generation of radical nationalists saw Westminster politics as increasingly arid and irrelevant to Irish concerns. John Redmond, the new leader of the Irish Party, articulated a clearer vision of Ireland's role in the Empire than any of his colleagues. He was a regular visitor to Canada and had a particularly close association with Australia. He and his brother both had Australian wives and Australia was one of the most generous sources of funds for the Irish Party. The Australian Irish had raised nearly £95,000 for Irish distress in 1879–80, far more than the American Irish. In 1883, on their first visit to Australia, the Redmonds raised £15,000 despite a very cold reception in the wake of the trials of the Phoenix Park murderers. Australia, however, was to affect profoundly Redmond's vision of Home Rule and Ireland's relationship with the Empire. 'Let us join every Imperial purpose', he declared in Melbourne, 'and defend the Empire, which is the heritage of both of us, but let each give up, once and for all, the attempt to rule the domestic affairs of each other. Let us have national freedom and Imperial unity and strength'.[34] In 1901, Australia became a federal Commonwealth and with Canada it presented, for Redmond, yet another tantalizing example of colonial self-government. He hailed the Australian case as an example of enlightened British statesmanship but wondered 'how the policy [might] be adopted with reference to Ireland of refusing to conciliate her people, and keeping her people constantly disaffected and disloyal to the interests of the Empire... Ireland is not a colony of fifty or a hundred years' growth. Why, Ireland has built up this Empire'.[35]

---

[33] Philip Bull, 'The United Irish League and the Reunion of the Irish Parliamentary Party, 1898–1900', *IHS*, XXVI (1988), p. 78.

[34] Denis Gwynn, *The Life of John Redmond* (London, 1932), p. 52; Patrick O'Farrell, *The Irish in Australia* (Kensington, NSW, 1987), pp. 221, 225–27.

[35] John Redmond, *Ireland and the Coronation* (Dublin, 1902), p. 1.

After almost twenty years of the Conservatives, the Irish Party were prepared to do anything to help the Liberals to power and they accepted a step-by-step policy on Home Rule. The Liberal electoral landslide in 1906, however, made even that policy redundant. The Irish Party was offered an Irish Councils Bill, a form of administrative Home Rule, drawn up by the Under-Secretary at Dublin Castle, Sir Antony MacDonnell, who had had a distinguished career in the Indian Civil Service before returning to Ireland. Redmond's deputy leader, John Dillon, dismissed MacDonnell's proposal as 'a kind of Indian council composed of that favourite abstraction of amateur solvers of the Irish problem, non-political business men'.[36] Redmond's disappointment was all the more keen as he had been deeply impressed by Campbell-Bannerman's restoration of self-government to the Transvaal in December 1906. 'We have the sympathy and the outspoken support of all the great self-governing colonies of the Empire', he said in August 1907. Every colonial leader from Laurier to Botha had declared in favour of Home Rule. Autonomy had proved to be a bond of Empire and the denial of colonial autonomy to Ireland was 'one of the strangest anomalies in British history'.[37]

Colonial models and federalism received a considerable airing from 1907 on. Recent research has indicated that Redmond was more interested in federalism than has been assumed, but his public utterances revealed all too clearly the confusion over its relationship to Home Rule. During a fund-raising visit to New York in the autumn of 1910, he gave an interview to the London *Daily Express* in which he stated that 'our demand for Home Rule does not mean that we want to break with the British Empire. We are entirely loyal to the Empire as such, and we desire to strengthen the imperial bonds through a federal system of government'. Redmond insisted that it was false to picture his movement as 'desiring to fight our Imperial kin'. On the contrary, he insisted, 'we shall do our best to strengthen the Empire by bringing Britain and America closer together'. What they wanted was the same measure of local government as an American state: Westminster could have final authority over local legislation: they were willing to forego the right to control tariffs and old

[36] A. C. Hepburn, 'The Irish Council Bill and the Fall of Sir Antony MacDonnell, 1906–07', *IHS*, XVII (1971), pp. 478–79.

[37] John E. Redmond, *Some Arguments for Home Rule* (Dublin, 1908), pp. 13, 20, 80–81.

age pensions and would support imperial charges such as the Army, Navy, and diplomatic service.[38]

In Ireland, the response to the interview was so hostile that Redmond was forced to deny its contents. Despite his transparent discomfort, however, the controversy was soon forgotten, as another General Election and the battle against the House of Lords veto were now imminent. The episode showed that, not for the first nor the last time, Redmond's conciliationist and imperialist views were out of tune with nationalist opinion in Ireland.[39] Redmond's American tour, which raised $100,000, provoked vitriolic comment. For alienated Liberals like Rosebery, Redmond's American support was 'Irish dictation subsidised by foreign gold', while Lord Ronaldshay, Unionist MP for Hornsey, referred to Redmond as 'the Irish political tramp who has returned with his pockets laden with American gold'.[40]

With the abolition of the House of Lords veto in 1911 the way was clear for a third Home Rule Bill. Although Ulster was to take centre stage from now on, the implications for the Empire were discussed by the two leading intellectual protagonists of the pro and anti-Home Rule case, Erskine Childers and L. S. Amery. Childers's *The Framework of Home Rule* was the ablest defence of Home Rule published since 1886. Childers, whose strong Unionist sympathies were evident at the time of Boer War, had converted to Home Rule in 1908. He dismissed the idea of a completely independent Ireland, a small state like Belgium, although he conceded that a prosperous friendly neighbour on a footing of independence was better than a discontented and backward neighbour on a dependent footing. He was equally dismissive of a federal solution: 'Before there is any question of Federation, Ireland needs to find herself, to test her own potentialities, to prove independence of character, thought and action'. Responsible government for Ireland, Childers considered, meant 'something in the nature of "Colonial" Home Rule', which was now enjoyed by states as varied as Canada, Newfoundland, and New Zealand.[41]

---

[38] *Daily Express*, 5 Oct. 1910, quoted in Michael Wheatley, 'John Redmond and Federalism in 1910', *IHS*, XXXII (2001), pp. 354–55. For the Conservatives and federalism, see John Kendle, *Walter Long, Ireland and the Union, 1905–20* (Dublin, 1992), pp. 46–51.

[39] Wheatley, 'John Redmond and Federalism', p. 363.

[40] Edward Pearce, *Lines of Most Resistance: The Lords, The Tories and Ireland, 1886–1914* (London, 1999), pp. 313–15.

[41] Erskine Childers, *The Framework of Home Rule* (London, 1911), pp. 189–203.

For Amery, Irish nationalism and the Irish Party were regressive developments in an era when imperial unity was moving towards a federation of smaller units. It was this which made any colonial parallels redundant. By what facts of geography, race, or history, Amery demanded, could the Irish claim to nationhood be justified? 'Ireland is most emphatically not a nation, but an integral part of a greater whole'. He recognized comparisons with South Africa but saw Irish nationalism as analogous to what he termed 'Krugerism', a nationalism based 'on a legend of hatred and hostility towards the nation to which the other half of the white population belonged... and towards that Imperial connection which was essential to the welfare and progress of South Africa'.[42]

The third Home Rule Bill was introduced in April 1912. How did the rest of the Empire see Home Rule? Walter Long, the most prominent standard-bearer of Empire among the Unionists, had always resented the ease with which Redmond and the Irish Party had raised money in North America. In August 1912 he embarked on a ten-week trip to Canada, where he laid particular stress on the Empire in his speeches. 'I am more than half an Irishman, and I love the land of Ireland', he told a Winnipeg meeting, 'and if I thought that by the concession of Home Rule the Empire would be benefited I would withdraw my opposition'. On 27 September, the day before the signing of the Ulster Covenant in Belfast, Long spoke to an overflow meeting in Toronto, where the Orange Order was particularly powerful. 'Ulster stops the way because she believes that home rule means the desecration of the Union Jack. If Canada with one voice declared itself in favour of home rule, those in Ulster would still oppose it... because it means the loss of British liberty and freedom'. However, he was disconcerted to find that the anti-Home Rule movement was treated in Canada with some scepticism and in various press interviews he attacked the Canadian analogies being applied to Irish Home Rule.[43]

In Australia, the Catholic Church dominated the various Irish-Australian organizations. Cardinal Moran of Sydney had opposed any commemoration of 1798, was deeply anti-Boer, and saw the British Empire as a civilizing agent. William Redmond's book *Through the New Commonwealth* (1905) was dedicated enthusiastically to Moran. The Irish

[42] L. S. Amery, *The Case against Home Rule* (London, 1912), pp. 59–70.
[43] Kendle, *Walter Long*, pp. 73–75.

Party was lauded for its firm parliamentary support of the Australian Commonwealth Act. Australia continued to be a lucrative source of funds for the Irish Party and Joseph Devlin and J. T. Donovan raised £22,000 on their 1906 tour. The last Irish Party delegation visited in 1911–12. Pro and anti-Home Rule meetings were held in Melbourne and Sydney, culminating in a monster meeting at Sydney Town Hall in June 1914 in support of Home Rule. Posters for the meeting asked whether Irish-Australians 'born in this free, self-governing Commonwealth' could ever feel free while Ireland was unfree?[44]

As in Australia, moderate Irish opinion in New Zealand had been alienated by the Phoenix Park murders when the Redmond brothers visited there in 1883. William Redmond, however, was well received in the Irish mining areas and raised nearly £1,500 from them. Despite the unpropitious circumstances, the Redmonds' respectable demeanour had made a favourable impression and Gladstone's conversion to Home Rule made their cause respectable again. When John Dillon, MP for East Mayo and later Redmond's long-time deputy leader of the party, visited New Zealand in 1889, he raised £6,000 from thirty-seven meetings in New Zealand. As Richard P. Davis has noted, Conservative and Orange fears in New Zealand about Home Rule tended to be expressed in a kind of domino theory: the concession of Home Rule to Ireland would, because of the fundamental disloyalty of Catholics, lead to the complete separation of Ireland from Britain; foreign powers would then use Ireland as a base against England; the antipodean colonies, deprived of their natural protector by Britain's collapse, would fall to the Asian hordes.[45]

In 1914, the third Home Rule Bill brought Ireland to the brink of civil war, with two paramilitary forces, the Ulster Volunteer Force in the north and the Irish Volunteers in the south, squaring up to each other. Civil war was averted by the outbreak of the First World War in August 1914. The Bill was passed a month later but was suspended for the duration of the war. For Redmond, the war was the opportunity to demonstrate that Home Rule Ireland could make its contribution alongside the other states of the Empire. Just as Botha and Smuts had been transformed from bitter enemies to loyal comrades in the Empire, so Ireland, he declared, 'has been transformed from "the broken arm of England" into one of the

[44] O'Farrell, *Irish in Australia*, pp. 240–51.

[45] Richard P. Davis, *Irish Issues in New Zealand Politics, 1868–1922* (Dunedin, 1974), pp. 7–10, 51–64, 99–119.

strongest bulwarks of the Empire'. The war in which the Empire was engaged was a 'just war...It is a war for the defence of the sacred rights and liberties of small nations, and the respect and enlargement of the great principle of nationality'. Redmond had two other beliefs which proved to be misconceived: that British public opinion would be so grateful for Irish support that after the war it would rally round Home Rule; and that the war might dissolve the sectarian tensions between Protestant and Catholic, nationalist and Unionist.[46]

Despite a rush of initial enthusiasm, support for the war became increasingly apathetic and Redmond, spending most of his time in London, soon became dangerously isolated and out of touch. The Irish Volunteers, the paramilitary force founded in 1913 as a counterpart to the Ulster Volunteer Force in order to engage the threat to Home Rule, split over Redmond's support for the war. A majority, approximately 150,000, sided with Redmond; the remainder, approximately 7,500, stayed with his opponent, the founder of the Volunteers, Eoin MacNeill. But this was by no means the whole picture, as the split was very confused at local level, with many units staying neutral. Others simply dropped out. With many of Redmond's Volunteers going off to fight in the war, MacNeill's faction soon filled the vacuum. The anti-war movement had many of the same personnel who had been involved fifteen years earlier in the Irish Transvaal Committee, including three who were to be executed after the 1916 rising, Thomas Clarke, James Connolly, and John MacBride. Others, however, notably Arthur Lynch and Tom Kettle, were now fighting in the British Army.

Redmond found lukewarm attitudes to the war among sections of his own party in 1914. His deputy, John Dillon, who had a surer grasp of the restlessness of Irish public opinion in the months after the outbreak of the war than did Redmond, was more clear-sighted about how long the war would actually last. Recruiting soon became a bone of contention. The War Office refused to arm and equip Redmond's Volunteers, and delayed granting them the same status and privileges as the anti-Home Rule Ulster Volunteers. Dismayed, Redmond warned the British Prime Minister, H. H. Asquith, of the impression this would create in Ireland, but to no avail. Despite the problems, initial recruitment was creditable, although there were marked regional differences and, as in the rest of the

[46] Gwynn, *Life of John Redmond*, pp. 384–86.

UK, a sharp drop in enlistment after the first rush. Conscription was introduced in March 1916 but was not applied to Ireland, thus highlighting the drop in Irish figures.[47] The disillusionment with the war reflected in the falling recruitment figures had complex reasons, not just annoyance at the conduct of the recruiting campaign, but foreboding at the formation of a new coalition government in Britain in May 1915 which saw obdurate opponents of Home Rule such as Edward Carson appointed to the British Cabinet. There was a growing feeling that the war had little to offer Ireland. Stephen Gwynn, the MP for Galway City, who enlisted at the age of fifty and saw active service, recalled that a common response at recruiting meetings was distrust of the government: 'Are you sure now they aren't fooling us again?'[48]

The 1916 rebellion was not the only imperial disturbance during the First World War. In October 1914 an Afrikaner rebellion had broken out in South Africa and there were disturbances in Nigeria, Egypt, and India. The task of dealing with the aftermath of the rebellion was given to Sir John Maxwell, who had been commander in Egypt when martial law had been declared there at the end of 1914. Because of concern to reassure opinion in America and the Dominions, the British government played down the true extent of the rebellion, which only made the treatment meted out to the rebels seem even more extreme. Redmond and Dillon both drew on South African parallels, particularly the recent pardon given to the Afrikaner rebels of 1914. 'The precedent of Botha's treatment of the rebels in S. Africa is the only wise and safe one to follow', Redmond urged Asquith on 3 May.[49] The editor of *The Times*, Geoffrey Dawson, was less impressed by this analogy. The Irish Party 'are in a far weaker position than before the Sinn Féin outbreak', he wrote. 'They are very much in the position which Smuts and Botha occupy in South Africa, except that the latter are far bigger and more dominant men'. The Royal Commission on the rebellion was chaired by Lord Hardinge, a choice that provoked considerable comment since, as Viceroy of India, he was much implicated in the Mesopotamia campaign, which led to the surrender of General Townshend at Kut in April 1916. It was suggested sarcastically that

[47] Jeffery, 'Irish Military Tradition', pp. 97–98.
[48] Stephen Gwynn, *John Redmond's Last Years* (London, 1919), p. 189.
[49] Gwynn, *Life of John Redmond*, p. 482.

Augustine Birrell, the luckless Chief Secretary who was vilified after the rising, should 'be sent to enquire into Mesopotamia'.[50]

The rebellion had profound consequences among the Irish communities in the Empire. In Australia, the radical Irish National Association, founded in 1915, had only 211 members in January 1916; by December 1916 its membership had trebled. The Australian Prime Minister, W. M. Hughes, blamed the Australian Irish for the defeat of the first conscription referendum in October 1916 and urged Lloyd George to seek a settlement. The Irish, he asserted in a fretful telegram, constituted 25 per cent of the population but 80 per cent of the labour movement in Australia. The Irish question was seriously affecting the prosecution of the war and prejudicing imperial developments. With a settlement, he wrote, 'we could get reinforcements; we could prosecute vigorous war policy, the air would be cleared, we should be a really united people and Australia could speak with one voice'. In reply to this and further telegrams from Hughes, Lloyd George simply stated that Ulster could not be coerced.[51] A second referendum was defeated later that year. The New Zealand Irish also faced allegations of treason and disloyalty. When conscription was introduced there in May 1916, controversy arose over the conscription of Catholic clergy and seminarians. These events increased sectarian tensions and in July 1917 the Protestant Political Association was founded with support from New Zealand's Orange Order. The following month the editor of *The Green Ray*, which had close links with the New Zealand Labour Party, was imprisoned for sedition. The magazine was suppressed by the government in 1918.[52]

In Canada on the outbreak of war, an Irish regiment, the Irish Canadian Rangers, was raised and its four companies were soon filled, intended initially for home defence. In 1916 it was decided to raise an overseas battalion, but recruiting for this was slow, reflecting a similar decline in overall recruiting. Shortly after its arrival in England in December 1916, the battalion was sent to Ireland for a two-week tour to spur flagging Irish enlistment. Canadian conscription was introduced in August 1917 to the delight of the Canadian Orange Order, which advised the government

[50] 10, 30 May 1916, Bodleian Library, Oxford, MSS Dawson 66. ff. 58–61.

[51] Dec. 1916-April 1917, House of Lords, Lloyd George Papers, F/32/4/14, 22, 40, 41, 47, 87.

[52] Davis, *Irish Issues in New Zealand Politics*, pp. 99–199; P. S. O'Connor, '"Protestants", Catholics and the New Zealand Government, 1916–18', in G. A. Wood and P. S. O'Connor, eds., *W. P. Morrell: A Tribute* (Dunedin, 1973), pp. 185–201.

to shoot at sunrise those guilty of treasonable utterances. The Canadian censors were particularly vigilant about Irish-American propaganda entering the country.[53]

There was a growing distrust of Irish soldiers after the 1916 rising. Although most reports at the time indicated that there was little support for the rising among Irish soldiers serving at the front, the executions caused much more concern. When soldiers from the 16th (Irish) Division returned on leave to Ireland, there were incidents in the streets and women became increasingly reluctant to be seen with men in British uniforms. Catholic Irish soldiers, like soldiers from Canada, Australia, and New Zealand, were generally regarded as shock troops with a reputation for indiscipline, but in the Irish case there was additional doubt about their loyalty, stirred not only by the rising but also by the attempts made by Roger Casement to recruit an Irish Brigade from Irish prisoners of war in Germany. In March 1918, the heavy defeats suffered by the 16th (Irish) Division in France led to insinuations that the men had been weakened by political disaffection. Terence Denman's research has shown that in fact the men were tired, overstrained, and holding poor strategic positions.[54] In April 1918, the British government finally decided to introduce conscription in Ireland in the wake of the huge losses on the Western Front. The decision led to the formation of an unprecedented alliance between the Irish Party, Sinn Féin, and the Catholic Church. The Inspector-General of the Royal Irish Constabulary reported that 'disloyalty and feelings of intense hatred towards England have been aroused' and that the police were unable to cope with the drilling and nightly parades against conscription.[55] The British Government was strongly advised against imposing conscription by the South African leader, General Smuts, who was also a member of the British War Cabinet, and by other imperial politicians with large Irish communities. Conscription was not imposed.

Historians have written about the amnesia which existed in Ireland for decades about Irish involvement in the First World War. This amnesia was

[53] Robin B. Burns, 'Who Shall Separate Us? The Montreal Irish and the Great War', in Robert O'Driscoll and Lorna Reynolds, eds., *The Untold Story: The Irish in Canada*, 2 vols. (Toronto, 1988), II, pp. 571–77.

[54] Terence Denman, 'The Catholic Irish soldier in the First World War: the "racial" environment', *IHS*, XXVII (1991), pp. 353–65 and *Ireland's Unknown Soldiers: The 16[th](Irish) Division in the Great War* (Dublin, 1992), pp. 153–70.

[55] Monthly reports, April, May 1918, CO 904/105, 106.

deceptive. Many of those who fought in the war of independence and on the republican side in the civil war had close connections with the First World War. Jack Hunt, who won the DSO at Guinchy in 1916, later joined the Irish Republican Army (IRA), as did Emmet Dalton and Tom Barry. Emmet Dalton's younger brother Charles, later a close associate of Michael Collins, started his career in the IRA with a revolver his brother Emmet had brought back from France. Barry, who was one of the IRA's most important commanders in the south, had joined the British Army in June 1915 and had served in Townshend's disastrous Mesopotamian campaign in 1916. Kevin O'Higgins's brother Michael was killed in the war as was the brother of John and Maurice Moynihan, members of a prominent republican family in Tralee who later had distinguished careers in the Irish civil service. Erskine Childers, his cousin Robert Barton, and their friend David Robinson, all from Anglo-Irish backgrounds, served in the British Army during the Great War and took the republican side in the civil war in 1922. Ernie O'Malley, author of two of the finest books about the 1916–23 period, *On Another Man's Wound* and *The Singing Flame*, had a brother in the Royal Dublin Fusiliers, was fascinated by armies and military manuals, and was planning to join up when the 1916 rising impelled him to change course and join the IRA.[56] These complex ties and allegiances, covering the First World War, the war of independence, and the civil war, were repeated in hundreds of families.

Shortly before the General Election in December 1918, Sir Hubert Gough was invited to stand as a Unionist parliamentary candidate in Belfast. A member of a prominent Anglo-Irish family from Co. Tipperary, Gough had been at the centre of the Curragh Mutiny of March 1914 (when protesting officers had threatened to resign if the Army were used to suppress Ulster opposition to Home Rule), and later fought with the 16th (Irish) Division. He explained to Sir Edward Carson why he would not accept: 'I told him how the war had somewhat changed my views on many things, including Ireland. He ... seemed to appreciate my viewpoint, saying "Of course a lot of water has flowed under London Bridge since the Curragh incident in 1914". I said, "Yes a lot of blood too!" '[57] Gough's class, the Anglo-Irish gentry, had suffered huge casualties during the war and it

---

[56] O'Malley's brother Frank served in the King's African Rifles after the war. The RIC asked the Colonial Office in 1921 whether there was any contact between Frank and his 'notorious rebel' brother. *On Another Man's Wound*, new edn. (Dublin, 2002), pp. 290–91.

[57] Sir Hubert Gough, *Soldiering On* (London, 1954), pp. 182–83.

was a measure of his alienation that he said he would never wear a British uniform again and was even thinking of settling in America (neither event happened), but Gough had recognized that with the end of the war some form of self-government for Ireland was inevitable. Where would this leave the Unionists of southern Ireland? Would they throw in their lot with the new order or become the first of the century's shipwrecked colonial minorities, left high and dry in surroundings that were familiar but uncongenial? It was the dilemma that George Birmingham had predicted in the *Westminster Gazette* in 1909.

Sinn Féin won seventy-three seats in the General Election of 1918 and annihilated the Irish Party. In January 1919, in line with Sinn Féin's policy of abstention from Westminster, those Sinn Féin TDs who were not in jail or on the run gathered in Dublin to set up their own Assembly, Dáil Éireann. The *Irish Times* described these proceedings as 'a solemn act of defiance of the British Empire by a body of young men who have not the slightest idea of that Empire's power and resources'.[58] More thoughtful observers considered Sinn Féin to be a far bigger threat than its ineffectual predecessors. How did the Sinn Féin leaders regard the Empire? As we have seen, Michael Collins had vivid childhood memories of the Boer War and greatly admired de Wet. In his various journals, Arthur Griffith devoted considerable space to Indian affairs. He had been an outspoken critic of the partition of Bengal in 1905 but was lukewarm about Gandhi.[59] De Valera, on the other hand, who spent eighteen turbulent months in the United States raising funds for the Dáil, was more interested in American parallels. The post-1916 Sinn Féin embraced a wide political spectrum, from moderate nationalists to radical republicans, which meant that any potential solution based on the Irish relationship with the British Empire would be fraught with difficulty.

The establishment of the Dáil was followed by guerilla war which lasted for two-and-a-half years. During that war there was a pervasive belief in political and military circles that the trouble was being caused by a minority of malcontents and that once they were under control, the cowed moderate majority would emerge. It was to be an enduring theme in later colonial wars. In 1956 the Governor of Cyprus, Sir John Harding, told a

---

[58] *Irish Times*, 23 Jan. 1919.

[59] Richard P. Davis, 'India in Irish Revolutionary Propaganda, 1905–22', *Journal of the Asiatic Society of Bangladesh*, 22, no. 1 (1977), pp. 66–89.

House of Commons committee that the EOKA terrorists consisted of about 'fifty wild men' whom he hoped to eliminate by the end of the year. Listening sceptically to Harding was the former Labour Prime Minister, Clement Attlee, who recalled being told in 1920 that Irish and Indian nationalism were 'artificial movements engineered by a handful of agitators'.[60]

When Lloyd George succeeded Asquith as Prime Minister in December 1916, it was hoped that he would give a greater impetus to the search for a settlement. William Redmond, MP, who described himself as 'an old friend' and was now at the front (at the age of 56), appealed to him, 'I DO BEG YOU TO SETTLE THE IRISH QUESTION... America, Australia the whole world calls for a truce with Ireland'. In his reply Lloyd George recalled that 'the Irish Members and I fought together on the same side in many a fierce conflict... but you know just as well as I do what the difficulty is in settling the Irish question'.[61] Redmond was killed two months later. Careful scrutiny of Lloyd George's career would have revealed that his views on Empire were of a somewhat different order from that of Redmond and other MPs with whom he had joined in opposition to the Boer War. In 1886 he had been a disciple of Joseph Chamberlain and was one of a minority of Welsh MPs who actually opposed Home Rule. In a speech in Belfast in February 1907 he warned against the dangers of separatism and said that the schism of Ireland from the Empire was 'unthinkable'. He never showed any insight into Irish affairs and on various occasions displayed anti-Catholic prejudice, particularly during the 1918 conscription crisis, which he blamed on the Catholic clergy. There is no evidence that Lloyd George was forced by his Conservative colleagues in the coalition government to take a hard line on Ireland; this was his own clear preference.[62]

The Colonial Secretary, Walter Long, had twice been invited by Lloyd George to take on the Chief Secretaryship (a post he had held briefly in 1905) but Long refused. Instead he became, in April 1918, chairman of the Cabinet's Irish Committee, which was drafting a new Government of

---

[60] Harold Nicolson, *Diaries and Letters, 1945–62* (London, 1968), p. 303.

[61] William Redmond–Lloyd George correspondence, 1–6 March 1917, Lloyd George Papers, F/94/1/64, 65.

[62] Kenneth O. Morgan, 'Lloyd George and the Irish', in n. a., *Ireland after the Union* (Oxford, 1989), pp. 83–103.

Ireland Bill and from then until the end of 1920 he was effectively the Cabinet's enforcer on Ireland. Long had by now become a convert to federalism; he dismissed Sinn Féin and thought that if only the government was 'Firm. Firm. Firm', it would fade away. He regarded Dominion Home Rule, which was now being widely canvassed as a possible solution, as 'blather'.[63] Lloyd George concurred. The war, as Kenneth Morgan has observed, fostered Lloyd George's imperial consciousness and he was, moreover, surrounded by imperialist prophets such as Smuts and Sir Alfred Milner, as well as leading members of the Round Table group: Philip Kerr, W. G. S. Adams, Edward Grigg, and L. S. Amery, who had joined the Cabinet secretariat. As peace returned, Dominion Home Rule for Ireland did not accord with Lloyd George's vision for the post-war world.[64]

For Kerr, one of the Prime Minister's closest advisers, Ireland was part of an Empire-wide threat: 'There is really an attack going on everywhere on Government as such', he wrote to Lloyd George in September 1920. 'It is obvious in Ireland, in Egypt, in Mesopotamia and in India, and we have reached such a stage that in all these places the revolutionaries are on the verge of success...I would turn your whole attention to the problems of Great Britain and the British Empire'. Kerr saw the American Irish as sinister manipulators of events who had linked up with 'Indians, Egyptians, Bolshies, and all the haters of England in France Germany etc.'. They knew that, by securing a republic for Ireland 'either by bamboozlement, or because they can tire England by murder and outrage', they could 'create a precisely similar movement in India, Egypt etc.'.[65] Throughout 1919, 1920, and 1921 the gloomy quartet of Ireland, Egypt, Mesopotamia, and India appeared with monotonous regularity on the Cabinet agenda. The fear of a domino effect in each theatre of imperial unrest gripped British ministers as they thrashed around for a solution.

By the end of 1920, Lloyd George was coming under increasing pressure from Dominion leaders to do something about the turmoil in Ireland, which was causing unrest in Irish communities in Australia, New Zealand, and Canada and, most prominently, the United States. But Long was adamant that Dominion Home Rule was 'impossible to grant unless we are prepared to go the whole length and accept the inevitable conclusion,

[63] Kendle, *Walter Long*, pp. 144–47.   [64] Morgan, 'Lloyd George and the Irish', p. 93.
[65] Kerr to Lloyd George, 2 Sept. 1920, 14 Sept. 1921, Lloyd George Papers, F/90/1/18.

namely practical, if not legal independence...sooner or later, Ireland would demand complete Dominion status...and this England could never concede'.[66] There was, however, no satisfactory definition of what Dominion Home Rule or Dominion status actually meant. At the Imperial Conference which assembled in London in June 1921, Smuts tried to seek such a definition and warned, prophetically, that the delay in reaching a satisfactory solution, 'which the example of Ireland gives to the whole Commonwealth, is one which we only neglect at our peril'.[67] Dominion status was offered to the Irish while the Imperial Conference was sitting, but apart from Smuts none of the Dominion leaders were consulted about it. No definition of Dominion status emerged from the seven weeks of the Conference deliberations.[68]

Following the truce which came into operation on 11 July 1921, Irish and British representatives, led by Eamon de Valera and Lloyd George respectively, spent a gruelling summer arguing about what sort of relationship Ireland would have with the Empire-Commonwealth. After de Valera's return from America in December 1920, Erskine Childers had become his principal constitutional adviser and, as is clear from his papers, Childers played a significant role in shaping the policy of external association which was to be the basis of the Irish negotiating position: Ireland would be associated with, but not be a member of, the British Empire. De Valera and Childers both believed that for reasons of geography and self-interest Britain would never treat Ireland on the same basis as the overseas Dominions. This point was underlined when Smuts visited Dublin early in July 1921 to try and persuade de Valera to accept Dominion status, urging him not to press for a republic. When de Valera replied that the matter was for the Irish people to decide, Smuts responded 'the British people will never give you this choice. You are next door to them'.[69]

On 20 July, Lloyd George made his first offer: Dominion status involving membership of the Empire and an oath of allegiance to the Crown, as well as a defence agreement. De Valera replied on 10 August asserting

---

[66] Long to Lloyd George, 26 Sept. 1920, Lloyd George Papers, F/34/1/46.

[67] 'The Constitution of the British Commonwealth', 1921, BL, Balfour Papers, Add. MSS. 49775.

[68] David Harkness, 'Britain and the Independence of the Dominions: The 1921 Crossroads', in T. W. Moody, ed., *Nationality and the Pursuit of National Independence: Historical Studies, XI* (Belfast, 1978), pp. 141–59.

[69] Thomas Jones, *A Whitehall Diary. Vol. III. Ireland, 1918–25*, ed. Keith Middlemas (Oxford, 1971), p. 83.

Ireland's indefeasible right to realize its own destiny. Dominion status for Ireland would be illusory, he argued, because the freedom enjoyed by the other Dominions was due to geography and not to legal enactments. He expressed his willingness to enter into a treaty of free association with the British Commonwealth, the basis of his idea of external association. After further exchanges, both sides agreed to enter negotiations without preconditions. The reaction of the other Dominion leaders was one of profound relief, though the New Zealand premier, W. F. Massey, who had an Ulster background, urged Lloyd George not to coerce Ulster: 'Any move in that direction will mean very serious trouble all over the Empire... people who are loyal [must] be treated fairly and justly'.[70]

During the negotiations, which started in October 1921, allegiance to the Crown, membership of the Empire, and defence guarantees were the core of the British demands. Throughout, Dominion status was never defined and neither was de Valera's alternative of external association, which was being constantly developed as the negotiations proceeded. In the end, under threat of immediate and terrible war, the Irish delegates were forced to concede to the British demands. The Anglo-Irish Treaty signed on 6 December 1921 established the Irish Free State as a self-governing Dominion within the British Empire. The Free State would have the same constitutional status as Canada: The Crown would be represented by a Governor-General; and members of the Free State Parliament would take an oath of allegiance. The terms created an immediate split which led directly to the civil war six months later.

The signing of the Anglo-Irish Treaty had profound repercussions in the wider imperial sphere. To the relief of the other Dominions, Irish agitation subsided and following the outbreak of the civil war in June 1922 there was a great revulsion among Irish communities in the diaspora. But the Irish Treaty had more immediate consequences in the case of both Egypt and India. In the autumn of 1921 British ministers faced negotiations not only with the Irish but with the Egyptians, led by their Prime Minister, Adli Pasha. Philip Kerr spoke with Adli at the end of October 1921 and urged Lloyd George to 'screw him up to going back and fighting for a reasonable settlement. If he doesn't Zaghlul [the radical nationalist leader] will go Sinn Féin, and though we can put him down, Zaghlul will begin to create a Pan-Islamic-Sinn Féin machine making mischief

[70] Jellicoe to CO, 11 Nov. 1921, Lloyd George Papers, F/10/1/44.

everywhere'.[71] In both sets of negotiations the problem was similar: how far could nationalist demands be met in Ireland and Egypt? British ministers were well aware that hostile sections of the British Conservative Party were monitoring both sets of negotiations in case unacceptable concessions were made. Lloyd George was afraid to make important concessions to Egypt, and Zaghlul was deported to the Seychelles in December 1921.

For India, the Irish negotiations and their aftermath had equally paralysing consequences. Just the week after the start of the Irish negotiations, Lloyd George telegraphed to the Viceroy, Lord Reading, in forthright terms: 'Our course in India is being watched in many other quarters, and we cannot afford to be misunderstood'. The British Empire, he argued, was 'passing through a very critical phase, and it will not survive unless it shows now in the most unmistakable fashion that it has the will and the power to stand by its policies and to deal conclusively with any who challenge its authority'.[72] In December 1921 the question of whether to start negotiations with Gandhi was under consideration. Although the Secretary of State for India, Edwin Montagu, was in favour of talks with Gandhi, the rest of the British Cabinet was not. Pressure to arrest Gandhi increased from Conservative MPs, who were emphatic that the surrender to Sinn Féin must not be repeated with the Indian Congress Party led by Gandhi. He was arrested in March 1922 just as the Irish Treaty was going through the British Parliament.

By the wave of a constitutional wand reminiscent of the first Home Rule debates in 1886, Ireland was given the same constitutional status as Canada under the Treaty signed on 6 December 1921. The Canadian analogy, however, was based on a profound misconception: Ireland, unlike Canada, was a Dominion by revolution not evolution. As critics such as Joseph Chamberlain had pointed out then, Canada was too distant and too big to prevent her seceding from the Empire. The Dominion settlement suffered from fatal flaws: as a concept Dominion status was still in the process of evolution; the Irish had never asked for it; it came too late; it was imposed; and it was accompanied by partition and civil war. The surprise is that it lasted as long as it did.

In the decade after 1921, Ireland played a major role in expanding the constitutional independence of the Commonwealth. The Cosgrave

---

[71] Kerr to Lloyd George, 28 Oct. 1921, Lloyd George Papers, F/34/2/9.
[72] Lloyd George to Reading, 21 Oct. 1921, Lloyd George Papers, F/41/1/30.

government, featuring such able ministers as Kevin O'Higgins, Desmond FitzGerald, and Patrick McGilligan, was very active at the various Imperial Conferences in 1926, 1929, and 1930. The 1926 Imperial Conference led to the Balfour Report, which at last produced the elusive definition of Dominion status: Following the 1930 Conference, the Statute of Westminster was passed, repealing the right of the British Parliament to legislate for the Dominions. The nature of these advances demonstrated, however, that for the new Irish Free State, Commonwealth membership resembled the chafing of an ill-fitting shoe. Allegiance to the Crown, insisted upon by the British negotiators in 1921 and underlined in the 1922 Constitution and the Balfour Report four years later, carried a weight of historical baggage which ensured that it would never be the same focus of loyalty as it was in Australia, Canada, and New Zealand. In 1921, British negotiators complained bitterly that the Irish were living in some fantasy land in their demand for a republic. Lionel Curtis, the constitutional adviser to the British delegation and later head of the Irish Branch at the Colonial Office, criticized their obsession with American models and ideas.[73]

The Irish were the realists: what they wanted, then as later, was precision. What they were to get consistently from British ministers and officials (until Ireland finally left the Commonwealth in 1948) was a lot of waffle about indivisible Crowns and indissoluble unity. Even if the Cosgrave administration had succeeded in eliminating the more objectionable aspects of the Treaty (and it is now known that they were considering some of the measures that de Valera later implemented), it is likely that the Commonwealth would have become a cul-de-sac for the Irish. As a forum for articulating Irish sovereignty, the League of Nations represented both an escape from the constitutional navel-gazing of the Imperial Conferences and more exciting opportunities for a new, small state anxious to make an impression on the world stage.[74]

When de Valera came to power in March 1932, it was barely eight years since he had been released from jail at the end of the Irish civil war, which had been fought over the terms of the Treaty and had led to the death of his friend Erskine Childers in one of the first executions of the civil war. Such painful, and recent, history made de Valera's innate wariness towards

---

[73] Deborah Lavin, *From Empire to International Commonwealth: A Biography of Lionel Curtis* (Oxford, 1995), pp. 194–203.

[74] Irish policy at the League is analysed by Michael Kennedy in *Ireland and the League of Nations, 1922–1946* (Dublin, 1995).

the Commonwealth understandable. He was also wary initially about the League of Nations, but he became an enthusiastic and active participant in its proceedings for the rest of the decade. America was the place outside Ireland that de Valera knew best and apart from Britain he did not visit any part of the Commonwealth until after he left office in 1948; he lacked an extensive acquaintance with Commonwealth statesmen, since he did not attend any of the Imperial Conferences in the 1930s. Within days of taking office de Valera introduced a Bill to abolish the oath of allegiance and disputed several substantial payments which were due to Britain. Over the next four years he introduced further Bills designed to chip away at the powers of the Crown in the internal affairs of the Free State.

These moves led to a six-year dispute with Britain during which the British government was forced to make a fundamental reassessment of the Commonwealth. If de Valera had opted for Irish secession from the Commonwealth, it would have made the British position clearer if not easier. The problem for all the sixteen years he was in office was that he never did. When drafting his new constitution in 1936, he told the British Dominions Secretary, Malcolm MacDonald, that his proposals, which were a variant of external association, were perfectly consistent with staying in the Commonwealth and that if the British government thought otherwise then it 'would have to turn them out'.[75] At the end of that year, during the abdication crisis, de Valera rushed the External Relations Act through the Dáil. The Act recognized the King as the symbol of the co-operation of the Commonwealth and confirmed certain of his functions in external affairs. In July 1937 de Valera's new constitution, which was republican in all but name, was passed by referendum. After consultation with the other Dominions, the British government stated that the new constitution did not affect Irish membership of the Commonwealth. This statement had the merit of papering over the immediate cracks in the Commonwealth at a time of worsening international tension. The dispute with Britain came to an end in April 1938 in an agreement which, *inter alia*, returned to Ireland the ports that had been retained under the 1921 Treaty. This made Irish neutrality possible the following year. When the Second World War broke out Ireland was the only Commonwealth state

---

[75] Memorandum by Malcolm MacDonald, July 1936, CAB 27/527, ISC(32) 108.

to remain neutral. By the end of the war the Irish relationship with the Commonwealth was almost invisible.

Developments in Ireland had a significant impact elsewhere in the Empire.[76] As early as 1929, Dominion status had become the goal of British policy in India, but there was considerable reluctance. Lord Birkenhead, Secretary for India and one of the signatories of the Irish Treaty in 1921, stated his belief in 1924 that it was 'frankly inconceivable that India will ever be fit for Dominion self-government'.[77] Die-hard Conservative MPs, notably Winston Churchill (another signatory of the 1921 Treaty), were implacably opposed to any further measure of self-government for India. When the Government of India Act was finally passed in 1935, no reference was made to Dominion status but the powers of the provincial legislatures were widened and the electorate was expanded. The Congress Party won most of the seats in the provincial elections of 1937 but its political rival, the Muslim League, was starting to consolidate support among the predominantly Muslim states of India. In March 1940 the Muslim League, led by Mohammed Ali Jinnah, made its first formal demand for a separate Muslim state, to be called Pakistan. The parallels with Ulster struck many observers at the time. The Congress Party, like Sinn Féin in 1919–21, paid no attention to this demand and believed, again like Sinn Féin over Ulster, that as a collection of Muslim states divided between India's eastern and western borders, Pakistan was simply unviable.[78]

In February 1948, de Valera was defeated in the General Election and was succeeded as Taoiseach by John A. Costello, who presided over a heterogeneous coalition of five parties. Costello had always disliked the External Relations Act, as did his new Minister for External Affairs, Seán MacBride. De Valera had considered repealing the Act after the war but he held his hand waiting to see what would happen with India. An Indian delegation had been sent to Dublin at the end of 1947 to consult de Valera about the country's future constitutional status. He urged them to consider some form of external association. In September 1948, during a

---

[76] On the popularity of Dan Breen in Bengal, for example, see National Archives of India, Home Rule (Political), 41/6/35, 10 Sept. 1935.

[77] Quoted in Anthony Read and David Fisher, *The Proudest Day: India's Long Road to Independence* (London, 1998), p. 205.

[78] Deirdre McMahon, 'A Larger and Noisier Southern Ireland: Ireland and the Evolution of Dominion Status in India, Burma and the Commonwealth, 1942–49', in Michael Kennedy and Joseph Morrison Skelley, eds., *Irish Foreign Policy, 1919–66* (Dublin, 2000), pp. 158–60.

visit to Canada, Costello announced that the External Relations Act would be repealed *and* that Ireland would be leaving the Commonwealth. In view of the discussions taking place about India, secession from the Commonwealth did not necessarily follow from the repeal of the Act, something that Costello apparently never considered. Ironically, British officials were actually suggesting to the Indians that they use the External Relations Act as a basis for staying in the Commonwealth.[79] Following talks in October and November 1948 between Irish, British, and other Commonwealth ministers, it was agreed that reciprocal arrangements regarding trade and citizenship rights were the best solution for the new Irish position. British ministers, resentful at the precipitate way Costello had announced the repeal of the Act, wanted to take a harder line with the Irish but found that the other Commonwealth leaders were opposed; they hoped that an informal relationship between Ireland and the Commonwealth might evolve, and even that the Irish might rejoin the Commonwealth.

After a winter of further argument and debate over what to do about India, the British government finally 'threw in the towel' and agreed on 8 April that the best solution would be for India to recognize the King as head of the Commonwealth and as the symbol of the free association of Commonwealth peoples.[80] Events moved swiftly after this. On 18 April 1949, Easter Monday, Ireland declared itself a republic and withdrew from the Commonwealth. On 27 April, the Commonwealth Prime Ministers' Conference in London issued a statement that India would stay in the Commonwealth as a republic and accept the King as the 'symbol of the free association of its independent member nations'. On 3 May the British government published its Ireland Bill, which revealed a bitter sting in the tail in the shape of the clause stipulating that in no event would Northern Ireland or any part of it cease to be part of the United Kingdom 'without the consent of the Parliament of Northern Ireland'.

In September 1949, a British Labour MP, A. L. Ungoed-Thomas, met de Valera at the Council of Europe in Strasbourg and reported their conversation to the Commonwealth Relations Office in London. De Valera emphasized that he 'had always been most careful to state that he did not

[79] Note by Sir Gilbert Laithwaite, 25 Oct. 1948, CAB 127/115.
[80] Cabinet Committee on Commonwealth Relations, 8 April 1949, CAB 1/45 D42.

wish to leave the Commonwealth so long as it was understood that no allegiance to the Crown of England was involved'. The Indian Commonwealth solution 'would have exactly met his position, and he was clearly angry at Mr Costello's action'. British ministers and officials were very encouraged by these comments and the British Ambassador in Dublin, Sir Gilbert Laithwaite, observed that if southern Ireland was prepared 'not only to come back into the Commonwealth on the same basis as India, but in addition to accept allegiance to the king', then 'subject to adequate guarantees to the North and to the agreement of the Northern Ireland Parliament', an all-Ireland Parliamentary Body might be established. Laithwaite, however, doubted whether, 'even if Southern Ireland came back into the Commonwealth on the Indian basis, the North would be prepared to whittle away its relation to The King or be satisfied with [his] position merely as "Head of the Commonwealth"'.[81]

Irish delegates continued to attend gatherings like the British Commonwealth Relations Conference. Lionel Curtis wrote that the inclusion of the Irish in the 1949 Conference in Canada was 'an unqualified success... everyone fell in love with the Irishmen'.[82] The historian Nicholas Mansergh, who held the Abe Bailey Commonwealth Chair at the Royal Institute for International Affairs, was critical of the way Irish participation in that conference had been reported in the influential Commonwealth journal *Round Table*. He described the journal's Irish correspondent, J. J. Horgan, as 'an unrepentant Redmondite who believes that everything went wrong in 1916'. It was a pity, Mansergh thought, that 'a periodical devoted to Commonwealth affairs and published in London should contain in every issue articles so very critical of almost anything that happens in Ireland'. Horgan had omitted to mention that the leader of the Irish delegation, Senator Michael Hayes, 'made it clear in Canada as in Ireland that while the Republic was not a member of the Commonwealth, she was, and wished to be, closely associated with it'.[83]

Such tenuous connections could not disguise the contraction of Ireland's international role after 1948. It had left the Commonwealth and was still excluded from the United Nations by a Soviet veto, which was eventually lifted in 1955. When Ireland joined the UN it had diplomatic

[81] Memorandum by Ungoed-Thomas, 5 Sept. 1948; minute by Laithwaite, 2 Nov. 1949, DO 35/3941.

[82] Curtis to J. J. Horgan, 30 Dec. 1949, Bodleian Library, MSS. Eng. Hist., c. 871 f. 186.

[83] Mansergh to Dermot Morrah, 23 Jan. 1950, Bodleian Library, MSS. Curtis, 98 ff. 217 a, b.

relations with only 20 countries but the UN—like the League of Nations before it—provided the Irish with valuable diplomatic contacts around the world. Even before the departure from the Commonwealth, formal diplomatic links had been established with Canada (1939) and Australia (1946). India opened an embassy in Dublin in 1949 and the first Irish embassy in Africa was opened in Nigeria in 1960. The civil war which erupted in Nigeria in 1967 provoked an Irish response to a foreign conflict not seen since the Spanish civil war. There were hundreds of Irish missionaries working in Nigeria and many had long-established connections with the eastern Igbo tribe which seceded to form the new state of Biafra. Despite enormous domestic pressure, the Irish government refused to recognize the new state and was considerably influenced by the parallels with Northern Ireland. It had great sympathy for Nigerian attempts to maintain the unity of their newly independent state, and Frank Aiken, the Minister for External Affairs, argued that if self-determination was conceded to the Igbos this would be an unfortunate precedent for other tribes. The Nigerians were also assured that the Irish would not raise the matter at the United Nations.[84]

Continuing their tradition from the League era, the Irish were strong defenders at the UN of small nations such as Hungary and Tibet which had been invaded by more powerful neighbours. They also took a strong line on apartheid in South Africa, which was criticized by a number of Irish people living there. Replying to one such letter in December 1957, de Valera stated that the Irish government 'was far too keenly aware, from our history, of the meaning of class segregation and the supremacy of one race over another, not to feel sympathy for those who are now treated as "second-class" citizens in their own country'.[85] Frank Aiken, during his long tenure as Minister for External Affairs (1957–69), took a particular interest in decolonization and told the French bluntly that they were doing a disservice to Western civilization by denying independence to Algeria. Ireland, he told the General Assembly in 1960, 'has a memory which gives us a sense of brotherhood with the newly emerging peoples of today... We stand unequivocally for the swift and orderly ending of colonial rule and other forms of foreign domination'.[86]

[84] Biafra is discussed in an illuminating article by Enda Staunton, 'The Case of Biafra: Ireland and the Nigerian Civil War', *IHS*, XXXI (1999), pp. 513–34.

[85] Quoted by Joseph Morrison Skelly, *Irish Diplomacy at the United Nations, 1945–65: National Interests and the International Order* (Dublin, 1997), p. 190.

[86] Skelly, *Irish Diplomacy at the United Nations*, pp. 21–22.

UN membership did not diminish Irish interest in the Commonwealth. The possibility that Ireland might rejoin the Commonwealth was discussed in 1957–58, during de Valera's last term as Taoiseach. In February 1957, Cardinal D'Alton of Armagh (who had known de Valera since their schooldays) gave an interview to the journalist Douglas Hyde and proposed, *inter alia,* that a reunited Ireland should rejoin the Commonwealth 'on the same basis as India'. D'Alton's statement was well received in the Irish and British press and by his fellow bishops, though official reactions in Dublin, Belfast, and London were more cool.[87] The British Ambassador in Dublin, Sir Alexander Clutterbuck, thought D'Alton's proposals 'courageous and sensible' but doubted if any Irish political party would support rejoining the Commonwealth, particularly with a General Election campaign under way.[88] The former Labour minister and historian of the 1921 Treaty, T. F. Pakenham (later Lord Longford), discussed the matter with de Valera in September 1957, but de Valera made it clear that rejoining the Commonwealth was dependent on the ending of partition. Neither Lord Home, the Commonwealth Secretary, nor the British Prime Minister, Harold Macmillan, exactly radiated enthusiasm at the prospect of the Irish rejoining the Commonwealth. While Macmillan thought that in theory it 'would be nice if Éire came in', he doubted if 'a united Ireland—with de Valera as a sort of Irish Nehru—would do us much good. Let us stand by our friends'. Home thought they were well rid of the Irish, who had been such a disruptive force in the Commonwealth before 1949. In any event, in a comment which showed how tenacious and out of date were British views on allegiance, Home stated his belief that the Irish 'would never politically accept allegiance to the Crown, or indeed accept her even as Head of Commonwealth'.[89]

The issue emerged again in March 1958 when, during a visit to London, de Valera and Frank Aiken proposed to Lord Home that 'Northern Ireland should surrender its direct allegiance to the Queen in return for a United Republic of Ireland within the Commonwealth, recognising the Queen as its head'.[90] The British response was negative. The proposal surfaced again in November 1959, just after Seán Lemass succeeded de Valera as

---

[87] My thanks to Daithi Ó Corráin of Trinity College, Dublin for these references to D'Alton from his forthcoming Ph.D. History thesis, 'The Churches and The Border'.
[88] Clutterbuck to CRO, 7 March 1957, DO 35/7845.
[89] Home to Macmillan, Aug. 1958, DO 35/7891.
[90] Memorandum by Home, 18 March 1958, DO 35/7891.

Taoiseach. Lemass was sure that a relationship between a reunited Ireland and the Commonwealth could be worked out but doubted if the Northern Ireland government would consider it. In May of the following year Lemass issued an invitation to the Commonwealth premiers, who were in London for the Commonwealth Conference, to visit Dublin. The Ghanaian leader, Kwame Nkrumah, accepted and paid a two-day visit.[91] A few years later, however, it was reported that the liberal Ulster Unionist MP, Henry Clark, had asked Paul Keating, counsellor at the Irish embassy in London, when the Irish would rejoin the Commonwealth, adding that Lemass 'would make a great impression at the Commonwealth Conference'.[92] In July 1965, Sir Joe Garner, Permanent Under-Secretary at the Commonwealth Relations Office (CRO), told the Irish Ambassador in London, J. G. Molloy, that he would like to see Ireland back in the Commonwealth.[93] But Europe was already beckoning. The first Irish application to join the Common Market was in 1961 and Ireland eventually joined in 1973. The question of Irish sovereignty had been a major issue for Irish officials and historical parallels were unavoidable. As the Irish Ambassador in Rome wrote in 1970: 'our entry into the EEC with all the rights of a member state is hardly on all fours with the act of Union of 1800 which has proved so difficult for Ireland to reverse'.[94]

Until the relevant archives are released, we do not know whether rejoining the Commonwealth was seriously discussed by the two governments during the Northern Ireland Troubles, although it did surface in the press from time to time. It received more attention immediately before and after the 1998 Belfast Agreement. Before she left office in 1997, the Irish President, Mary Robinson (whose family had close links with the British colonial service), suggested that the Irish government should seriously consider the idea. The Taoiseach, Bertie Ahern, seemed willing to consider

---

[91] Sir Ian Maclennan (Dublin) to G. W. Chadwick (CRO, formerly the Dominions Office, London) 24 May 1960, DO 35/7854.

[92] Quoted by John Horgan, 'Irish Foreign Policy, Northern Ireland, Neutrality and the Commonwealth: The Historical Roots of a Current Controversy', *Irish Studies in International Affairs*, 10 (1999), pp. 146–47.

[93] Ó Corráin, 'The Churches and the Border'. Garner had been dealing with Irish affairs since the 1930s and in *The Commonwealth Office, 1925–68* (London, 1978) wrote sympathetically about Irish relations with the CRO.

[94] Quoted by Gary Murphy, '"A Measurement of the Extent of our Sovereignty at the Moment": Sovereignty and the Question of Irish Entry to the EEC, New Evidence from the Archives', *Irish Studies in International Affairs*, 12 (2001), p. 202.

rejoining but did not subsequently expand on this in any detail. In an article in the *Irish Times* in November 2001, a Canadian law professor, Robert Martin, urged the Irish to rejoin, pointing out that all but one of the priority recipient countries for Irish overseas aid were members of the Commonwealth. The Commonwealth, he wrote, 'is not, as many Irish people imagine it to be, the British Empire in drag; it is not the resurrected cadaver of Empire. It's over half a century since Ireland left the Commonwealth. It's time for the Irish to take another look'.[95]

Select Bibliography

DONALD HARMAN AKENSON, *The Irish Diaspora: A Primer* (Belfast, 1994).

ANDY BIELENBERG, ed., *The Irish Diaspora* (Harlow, 2000).

RICHARD P. DAVIS, *Irish Issues in New Zealand Politics, 1868–1922* (Dunedin, 1974).

TERENCE DENMAN, *A Lonely Grave: The Life and Death of William Redmond* (Dublin, 1994).

DENIS GWYNN, *The Life of John Redmond* (London, 1932).

DAVID HARKNESS, *The Restless Dominion: The Irish Free State and the British Commonwealth of Nations, 1921–31* (London, 1969).

KEITH JEFFERY, ed., *'An Irish Empire? Aspects of Ireland and the British Empire* (Manchester, 1996).

MICHAEL KENNEDY, ed., *Documents on Irish Foreign Policy. Vol. 1, 1919–22* (Dublin, 1998); *Vol. 2, 1923–26* (Dublin, 2000); *Vol. 3, 1926–32* (Dublin, 2002).

MICHAEL KENNEDY and JOSEPH MORRISON SKELLY, eds., *Irish Foreign Policy, 1919–1966: From Independence to Internationalism* (Dublin, 2000).

DIANA MANSERGH, ed., *Nationalism and Independence: Selected Irish Papers by Nicholas Mansergh* (Cork, 1997).

NICHOLAS MANSERGH, *The Unresolved Question: The Anglo-Irish Settlement and its Undoing, 1912–72* (London, 1991).

IAN McCABE, *A Diplomatic History of Ireland, 1948–49: The Republic, the Commonwealth and NATO* (Dublin, 1991).

DONAL P. McCRACKEN, *The Irish Pro-Boers* (Johannesburg, 1989).

ALAN O'DAY, *Irish Home Rule, 1867–1921* (Manchester, 1998).

PATRICK O'FARRELL, *The Irish in Australia* (Kensington, NSW, 1987).

G. K. PEATLING, *British Opinion and Irish Self-Government, 1865–1925: From Unionism to Liberal Commonwealth* (Dublin, 2001).

---

[95] *Irish Times*, 23 Nov. 2001.

8

Historiography

STEPHEN HOWE

Most historians would concur that the history of modern Ireland has been intimately associated with that of the British Empire. Beyond that minimal consensus, there is wide, often deep, sometimes bitter dispute. Some scholars, especially many of those in literary and cultural studies, view the entirety of Ireland's past in colonial terms and its present as distinctively 'postcolonial'. Many political writers and activists, especially those from the republican tradition, share this view but express it in a very different idiom, being often especially concerned to press the case that contemporary Northern Ireland remains subject to British imperialism. A growing body of historical work, especially that focused on the sixteenth and seventeenth centuries, seeks to integrate Ireland's story into that of English, then British, attempts at empire-building, both within the British-Irish islands themselves and across the whole Atlantic world. Some other authorities on the same periods, however, remain deeply sceptical about the very use of colonial labels for Ireland's past, or urge that such terminology is too vague, or too subjective, to be of value.[1]

The limits and boundaries of this chapter are therefore hard to set. An enormous body of historical writing—or rather, several different bodies, plus material from political, economic, and cultural theorists, anthropologists, and others—is evidently relevant. A far smaller body of work, of varied origins, uneven quality, and often highly partisan character, takes Ireland and Empire as its explicit focus, in the sense of using concepts such as imperialism and colonialism in analysing the Irish past, or of seeking substantially to incorporate Ireland into general histories or

---

[1] For instance, T. C. Barnard, 'Crises of Identity among Irish Protestants, 1641–1685', *Past and Present*, 127 (1990), p. 40; Steven G. Ellis, 'Writing Irish History: Revisionism, Colonialism, and the British Isles', *Irish Review* (hereafter *IR*), 19 (1996), pp. 1–21.

theories of British imperialism.[2] These different kinds of writing have often pursued parallel rather than intersecting tracks. The ensuing controversies have intertwined with others, including the long dispute between so-called 'revisionists' in Irish history and their opponents, and that over whether the island of Ireland contains 'two nations' or just one. These are often highly politically charged debates, with strands of republican and cultural nationalist thought inclined to welcome colonial models for understanding Ireland, and Ulster Unionists rejecting them. Some commentators even suggest that others' failure to adopt colonial models—especially in relation to modern Northern Irish history—must necessarily be a quite direct result of political censorship or self-censorship, of a pro-Unionist or 'British Establishment' kind.[3] The very terminology involved—colonialism, imperialism, postcoloniality, neo-colonialism and so on—is intensely, complexly contested in global as well as in specifically Irish debates. These terms, moreover, are often used in loosely allusive or even metaphorical ways.[4]

This chapter will offer a critical survey of the field, giving fairly brief treatment to broad themes in the extensive literature relevant to, but not explicitly focused on, 'Ireland and Empire', and focusing in more detail on major instances of the work which does make colonialism in Ireland its explicit focus. The emphasis will be on fairly recent writings, since substantive historical, or historically informed, investigation of Ireland employing such concepts as colonialism and imperialism has, for the most part, emerged only in the past few decades. The chapter will review the scholarly literature on each of four periods: early-modern, eighteenth-century, the period of Union, and the era since independence. It will then turn to an analysis of postcolonial theory and a consideration of some new contexts and directions for the subject.

---

[2] See Stephen Howe, *Ireland and Empire: Colonial Legacies in Irish History and Culture*, second edn. with new Preface (Oxford, 2002) and 'The Politics of Historical "Revisionism": Comparing Ireland and Israel/Palestine', *Past and Present*, 168 (2000), pp. 227–53.

[3] David Miller, 'Colonialism and Academic Representations of the Troubles' and Pamela Clayton, 'Religion, Ethnicity and Colonialism as Explanations of the Northern Ireland Conflict', both in David Miller, ed., *Rethinking Northern Ireland: Culture, Ideology and Colonialism* (Harlow, 1998); Robbie McVeigh, 'The British/Irish "Peace Process" and the Colonial Legacy', in James Anderson and James Goodman, eds., *Dis/Agreeing Ireland: Contexts, Obstacles, Hopes* (London, 1998).

[4] Stephen Howe, *Empire: A Very Short Introduction* (Oxford, 2002).

Much recent writing on early-modern Irish history has sought to move away from insularity, or from near-exclusive focus on a bipolar English-Irish relationship, through a 'four nations' or 'archipelagic' approach, or through one which relates Irish and British developments to patterns of change across Europe and, later, the Atlantic world. Each of these approaches has yielded a range of both complementary insights and competing views on the appropriateness of colonial models for understanding early-modern Ireland. It is the framework of Atlantic history, however, pioneered by David Beers Quinn and most influentially explored by Nicholas Canny, which has had the strongest impact on that debate.[5]

The 'archipelagic' model, initially inspired by the work of J. G. A. Pocock, has sometimes seemed complementary to Atlantic and colonial ones; though other practitioners, including Canny and Steven Ellis, have viewed the relationship as a more antagonistic one. Ellis tends to stress how English policies in Ireland resembled those pursued within England itself, and how different they were from those undertaken in the Americas, let alone the characteristic patterns of later colonial expansion. Neither the language of 'colonization' nor that of 'colonialism', in his view, well fits early-modern Ireland.[6] Canny, for his part, sees a residual 'Greater British' nationalism lurking behind at least some uses of the archipelagic approach, including Pocock's own, and therefore avows himself a 'Brito-sceptic'.[7]

Resolution of such arguments depends not only on evaluation of English-British policies in Ireland or the actual course of events there, but

---

[5] D. B. Quinn, *The Elizabethans and the Irish* (Ithaca, NY, 1966). By Nicholas Canny, see: 'The Ideology of English Colonization: From Ireland to America', *William & Mary Quarterly* (hereafter *WMQ*), Third Series, XXX (1973), pp. 575–98; *Kingdom and Colony: Ireland in the Atlantic World, 1560–1800* (Baltimore, 1988); 'The Origins of Empire: An Introduction' and 'England's New World and the Old, 1480s–1630s', in Canny, ed., *OHBE. Vol. I. The Origins of Empire: British Overseas Enterprise to the Close of the Seventeenth Century* (Oxford: 1998), pp. 1–33, 148–69; and *Making Ireland British, 1580–1650* (Oxford, 2001).

[6] Steven Ellis, *Tudor Ireland: Crown, Community and the Conflict of Cultures, 1470–1603* (London, 1985); 'Nationalist Historiography and the English and Gaelic Worlds in the Late Middle Ages', *Irish Historical Studies* (hereafter *IHS*), XXV, no. 97 (1986), pp. 1–18; and 'Representations of the Past in Ireland: Whose Past and Whose Present?', *IHS*, XXVII, no. 108 (1991), pp. 289–308.

[7] Canny, 'Irish, Scottish and Welsh Responses to Centralisation, c.1530–c.1640: A Comparative Perspective', in Alexander Grant and Keith Stringer, eds., *Uniting the Kingdom? The Making of British History* (London, 1995); Canny, 'Commonwealth Fund lecture', University College London, 5 April 2002.

on what view is taken of English, Irish, and later British, identity-forma-
tion, and of the national groups' images of one another. For the start of
the period, the very categories 'English' and 'Irish' may be anachronisms.
Historians argue energetically over how far back in time such national
labels can aptly be applied. Even later, particular individuals and groups
evidently had changeable or hybrid identities: the same person might be
viewed as English, as Irish, as both, or indeed as neither, from different
perspectives or at different times. 'Old English' and later 'Anglo-Irish' identities in early-modern Ireland are the most obvious examples. A fine recent
historical study of Ulster Scots migration and settlement on both sides of
the Atlantic is entitled *The People With No Name*, precisely to underline the
mutability of their collective identities, as viewed both by the migrants and
by others.[8] Yet it is plausible to argue that a sense of English identity and
indeed superiority was forged very early, perhaps, on comparative perspective, uniquely early. It was formed, on this view, not least through conflict
and conquest in Ireland, suggesting that ideas of profound cultural, even
racial, difference—later overlaid or intermingled with religious schisms—
not only marked English attitudes and policies in Ireland, but made these
qualitatively different from those operating in other early-modern European 'ethnic frontiers', and indeed more aptly comparable to those which
came to hold sway in non-European zones of colonial conquest. Parallel
historical investigations into the development of Irish national self-images
have offered widely divergent accounts, with earlier romantic nationalist
chroniclers tending naturally to proclaim or assume their great antiquity,
but perhaps the most influential modern studies seeing them as mainly
eighteenth and nineteenth-century creations.[9]

Literary critics and cultural historians have contributed vigorously, and
disputatiously, to these debates, with a considerable outpouring of work
on the attitudes towards Ireland of major English literary figures such as
Shakespeare, Milton, and above all Edmund Spenser.[10] The latter's *View of*

[8] Patrick Griffin, *The People with No Name: Ireland's Ulster Scots, America's Scots Irish, and
the Creation of a British Atlantic World, 1689–1764* (Princeton, 2001).

[9] Joep T. Leerssen, *Mere Irish and Fíor-Gael: Studies in the Idea of Irish Nationality, its
Development and Literary Expression Prior to the Nineteenth Century* (Amsterdam, 1988) and
*Remembrance and Imagination: Patterns in the Historical and Literary Representation of Ireland
in the Nineteenth Century* (Cork, 1996).

[10] Amidst a vast literature, see Willy Maley, *Salvaging Spenser: Colonialism, Culture and
Identity* (Basingstoke, 1997); Andrew Hadfield, *Spenser's Irish Experience* (Oxford, 1997); and
Canny, *Making Ireland British*, pp. 1–58.

the Present State of Ireland (which remained unpublished until 1633) advocated a harsh policy of repression or even extermination. Historians have differed sharply over how representative or influential such extreme proposals may have been, and on how far Spenser's epic *Faerie Queene* (1590–96) should be read as presenting a similar view in allegorical form. Much of the debate resolves itself into the question: how far was early English writing about Ireland a colonialist literature? Some commentators, including in recent years those influenced by postcolonial theory, would emphasize its general tendency to stereotype, denigrate, and scorn its subjects. They see a great deal of this literature as directly linked to and supporting England's attempts at conquest, domination, and exploitation. A hard-edged division of the world between civilized and barbarian, the foundation for all subsequent imperialist ideology, was on this view already evident in sixteenth-century English ideas about Ireland.[11]

Other scholars, looking at the same English literary sources from the sixteenth and seventeenth centuries, have drawn quite different conclusions. David Armitage, for instance, believes that the idea of Empire and specifically colonial themes feature only very marginally in early modern English literature. Where such themes do appear, the writers are often critics, not supporters, of the colonial enterprise. We should, he implies, be more impressed by the weakness than by the strength of early English ideologies of Empire.[12] However the general claim about early colonial discourses' strength or weakness may be judged, it is undoubtedly true that, Spenser aside, few major English writers of the era gave close attention to Ireland. To note this is not, however, to deny the extensive English efforts to impose a policy of what some would call 'linguistic colonialism'.[13]

Moving beyond literary sources to the wider historical debate, there has been almost as much disagreement. Much recent historical work,

---

[11] See for instance Seamus Deane, 'Civilians and Barbarians', in *Ireland's Field Day*, ed. Field Day Theatre Company (London, 1985), pp. 33–42.

[12] David Armitage, 'Literature and Empire,' in Canny, ed. *OHBE. Vol. I*, pp. 99–123; Armitage, *The Ideological Origins of the British Empire* (Cambridge, 2000); and Armitage, 'John Milton: Poet Against Empire', in David Armitage, Armand Himy, and Quentin Skinner, eds., *Milton and Republicanism* (Cambridge, 1995). For comparative perspectives, see Anthony Pagden, *Lords of All the World: Ideologies of Empire in Spain, Britain and France, c.1500–c.1800* (New Haven and London, 1995).

[13] Clare Carroll, *Circe's Cup: Cultural Transformations in Early Modern Ireland* (Cork, 2001); Patricia Palmer, *Language and Conquest in Early Modern Ireland: English Renaissance Literature and Elizabethan Imperial Expansion* (Cambridge, 2001).

especially by Canny, has looked closely at the ways in which Ireland came to be viewed by policy-makers and would-be rulers as part of England's emerging overseas Empire, and how this process interacted with Ireland's status as both a part of a larger British state and a separate though subordinate kingdom in itself. Two distinct images of Ireland persisted and contended right across the early-modern era: as a sovereign entity, and as a field of colonial settlement or exploitation. Neither image ever wholly predominated over the other.[14] Though Henry VIII had taken the title King of Ireland in 1541, this did not mark, as his advisers had hoped, Ireland's full incorporation under English rule. Neither did the Protestant Reformation (which, of course, failed to win majority support or even acquiescence in Ireland) nor the defeat of O'Neill's rising and of Spanish intervention in 1600–01. Although much recent historical work—perhaps, again, above all Canny's—has emphasized the power and purposefulness of an English Protestant ideology of colonization in Ireland, some historians have nonetheless concluded that the result was what Lennon calls an 'incomplete conquest', while the drive to 'make Ireland British' was in the end, in Canny's own words, 'a costly failure'.[15]

In an argument closely paralleling an influential interpretation of nineteenth-century colonial expansion, some recent scholars see the whole course of events in early-modern Ireland as driven far more by unforeseen crises on the periphery than by English officials' aims or ideologies.[16] Others—perhaps most forcefully, in recent years, Brendan Bradshaw—continue to urge the centrality of English rulers' ideas, especially religious ones.[17] Canny stresses that much of the English conquerors' motivation was, by their own lights or at least in their own rhetoric, benign: 'where

[14] Ciaran Brady and Raymond Gillespie, eds., *Natives and Newcomers: The Making of Irish Colonial Society, 1534–1641* (Dublin, 1986); Karl Bottigheimer, 'Kingdom and Colony: Ireland in the Westward Enterprise, 1536–1660,' in K. R. Andrews, N. P. Canny, and P. E. Hair, eds., *The Westward Enterprise: English Activities in Ireland, the Atlantic and America, 1480–1650* (Liverpool, 1978).

[15] Colm Lennon, *Sixteenth-Century Ireland: The Incomplete Conquest* (Dublin, 1994); Canny, *Making Ireland British*, p. 578.

[16] See for instance Ciaran Brady, *The Chief Governors: The Rise and Fall of Reform Government in Tudor Ireland, 1536–1588* (Cambridge, 1994).

[17] Brendan Bradshaw, *The Irish Constitutional Revolution of the Sixteenth Century* (Cambridge, 1979) and 'The Tudor Revolution and Reformation in Wales and Ireland: The Origins of the British Problem', in Brendan Bradshaw and John Morrill, eds., *The British Problem, c.1534–1707: State Formation in the Atlantic Archipelago* (Basingstoke, 1996).

to the twentieth-century mind the term "colonization" conjures up the image of primitive people being exploited by Europeans', he writes, 'this was not necessarily the association with the word in the sixteenth century, and English advocates of colonization were clearly concerned to convince their superiors in government that they fostered no exploitative intentions'.[18] Yet, as with many other episodes of conquest across the globe, protestations of, or even sincere belief in, rulers' benevolent intent could readily coexist with a reality of extreme violence.

By the late seventeenth century, in the aftermath of the Williamite wars, the 'incomplete conquest' of previous centuries had apparently been made total, at least on the level of a temporarily almost unchallenged British political overrule, while Ireland's demography and social structure had been transformed by the devastation of the long seventeenth-century wars, large-scale Catholic dispossession, transplantation, emigration, and substantial Anglo-Scottish settlement especially in the north-east. The last of these has become a special focus for debate among historians interested in the applicability of comparative colonial models for Ireland. How did the social, economic, and ideological patterns established by these migrants and their descendants relate to those of settler-colonial communities elsewhere?

Meanwhile, among the Catholic majority, cultural changes were unleashed which some modern writers have identified as distinctively colonial: the decline of the Irish language, the marginalization and persecution of the majority religion (most obviously under a series of anti-Catholic penal laws), and the ever-increasing association of social status and power with Englishness, Britishness, and/or Anglican Protestantism. Yet if some observers—perhaps more often wide-ranging cultural critics than specialist historians of the eighteenth century—have seen here a pattern of cultural colonialism very like that later visited on Africa and Asia, others stress that there was no stark, simple cultural opposition of colonizers to colonized, but rather numerous forms of cultural hybridity and syncretism. These included an 'Anglo-Irish' milieu whose distinguished intellectual products featured such figures as Burke, Goldsmith, Sheridan, and Swift, a 'hidden Ireland' and 'underground gentry' among Catholics, and Ulster Dissenters' development of a distinctive politico-religious radical-

---

[18] Canny, *Kingdom and Colony*, p. 14.

ism with close links to Scotland.[19] Some historians have countered that emphasis on this diversity does not necessarily disable the applicability of colonial models to eighteenth-century Ireland, for multiple modes of cultural interaction and mingling characterized many other, later colonial situations too. Historians such as Seán Connolly and C. D. A. Leighton suggest that this society—pre-industrial, dominated by structures of patronage and clientship rather than class, ruled by a landed élite and a confessional state—resembles continental Europe's *ancien régimes* more than it does the 'colonial societies' either of the time or later.[20] Yet, as Tom Bartlett points out, this need not be an 'either/or' argument: a single society can include attributes of both models, colonial and *ancien régime*.[21]

At the heart of these controversies lie the identities and ideologies of the Protestant élites, because it was they who held most of the wealth and local power and consequently have been more intensely studied than have subaltern groups. How far and in what ways did they come to identify themselves as Irish? How far did they conceive of their situation as distinctively colonial, and develop a 'colonial nationalism' like that emerging in the Americas? In so far as nationalism did become powerful in Ireland, why did it fail to achieve legislative independence as its American counterparts did?[22] For most historians of eighteenth-century Ireland, the idea of colonial nationalism has indeed become an organizing principle.

[19] Daniel Corkery, *The Hidden Ireland: A Study of Gaelic Munster in the 18th Century* (Dublin, 1925); Kevin Whelan, *The Tree of Liberty: Radicalism, Catholicism and the Construction of Irish Identity, 1760–1830* (Cork, 1996); Breandán Ó Buachalla, 'Irish Jacobitism and Irish Nationalism: The Literary Evidence', in Michael O'Dea and Kevin Whelan, eds., *Nations and Nationalisms: France, Britain, Ireland and the Eighteenth Century Context* (Oxford, 1995); I. R. McBride, *Scripture Politics: Ulster Presbyterian Radicalism in the Late Eighteenth Century* (Oxford, 1998); Leerssen, *Mere Irish and Fíor-Gael*.

[20] C. D. A. Leighton, *Catholicism in a Protestant Kingdom: A Study of the Irish Ancien Régime* (Dublin, 1994); S. J. Connolly, *Religion, Law and Power: The Making of Protestant Ireland* (Oxford, 1992).

[21] See chap. 3, above, p. 72.

[22] For a range of views see, *inter alia*, Nicholas Canny, 'Irish Resistance to Empire? 1641, 1690 and 1798', in Lawrence Stone, ed., *An Imperial State at War: Britain from 1689 to 1815* (London, 1994); Aidan Clarke, 'Colonial Identity in Early 17th-century Ireland', in T. W. Moody, ed., *Nationality and the Pursuit of National Independence. Historical Studies, XI* (Belfast, 1978); J. L. McCracken, 'Protestant Ascendancy and the Rise of Colonial Nationalism', in T. W. Moody and W. E. Vaughan, eds., *A New History of Ireland. Vol. IV. Eighteenth-Century Ireland, 1691–1800* (Oxford, 1986); R. B. McDowell, *Ireland in the Age of Imperialism and Revolution, 1760–1801* (Oxford, 1979); Thomas McLoughlin, *Contesting Ireland: Irish Voices against England in the Eighteenth Century* (Dublin, 1999).

A minority view, however, well represented by Toby Barnard, doubts the applicability of such models beyond a very restricted and short-lived context, and sees them as implying a mistaken teleology (by which Irish independence 'should' naturally have eventuated), and thinks that continental European parallels, such as that with Bohemia, are more apt.[23]

Perhaps the sharpest divergence among historians of the eighteenth century—one that is very relevant to debate on the earlier and later periods as well—is over how far Ireland's ethnic and confessional divisions were seen by contemporaries, or should be analysed by us, as 'racial'. Are terms like 'apartheid', whether used as broad (and emotive) analogies, or as would-be close structural comparisons, at all appropriate?[24] There is dispute, moreover, about how far Ireland was treated as an inferior colonial possession in either constitutional or economic terms, though almost everyone agrees on its hybrid, even unclassifiable position. Britain discriminated against Irish agricultural imports, but Ireland was not shut out from Atlantic trade, including the slave trade (Irish participation in which has attracted new attention in recent historiography).[25] Although in theory Ireland retained the status of a separate kingdom with its own Parliament, in practice the Irish legislature had less real power than did the Assemblies of many American colonies.

Across these disagreements, there is a more general concurrence that it is anachronistic to use labels such as 'imperialism', 'anticolonialism', and perhaps even 'nationalism', at least before the later eighteenth century.[26] Most varieties of Irish political thought were variants on British ones, from Jacobitism through 'Patriot' invocations of citizen virtue, to the influence of Scottish theological disputes in Ulster. Even 'Whiteboys' were known to declare their loyalty to the Crown, and some United Irishmen

---

[23] Barnard, 'Crises of Identity' and 'New Opportunities for British Settlement: Ireland, 1650–1700', in Canny, ed., *OHBE. Vol. I*, pp. 309–27.

[24] Canny, 'Protestants, Planters and Apartheid in Early Modern Ireland', *IHS*, 22, 98 (1986), pp. 105–15.

[25] R. C. Nash, 'Irish Atlantic Trade in the Seventeenth and Eighteenth Centuries', *WMQ*, Third Series, XLIII (1985), pp. 329–56; Nini Rodgers, 'Ireland and the Black Atlantic in the Eighteenth Century', *IHS*, 32, 126 (2000), pp. 174–92. See also chap. 3, above, pp. 63–68.

[26] On the other hand, Joe Cleary is correct that we cannot 'settle' disputes over the applicability of analytical terms simply by asking whether contemporaries would have recognized them; see his 'Misplaced Ideas? Locating and Dislocating Ireland in Colonial and Postcolonial Studies', in Crystal Bartolovich and Neil Lazarus, eds., *Marxism, Modernity and Postcolonial Studies* (Cambridge, 2002).

dreamed of a future free Ireland building its own overseas Empire. Yet much the same could be said of political argument in Britain's American colonies. The existence of a substantially shared discourse, most historians would now concur, was no necessary barrier to the rise of separatism. A mass of recent scholarship on the United Irish movement, the 1798 rising, the Act of Union, and their backgrounds underlines how complex and often unexpected Irish political alignments were in these years. Not the least surprising of these phenomena, in light of the allegiances of later decades, is the fierceness of opposition to Union among Irish Protestants and, indeed, Orangemen.[27]

Legislative Union with Britain made Ireland part of a unitary Kingdom: on a constitutional level Ireland's ambiguous 'colonial' status had come to an end. Advocates of Union indeed stressed that it would enable Ireland to play a fuller role in Britain's imperial expansion beyond Europe. Yet scholarly debate over Ireland and colonialism is no less intense and complex for the nineteenth century than for earlier eras, for evidently enough, in some ways and by some definitions, the country's position as a subordinated part of the British imperial system was intensified, not ended, by Union. Debate on these questions has intermingled with several others: notably on the character of nineteenth-century Irish nationalism, on how British policies and 'official minds' treated Ireland, and on changing attitudes to 'race'. And the closer one gets to the present, the more one finds that contemporaries, not just later commentators, deployed the language of imperialism and anti-imperialism in relation to Ireland. Three kinds of difficulty or ambiguity in definition and conceptualization have especially complicated this emerging structure of debate on Ireland's position under the Union: firstly, the sheer complexity and heterogeneity of Britain's imperial system; secondly, the shifts and mixtures of language involved in nineteenth and early twentieth-century discourse on Empire (where the idea of empire did not mean only territories outside the 'core' state, but— not least in debates on Irish Home Rule—encompassed the 'core' too and often had it as its primary referent); and, thirdly, the lack of consensus or sometimes even basic information on the impact of the Empire within Britain itself.

---

[27] On the Union, see chap. 3, above, pp. 82–88.

Historians find it hard to place British thought about Ireland in relation to a general discourse of Empire, simply because there was no such generalized discourse. Neither British colonialism's political structures nor its contemporary cultural representations formed a coherent, let alone homogenous, system. Britain's overseas possessions included an extraordinary variety of types of territory and forms of rule, and British attitudes to them, whether official or popular, were equally heterogenous.[28] Thus, arguments over whether or in what ways Ireland's position was 'colonial' have often been weakened by a tendency to assume a generalized or homogenized picture of 'the colonial situation' against which Irish experience can be compared, whereas in reality no such singular situation obtained across the vast variety of colonial systems. There is, though, something of a paradox here. Some critics have seen this diversity as a major argument against many applications of colonial and postcolonial theory to Ireland, and indeed against some very influential currents in cultural studies of Empire more generally; others, conversely, see it more as an argument against 'naïve *objections* to the thesis that Ireland was a colony'.[29]

To what degree, and in what ways, did Victorian and Edwardian British official opinion and policy-making perceive Irish questions as colonial ones? There is, as yet, no substantial body of historical writing that illuminates this question.[30] The literatures on British domestic statecraft, on policy towards Ireland, and on the 'official minds' of British imperialism are generally quite distinct, with strikingly little interconnection. It is surprising that this has remained so, especially for work dealing with the later nineteenth century and the start of the twentieth, for surely this was just the period when the discourse of Empire fused most fully with that of British nationality, through the ideas of 'Greater Britain' and of 'Commonwealth'.[31] Meanwhile it was precisely Ireland's 'hybrid' position which

---

[28] See, for instance, Andrew S. Thompson, *Imperial Britain: The Empire in British Politics, c.1880–1932* (London, 2000).

[29] Howe, *Ireland and Empire*; Cleary, 'Misplaced Ideas?', p. 109 (emphasis added).

[30] For the era of the Union an early, partial exception is Nicholas Mansergh, *The Irish Question, 1840–1921* (London, 1965). More recent exceptions include John Kendle, *Ireland and the Federal Solution: The Debate over the United Kingdom Constitution, 1870–1921* (Kingston and Montreal, 1989) and *Federal Britain: A History* (London, 1997).

[31] The term 'Commonwealth' in this period referred to a 'family of British-descended peoples' rather than, as later, a multiracial association of states. On Greater Britain, see

made it an important hinge between debates on domestic politics and those on the future of the Empire. It can safely be predicted that, in the near future, a growing body of scholarly work will seek to investigate the place of Ireland and Irishness in this complex.

The same might well be said of the domestic impacts of the Empire. Until quite recently, most British history-writing largely overlooked the ways in which the Empire and its aftermaths permeated and shaped many aspects of British life. Latterly, this omission has been corrected, perhaps in some cases overcorrected, with some proponents of a 'new imperial history' taking it as an article of faith that colonialism's domestic influences were all-pervasive, the very ideas of Englishness and Britishness being entirely products of imperialism. Yet there have also been important, innovative recent studies of these themes, such as those by John MacKenzie and Catherine Hall, which avoid such sweeping assumptions.[32] More recently still, similar kinds of work have begun to be undertaken for Ireland, and these seem likely to proliferate in the future.[33]

Equally, few substantial studies on British perceptions of Irish questions as 'colonial' ones have extended beyond the particular context of debates on Home Rule or imperial federation to a wider pattern of interconnection with other parts of the Empire. It still proves possible, therefore, for serious scholars to propose entirely contrary answers to quite restricted questions in this sphere (such as whether there was any significant Irish influence on British colonial policing) despite the apparent lack of any sharp ideological or paradigmatic divergence between them, and despite their appealing to much the same body of evidence.[34] More contentiously, it may be (but so far has not often been) asked what place, if any, a

Charles Dilke, *Greater Britain* (London, 1868) and *Problems of Greater Britain*, 2 vols. (London, 1890); J. R. Seeley, *The Expansion of England* (London, 1883); and the broad historiographical discussion in David Armitage, 'Greater Britain: A Useful Category of Historical Analysis?', *American Historical Review*, 104 (April 1999), pp. 427–45.

[32] See, for instance, John Mackenzie, ed., *Imperialism and Popular Culture* (Manchester, 1986) and several later volumes in the Manchester 'Studies in Imperialism' series under Mackenzie's editorship; Catherine Hall, *Civilising Subjects: Metropole and Colony in the English Imagination, 1830–1867* (Oxford, 2002).

[33] See several of the contributions to Keith Jeffery, ed., *'An Irish Empire'? Aspects of Ireland and the British Empire* (Manchester, 1996).

[34] Compare Richard Hawkins, 'The "Irish Model" and the Empire: A Case for Reassessment', in David Anderson and David Killingray, eds., *Policing the Empire: Government, Authority and Control* (Manchester, 1992) with Keith Jeffery's 'Introduction' to Jeffery, ed., *Irish Empire?*

'colonialist' mindset played in British government failure to provide effective relief in the great Irish Famine of the 1840s. A recent study by S. B. Cook is perhaps the most important attempt to extend the enquiry, focusing on land policies and arguing for a close interaction between attitudes to Ireland and those toward India.[35]

Somewhat more widely analysed, though again historiographically contentious, have been Irish nationalists' international attitudes and contacts, including those with anticolonialist movements elsewhere in the British imperial system. Most historians agree that the closest Irish imperial links and sympathies tended to be with movements in the colonies of white settlement, sometimes involving racially exclusivist or supremacist ideas, including complaints that Ireland's lack of self-rule was peculiarly intolerable precisely because the Irish were white.[36] Little explicitly 'anti-imperialist' thought or writing of a global or general kind is to be found in nineteenth or early-twentieth century Irish nationalism, even if some important individuals, from Daniel O'Connell to early Irish socialist thinkers such as James Connolly or Liam Mellows, expressed broad internationalist sympathies (and, at least in Mellows's case, a programmatic anticolonialism).[37] Several historians have investigated contacts and mutual influences between Irish and Indian nationalists.[38] They have

---

[35] Scott B. Cook, *Imperial Affinities: Nineteenth Century Analogies and Exchanges Between India and Ireland* (New Delhi, 1993) and '"The Irish Raj": Social Origins and Careers of Irishmen in the Indian Civil Service, 1855–1919', *Journal of Social History*, 20, 3 (1987), pp. 507–29. John Turner attempts a wider-ranging but less well documented argument in 'Letting Go: The Conservative Party and the End of the Union with Ireland', in Grant and Stringer, eds., *Uniting?*, pp. 255–74. For a contrary view to Turner's see Stephen Evans, 'The Conservatives and the Redefinition of Unionism, 1912–21', *Twentieth Century British History*, 9, 1 (1998), pp. 1–27.

[36] See Howe, *Ireland and Empire*, especially pp. 42–54, which concurs with Cleary ('Misplaced Ideas?', pp. 104–05, 108–09) that such attitudes were neither surprising nor unusual when placed in context.

[37] For Connolly as a thoroughgoing and indeed pioneering anticolonialist, see for instance Robert J. C. Young, *Postcolonialism: An Historical Introduction* (Oxford, 2001), pp. 303–07. For a more sceptical view, see Austen Morgan, *James Connolly: A Political Biography* (Manchester, 1988) or Howe, *Ireland and Empire*, pp. 62–64, 159; and on Mellows's anticolonialism, C. Desmond Greaves, *Liam Mellows and the Irish Revolution* (London, 1971), pp. 205–08, 278, 365–69.

[38] H. V. Brasted, 'Indian Nationalist Development and the Influence of Irish Home Rule, 1870–1886', *Modern Asian Studies*, 14, 1 (1980), pp. 24–45; 'Irish Nationalism and the British Empire in the Late 19th Century', in Oliver MacDonagh, W. F. Mandle, and Pauric Travers, eds., *Irish Culture and Nationalism, 1750–1950* (Dublin, 1983); and 'Irish Models and the Indian

come to divergent conclusions about the significance of such contacts, though the dominant impression is that Irish experience influenced Indian nationalist politicians rather more than vice versa. Some scholars in literary and cultural studies have also recently turned to such themes, but in ways that, to some critics, risk overstating the *political* significance of individuals' *cultural* contacts or interests. While some Irish writers— most obviously, W. B. Yeats—were fascinated by Indian and other eastern cultures, this did not necessarily carry clear political implications or have a wider influence on political or intellectual debate.[39]

These scholarly exchanges relate to a broader one, about the place of racial attitudes in British-Irish-Empire relations, including the roles of anti-Irish racism and of Irish people's own racial ideas. Here a multidirectional and sometimes heated debate has been staged, with some urging very close parallels between anti-Irish and anti-black racisms in nineteenth (and indeed twentieth) century Britain and that such parallels are a central component in the case for seeing Ireland's position as colonial.[40] Others dispute the details of such a case, the claims about the nature or relative intensity of the different forms of prejudice, and the suggested necessary link between colonialism and racism or even, as with Sheridan Gilley, argue that 'racism' is not the applicable label for English attitudes to the Irish.[41] Such debates have intersected increasingly not only with

National Congress, 1870–1922', in Jim Masselos, ed., *Struggling and Ruling: The Indian National Congress, 1885–1985* (Delhi, 1987), pp. 24–46. See also Michael Holmes, 'The Irish and India: Imperialism, Nationalism and Internationalism', in Andy Bielenberg, ed., *The Irish Diaspora* (Harlow, Essex, 2000), pp. 235–50. Bolder, less well evidenced claims about such links have been made by, for instance, Richard Davis, *Arthur Griffith and Non-Violent Sinn Féin* (Dublin, 1974) and Liz Curtis, *The Cause of Ireland: From the United Irishmen to Partition* (Belfast, 1994).

[39] Elleke Boehmer, *Empire, the National, and the Postcolonial: Resistance in Interaction* (Oxford, 2002). See also *Interventions*, 4, 1 (2002), a special issue devoted to 'Postcolonial Studies and Transnational Resistance', where Stephen Howe's 'Transnationalisms Good, Bad, Real, Imagined, Thick and Thin' (pp. 79–88) rehearses some of the reasons for scepticism alluded to above.

[40] Major instances include L. P. Curtis, *Anglo-Saxons and Celts: A Study of Anti-Irish Prejudice in Victorian England* (Bridgeport, Conn., 1968); Luke Gibbons, 'Race Against Time: Racial Discourse and Irish History', *Oxford Literary Review* (hereafter *OLR*), 13, 1–2 (1991), pp. 95–117; R. N. Lebow, *White Britain and Black Ireland: The Influence of Stereotypes on Colonial Policy* (Philadelphia, 1976); David Lloyd, 'Race under Representation', *OLR*, 13, 1–2 (1991), pp. 62–94; H. L. Malchow, *Gothic Images of Race in Nineteenth-Century Britain* (Stanford, 1996).

[41] Gilley, 'English Attitudes to the Irish in England, 1780–1900', in Colin Holmes, ed., *Immigrants and Minorities in British Society* (London, 1978).

wider arguments about the role of 'race' in colonial discourse, but with those over racial attitudes among, and towards, the Irish in the United States and other places of emigration. This has included dispute over whether, or how, claims made in the recent, mainly North American literature of 'whiteness studies' are applicable to Ireland and its diaspora.[42] Meanwhile historical investigation into Ireland's own race relations remains in its infancy.[43]

Interacting with these discussions over race has been increasing attention to gender and its imagery, with some critics stressing how British writers and administrators viewed the land and people of Ireland as feminine, with this implying inferiority, passivity, and openness to possession or violation. This, in some eyes, was a distinctively colonialist structure of imagining. Yet conversely, Irish nationalist rhetoric too habitually imagined Ireland as a woman. Again, literary scholars have been especially interested in these themes, as with Marjorie Howes's discussion of the gendered imagery of nationhood in Yeats, Margaret Kelleher's study of Famine narratives, or Colin Graham's analysis of Maria Edgeworth's *Castle Rackrent*. The latter, under the influence of Homi K. Bhabha's notion of 'sly civility', sees the colonizer-colonized relationship as interlinked with gender relations and ideas about marriage.[44] In a more political and sometimes polemical vein, it is sometimes argued that there was a special and even necessary relationship between the causes of women's emancipation and of Irish freedom; or that feminism in Ireland today must, because of the country's colonial history, take distinctively 'postcolonial' forms radically different from those in, say, Britain or the United States.[45]

[42] See David R. Roediger, *The Wages of Whiteness* (London, 1991) and the much cited but far less careful Noel Ignatiev, *How the Irish Became White* (New York, 1995).

[43] The broadest, if somewhat superficial and polemical, survey is Bill Rolston and Michael Shannon, *Encounters: How Racism Came to Ireland* (Belfast, 2002). See also Ronit Lentin and Robbie McVeigh, eds., *Racism and Anti-Racism in Ireland* (Belfast, 2002).

[44] Marjorie Howes, *Yeats's Nations: Gender, Class, and Irishness* (Cambridge, 1996); Margaret Kelleher, *The Feminization of Famine: Representations of Women in Famine Narratives* (Cork, 1997); Colin Graham, 'History, Gender and the Colonial Moment: *Castle Rackrent*', *Irish Studies Review* (hereafter *ISR*), 14 (1996), pp. 21–24; Homi K. Bhabha, *The Location of Culture* (London, 1994), especially chap. 6.

[45] See, for instance, Carol Coulter, *The Hidden Tradition: Feminism, Women and Nationalism in Ireland* (Cork, 1993); Timothy P. Foley, Lionel Pilkington, Seán Ryder, and Elizabeth Tilley, eds., *Gender and Colonialism* (Galway, 1995). For a sceptical historical appraisal of such arguments, see Linda Connolly, *The Irish Women's Movement* (Basingstoke, 2001).

After the British-Irish conflict of 1919–21, Partition, and the Treaty, political argument over Ireland's relations to Britain became—no doubt inescapably—quite sharply bifurcated. Subsequent scholarly and polemical writing about 'Ireland and colonialism' has been no less so. Relevant debate relating to the Free State and, later, Republic revolved around whether the polity and society should appropriately be analysed as 'neocolonial', 'postcolonial', both, or neither. The debate attending to Northern Ireland engaged with two principal issues, while a subsidiary controversy asked just how distinct the two issues really were: whether the Union and British policies should be thought of as imperialist or not; and whether the structural position, or the dominant ideologies, of Ulster Protestants were settler-colonialist ones. Most analysts, from all political persuasions, have concurred that the southern Irish state after 1921 exercised most if not all of the attributes of political sovereignty, even before full sovereignty was formally attained, by stages, in the 1930s and 1940s. The economy and social structure underwent dramatic transformations, especially from the 1960s onward, and (on most views and in most respects) Ireland came to qualify as an economically advanced capitalist democracy. Some have argued, none the less, that its pattern of development remained distinctively neocolonial or postcolonial. These arguments always had only a minority place in the Republic's intellectual life, but their proponents were diverse, vigorous, and in some cases highly sophisticated.

One line of attack focused on economic and social structure, seeking to show that the changes which have taken place since the 1920s, despite their ostensibly autonomous, developmentalist, and 'modernizing' character, have none the less retained or intensified a distinctively dependent or neocolonial pattern. Such arguments came primarily on the pro-republican and Marxist left, and paralleled or were influenced by Marxist theory and later by Latin American and other 'Third World' theories of underdevelopment and dependency. A more indigenous ancestry was sometimes claimed, drawing on the ideas of pioneer Irish socialists such as James Connolly or even the nineteenth-century nationalist critique of orthodox political economy.[46] In the 1960s the republican intellectuals Roy Johnston and Anthony Coughlan sought to influence the IRA (and,

---

[46] Thomas A. Boylan and Timothy P. Foley, *Political Economy and Colonial Ireland: The Propagation and Ideological Function of Economic Discourse in the Nineteenth Century* (London, 1992).

less directly, the early Northern civil rights movement) with an analysis of this kind. Related arguments that British imperialism remained a crucial influence on the economies of both parts of Ireland emerged from the 1970s onward in the work of Marxist intellectuals including D. R. O'Connor Lysaght.[47]

A central object of critique was the economic reform programme instigated under Seán Lemass, which was viewed as merely strengthening the hold of neocolonialism in Ireland. First the Official wing of the republican movement, and then the Provisionals and Sinn Féin, came to espouse similar, though perhaps cruder, versions of this view of the Republic as neocolonial.[48] The most sustained and independent-minded such analysis was undoubtedly Raymond Crotty's 1986 book *Ireland in Crisis*.[49] Ranging across a broad sweep not only of Irish but of world history, Crotty's ambitious project was, however, apparently viewed by most other Irish economic historians as simply eccentric. It was criticized not only for its intense economic and cultural nationalism (some said xenophobia), but for its questionable insistence that Ireland's past as a victim of 'capitalist colonialism' made it unique in Europe. More recently, some other scholars have argued for the pertinence of dependency theory to analysing Ireland's development—though usually in more partial or nuanced forms than Crotty had done—or argued that Ireland's pattern of economic growth retained 'peripheral' or even 'Third World' characteristics. But theirs have remained somewhat isolated voices.[50] One critic, Dermot McAleese, described their views as only 'a strong body of sentiment, buttressed by flimsy but suggestive economic reasoning'.[51]

If there seemed, at least in academically orthodox eyes, little to support a case for Ireland's post-independence economic structures as neocolonial, a stronger argument could perhaps be made that the political system had characteristically postcolonial features. This view was most powerfully

---

[47] D. R. O'Connor Lysaght, *The Republic of Ireland* (Cork, 1970).

[48] Perhaps the best account is Henry Patterson, *The Politics of Illusion: A Political History of the IRA* (London, 1997); see also Howe, *Ireland and Empire*, pp. 158–63.

[49] Raymond Crotty, *Ireland in Crisis: A Study of Capitalist Colonial Underdevelopment* (Dingle, 1986).

[50] See, for instance, Denis O'Hearn, 'The Irish Case of Dependency: An Exception to the Exceptions?', *American Sociological Review*, 54, no. 4 (1989), pp. 578–96 and *Inside the Celtic Tiger: Reality and Illusion in the Irish Economy* (London, 1998).

[51] Dermot McAleese, 'Political Independence, Economic Growth, and the Role of Economic Policy', in P. J. Drudy, ed., *Ireland and Britain Since 1922* (Cambridge, 1985), p. 89.

propounded by Tom Garvin.[52] Noting how atypical of Western Europe
were Ireland's party system and political culture—he pointed to features
such as the powerful role of the Church, the weakness of social bases for
party alignments, and the salience of nationalist issues—Garvin suggested
that Ireland had more in common with the countries of the postcolonial
world. He did, however, concede that it differed starkly from most of
those in possessing a stable democratic system: and in fact his later
work focused ever more on the origins of Irish democracy.[53] His earlier
argument found little support. Indeed many of the traits which it had
emphasized seemed to erode in significance in subsequent decades, as
Ireland's 'modernization' and 'Europeanization' were accompanied by
secularization and the 'detraditionalization' of attitudes.

It remained possible, however, to suggest that the international attitudes
of important sectors of the Irish people, or of the state itself, could be
seen as distinctively postcolonial. Irish foreign policy was generally neutra-
list and at times, especially in the late 1950s, actively anticolonialist.
Clearly this could be linked to perceptions of the country's own past, and
was so linked by some politicians and analysts. Similar claims could be
made in relation to the strong popular support gained in Ireland for
movements like those for famine relief, for various national liberation
struggles, and against apartheid. International religious networks, involving many Irishmen and women working in poor countries, may have
furthered these sympathies. Yet other commentators doubted whether all
this amounted to a 'Third Worldist' foreign policy or popular attitudes.
Links with Britain (fraught though these, and Ireland's association with
the Commonwealth, often were), the United States, and latterly the European Union, were always more important than ones with postcolonial
countries.[54] Neither the budget for development aid, nor the policy towards refugees, was ever very generous. Ireland's United Nations voting

[52] Tom Garvin, 'The Destiny of the Soldiers: Tradition and Modernity in the Politics of de
Valera's Ireland', *Political Studies*, 26, 3 (1978), pp. 328–47 and *The Evolution of Irish Nationalist
Politics* (Dublin, 1981).

[53] See especially Tom Garvin, *1922: The Birth of Irish Democracy* (Dublin, 1996).

[54] The complex 'triangle' of British-Irish-Commonwealth relations, especially in the Free
State era, is now one of the most closely researched themes in the general field. See David
Harkness, *The Restless Dominion: The Irish Free State and the British Commonwealth of
Nations, 1921–31* (London, 1969); Deirdre McMahon, *Republicans and Imperialists: Anglo-Irish
Relations in the 1930s* (New Haven, 1984).

record conformed to a broadly European pattern rather than a 'Third World' one.[55]

An alternative way of arguing that southern Ireland remains profoundly shaped by colonialism is to shift the ground of debate from economic and political structures to cultural and psychological questions. This has been done by a range of contemporary writers, including both traditional cultural nationalists and, in a more sophisticated style, by a very influential current in cultural theory. The latter body of writing is discussed separately below. The former, in arguing a general case for the persisting power of British cultural imperialism, has tended to be polemical and pamphleteering rather than analytical in style.[56] More substantial, if still much contested, arguments have been made for seeing the 'language question' as being at the heart of a continuing colonial legacy; for believing that a colonial past accounts substantially for the alleged failure or incompleteness of cultural modernity in Ireland; and for thinking that colonialism has had abiding and damaging effects on Irish psychological characteristics.[57]

Arguments over colonial models for understanding Northern Ireland after 1921 have, naturally, carried an even stronger political charge than those relating to the Republic. It has been in relation to the Northern

[55] On various aspects of this record see Edmund Hogan, *The Irish Missionary Movement: A Historical Survey, 1830–1980* (Dublin, 1990); Michael Holmes, Nicholas Rees, and Bernadette Whelan, *The Poor Relation: Irish Foreign Policy and the Third World* (Dublin, 1993); Michael Holmes and Denis Holmes, eds., *Ireland and India: Connections, Comparisons, Contrasts* (Dublin, 1997); Brigid Laffan, *Ireland and South Africa: Irish Government Policy in the 1980s* (Dublin, 1988); Trevor C. Salmon, *Unneutral Ireland: An Ambivalent and Unique Security Policy* (Oxford, 1989).

[56] For a sample, see Kieran Allen, *Is Southern Ireland a Neo-Colony?* (Dublin, 1990); Therese Cahery and others, eds., *Is Ireland a Third World Country?* (Belfast, 1992); Kevin Collins, *The Cultural Conquest of Ireland* (Cork, 1990); Jack O'Brien, *The Unionjacking of Ireland* (Cork, 1993).

[57] On language, see Tomás MacSiomoin, 'The Colonised Mind—Irish Language and Society', in Daltún O'Ceallaigh, ed., *Reconsiderations on Irish History and Culture* (Dublin, 1994); Clair Wills, 'Language Politics, Narrative, Political Violence', *OLR*, 13, 1–2 (1991), pp. 20–60. For arguments about colonial legacies and modernity, amidst a rapidly growing literature, see Conor McCarthy, *Modernisation: Crisis and Culture in Ireland, 1969–1992* (Dublin, 2000); Jim MacLaughlin, 'The "New" Intelligentsia and the Reconstruction of the Irish Nation', *IR*, 24 (1999), pp. 53–66. On colonialism's supposed enduring psychic effects, see Geraldine Moane, *Gender and Colonialism* (Basingstoke, 1999); Liam O'Dowd, 'New Introduction' to Albert Memmi, *The Colonizer and the Colonized* (London, 1990); and, as part of a much wider-ranging, more subtle, and more influential argument, J. J. Lee, *Ireland, 1912–1985: Politics and Society* (Oxford, 1989).

'Troubles' after 1969 that reference to colonialism and anticolonialism in Ireland has become most pervasive, and most intensely contentious. This has included a great deal of writing from outside Ireland, not least from revolutionary groups in Britain and elsewhere which supported the republican struggle on the basis of its 'anti-imperialist' character. There were numerous evocations of the idea of Northern Ireland as 'Britain's last colony'—the last as Ireland had supposedly been the first. On this view, the province must itself be destined for imminent decolonization, in the form of British withdrawal and Irish unification.

Amidst the mass of polemical writing (by no means all of which, it should be emphasized, came from pro-republican sources, let alone implied that the writers necessarily supported anyone's acts of violence) there were few extended or substantial analyses of the Ulster conflict as an anti-imperialist one. The exceptions included Michael Farrell's *Northern Ireland: The Orange State*, and—perhaps the earliest such effort, and one which did not fit any conventional political mould—*Divided Ulster*, by the distinguished archaeologist Líam de Paor.[58] On the related but distinct theme of the 'settler colonial' character of Ulster Unionist ideologies, a major, historically informed study did not appear until almost thirty years after the conflict's eruption, with Pamela Clayton's *Enemies and Passing Friends*, and even then it came under heavy criticism for the weakness of its empirical and comparative material.[59] Meanwhile, the more agitational or emotive uses of the Ulster settler colonial thesis seemed to hostile observers to imply the conclusion that an Algerian-style mass exodus of the *colons* was, in nationalist eyes, the most likely or desirable outcome of the conflict. If this was so, however, very few nationalist, or indeed republican, thinkers explicitly advanced such a view.[60]

Much of this writing had, or proclaimed, a Marxist lineage; but other Marxists writing on Northern Ireland took sharply opposed stances, arguing, for instance, that Marxist theories of imperialism, properly understood, did not sustain the interpretation of the conflict as anti-imperialist;

[58] Michael Farrell, *Northern Ireland: The Orange State* (London, 1976; second edn., 1980); Líam de Paor, *Divided Ulster* (Harmondsworth, 1970; second edn., 1971).

[59] Pamela Clayton, *Enemies and Passing Friends: Settler Ideologies in Twentieth Century Ulster* (London, 1996).

[60] On modern republican political thought and its attitudes to Unionists, see Patterson, *Politics of Illusion*, and Richard English, *Armed Struggle: A History of the IRA* (London, 2003).

or that Ulster Protestants were a distinct nationality with a right to self-determination, rather than a mere settler-colonial implant.[61] Probably the most influential and contentious repudiation of colonial conceptions of the Ulster conflict, though, came from someone who was never a Marxist but was—in his earlier career—strongly associated with the Irish left and with anti-imperialist causes. This was Conor Cruise O'Brien, with his 1972 book *States of Ireland* and a mass of subsequent analysis and polemic. He sought to turn the tables on anticolonialist arguments, avowing that in 'combating an Irish Catholic imperialist enterprise: the effort to force the Protestants of Northern Ireland... into a United Ireland they don't want', he was acting in the same spirit and upholding the same values as when he had earlier opposed Britain's imperialism in Africa or America's in Vietnam.[62]

More empirical questions over how far, if at all, Unionists saw *themselves* as colonists, identified with the British Empire, or with 'settler' populations elsewhere, remained controversial and clouded, with clear answers made elusive by both the dearth of serious research and the conceptual vagueness of much that was written on the subject. The studies—and, once again, polemics—which exist have tended to note the lack of a full-fledged racial ideology or 'frontier tradition' analogous to those developed among many colonial-settler communities elsewhere. And although Donal Lowry, for instance, has traced the degree to which Unionists drew parallels between their situation and those of white settlers in conflict with anticolonial nationalists, the expressions of solidarity or identification he cites are mainly from extreme loyalist currents rather than the mainstream of Unionism.[63]

On the other hand, Unionists were clearly keen to celebrate the Empire, and as Alvin Jackson says were 'bombarded at every stage in their lives

[61] For the former, see Paul Bew, Peter Gibbon, and Henry Patterson, *The State in Northern Ireland* (Manchester, 1979); for the latter, Tom Nairn, *The Break-Up of Britain: Crisis and Neo-Nationalism* (London, 1981) and many writings by members of the British and Irish Communist Organisation.

[62] Conor Cruise O'Brien, *Ancestral Voices: Religion and Nationalism in Ireland* (Dublin, 1994), p. 5 and *States of Ireland* (London, 1972). It is surprising how few Unionist writers have so far followed O'Brien's lead in proclaiming themselves victims of imperialism; but see Gavin Adams, et al., *Ulster—The Internal Colony* (Belfast, 1989); Arthur Aughey, *Irish Kulturkampf: A Critique of Irish Cultural Imperialism* (Belfast, 1995).

[63] Donal Lowry, 'Ulster Resistance and Loyalist Rebellion in the Empire', in Jeffery, ed., *Irish Empire?*

and in every sphere of their activity with the image of Empire'.[64] But it is less clear whether this propaganda bombardment and popular responses to it were more intense among Ulster Unionists than in England or Scotland. A wide range of contemporary analyses of Unionist ideologies more generally have tended to stress complexity and internal division, with supremacist or settler-colonialist ideas seen as only one of several contending currents.[65] And Frank Wright's influential studies have concluded that a settler-colonial *past* was important in shaping Ulster's development, but that most of the region's specifically colonial features long since withered away, while the concept of an 'ethnic frontier' is a better analytical key today than that of a 'colonial situation'.[66] Scholars analysing Northern Irish literature and culture, including the modern literature of the 'Troubles', have in recent years increasingly adopted colonial and postcolonial models or analogies. Political, social, and economic historians, political scientists, and social theorists, by contrast, still rarely do so. The majority of them see the roots of conflict as mainly internal to Northern Irish society rather than, or more than, deriving from external forces such as British imperialism. Yet John Whyte's comment from 1990 remains largely true today: those authors who do not adopt the view that Northern Ireland is a colonial situation rarely argue the case against it, but 'simply remain silent on the subject'.[67] Where this view is openly addressed, dispute over it is perhaps still more sharply politicized than any other aspect of the subject.

Probably the most widely influential mode of argument over 'Ireland and imperialism' since the 1980s has come from literary and cultural studies, in the form of applications to Irish contexts of postcolonial theory and its close intellectual relative, colonial discourse analysis.[68] The most

---

[64] Alvin Jackson, 'Irish Unionists and the Empire, 1880–1920: Classes and Masses', in Jeffery, ed., *Irish Empire?*, p. 143.

[65] Major instances include John McGarry and Brendan O'Leary, *Explaining Northern Ireland: Broken Images* (Oxford, 1995); Joseph Ruane and Jennifer Todd, *The Dynamics of Conflict in Northern Ireland: Power, Conflict and Emancipation* (Cambridge, 1996).

[66] Frank Wright, *Northern Ireland: A Comparative Analysis* (Dublin, 1987) and *Two Lands on One Soil: Ulster Politics Before Home Rule* (Dublin, 1996).

[67] John Whyte, *Interpreting Northern Ireland* (Oxford, 1990), p. 178.

[68] Often now the broader labels 'postcolonial studies' or just 'postcolonialism'—signalling the transdisciplinary ambitions of much such work—are employed. The most historically detailed survey of the field is Young, *Postcolonialism*. Howe, *Ireland and Empire*,

important single inspiration for such studies, internationally, has been the work of Edward W. Said, though other developments, such as a revived interest in the ideas of Frantz Fanon, were also important. A wide range of poststructuralist, deconstructionist, and postmodernist theories have also had a major influence on much of this work, as have 'new historicist' and 'cultural materialist' currents in literary studies. In relation to Ireland, formative elements included the early activities of the Field Day collective from the early 1980s, and the publications of David Cairns and Shaun Richards's *Writing Ireland* in 1988, of Field Day pamphlets by Terry Eagleton, Fredric Jameson, and Said himself, also in 1988, and of essays by Luke Gibbons, David Lloyd, and Clair Wills in the *Oxford Literary Review* in 1991.[69] There were, naturally, wider shaping contexts too, political, cultural, and more specifically academic. On the academic front, the rapid growth in attention to colonial themes evidently stemmed in part from the burgeoning internationalisation of 'Irish studies': several of the key participants either worked in or were frequent visitors to American campuses.

Despite the pioneering position of Cairns's and Richards's book, and despite the attention commanded by Eagleton's, Jameson's, and Said's interventions (though in fact the last two displayed disconcertingly little familiarity with Irish history, while Eagleton's attitude to postcolonial theorizing was ambivalent and later became downright hostile), three other scholars have over the past decade or so come to dominate the field. These are Seamus Deane, Declan Kiberd, and David Lloyd. A mass of further studies following broadly similar approaches has also appeared, including numerous monographs studying particular major Irish writers through the prism of postcolonial theory, dissecting the alleged anti-Irish racism and colonialism of major figures in the English canon, or offering sometimes rather formulaic additions to the literature. Some younger scholars have recently offered fresh perspectives, registered more fully than

---

chap. 7, offers a sharply critical overview of this endeavour in relation to Irish studies. David Washbrook, 'Orients and Occidents: Colonial Discourse Theory and the Historiography of the British Empire', in Robin W. Winks, ed., *OHBE. Vol. 5. Historiography* (Oxford, 1999), pp. 596–611, attempts something similar in relation to imperial history.

[69] David Cairns and Shaun Richards, *Writing Ireland: Colonialism, Nationalism and Culture* (London, 1988); Terry Eagleton, *Nationalism, Irony and Commitment*, Fredric Jameson, *Modernism and Imperialism*, and Edward Said, *Yeats and Decolonization* (Field Day pamphlets, Derry, 1988). The essays by Gibbons, Lloyd, and Wills are cited above at nn. 40 and 57.

hitherto the historical complexity of the issues involved, and in some cases criticized assumptions about the 'easy transferability' to Ireland of post-colonial theories originally developed in relation to Africa or India.[70] For reasons of space, the analysis here is confined to a brief discussion of the main themes advanced by Deane, Kiberd, and Lloyd.

In a series of books and essays, Seamus Deane, who is also a noted poet and novelist, proposed a view of Irish history centred on the centuries-long clash between colonialism and nationalism. It was none the less, he insisted, an open, complex, pluralist model rather than a stark maniche-ism, since colonialisms and conquests in Ireland's past had been multiple, since he saw each wave of colonizers as having intermingled culturally with previous inhabitants, since nationalism too had taken multiple forms (the dominant ones largely sharing the élitist outlook of the imperialists), and since the vision of Ireland's past which he and the Field Day group espoused was itself open, critical, flexible, and theoretically informed.[71] This last claim was the one which aroused the most controversy, for in a series of polemics Deane repeatedly counterposed it to the ways of the majority of Ireland's academic historians, especially those labelled 'revisionists'. These, he argued, typically espoused a naïve and dogmatic positivism, blind to the demands of critical theory and to the essentially fictional or mythological nature of all historical narrative. This was intim-ately linked to the historians' pervasive pro-Unionist, anti-nationalist political bias, which even led them, Deane charged in one place, into legitimizing loyalist violence. 'The rhetoric of revisionism', he believed, 'obviously derives from the rhetoric of colonialism and imperialism'.[72]

[70] Notable instances include Colin Graham, *Deconstructing Ireland* (Edinburgh, 2001); Joe Cleary, *Literature, Partition and the Nation-State: Culture and Conflict in Ireland, Israel and Palestine* (Cambridge, 2002); and Glenn Hooper and Colin Graham, eds., *Irish and Postcolonial Writing: History, Theory, Practice* (Basingstoke, 2002). The quotation is from Richard Kirkland, 'Frantz Fanon, Roger Casement and Colonial Commitment', in Hooper and Graham, eds., *Irish and Postcolonial Writing*, p. 53.

[71] The argument is most succinctly and accessibly made in Deane's 'General Introduction' to vol. I of *The Field Day Anthology of Irish Writing*, 3 vols. (Derry, 1991), ed. Seamus Deane. The critique of hegemonic nationalism is most fully expounded in Seamus Deane, *Celtic Revivals* (London, 1985).

[72] Seamus Deane, *Strange Country: Modernity and Nationhood in Irish Writing Since 1790* (Oxford, 1997), p. 193, where the charge about legitimating violence also appears. Related 'anti-revisionist' arguments are made in the 'Introduction' to Seamus Deane, ed., *Nationalism, Colonialism, and Literature* (Minneapolis, 1990) and in Seamus Deane, 'Wherever Green is Read', in Mairín Ní Dhonnchadha and Theo Dorgan, eds., *Revising the Rising* (Derry, 1991).

Unfriendly observers thought such attacks revealed not only an idiosyncratic conception of historical study, but the assailant's own strong political agenda. Such critics thus charged that despite, or behind, all the theoretical sophistication of Deane's work and that of some of his Field Day associates, there lay a simple, even anachronistic, nationalist worldview. In supposedly contesting and disaggregating the great mythographies of colonialism and nationalism, Deane and other Field Day writers, it was alleged, remained trapped in their assumptions. Even where Deane was critical of nationalism, it was mainly for being too conservative, too much indebted to the British ideas it claimed to contest. And the Field Day image of Irish culture, hostile reviewers added, was itself disconcertingly monolithic: Deane's *Celtic Revivals* had just one passing reference to Ulster Unionists, who were identified only by their 'clamant imperialism'.[73]

Similar complaints—that the novel emphases and procedures of a complex, transnational postcolonial theory, as applied to Ireland, coexisted with a highly traditional nationalist worldview—were directed at Declan Kiberd. Kiberd's magnum opus, *Inventing Ireland*, published in 1995, was the most extensive and detailed attempt thus far to apply ideas about colonialism and postcoloniality to Irish culture.[74] Drawing heavily on Edward Said and Frantz Fanon, Kiberd saw the impact of British colonialism on Ireland as all-determining. Every aspect of modern Irish cultural life and art (the book and Kiberd's other works included many detailed and, as even hostile responses conceded, acute analyses of individual literary works) was shaped by Empire and the attempts to challenge it. Critics argued that Kiberd's insistence on reading most major Irish writers as colonial or postcolonial was procrustean, that though far more nuanced and detailed in execution than many other exercises in the genre of postcolonial theory, the result was oddly homogenizing and monolithic, and that the work's allusions both to Irish history and to colonial situations elsewhere were often empirically suspect.[75] Some, though, found attractive

---

[73] Deane, *Celtic Revivals*, p. 66. Among many such critiques of Deane and Field Day, perhaps the most widely debated were in Francis Mulhern, *The Present Lasts a Long Time: Essays in Cultural Politics* (Cork, 1998) and Edna Longley, *The Living Stream: Literature and Revisionism in Ireland* (Newcastle upon Tyne, 1994).

[74] Declan Kiberd, *Inventing Ireland: The Literature of the Modern Nation* (London, 1995).

[75] Such critiques include Colin Graham, 'Post-Colonial Theory and Kiberd's *Ireland*', *IR*, 19 (1996), pp. 62–67, and Bruce Stewart, 'Inside Nationalism: A Meditation upon *Inventing Ireland*', *ISR*, 6, 1 (1998), pp. 5–16.

the optimism with which Kiberd viewed a possible future after Ireland had finally shaken off its colonial legacies: 'When this happens, an end will come to that restless arraignment of the English Other and to the consequent purging of heresy within: instead there will emerge a self-creating Ireland produced by nothing but its own desire'.[76]

David Lloyd acknowledged a wider range of theoretical sources, and ranged more broadly across the postcolonial world in his drawing of parallels with Irish experience, than did Deane or Kiberd, and gave his version of Irish postcolonialism a yet sharper political point. In his argument, 'bourgeois' Irish nationalists had contested only the political authority of colonial rule, not its cultural power. They had done so in the name of a mythically united national will, whose leadership they claimed, and a rationalist, Enlightenment spirit, which perpetuated the imperialism they claimed to oppose. Thus, they colluded with colonialism in destroying Ireland's ancient, oppositional, underground, or 'subaltern' popular culture. That culture, whose continuing resistance Lloyd celebrated, is represented by past agrarian rebels like the 'Whiteboys' and—the link became increasingly explicit in his more recent work—republican insurgency in modern Northern Ireland.[77] Lloyd is perhaps the most theoretically sophisticated of Irish postcolonial critics. Yet quite apart from the fierce political contention his work engendered, it seemed open to some of the same complaints as were directed against other writers in the field: that its command of non-Irish historical evidence and indeed of empirical data on Ireland was questionable, its conception of colonialism itself unduly homogenizing and ahistorical, its view of historians' method unduly dismissive.

It could also, more generally, be argued that, so far, few of the literary scholars who have adopted colonial models for thinking about Ireland appear to have engaged sufficiently closely with the international literature on colonialism, or sought carefully to define the concept itself. There are few references, in this Irish literature, to the substantial body of historical writing that seeks to clarify the term. In failing to define it, Irish-colonial

---

[76] Kiberd, *Inventing Ireland*, p. 124.

[77] See, for instance, David Lloyd, *Anomalous States: Irish Writing and the Post-Colonial Moment* (Dublin, 1993), p. 3; 'Outside History: Irish New Histories and the "Subalternity Effect"', in Shahid Amin and Dipesh Chakrabarty, eds., *Subaltern Studies, IX* (Delhi, 1996), p. 262; and *Ireland After History* (Cork, 1999), p. 106.

cultural theorists often seemingly imply that Ireland's position was precisely the same as that of all Britain's African, Asian, or Caribbean colonies; or that Ireland today is an undifferentiated part of a similarly
homogenized postcolonial world. At worst a strange, almost oxymoronic
combination of assumptions about global sameness and about Irish
uniqueness (especially its uniqueness when set against an undifferentiated
'Europe') operates in some of this writing. Even so, Irish colonial and
postcolonial cultural theory might be welcomed as offering the potential
for a wider international perspective than had often been evident in the
Irish studies of the past.

Thinking about Irish history in relation to the global reach of the British
Empire, and indeed to other imperial systems in world history, evidently
requires both a comparative and, more challengingly, an integrative historical awareness. As is often lamented, neither British (meaning, usually,
mainly English) nor Irish history-writing has in the past been strong on
these qualities. Conversely, the major international theorists of imperialism rarely integrated Ireland into their arguments or, for that matter, even
mentioned the place. Marx and Engels did write extensively on Ireland,
though mainly in private letters and in their journalism. Those writings
have attracted a vast body of subsequent commentary, but despite some
rather pious claims by later Irish Marxists, they do not amount to a
comprehensive treatment of the Anglo-Irish question, or its placement in
some general theory of imperialism.[78]

   The two most influential twentieth-century theories of imperialism
have been those of J. A. Hobson and V. I. Lenin, the latter somewhat
derivative of the former. Neither Hobson's 1902 *Imperialism* nor Lenin's
relevant writings makes more than the briefest, most casual allusions to
Ireland; and in neither case do those brief references feature the country as
a victim of colonial oppression.[79] Bukharin's *Imperialism and World Economy* follows Lenin's *Imperialism* in making no reference to Ireland at all.[80]
The same is true of major early non-Communist writings like Parker

---

[78] Karl Marx and Friedrich Engels, *On Ireland* (Moscow, 1971). On subsequent developments see Anthony Brewer, *Marxist Theories of Imperialism: A Critical Survey*, second edn.
(London, 1990).

[79] J. A. Hobson, *Imperialism, A Study* (London, 1902).

[80] Nikolai Bukharin, *Imperialism and World Economy* (Moscow, 1918), cited from the 1973
New York edn.

Thomas Moon's 1926 *Imperialism and World Politics*.[81] Very little indeed in the mass of British left-wing, anticolonialist writing and agitation from the 1880s to the 1960s features Irish affairs. This near-exclusion of Ireland from the work of classical theorists of imperialism is echoed by almost all modern historians of the British Empire. The recent, five-volume *Oxford History of the British Empire*—and, still more, the present volume—breaks new ground in this respect.

Even within the 'north Atlantic archipelago', neither comparative nor integrative studies relating Irish, Scottish, and Welsh experiences of rule from England—whether or not these are seen as experiences of colonialism—had a substantial presence until very recently.[82] Today, such work is beginning to proliferate, but even now almost nothing compares Irish and Scottish attitudes to or participation in Empire, while the Scots literature on the subject remains considerably more extensive than the Irish.[83] Several commentators have emphasized how attention to the Scottish dimension challenges the polarities of much Irish historiography, including that which adopts simple colonial models.[84] Others have suggested that a 'pan-Celtic' approach to the subject, though one shorn of *Braveheart*-style romantic cultural nationalism, may offer a fruitful way forward.[85] It might even be asked whether there is merit in bringing into the debate conceptions of the *English* past as a colonized one; or of adopting a broad historical view on which a great deal, if not all, of Europe's history is a story of conquest and colonization.[86] One consequence might be to come

---

[81] William Parker Moon, *Imperialism and World Politics* (New York, 1926).

[82] A pioneering if contentious example was Michael Hechter's *Internal Colonialism: The Celtic Fringe in British National Development, 1536–1966* (London, 1975).

[83] John Mackenzie, 'On Scotland and the Empire', *International History Review*, 15, 4 (1993), pp. 714–39 and 'Empire and National Identity: The Case of Scotland', *Transactions of the Royal Historical Society*, Sixth Series, VIII (Cambridge, 1998); Richard J. Finlay, ' "For or Against?" Scottish Nationalists and the British Empire', *Scottish Historical Review*, 71, 1, 2 (1992), pp. 184–206 and 'The Rise and Fall of Popular Imperialism in Scotland, 1850–1950', *Scottish Geographical Magazine*, 113 (1997), pp. 13–21; Michael Fry, *The Scottish Empire* (Edinburgh, 2001).

[84] See for example Richard English, 'Shakespeare and the Identity of Ireland', in Mark Thornton Burnett and Ramona Wray, eds., *Shakespeare and Ireland: History, Politics, Culture* (Basingstoke, 1997); Willy Maley, 'Rebels and Redshanks', *ISR*, 6 (1994), pp. 7–11.

[85] John S. Ellis, 'Reconciling the Celt: British National Identity, Empire, and the 1911 Investiture of the Prince of Wales', *Journal of British Studies*, 37, no. 4 (1998), pp. 391–418; Murray G. H. Pittock, *Celtic Identity and the British Image* (Manchester, 1999).

[86] Francis James West, 'The Colonial History of the Norman Conquest?' *History*, 84, no. 274 (1999), pp. 219–36; Robert Bartlett, *The Making of Europe: Conquest, Colonization and Cultural Change, 950–1350* (London, 1993).

to see the question often recently and polemically posed about Ireland, 'postcolonial or European?', as involving a false antithesis.[87]

Some comparative studies, linking Ireland (or often, more specifically, Northern Ireland) to historical case studies elsewhere, have also been enlightening, although only a minority of the major works concerned make comparison in specifically imperial or postcolonial frameworks, and many of them seem to critics to be severely flawed in various ways.[88] Thus Donald Akenson's study of 'covenantal' ideologies among settler communities in Ireland, Israel, and South Africa, and Ian Lustick's successive attempts to analyse state strategies and settler lobbies' influence in ethnically disputed territory, both offer important insights on northern Irish developments and Britain's role there.[89] So may comparative analyses of international law and practice in decolonization, where numerous other twentieth-century controversies provide partial parallels with aspects of the Irish situation.[90] A recent proliferation of writings exploring correspondences between 'peace processes' in various parts of the world, several of them also involving (at least in the eyes of some protagonists) processes of decolonization, offer a fresh perspective on Ireland's historical conflicts and its relationship with imperial Britain.[91]

Many of these intellectual developments and discourses, however, still operate in relative isolation from one another or, as with the exchanges between postcolonial theorists and 'revisionist' historians, in a state of

[87] For instance, Brian Walker, 'Ireland's Historical Position—"Colonial" or "European"?', *IR*, 9 (1990), pp. 36–40.

[88] My own frankly often caustic survey of some of this literature may be found in *Ireland and Empire*, chap. 11.

[89] Donald Harman Akenson, *God's Peoples: Covenant and Land in South Africa, Israel, and Ulster* (London, 1992); Ian Lustick, *State-Building Failure in British Ireland and French Algeria* (Berkeley, 1985) and *Unsettled States, Disputed Lands: Britain and Ireland, France and Algeria, Israel and the West Bank-Gaza* (Ithaca, NY, 1993). See also Thomas G. Mitchell, *Native versus Settler: Ethnic Conflict in Israel/Palestine, Northern Ireland, and South Africa* (Westport, Conn., 2000).

[90] Michael Gallagher, 'Do Ulster Unionists Have a Right to Self-Determination?', *Irish Political Studies*, 5 (1990), pp. 11–30; Hurst Hannum, *Autonomy, Sovereignty, and Self-Determination* (Philadelphia, 1990); and, less valuably, Anthony Carty, *Was Ireland Conquered? International Law and the Irish Question* (London, 1996).

[91] See for example Hermann Giliomee and Jannie Gagiano, eds., *The Elusive Search for Peace: South Africa, Israel, Northern Ireland* (Cape Town, 1990); Adrian Guelke, *Northern Ireland: The International Perspective* (Dublin, 1988); John McGarry, ed., *Northern Ireland and the Divided World* (Oxford, 2001); Brendan O'Leary, Ian S. Lustick, and Thomas Callaghy, eds., *Right-Sizing the State: The Politics of Moving Borders* (Oxford, 2001).

antagonism. Over a decade ago, surveying some of the literature on Ireland and colonialism, Joseph Ruane felt forced to conclude that it 'points to the questions that are outstanding and have to be answered, but it does not let us answer them. At the current stage of research in Irish historical studies, the questions of whether, for what period, or in what sense Ireland should be viewed in colonial terms are unanswerable'.[92] Relevant research and debate have subsequently proliferated so far that we need, surely, no longer think of these as 'unanswerable' conundrums. But we still have far more questions than answers.

Select Bibliography

DONALD HARMAN AKENSON, *God's Peoples: Covenant and Land in South Africa, Israel, and Ulster* (London, 1992).

DAVID CAIRNS and SHAUN RICHARDS, *Writing Ireland: Colonialism, Nationalism and Culture* (London, 1988).

NICHOLAS CANNY, *Making Ireland British, 1580–1650* (Oxford, 2001).

SCOTT B. COOK, *Imperial Affinities: Nineteenth Century Analogies and Exchanges between India and Ireland* (New Delhi, 1993).

RAYMOND CROTTY, *Ireland in Crisis: A Study of Capitalist Colonial Underdevelopment* (Dingle, 1986).

SEAMUS DEANE, *Strange Country: Modernity and Nationhood in Irish Writing Since 1790* (Oxford, 1997).

MICHAEL HECHTER, *Internal Colonialism: The Celtic Fringe in British National Development, 1536–1966* (London, 1975).

GLENN HOOPER and COLIN GRAHAM, eds., *Irish and Postcolonial Writing: History, Theory, Practice* (Basingstoke, 2002).

STEPHEN HOWE, *Ireland and Empire: Colonial Legacies in Irish History and Culture*, second edn. with new Preface (Oxford, 2002).

KEITH JEFFERY, ed., *'An Irish Empire'? Aspects of Ireland and the British Empire* (Manchester, 1996).

DECLAN KIBERD, *Inventing Ireland: The Literature of the Modern Nation* (London, 1995).

JOEP T. LEERSSEN, *Mere Irish and Fíor-Gael: Studies in the Idea of Irish Nationality, its Development and Literary Expression Prior to the Nineteenth Century* (Amsterdam, 1988).

---

[92] Joseph Ruane, 'Colonialism and the Interpretation of Irish Historical Development', in Marilyn Silverman and P. H. Gulliver, eds., *Approaching the Past: Historical Anthropology through Irish Case Studies* (New York, 1992), p. 319.

DAVID LLOYD, *Anomalous States: Irish Writing and the Post-Colonial Moment* (Dublin, 1993).

IAN LUSTICK, *Unsettled States, Disputed Lands: Britain and Ireland, France and Algeria, Israel and the West Bank-Gaza* (Ithaca, NY, 1993).

JOHN McGARRY, ed., *Northern Ireland and the Divided World* (Oxford, 2001).

PATRICIA PALMER, *Language and Conquest in Early Modern Ireland: English Renaissance Literature and Elizabethan Imperial Expansion* (Cambridge, 2001).

FRANK WRIGHT, *Two Lands on One Soil: Ulster Politics Before Home Rule* (Dublin, 1996).

9

Postcolonial Ireland

JOE CLEARY

The application of colonial and postcolonial perspectives and methodologies to the study of modern Irish literature and culture represents one of the more significant, and controversial, developments in the Irish humanities in recent decades. For many, this has been a positive and welcome phenomenon, one that has allowed Irish critics to draw upon and to contribute to a wider body of international theory and criticism in order to advance new ways of thinking about the evolution of modern Irish culture and society. For others, the emergence of Irish colonial and postcolonial studies is a retrograde development. Excoriated by cultural conservatives as a crude and unwarranted 'politicization' of literary and aesthetic debate, postcolonial studies has also been dismissed by revisionist and some leftist critics as a spurious renovation of a jaded Irish cultural nationalism in a new academic jargon. It has, in other words, been characterized by some as too politically radical and militant, and by others as a conservative last-ditch attempt to renovate an Irish cultural nationalism increasingly out of kilter with contemporary domestic and global realities.

Although this chapter will engage with some of the various challenges and objections posed to the conception of modern Irish culture in postcolonial terms, its primary purpose is neither to track the development of Irish postcolonial studies in recent decades nor to review the controversies that this body of scholarship has generated. Instead, its purpose is to indicate some of the ways in which postcolonial readings of modern Irish literary culture in the period that stretches from the Irish Literary Revival through the Counter-Revival and up to the contemporary 'Troubles' in Northern Ireland can help to reconfigure received versions of modern Irish literary and cultural history. Postcolonial readings of Irish culture, it will be suggested, have the capacity not only to critique established versions of Irish literary history, but also to extend the scope of inquiry to engage with the cultural dilemmas of subaltern groups—such as women, workers, and emigrants—that were typically either elided or under-represented within nationalist literary history. Irish postcolonial analysis is conceived here, therefore, not as a renovated cultural nationalism but as the most expansive and outward-looking of the various modes of socio-cultural analysis currently shaping Irish studies. Based on the premise that it is the wider historical and geographical span of modern colonial capitalism that constitutes the proper contextual frame for the study of modern Irish literature and society, postcolonial modes of analysis impel Irish studies in the direction of a conjunctural global analysis in which Irish literary history must be assessed in terms of the ongoing cultural traffic between metropolitan literary cores and colonial or postcolonial cultural peripheries and semi-peripheries.

It is as well to begin with some of the more frequently reiterated objections to the conceptualization of modern Irish society in postcolonial terms. These objections take a variety of forms but three broad categories recur with particular frequency. The first is that the development of twentieth-century Irish society has more in common with other small, peripheral, mainly agrarian European societies than with that of the African and Asian colonies of the British Empire. In these distant overseas colonies, it is argued, the scale of poverty and the levels of violence and racial oppression endured by the colonized peoples were incommensurate with anything experienced in nineteenth or twentieth-century Ireland. A second objection is that conceptions of twentieth-century Ireland as a postcolonial society carry an inevitable conservative undertow. To conceive of matters thus, it is suggested, serves conveniently to mitigate Irish responsibility for Irish problems by displacing blame on to an oppressive past or on to the United Kingdom. According to a third argument, even if it is conceded that Ireland was a British colony prior to the establishment of Northern Ireland and the Irish Free State in the early 1920s, it remains the case that Ireland won its independence quite early in the twentieth century and has long since had ample time to overcome its 'postcolonial' legacies and hangovers.[1]

These arguments have their importance, but they rest nevertheless on poorly developed conceptions of Empire, colonization, and decolonization. The argument that Irish subjection to British rule cannot really be

---

[1] Líam Kennedy, *Colonialism, Religion and Nationalism in Ireland* (Belfast, 1996).

considered 'colonial' because social and economic conditions in Ireland were not quite the same as those in Britain's distant overseas colonies assumes that there is some sort of 'classical' colonial or post-colonial condition to which Ireland somehow fails to correspond. Some versions of postcolonial theory have correctly been criticized for their abstractly homogenized conception of colonization and decolonization; yet this same criticism can also be applied to those critics who dismiss the idea of 'postcolonial Ireland' on the grounds that Ireland was never a typical 'Third World' society.[2] What both of these conceptions of colonialism fail to acknowledge is that there never was any 'classical' colonial society or generic colonial condition to begin with. The British Empire comprised a heterogeneous collection of trade colonies, Protectorates, Crown colonies, settlement colonies, administrative colonies, Mandates, trade ports, naval bases, Dominions, and dependencies. These constituent parts of the Empire had quite diverse pre-colonial and pre-capitalist histories; their economic, political, and juridical relations with the British metropolis varied considerably from one region to another and sometimes from one epoch to the next; and their independence struggles and subsequent post-colonial histories, depending as they did on diverse concatenations of domestic and metropolitan circumstances, developed along quite hetero-geneous trajectories as well.

Given that a wide diversity of colonial situations can exist even within a single Empire, the fundamental predicate of postcolonial studies in an Irish context is not that Ireland's historical profile corresponded exactly to that found in other colonies, but, rather, that twentieth-century Ireland has wrestled with a complex of colonial structures, legacies, and dilemmas, many of which have also occurred, in variant forms obviously, in other former colonies across the world. The Irish case, in other words, may not be identical to that of any other colony or set of colonies in particular, but the claim on which postcolonial studies rests is that some facets of Irish development since independence will bear useful comparative evaluation with broadly parallel developments in various ex-colonies. Comparative analysis with other small European societies may also be instructive, but the development of twentieth-century Irish society has been most deeply

[2] Stephen Howe's *Ireland and Empire: Colonial Legacies in Irish History and Culture* (Oxford, 2002) develops the most wide-ranging and comprehensive critique of Irish colonial and postcolonial studies.

conditioned by attempts either to preserve or to surmount Ireland's
centuries-old relationship with Britain and the British Empire. This
circumstance lends real weight to attempts to evaluate the Irish situation
in terms of other societies whose modern histories have been shaped and
constrained by similar postcolonial imperatives.

Ireland shares several postcolonial legacies and dilemmas with other
erstwhile colonial societies that include broad issues such as state formation, emigration, economics, and culture. Firstly, twentieth-century Irish
state formation was determined by a context in which the retraction
of British rule was accompanied by a partition of the island. The task of
nation and state-building in such a context is clearly one with suggestive
parallels with processes of state formation in former British colonies and
partitioned territories such as India, Palestine, and Cyprus.[3] Secondly,
because of its extended history of economic subordination and underdevelopment under British rule, Ireland was one of a series of ex-colonies
that would experience a major and continuous haemorrhage of population to the industrial core areas of the modern world economy. The
massive waves of economically impoverished Irish emigrants drawn to
work as cheap labour in nineteenth-century England and the United
States especially, but also in the 'white' Dominions of Canada, New Zealand, Australia, and South Africa, reflected deeply embedded patterns of
migration that were to remain central to Irish social, political, and cultural
development right across the twentieth century. The stream of Irish
emigration to Britain and the overseas Empire in the nineteenth century
can be seen as an early historical forerunner to later large-scale migrations
from colony to centre, such as that of Afro-Caribbean or South Asian
migrants to England in the period since the Second World War. In all of
these cases, the British reception of the immigrant communities was conditioned by attitudes to their regions of origin that had been shaped by
the history and ideology of Empire, and in turn the relations of these
migrant communities themselves both to the United Kingdom and to
their own countries of origin have been powerfully inflected by an inherited sense of colonial history. Thirdly, the attempt by the Irish
Free State in the first four decades of its independence to overcome the

---

[3] T. G. Fraser, *Partition in Ireland, India and Palestine: Theory and Practice* (London, 1984);
Joe Cleary, *Literature, Partition and the Nation State: Culture and Conflict in Ireland, Israel and
Palestine* (Cambridge, 2002).

debilities of an agrarian, export-oriented, industrially underdeveloped, and British-centred economy by way of autarkic economic development (an experiment accompanied by a good deal of cultural protectionism and nativism as well) finds suggestive parallels in other ex-colonies, such as Tanzania, Ghana, or Cuba, where an introverted turn of this kind, especially just after independence, was quite common.

Encompassing these three themes of state formation, migration, and economic development was a fourth, the task of establishing a national culture and the attendant dilemma of what is sometimes called 'the language question'. In Ireland, as in many other regions of the British Empire, colonization was accompanied by extensive Anglicization. But whereas Anglicization in some cases was restricted mainly to the élite and upper middle-class sections of native society, in Ireland an indigenous Gaelic culture had suffered calamitous collapse in the nineteenth century. Irish nationalist cultural and literary self-assertion throughout the post-Union period, therefore, has continuously and anxiously returned to the bedevilled issue of language and cultural authenticity. For some Irish nationalists, there could be no adequate decolonization that did not involve the revival of Irish as a living vernacular and as the chief medium of Irish writing. For others, the real challenge was to establish an internationally distinguished Irish national literature in English. More recently, many Irish writers have stressed the importance of moving beyond the oppressive sense that the choice must always be between either one language or the other, and some have argued that a genuinely bilingual society would be the most worthwhile goal for which to aim.

In the early twentieth century, a young James Joyce captured the dilemma nicely: '"Condemned to express themselves in a language not their own", he wrote, "[the Irish] have stamped on it the mark of their own genius and compete for glory with the civilised nations. This is then called English literature".'[4] The remark catches that peculiar combination of linguistic assertion and linguistic alienation that attends the task of constructing a national literature in the language of the former imperial power, and notes as well the ways in which powerful metropolitan cultures annex the 'minor literatures' of their former colonies to augment their

---

[4] Cited in C. L. Innes, 'Modernism, Ireland and Empire: Yeats, Joyce and their Implied Audiences', in Howard J. Booth and Nigel Rigby, eds., *Modernism and Empire* (Manchester and New York, 2000), p. 137.

own national prestige. The anxieties registered here are ones that have attended the development of postcolonial literatures in many parts of the world, and not just in 'white' Anglophone ex-colonies such as Canada, Australia, and New Zealand, but also in Latin America, in the Anglophone and Francophone Caribbean, and in many parts of Africa and the Arab world.

Among those critics who concede Ireland's 'postcolonial' status, some have argued that the appellation is valid only for the decades immediately following independence. These arguments are hardly convincing. If colonialism is used in the restricted sense of the imposition of British governance on Ireland, then it is certainly true that this form of rule retracted, however unevenly, in both regions of the island after the 1920s, at least until the outbreak of the 'Troubles' in Northern Ireland and the re-imposition of direct rule from London in 1972. But if colonialism is taken to mean not just an oppressive system of foreign rule or interference, but rather the combined economic, military, political, and cultural forces deployed by an imperial centre to dismantle pre-colonial societies and to replace them with new social orders more amenable to imperial interests, then it follows that what is called 'decolonization' must also inevitably be the work of a long rather than a short *durée*. The drive to postcoloniality, in this sense, refers to an extended process of social reconstruction that is just as much a feature of the Irish Free State and Republic as of contemporary Northern Ireland. Hence, perhaps, Thomas Kinsella's wry observation that '"it is one of the findings of Ireland's dual tradition that an empire is a passing thing, but that a colony is not"'.[5]

Decolonization in twentieth-century Ireland, then, is best understood not as a singular and linear but as a multi-stranded, multi-directional process that has meant quite different things, and that has posed quite different challenges, for different sections of Irish society. The drive towards postcoloniality has entailed something quite different for southern Irish nationalists, for southern Irish Unionists, for Northern Unionists and Northern nationalists, for Irish women, for the Irish subaltern and working classes, and for Irish people living overseas. These different vectors of Irish postcoloniality ought not to be segmented into entirely discrete 'experiences' since their relationship to each other is mutually

---

[5] Thomas Kinsella, *The Dual Tradition: An Essay on Poetry and Politics in Ireland* (Manchester, 1995), p. 111.

constitutive. Nevertheless, it is only by attending to the quite diverse ways in which different sectors of Irish society have responded to the protracted collapse of the British Empire, and by tracking the various Irish attempts to create a society different from that which had emerged in the shadow of Empire, that the lived texture and complexity of twentieth-century Irish postcoloniality can fully be appreciated.

The Irish Literary Revival, which extended from about 1880 to approximately 1930, is usually deemed the constitutive moment in the development of a modern Irish post- or anti-colonial culture. As a broad cultural movement, the Revival owed much to earlier nineteenth-century cultural developments such as antiquarian and folkloric studies, the cultural nationalism of Young Ireland, and German and Irish philological studies of Celtic languages and civilization. In this particular instance, however, the cultural revival extended beyond narrow intellectual coteries and acquired real political impetus from several events: the final destruction of Gaelic culture during the Famine; the settlement of the land issue, which undermined Ascendancy political hegemony and saw the consolidation of an assertive Catholic middle class; and the successive Home Rule crises that inflamed the demand for national autonomy. The literary revival associated with figures such as Standish O'Grady, Douglas Hyde, W. B. Yeats, Lady Gregory, John M. Synge, Patrick Pearse, and others emerged as part of a wider cultural ferment produced by a series of overlapping cultural and political organizations that included the Gaelic League, the Gaelic Athletic Association, the Irish Literary (later Abbey) Theatre, the co-operative movement, and Sinn Féin.

The character and achievements of the Revival remain matters of intense controversy in Irish cultural criticism, and even among so-called 'postcolonial' critics assessments of the period vary considerably. On the whole, despite the huge critical esteem accorded especially to Joyce and Yeats, the Revival period was viewed in largely negative light in later twentieth-century Ireland, in critical terms supplied mainly by the Counter-Revivalist critique that developed between 1930 and 1960. From this perspective, the Revival is usually perceived as a local Irish version of a wider morbid *fin de siècle* European romanticism and cultural nationalism. For many, the Revival represents a costly 'flight from reality' in which Irish cultural nationalists constructed highly idealized versions of Ireland's premodern past and totally impractical visions of its future destiny.[6] When this Revivalist literature was later institutionalized as the official culture of the Free State, its narcotic effect, it is suggested, served to impede or to delay Irish society from coming to any sort of realistic appraisal of its most pressing social problems.[7] Others have concentrated critical fire on the celebration of heroic action, martyrdom, and self-sacrifice in some important strands of Revival literature, especially in works by Yeats and Pearse. This cult of sacrifice, it has been argued, was to have socially destructive consequences, lending unwarranted glamour to physical force nationalism and to the more militant and authoritarian stands of Irish political republicanism.[8] From this perspective, the Revival is usually characterized as an insular, romantic, cultural nationalist *cul de sac*, the more positive cultural antitheses and antidotes to which are Irish modernism (exemplified by Joyce and Beckett), with its broader European and internationalist and humanist value system, and the more realistic, naturalistic, anti-heroic, or satirical and 'de-mythologizing' literary currents consolidated by Counter-Revivalists such as Sean O'Faolain, Frank O'Connor, Patrick Kavanagh, or Flann O'Brien.[9]

From a postcolonial studies perspective, this particular construction of modern Irish cultural history suffers from several deficiencies. In keeping with Irish revisionist historiography generally, this version of literary history tends to isolate Irish republican politics and political and cultural nationalism as the prime causes of the country's twentieth-century social ills, obscuring the degree to which other socio-cultural factors contributed to the conservative society that emerged after independence. The tendency to characterize the Revival in terms of an undifferentiated romantic cultural nationalism, moreover, obscures the fact that it was never a homogenous cultural movement, but rather a socially and ideologically

[6] John Wilson Foster, *Colonial Consequences: Essays in Irish Literature and Culture* (Dublin, 1991), p. 50.

[7] Terence Brown, 'Cultural Nationalism, 1880–1930', in Seamus Deane, ed., *The Field Day Anthology of Irish Writing*, 3 vols. (Derry, 1991), II, pp. 516–20.

[8] Representative works include Conor Cruise O'Brien, 'Passion and Cunning: An Essay on the Politics of W. B. Yeats', in A. N. Jeffares and A. S. Knowland, eds., *In Excited Reverie: A Centenary Tribute to W. B. Yeats* (London, 1965), pp. 207–78; W. I. Thompson, *The Imagination of an Insurrection: Dublin, Easter 1916; A Study of an Ideological Movement* (London and New York, 1967); Ruth Dudley Edwards, *Patrick Pearse: The Triumph of Failure* (London, 1979); Richard Kearney, 'Myth and Motherland', in Seamus Deane, ed., *Ireland's Field Day* (London, 1985), pp. 61–80.

[9] Richard Kearney, *Transitions: Narratives in Modern Irish Culture* (Dublin, 1988).

variegated one in which a wide spectrum of personalities and organizations vied with each other to offer different socio-cultural visions of what
an independent Ireland might become.[10]

Some have argued, indeed, that the most romantic, anti-democratic,
and politically reactionary elements of the Revival were not those associated with militant Irish republicanism but rather those associated with an
Anglo-Irish Ascendancy élite. The impetus of the former was in the main
both democratic and socially transformative, while the Ascendancy Revivalists were often bitterly hostile to a twentieth-century modernity identified with the decline of Protestant landlord leadership and the increasing
threat of 'mob rule' and demagogic mass politics associated with the rise
of the Irish Catholic middle classes. Hence, the most socially reactionary
elements of the Revival are not to be found in the works of militant
separatist republicans such as Patrick Pearse or revolutionary socialist
republicans such as James Connolly, but rather in those Revivalist strands
that issued from the patrician 'constructive Unionism' of individuals like
Standish O'Grady or from Ascendancy elegists such as W. B. Yeats.[11] Pearse
shared O'Grady's and Yeats's enthusiasm for the heroic past, and
bemoaned, as did they, the putative decadence of the modern age. He
was, however, committed to a radical transformation of Irish society,
while Yeats and O'Grady embraced an anti-democratic social vision in
which a symbiotic fusion of landlord and peasant classes would lead to a
renovated Irish neo-feudalism. The Revival can therefore best be seen as
a complex cultural moment in which a declining Ascendancy colonial
élite, an emergent anti-colonial, constitutionally democratic, but socially
conservative Irish middle-class bourgeois nationalism, and more radical
republican and socialist versions of anti-colonial nationalism engaged in a
protracted contest for dominance within the Irish national movement.

Those committed to a postcolonial perspective on this period would
also contest the revisionist tendency to construe the Literary Revival
(associated with an insular Hiberno-Victorian late romanticism) and
Irish modernism (associated with a cosmopolitan European humanism)
as polar opposites. If European modernism refers to that broad spectrum
of vanguardist cultural movements that emerged in response to the

[10] Luke Gibbons, 'Challenging the Canon: Revisionism and Cultural Criticism', in Deane,
ed., Field Day Anthology, III, pp. 561–68.
[11] Seamus Deane, Celtic Revivals: Essays in Modern Irish Literature, 1880–1980 (London,
1980).

convulsions of the nineteenth-century social order brought about by the technological innovations of the second industrial revolution, the trauma of the First World War, and the spectre of socialist revolution, then the Irish Revival may also be seen not so much, or certainly not only, as a belated provincial romanticism but also as a vernacular regional instance of that broader modernist current. Having passed, a mere generation earlier, through the appalling devastation of the Great Famine and the turbulent social revolution of the Land Wars, late nineteenth-century Irish society was undergoing a process of social transformation as sweeping, convulsive, and far-reaching as any in metropolitan Europe.[12] Revivalist literature, moreover, shared with modernism generally an anti-realist, anti-naturalistic, self-reflexive, and experimental aesthetic thrust. The same calamitarian spirit, sense of civilizational shipwreck, and impetus to comprehensive socio-cultural renovation that animated modernism also animated the literature of the Revival.

Rigidly to set off Yeats and the Revival against Joyce, Beckett, and European modernism, therefore, is to construct an artificially schematic literary history that obscures both the correspondences between the two movements and the critical engagement of leading modernists such as Joyce and Beckett with at least some fundamental preoccupations of the Revival. Joyce, for instance, was certainly implacably hostile both to the Ascendancy and to Irish-Ireland variants of Revivalist cultural nationalism, but he was at the same time an advocate of Irish independence and a stringent critic not only of the imperial Roman Catholic Church but also of the British Empire. Whereas he has conventionally been viewed as someone who developed a relentlessly hostile critique of Irish nationalism from the vantage point of a more cosmopolitan European humanism, in recent years a number of critics have developed postcolonial readings of Joyce that suggest that he can better be understood as someone who shared with Irish separatist nationalists a resentful sense of the damaging consequences of British rule in Ireland, though always remaining critically alert to the repressive ways in which many Irish nationalist movements conceived of independence.[13]

---

[12] On connections between the Famine and the Revival, see Luke Gibbons, 'Montage, Modernism and the City', in his *Transformations in Irish Culture* (Cork, 1996), pp. 165–69; Kevin Whelan, 'The Memories of "The Dead"', *The Yale Journal of Criticism*, 15, 1 (2002), pp. 59–97.

[13] Representative works include Enda Duffy, *The Subaltern Ulysses* (Minneapolis, 1994); Vincent Cheng, *Joyce, Race, and Empire* (Cambridge, 1995); Emer Nolan, *James Joyce and Nationalism* (London, 1995).

The cultural nationalism of the Irish Revival had much in common with other anti-colonial nationalisms. Throughout the nineteenth century, the Irish, like other colonized peoples, had been dually constructed, both as a virile, military race, exercising its natural martial qualities in the wars and adventures of Empire, and as an essentially emotional, irrational, and feminized people incapable of self-government. The one set of images finds its most potent expression in Kipling's celebration of the loyal Irish imperial foot-soldier; the other, weightier strand was popularized by Matthew Arnold's influential, Ernest Renan-inspired essay, *On the Study of Celtic Literature* (1867). For Arnold, the language of the Celts in Ireland and Wales was 'the badge of a beaten race', and its decline was therefore desirable because the 'fusion of all the inhabitants of these islands into one homogenous English-speaking whole... is a consummation to which the natural course of things irresistibly tends'.[14] In Arnold's work, Celticism was designed to endorse British Unionist state politics: the more spiritual Celtic race would leaven the philistinism inherent in Saxon culture, but since Celts were ineffectual in the arts of material progress, they were destined to remain politically subordinate to the English. For the domestic Anglo-Irish Protestant Ascendancy, the same Celticist discourse could be reworked to legitimate their patrician sense of themselves as Ireland's resident Saxons or Teutons, safeguarding the emotional Celts from their racial disposition to anarchy and excess.

In the late nineteenth century, in the hands of Ascendancy Revivalists such as O'Grady, Gregory, and Yeats, Celticism was re-deployed in yet another variant as a counter to middle-class Catholic nationalism. The stress on an ancient, imaginative, anti-materialist Celtic race allowed the Ascendancy Revivalists to define the Irish as a quintessentially aristocratic people, naturally receptive to the virtues of a feudal rather than a modern industrial or democratic social order. The emphasis on a common Celticism also served in these quarters to combat a nascent Irish political nationalism that was increasingly prepared to dismiss the whole cultural world of the Anglo-Irish Protestant élite as that of an alien colonial garrison. In the more middle-class Irish-Ireland factions of the Revival, the Ascendancy cult of the Celt was excoriated as an attempt to substitute the practical hard-headed aims of Irish political nationalism with a dilettante mysticism or, alternatively, the Celtic element was simply

[14] Matthew Arnold, *Lectures and Essays in Criticism*, ed. R. H. Super (Ann Arbor, 1962), pp. 293, 296.

assimilated and subordinated into the Gaelic and Catholic dimensions of the Irish national heritage.[15]

In contrast to the Irish Literary Revival, which was determined to furnish a distinct Irish national literature in English, the Gaelic Revival sought to resurrect an Irish national culture in the medium of Irish. Some of the leading intellectuals in the Gaelic Revival, such as Douglas Hyde, were also drawn from the Ascendancy, though the majority of the membership of the Gaelic League, established in 1893 to restore Irish as the vernacular national language, were middle-class Catholics. Hyde's lecture 'The Necessity for De-Anglicising Ireland' (1892) became a defining manifesto for the League, which quickly became one of the most popular nationalist organizations of its day. For Hyde, as for Pearse, Irish political independence would never be complete without the restoration of the Gaelic tongue, deemed the essential link with the pre-colonial past, the fundamental carrier of the intrinsic values and cultural memory of the nation from one epoch to another, and an indispensable bulwark against the pollutions of Anglo-American commercial mass culture. For its opponents, the attempt to restore Gaelic as the nation's spoken tongue, after a century during which the language had suffered a catastrophic and seemingly irreversible decline, seemed yet another example of a quixotic Irish nationalist proclivity to fetishize the past; for its supporters, it was an attempt to restore to dignity one of the oldest vernacular literatures in Europe. For some Irish Protestants, the emphasis on Gaelic served, as did Celticism for Yeats and O'Grady, as a means to counteract a more confessional nationalism in which Catholicism rather than language would become the defining touchstone of national identity.

The political and cultural negotiations that lent impetus to the Revival correspond in broad outline to those that shaped other decolonizing nationalist movements in the lead-up to independence. In Ireland, as elsewhere in the colonial world, the encounter between the subject culture and the imperial metropolitan culture was conceived of in terms of an essentialized civilizational difference. In English and Unionist discourse, 'Celtic' or 'Gaelic' culture might sometimes be praised for its lyrical and spiritual qualities, but it had long been traduced as belonging irremediably to the past and dismissed as singularly lacking in those qualities that

---

[15] David Cairns and Shaun Richards, *Writing Ireland: Colonialism, Nationalism and Culture* (Manchester, 1988), pp. 42–57.

equipped English culture for power and progress. Simultaneously assimilating and inverting this essentialist value-system, Irish nationalist discourse accepted that the essence of English culture was its materialism (its science, technology, industry), but claimed that Celtic culture was spiritually and imaginatively preeminent. Since Englishness was associated with modernity and Irishness with backwardness, nationalists were led to assert either that they could develop their own superior national culture by combining the material qualities of English industrial society with the spiritual superiority of Irish tradition; or that English material progress had been attained at the cost of human and spiritual degradation and that Ireland, precisely because it alone in Western Europe was not modern, had thereby preserved a unique culture that could regenerate a now decadent metropolitan Europe. Depending on their aspirations and interests, the different factions manœuvering for position within Irish nationalism variously identified the lodestone of the supposed spiritual distinction of Irish culture with Catholicism, with the vitalistic or spiritually pure peasant, with the heroic Celtic past, or with the Gaelic language. In many cases, however, the fundamentally racialist and essentialist cultural template elaborated to legitimate centuries of British administrative dominance and moral and civilizational superiority was preserved, even if now elaborately reworked to serve new social agendas.[16]

As in colonial situations elsewhere, antiquarian, arcadian, anthropological, or folkloric preoccupations with ancient and epic tradition, with pre-colonial golden ages and their cultural achievements, with the putative qualities of a rural peasantry conceived as the social element that preserved the residual vitalism or organic purity of the pre-colonial period, can easily be dismissed as regressive and reactionary. But while such preoccupations certainly did sometimes lend themselves to reactionary articulation, they were, on the whole, driven less by a rejection of modernity than by the need for a fundamental revaluation of a long-disparaged subject culture, and by the effort to effect this transvaluation within the received intellectual and aesthetic orthodoxies of the day, which were after all those elaborated and regnant within the imperial metropoles.

Moreover, in Ireland as elsewhere the attempt to develop a national culture that would legitimate political independence was inevitably

---

[16] Partha Chatterjee, *Nationalist Thought and the Colonial World: A Derivative Discourse?* (Minneapolis, 1986).

fraught with tension, since whatever was selected to be the cornerstone of a renovated national culture was almost certain to favour some constituencies of the local population over others. In both settlement and administrative colonies, the construction of a distinct indigenous national culture always risks giving priority to one ethnicity as more authentically representative of the people-nation than another, and the struggle to imagine the new nation, therefore, is invariably accompanied by an attendant struggle between various ethnic or confessional groups to establish position within the emergent society. In the decades of the Literary Revival this internal war of manoeuver between different ethnic-confessional segments and between various social movements was as important as the common struggle against British imperial rule. As was also to happen in diverse ways in other places, such as India and Palestine, the clash of contending sub-nationalisms within Ireland was ultimately to issue in state partition. This partition in turn transformed the terms and terrain on which the Revivalist struggle to define Irish national culture was conducted, but it also aggravated and extended that struggle. In this sense at least, the cultural struggles that lent momentum to the Revival did not cease in the 1930s; they have continued to exercise Irish society right into the present.

The elements of ethnic essentialism and social conservatism that undoubtedly coloured some Revivalist cultural production ought not to obscure the many really impressive and enduring achievements of the period. Domestically, the Revivalist generation successfully challenged London's cultural dominance by helping to make Dublin a rival cultural capital and, in Declan Kiberd's words, 'achieved nothing less than a renovation of Irish consciousness and a new understanding of politics, economics, philosophy, sport, language and culture in its widest sense'.[17] The period witnessed a level of sustained and vigorous intellectual debate and an efflorescence of literary production of a quality not again matched in twentieth-century Ireland. Even those modernists who rejected the Revival and went into exile mostly bypassed London (O'Casey is the obvious exception here), reinserting Ireland into the mainstream of European culture from which centuries of British rule were felt to have detached it.

---

[17] Declan Kiberd, *Inventing Ireland: The Literature of the Modern Nation* (London, 1995), p. 3.

Internationally, the Irish political and cultural struggle for independence was much admired by many anti-colonial intellectuals and movements across the world. Writing in 1921, Cyril Briggs, a Caribbean-born socialist leader of the African diaspora, could enthuse about the 'the Irish fight for liberty' as 'the greatest Epic of Modern History'.[18] Briggs's ebullient assessment of that struggle was predicated on his belief that it pointed the way towards the wider global demise of the British Empire and hence towards the imminent liberation of Africa and Asia. The Indian nationalist leader, Subhas Chandra Bose, claimed that in his native Bengal there was scarcely ' "an educated family where books about the Irish heroes are not read" '.[19] Jawaharlal Nehru visited Ireland in 1906 and declared himself ' "impressed by the *Sinn Féin* movement" '. His father, Motilal Nehru, headed a committee in the 1920s that tried to draft a constitution, modelled closely on that of the Irish Free State, for an independent India.[20] Culturally, as Edward Said and others have argued, many 'Third World' writers and artists saw in the Irish Revival an inspirational template for their own countries.[21] The literary achievements of the Revival had demonstrated that a vibrant national literature, even when expressed in the language of the imperial overlord—though reworked to express the vernacular speech patterns and idioms of the colony—could lend dignity to a national movement and compete with the great metropolitan literatures as well.[22]

The period of Irish literary and cultural reaction to the Revival, usually deemed to extend from the late 1920s to the mid-1960s, has been much less extensively studied in postcolonial terms than has either the period of the Revival itself or that of the contemporary Northern Irish 'Troubles'. There is a wide consensus in contemporary Irish cultural historiography that the literature of the Counter-Revival attempted to challenge the climate of rigid social conservatism and moral puritanism that dominated

---

[18] Cyril Briggs, 'Heroic Ireland', *The Crusader*, 4 (Feb. 1921), p. 5.

[19] Cited in Michael Holmes 'The Irish and India: Imperialism, Nationalism and Internationalism', in Andy Bielenberg, ed., *The Irish Diaspora* (Harlow, Essex, 2000), p. 242.

[20] Holmes, 'The Irish and India,' p. 242.

[21] Edward W. Said, *Culture and Imperialism* (London, 1994), p. 281. See also Elleke Boehmer, *Empire, The National and the Postcolonial, 1890–1920* (Oxford, 2002), pp. 169–214.

[22] The cultural achievements of the Revival were inspirational to the Harlem Renaissance, and later to many Anglophone Caribbean writers, while Joyce's work, especially *Ulysses*, was to have a decisive influence on the development of the modernist novel across Latin America.

life in the new Irish Free State, and later Republic, though some have contended that the literature of this period was itself shaped, often stunted, by the very conservatism it contested.[23] More recently, some have also suggested that contemporary assessments of the post-independence period are unduly tinted by the more permissive value-system of the post-sixties world, and that the religiously, socially, and sexually conservative climate that undoubtedly blighted Irish life in this era also prevailed in Britain, Europe, and America until the Second World War.[24] Be that as it may, it is generally agreed that from 1945 onwards, when social democracy in Europe and the welfare state in Britain were developed, the independence project in the twenty-six counties was gripped by a deepening sense of failure. In the face of economic stagnation, drastic emigration levels, and declining population rates, the economic autarky and official cultural nationalism that the new Irish state had cultivated since independence came under increasing pressure. Endorsed by the state and the Roman Catholic Church, and articulating the interests of a hegemonic bloc of the national bourgeoisie (agrarian, professional, clerical, and small business), Irish cultural nationalism had tried to consolidate an 'Irish-Ireland' identity premised on the negation of a British Unionist culture. This recuperated national identity was supposed to be Gaelic not Anglo-Saxon, Catholic not Protestant, agrarian not industrial, religious not secular, and ascetic and pure rather than consumerist and permissive.

While postcolonial critics have tended to overlook this period, a comparative analysis of post-revolutionary Ireland and ex-colonies elsewhere has evident merits. In his study of modern African writing, Neil Lazarus comments on a recurring pattern whereby a sense of initial exhilaration in the immediate wake of independence rapidly surrendered to a sense of postcolonial dejection. Like all revolutionaries, Lazarus remarks, African anti-colonial nationalists had a much clearer idea about what they wanted to end than what they wished to put in its place.[25] This swing from euphoria to despair certainly finds suggestive parallels in Irish writing in the Counter-Revival period. Sean O'Casey's trilogy of Dublin tragedies,

---

[23] Seamus Deane, *A Short History of Irish Literature* (1986; Notre Dame, 1994), pp. 210–49. The most authoritative cultural history of the Counter-Revival period is Terence Brown's *Ireland: A Social and Cultural History, 1922–1985* (London, 1985).

[24] See esp. Brian Fallon, *An Age of Innocence: Irish Culture, 1930–1960* (Dublin, 1999).

[25] Neil Lazarus, *Resistance in Postcolonial African Fiction* (New Haven and London, 1990), pp. 1–26.

The Shadow of a Gunman (1923), Juno and the Paycock (1924), and The Plough and the Stars (1926) is the most distinguished example of a new literary revisionism that challenged heroic conceptions of the struggle for independence. Set in the Dublin slums in the turbulent period from Easter 1916 to the civil war, these works indict the independence struggle as a compound of bombast and bloodlust that did nothing to alter the lives of the Dublin poor except to visit even greater hardship on them. Yet O'Casey's critique of the independence struggle tends in the end to reduce all politics to cant and to settle into a resigned humanitarian cynicism predicated on 'a vision of the world as chaotically absurd', redeemable, if at all, only by the comic energy, linguistic vitality, and occasional generosity of the Dublin poor, especially the women.[26]

Whereas the more combative literature of the Revival had valorised the ideal of noble self-sacrifice, this period sees instead the emergence of a literature focused on the human costs of revolutionary violence. In Frank O'Connor's Guests of the Nation (1931) emphasis falls on the young revolutionary disillusioned by the act of having to kill an enemy with whom he feels a common human bond; in Liam O'Flaherty's The Informer (1925) it is those unfortunates trapped and terrorized between the warring factions in the independence struggle that win the reader's empathy. In the literature of the Counter-Revival, the emphasis is not on the heroics and achievements of the revolution, but on its victims and atrocities, and on a general sense of betrayal. The outstanding figure of this generation of writers, many of whom had been republican activists in the independence struggle, was Sean O'Faolain. Whereas the more left-wing republican writers, such as O'Casey and O'Flaherty, tended to ascribe the derailing of the revolution to the comprador or gombeen (a pejorative term for small-time money lenders in rural Ireland) mentality of its middle-class leadership, O'Faolain, in his novels and even more so in his biographies, attempted a longue durée analysis of the collapse of Gaelic civilization and the emergence of a stunted and introverted modern Ireland. Daniel Corkery, O'Faolain's nationalist mentor, had contended in his critical work The Hidden Ireland (1924) that an underground Gaelic cultural tradition had survived the wreckage of conquest and defeat until the eighteenth century and that this, rather than the Anglo-Irish literary achievements of

[26] Terence Brown, 'The Counter-Revival, 1930–60: Drama', in Deane, ed., Field Day Anthology, III, p. 175.

Berkeley, Swift, and Burke—and by extension of Yeats and Synge—was the true foundation on which a modern national literature ought to build. In *The King of the Beggars* (1938), his life of Daniel O'Connell, and *The Great O'Neill* (1942), O'Faolain, in contrast, presented the old Gaelic world as one bereft of the resources to meet the challenges of the modern era, and as a world that the creators of modern Ireland and their followers had therefore no option but to abandon. Where Corkery had promoted 'religion', 'nationalism', and 'the land' as the touchstones of national culture and writing, O'Faolain's works yearn for a more cosmopolitan, secular, and culturally sophisticated dispensation, something increasingly identified with continental Europe, which became the yardstick by which to measure the shortcomings and inadequacies of the new Ireland.

If epic, saga, heroic tragedy, mythic realism, manifesto, and political ballad had been the major forms cultivated in the Revival period, the dominant forms of the Counter-Revival were comic satire and farce, the short story, and, in the novel and drama especially, a dogged literary naturalism that stressed the bleak and repressive nature of modern Ireland. Some of the major satirical achievements in this era include Flann O'Brien's *At-Swim Two-Birds* (1939) and *An Béal Bocht* (*The Poor Mouth*, 1941), and Brendan Behan's *An Giall*, later produced as *The Hostage* (1958). O'Brien's works heap scorn on the mixture of incompetent ignorance and reverence with which the new state venerated both ancient Gaelic literature and the modern *Gaeltacht*. These works are permeated by a sense that the only energy left in modern Ireland is the linguistic, yet even this linguistic vitality is ultimately vitiated 'for want of anything truly worthwhile to say'.[27] The works of O'Brien's contemporary, Samuel Beckett, are grounded in an analogous sense of inertia, stasis, and linguistic futility, though in Beckett this is conceived as a universal rather than peculiarly Irish condition.

If satire offered one way to handle post-independence disillusion, naturalism would ultimately prove the dominant literary aesthetic of the Counter-Revival. In poetry, Patrick Kavanagh's *The Great Hunger* (1942) offered a savagely satiric and naturalistic riposte to Revivalist pastoral and its cult of the ascetic and vitalistic peasant. Dismissing the whole Revival as ' "a thorough-going English-bred lie" ', but unable to sustain

---

[27] Terence Brown, 'The Counter-Revival: Provincialism and Censorship: 1930–65', in Deane, ed., *Field Day Anthology*, III, p. 93.

any alternative social vision, Kavanagh's later work increasingly celebrated the saving graces of the local and quotidian, his example later being taken up by a long line of modern Irish poets who have cultivated the short lyric of private disengagement. In the novel, the immediate post-revolutionary generation dominated by O'Faolain gave way to a new one—in which the leading novelists include Edna O'Brien, John McGahern, and Brian Moore—whose works were steeped in an atmosphere of provincial misery and renunciation, religious repression, stifled and loveless sexuality, and imaginative and libidinal immiseration. In their works, the characters live thwarted lives or go into exile to escape a claustrophobic world where Irish nationalism and Catholicism have become hopelessly autocratic, ingrown, and spiritually death-dealing.

Critical evaluations of the literary achievements of the Counter-Revival period vary, though most critics stress its importance as a necessary demythologization of either unattainable or regressive Revivalist aspirations. The writers of the period undoubtedly operated in a censorious clerical and nativist climate and their works were part of a larger struggle to counter the philistinism of the new state. But despite the emotional power and ethical commitment that distinguishes the best of these works, the limits of the Counter-Revivalist analysis of the post-independence condition are now increasingly evident. The mendacity, vulgarity, and intellectual bankruptcy of the post-colonial establishment and the degraded texture of ordinary life in the new state are usually diagnosed with clinical skill. With few exceptions, however, there is little sense in the writings of this period of the more complex structural relationship between internal failures and the longer historical background or wider global forces that weighed on the new society.

The new Irish state, after all, was born of military struggle against the world's most powerful imperial centre; independence was accompanied by territorial partition and a bloody civil war. The Free State inherited, moreover, an agrarian economy structurally dependent on Britain after centuries of colonial rule. Burdened with an unenviably obdurate complex of problems not all of its own making, the state had very formidable political and economic challenges to face. To attribute all of its failings, then, either to a regressive nationalism (as revisionists tend to do) or to a worthless *comprador* bourgeoisie (as most socialist and postcolonial critics tend to do) is to lose sight of the more intractable structural dilemmas involved. Whereas the literature of the Counter-Revival period has been commonly regarded until recently as essentially a dissident literature that bravely defied the clericalist post-independence state order, some postcolonial critics seem increasingly to regard much of that literature as itself steeped in the counter-revolutionary mentality of that new order. It is viewed, in other words, as a literature of diminished expectations, one which had lost the utopian ambition, self-assurance, and experimental daring of the greater Revivalists.[28]

Those Irish writers and intellectuals who looked beyond Ireland in this period were more concerned with its relationship to England, Europe, and the United States than with any affinities between Ireland and Europe's overseas colonies. When they left Ireland, the writers and intellectuals did so to live in Europe or to find work in British and American universities. It is important to remember, however, that the Irish independence struggle was waged many decades before the great wave of anti-colonial independence movements that gathered momentum after the Second World War and that climaxed in the late 1950s and 1960s. Moreover, just when the British Empire finally began to come asunder with Indian independence in 1947, southern Ireland withdrew from the British Commonwealth, removing it from the wider nexus of Empire at the very moment when the political and cultural impact of the new African and Asian decolonizing movements was to attain its widest global reach and impact. Moreover, by the time the new wave of postcolonial writers and intellectuals that emerged from these later independence struggles made their impact on Europe, the most ambitious literary achievements of the Irish Revival and immediate post-Revival period—those of Synge, Yeats, Joyce, O'Casey, and Beckett—had already been incorporated into the canons of European and Anglophone modernism.[29] This has undoubtedly discouraged comparative postcolonial cultural analysis, since the Irish writers were thereby often viewed as integral to the Eurocentric canon of 'world literature' that many new postcolonial writers regarded as restrictively 'Western' and were determined to contest.

Hence, the most telling correspondences between Ireland and the overseas British ex-colonies have much less to do with direct contacts or

---

[28] Arguments along these lines may be found in Seamus Deane, *Strange Country: Modernity and Nationhood in Irish Writing Since 1790* (Oxford, 1997) and Lionel Pilkington, *Theatre and the State in Twentieth-Century Ireland* (London, 2001).

[29] See Innes, 'Modernism, Ireland and Empire', pp. 137–55.

influence, though these are not at all negligible, than they do with certain broad affinities of literary genre, structures of feeling, and intellectual problems that emerge when anti-imperial revolutionary excitement succumbs to post revolutionary *tristesse* and despair. Commenting on a wide body of postcolonial literature, Chidi Okonkwo has remarked that '[d]isillusionment has been so established in post-independence literature that there is a danger of accepting it as the only discourse on the performance of post-colonial states'.[30] The literature of the Irish Counter-Revival certainly exudes a sense of disillusion comparable to that which Okonkwo remarks upon, and, until recently, social and cultural historical writing on Ireland has tended to see this discourse of disappointment as the only discourse on the post-independence period worth consideration.

If the post-independence Irish nationalist literary tradition has centred on *bildung* narratives of stunted growth and damaged development, a southern Irish Unionist tradition emphasized, in contrast, lingering decline, and delicate but irreversible deliquescence. The obsessive concern of these 'Big House' fictions, centred on the old Anglo-Irish Ascendancy houses bathed in the auratic sunset of their last days, is the disempowerment of the Protestant ruling élite in the new Irish Free State and the struggle of that class to accommodate itself to diminished circumstances. Whereas the nineteenth-century 'Big House' form was closely affiliated to the Gothic tradition, the twentieth-century version acquired a more elegiac Chekhovian cadence: a rueful emphasis on the grace of a lost civilization tending to soften memories, sometimes to the point of willed amnesia, of the violent monopoly of power that sustained the Ascendancy world. Yeats lent the tradition new energy and authority, but women writers—Somerville and Ross, Elizabeth Bowen, and Molly Keane—predominate. The Anglo-Irish 'Big House' novel is best situated within the context of a wider Anglophone literature of imperial collapse that encompasses both domestic British fictions of loss and those that deal with the fate of the ruling colonial castes in the various outposts of Empire in its final days. Viewed in this wider archipelagic and imperial context, the early twentieth-century Anglo-Irish 'Big House' tradition might be regarded as an early but significant Irish tributary to the ever-swelling tide of Anglophone literature suffused with a sense of post-imperial and

---

[30] Chidi Okonkwo, *Decolonization Agonistics in Postcolonial Fiction* (Basingstoke, 1999), p. 166.

post-aristocratic melancholy. The genre has enjoyed a remarkable second lease of life since the outbreak of the contemporary 'Troubles' in Northern Ireland, even though these 'second-wave' fictions—by authors such as Aidan Higgins, J. G. Farrell, John Banville, William Trevor, Leland Bardwell, and Jennifer Johnston—continue to be set mainly during the earlier 'Troubles' when the war of independence was underway.[31]

This recent 'wave' of Big House novels has coincided with a wider resurgence of what Salman Rushdie described, in a controversial 1984 essay, as British 'Raj nostalgia'. Rushdie was referring to what he saw as a common structure of feeling shared by a conservative establishment under Margaret Thatcher and by historians, writers, and filmmakers anxious to return English people to 'the lost hour of their precedence'.[32] Works such as *The Far Pavilions, The Jewel in the Crown, Gandhi*, and *A Passage to India* conspired, Rushdie contended, to retell the story of British involvement in India in glamorous, gentlemanly terms that elided much of the violence and racism involved. This was also the decade, as Ian Baucom has noted, when Prince Charles led a conservative heritage industry campaign that lamented the post-war mutilation of Britain's noble architecture and decried a supposedly vanishing country-house England.[33] It was in this context that a whole slew of Anglo-Irish Big House dramas found their way onto the British screen in the 1980s. These include a BBC dramatization of Keane's *Good Behaviour* in 1982, Channel 4's serializations of *The Irish R.M.* in 1983, 1984, and 1985, and versions of Farrell's *Troubles* in 1988, Somerville and Ross's *The Real Charlotte* in 1990, and Trevor's *Fools of Fortune* in 1991. Against the backdrop of an ongoing war in the North of Ireland, the effect of this spate of Irish Big House novels and films was

---

[31] W. B. Yeats, *The Tower* (London, 1928), *The Winding Stair* (London, 1933), and *Purgatory* (Dublin, 1939); Edith Somerville, *The Big House of Inver* (London, 1925); Elizabeth Bowen, *The Last September* (New York, 1929); Molly Keane, *Mad Puppetstown* (London, 1931) and *Two Days in Aragon* (London, 1941); Aidan Higgins, *Langrishe, Go Down* (London, 1966); J. G. Farrell, *Troubles* (London, 1970); John Banville, *Birchwood* (London, 1973); William Trevor, *Fools of Fortune* (London, 1983) and *The Story of Lucy Gault* (London, 2002); Leland Bardwell, *The House* (Dingle, Co. Kerry, 1984); Jennifer Johnston, *Fool's Sanctuary* (London, 1987). Two major non-fiction works, Elizabeth Bowen's *Bowen's Court* (London, 1942) and David Thomson's *Woodbrook* (London, 1974) are also classics in this line.

[32] Salman Rushdie, 'Outside the Whale', in Rushdie, *Imaginary Homelands: Essays and Criticism, 1981–1991* (London, 1991), p. 92.

[33] Ian Baucom, 'Among the Ruins: Topographies of Postimperial Melancholy,' in Baucom, *Out of Place: Englishness, Empire and the Locations of Identity* (Princeton, 1999), pp. 164–89.

undoubtedly conservative. By filtering the current Northern 'Troubles' through the earlier Irish war of independence, these works may have subliminally linked contemporary events in the North to a longer history of Irish nationalist and anti-imperial struggle. But in a manner compatible with the nostalgic Raj fictions diagnosed by Rushdie, they did so generally in a way that reinforced domestic English conservative anxieties about the surrender of old civilization to new barbarism and that pandered to a sense of embattled grandeur on the wane.

Critics of the Big House tradition have censured it for its melancholy devotion to the past and for its manichean construction of the world in terms of élite culture besieged by faceless barbarity. Others, however, have stressed that these fictions sometimes focus less on an external enemy than on the collaboration of a class in its own destruction and hold that in some works at least there are also attempts to accept loss and to reach accommodation with the new Ireland. Lionel Pilkington has argued that for the southern Irish Protestant community, thinking of its identity in terms of the twilight of the Ascendancy was a psychologically attractive salve to the damage inflicted on it by the Catholic *Ne Temere* decree and to the serious isolation it experienced within a state increasingly and dogmatically influenced by the Catholic Church. The insistent topos of the ancient home in the genre, in other words, might be seen as a form of aesthetic compensation for an increasing sense of political and cultural homelessness in the new state. Nevertheless, Pilkington argues, thinking of the southern Protestant community in this manner allowed a small élite to shape southern Protestant identity in ways that 'flatly contradicted the lived experiences of the majority of Irish Protestants for whom contact with the Big House was often non-existent'.[34]

Both imperialist and nationalist political and literary historiography have conventionally tended to view the story of Empire and of anti-imperial freedom struggles in extremely masculinist terms. Contemporary postcolonialist critique, however, has been deeply influenced by both 'third world' feminist criticism and by subaltern and disapora studies, and these have directed attention towards the specific effects of Empire, colonialism, and anti-colonial struggles on a whole series of groups—women, workers,

[34] Lionel Pilkington, 'Imagining a Minority: Protestants and Irish Cultural Politics', *Graph*, 3 (Autumn/Winter 1988), p. 16.

migrants, nomads, and so on—whose histories complicate any triumphal, bourgeois nationalist linear narrative of transition from oppressed colony to emancipated nation-state. In the case of Ireland, inquiries of these kinds have, to date at least, been concentrated mainly on questions of women, gender, and the nation-state, and on the issue of Irish emigrant history.

Writing in *The Irish Citizen* in 1914, Helena Moloney, socialist and feminist, contended that '"there can be no free women in an enslaved nation"'.[35] At a time when the fight for Irish independence was developing concurrently with an already active, militant campaign for women's suffrage, Moloney argued that Irish women should fight first for an Ireland free from colonial rule, since the emancipation of women could not be attained without that of the people as a whole. Other Irish women linked Irish oppression at home to a wider global politics of imperial capital. Thus, for Maud Gonne, 'The British Empire [cannot] stand or go without famine in Ireland, opium in China, pauperism in England, disturbance and disorder in Europe, and robbery everywhere.'[36] Yet the determined anti-imperialism and advocacy for Irish nationalism of Irish feminists such as Moloney and Gonne was by no means undisputed among feminist activists at the time. Some feminists were Protestant and Unionist or at least non-nationalist; others were vehemently opposed to militaristic nationalism. Along with communism, feminism was an internationalist political discourse, and many in the movement regarded the nation itself as a bulwark of the patriarchal system. The degree to which women's struggles coincide with those of anti-colonialism, or to which the two are actually in tension with each other, has always been a central issue for feminists in the colonial world. In Ireland, this subject has also recurrently complicated the development of the women's movement, and, in recent times especially, wider currents of postcolonial analysis have received considerable attention in Irish women's studies.

Many of the movements central to the Irish national struggle were strongly patriarchal in institutional structure and ideological sentiment. The Irish Republican Brotherhood had, as its name suggested, a masculinist ethos and no serious commitment to women's rights.

---

[35] Helena Moloney, *The Irish Citizen*, 25 July 1914, cited in Roger Sawyer, *We are but Women: Women in Ireland's History* (London, 1983), p. 83.

[36] Maud Gonne, *A Servant of the Queen* (London, 1938), p. i.

Women were largely excluded from the Irish Volunteers, and many of the women involved in the major nationalist women's organization, *Cumann na mBan*, regarded its role as essentially supportive. The constitutionalist nationalist Home Rule Party was monolithically male and hostile to women's suffrage. The emergent and more radical Sinn Féin attracted far more support from women than the Home Rulers did, but only Connolly's socialist Irish Citizen Army, on the left wing of the national movement, accepted women on an equal footing. The Catholic Church was hostile to women's suffrage and to modernization generally. Moreover, since nationalist cultural revivals often tend to celebrate more traditional forms of social life as sources of resistance to the 'imposed' and 'alien' culture of the imperialist, the idealization of women as national icons and custodians of tradition also tended to create real and enduring dilemmas for the women's movement.

The republican proclamation of 1916, a radical democratic document, addressed itself to both 'Irishmen and Irishwomen' and promised 'equal rights and equal opportunities' to all its citizens, and the 1919 Sex Disqualification Act intended to safeguard equal opportunities regardless of sex. Yet, after independence, the Irish Free State introduced a raft of measures that discriminated against women. They were exempted from jury service; all married women were later excluded from teaching and the civil service; women were also restricted entry to a number of industrial professions. Eamon de Valera's 1937 Constitution compounded this already well-established trend when it idealized women's domestic roles as home-makers and mothers. In the newly independent state, the Catholic Church was determined to consolidate its role as the decisive moral authority in southern Irish society and this was achieved primarily through the control of education and health services, and the regulation of sexuality, especially women's sexuality. Hence the post-independence period witnessed the state banning of contraceptive devices and of information on such devices, the outlawing of divorce, and a stringent emphasis on female sexual purity and the sanctity of mother-hood. These were all to be pivotal issues for the 'second wave' Irish feminist movement that emerged in the late 1960s and were later to become the subject of some of the most bitterly divisive social struggles fought within southern Irish society in the contemporary period. Although the state prohibitions against contraception and divorce were eventually overturned, abortion remains illegal in both the Irish Republic and Northern Ireland.[37]

These developments have led some Irish feminists to conclude that the independence struggle was detrimental to the women's movement: a budding feminist political consciousness, it has been argued, was absorbed into and strangled by a new nationalist hegemony.[38] Some have contended that once Irish national independence was achieved, the struggle was commemorated largely in terms of masculinist heroics and women's involvement deleted or downplayed, in conformity with patterns common in revolutionary national situations elsewhere. It has also been suggested that the feminization of the colonized male under Empire produced an insecure and aggressive masculinity in the nationalist movements, something which expressed itself in post-independence Ireland in a determined drive by the Church-State nexus to control women.[39]

While these arguments undoubtedly have explanatory power, they tend to isolate nationalism and Catholicism as the decisive factors that determined Irish women's oppression between the 1920s and 1970s. Some feminists have suggested that this tendency downplays equally compelling factors and that it overstates the conservatism and exceptionalism of the Irish situation. The inter-war years saw a decline of feminism generally across the Western world once the suffrage was attained. In the dire economic circumstances and high unemployment levels of the twenties and thirties many Western states other than Ireland, including Britain and the United States, took measures to exclude or force women from jobs in some sectors of the economy. By remaining neutral, the Free State escaped the devastation of the Second World War, but non-involvement meant that it did not experience either the high levels of women's participation in the workforce compelled by the war, or the post-war economic boom experienced by many European countries. The combination of economic stagnation, a predominantly agricultural-based economy, and the massive levels of emigration which acted as a social safety-valve and diluted pressure for change, may therefore have impeded the development of the

---

[37] For a useful overview, see James Drewett, 'Free Nations and Enslaved Women: Gender Constraints in Independent Ireland', *Études Irlandaises*, 27 (Spring 2002), pp. 123–37.

[38] Frances Gardiner, 'Political Interest and Participation of Irish Women, 1922–1992: The Unfinished Revolution', in Ailbhe Smyth, ed., *Irish Women's Studies Reader* (Dublin, 1993), pp. 45–78.

[39] Geraldine Meaney, *Sex and Nation: Women in Irish Culture and Politics* (Dublin, 1991).

women's movement until the seventies as much as nationalism and Catholicism did. These impediments are best seen in the Irish case as features of a decolonizing society struggling with the embedded structural legacies bequeathed by colonial dependency.

Given this history, a great deal of women's writing in the Free State and Republic has been concerned to challenge oppressive inscriptions of women as religious and nationalist icons. This challenge has been directed at a nationalist literature that feminized the national territory or represented women as heroic mothers willingly sacrificing children to the national cause, and at the Yeatsian 'Big House' genre, where women were also conceived as custodians of ancestral heritage.[40] Though historical novels such as Kate O'Brien's *The Ante-Room* (1934) have sometimes traced the development of post-independence Irish middle-class mores back to the nineteenth century, twentieth-century Irish women's writing has much more commonly dwelled, in keeping with a wider Counter-Revivalist naturalist aesthetic, on the immediate forms of repression suffered by women in the southern state. Edna O'Brien's *The Country Girls* trilogy (1960–64) was a decisive influence in developing this particular naturalistic mode, but the resurgence of right-wing Catholicism, the conservative backlash in the 1980s, and the litany of clerical scandals disclosed in recent decades have encouraged an even bleaker and more gothic register in contemporary narrative. The Northern 'Troubles' have also directed renewed attention to an older concern with the relationship between women and republican nationalism. In many literary and cinematic narratives, from Pat Murphy's *Maeve* (1981) and *Anne Devlin* (1984), to Anne Devlin's *Ourselves Alone* (1985) and *After Easter* (1994), to Margo Harkin's *Hush-a-Bye Baby* (1989), this relationship remains an abiding preoccupation. Poets such as Eavan Boland have engaged the thematic of the nation to extend it to make room for women's experience, while Nuala Ní Dhomnaill has set out to release not only women but also the Gaelic language from the oppressive sense of joyless and puritanical reverence that had attached to both in official state culture.

The characteristic concerns and forms of Irish women's writing overlap with those in both Euro-American and postcolonial women's writing, though the issues clustered around the nexus of national struggle and religion are perhaps more prominent in the Irish case than in Euro-American

[40] See Marjorie Howes, *Yeats's Nations: Gender, Class, and Irishness* (Cambridge, 1996).

women's writing generally. Some feminists have argued that attempts to align the Irish experience with that of other postcolonial women's movements, rather than with Anglo-American traditions that have exerted a more obvious intellectual influence, tend to reduce the Irish experience to colonial oppression and nationalism and to ignore other issues and other Irish feminisms (whether Unionist, pacifist, or non-nationally defined versions) that fit less well into this paradigm.[41] Against this, it could be argued, however, that the 'third world' or postcolonial versions of feminism, which have insisted on forms of experience and oppression not accommodated in 'Western' feminist analysis, have themselves strongly contributed to a wider feminist appreciation of the diversity of women's experiences, and that postcolonial feminism has spoken powerfully to the concerns of some Irish women especially—Northern republicans, Irish speakers, and others—in ways that Anglo-American versions simply have not done. It is also the case that a great deal of work centred not just on women and nationalism, but also on the involvement of women from Ireland in Empire—whether as Unionists, missionaries, travelers, or settlers in the colonies—can also usefully be explored within a wider postcolonial framework.

The issues of migration, diaspora, and Empire that are centrally important to contemporary postcolonial studies have an obvious relevance to Irish history, though these are subjects with which Irish postcolonial studies has only recently begun to engage.[42] From a postcolonial perspective, the story of Empire is not simply a narrative of Western migration to the colonial 'peripheries', but also one whereby many in the former colonies have migrated to the metropole, either because of economic uneven development or in search of other opportunities not available in the home country. The subject of emigration looms very large in Irish culture, much of it expressed in oral and song tradition, and much in an extensive written literature. The most celebrated work of this kind is that of the modernist literary 'exiles': Moore, Wilde, Joyce, O'Casey, Beckett, and others. The literature of cultural expatriation is now widely regarded as intrinsic to the development of postcolonial literatures worldwide, and the Irish writers who left to establish major international reputations in Europe and America had much in common with contemporary

---

[41] Linda Connolly, *The Irish Women's Movement* (Hampshire, 2002), p. 30.
[42] For a fuller treatment, see chap. 4, above, pp. 95–101.

Western-resident writers from 'the once-colonized world' like Achebe, Rushdie, Walcott, Ngugi wa Thiongo, Soyinka, and Naipaul.

The exilic situation has frequently allowed such writers a standpoint from which to deliver powerful critiques of the new postcolonial societies, eliciting from those countries in return the accusation of rootless cosmopolitanism. Many critics have observed that metropolitan audiences have proved much more receptive to postcolonial expatriate writing produced in metropolitan precincts than to the literatures domestically produced within the new ex-colonial states, and here again there are suggestive parallels with the Irish case. Moreover, the critical celebration of much contemporary postcolonial migrant writing often overlooks the fact that these are also literatures of retreat, products of the writers' disillusionment with or rejection by their own new states.[43] Irish modernism, for instance, might usefully be contextualized in terms of a similar dialectic of critique and retreat during the initial stages of independent statehood.

There is a much more extensive literature, produced both domestically and overseas, that deals not with the travails of the relatively privileged expatriate writer, but with the subaltern masses who left Ireland to become the proletariat and lumpen-proletariat of the Anglo-American industrial core countries. Very few texts by Irish women have entered into the more familiar canons of emigrant Irish writing: though their relationship to each other is often conceived antagonistically, the canons of Irish national literature and of the literature of Irish emigration have tended, on the whole, to be equally masculinist. Emigration literature deals with the trauma of departure and the costs of adaptation to the host societies, and the anguish or impossibility of returning 'home'. More often than not, this is a literature of redoubled alienation: the emigrant's embittered rejection of socially 'backward' and claustrophobic Ireland intensified by a sense of the existential homelessness of the more 'modern' world beyond.

While the domestically produced literature of departure and return has sometimes as much to do with Irish writing's obsessive preoccupation with the thematics of tradition and modernity as with the social actualities of emigrant life, there is a considerable literature that does engage those actualities. Patrick MacGill's *Children of the Dead End* (1914), Dónall Mac Amhlaigh's *Dialainn Deoraí* (1960), and Tom Murphy's *A Whistle in the*

---

[43] See Elleke Boehmer, *Colonial and Postcolonial Literature* (Oxford and New York, 1995), pp. 236–37.

Dark (1961) are among the 'classics' dealing with twentieth-century Irish settlement in Britain. Although this literary archive remains seriously understudied, its characteristic preoccupations overlap suggestively with those of Caribbean or South Asian writers dealing with their communities' inward migrations to the imperial 'motherland' after the Second World War. In all of these literatures, the experience of diaspora remains imbricated in the rhetorics of Empire and nation. In all cases, moreover, the characteristic worldviews or structures of feeling that they express are both ethno-parochial and cosmopolitan in a manner typical of communities who live in a time-space constituted by continuous reference to both 'home' and 'host' nations.

The degree to which Northern Ireland can be considered a colonial settler society, and hence included in the postcolonial paradigm, has been a matter of much controversy. Broadly speaking, the contrast between the Irish Free State and Northern Ireland resembled that between, on the one hand, those colonial societies that were to fight wars of independence to extricate themselves from Empire; and, on the other hand, Dominions such as Canada or New Zealand that identified more closely with the imperial idea and that had only more limited and gradualist aspirations towards independence. In the Free State, it was generally felt that Ireland must develop its own independent literature in the English language, as the United States had already done. The new Northern establishment, however, was more anxious to stress that state's cultural connections to Britain than to distance itself from it. In colonial societies, it is typically the intellectual classes who mobilize popular support for a new nation-state, working thereafter to consolidate a national culture that will lend the new state cultural capital and establish its difference from the metropolitan power. In the North, the intellectuals, working within the framework of an already consolidated and distinguished British national culture, had no language to restore to glory, no ancient national traditions to resuscitate or invent. The major clerical and teaching professions remained deeply split along sectarian lines, moreover, and this may well have diminished the impact of the intellectual sector as a whole on the subsequent development of the new state.[44]

---

[44] Liam O'Dowd, 'Intellectuals and Political Culture: A Unionist-Nationalist Comparison', in Eamonn Hughes, ed., *Culture and Politics in Northern Ireland, 1960–1990* (Milton Keynes and Philadelphia, 1991), pp. 151–73.

The civic and official culture of the new Northern state was exclusively British and Protestant, its state rituals were based on British 'high' culture, and its more populist expressions were compounded of Orange marches, evangelical missions, and commemorations of Protestant siege and victory. The massive Ulster Regiment losses on the Somme, a blood sacrifice sanctifying the Northern state as Easter 1916 did the Free State, were construed as 'Ulster's sacrifice for Empire' and contrasted with the perfidy of the South. The sense of an overarching imperial unity welding the North to the United Kingdom was intensified by a common defence effort during both World Wars. Thereafter the tendency of the Dominions to go their own way decreased that sense of common identity, every subsequent shrinkage of the Empire tending to be celebrated by Irish nationalists as yet another overdue break-up of the behemoth, but viewed by Irish unionists as a dread omen of their own eventual betrayal.

Attempts to classify Northern Ireland as a colonial 'settler society' have been confused by the difficulty of processing all such societies through a single equation. Northern Ireland was patently not a recently established colonial settler society in the same way as Kenya, Rhodesia, or Israel were; the local 'native' population had not been genocidally devastated as were those in Australia or America. The new state was clearly not a self-renewing immigrant society with vast stretches of frontier to be settled, as were Canada, South Africa, Australia, or even New Zealand. Like Algeria, Northern Ireland was not legally a colony, but part of the metropolitan state; yet in Northern Ireland, unlike Algeria, the settler-descended community was not a tiny *colon* minority, but a demographic majority. Given the heterogeneity of settler colonies, as of colonies *per se*, therefore, generalizations about 'settler mentalities', 'settler ideologies', and 'settler cultures' that are not historically and contextually situated always risk becoming bad abstractions.

Nevertheless, the history of the territory that became Northern Ireland did share certain broad similarities with that of other settler societies. Historically, Ulster had been subjected to a well-planned state-devised colonization process in the early seventeenth century. Its earlier Catholic inhabitants were subjected to massive land-transfers to new Protestant settlers; for centuries, discriminatory systems of property laws and religious prohibition had contrived to maintain Catholic subordination and Protestant domination. Even those who argue that the original colonial settlement structures began to shatter after the repeal of the penal laws and the passing of the Act of Union allow that 'some of these features, the marks of that past, remained deeply ingrained' in modern Northern society.[45] The Ulster Protestant community's tendency to construe itself as an 'elect nation' embattled in the wilderness; its sense of racial superiority and fears of being 'outbred'; the strong taboos in both loyalist and nationalist communities against intermarriage; not least, the populist ideologies of 'planter' and 'Gael', 'settler' and 'native', cultivated on both sides—all of these combined have lent the region a colonial-settler quality of sorts that has lasted well into the twentieth century.

In *The Wretched of the Earth*, Frantz Fanon notes that in the settler colony, the settler is always 'the absolute beginning', the one who makes history.[46] In settler societies everywhere, history has typically been deemed largely immobile before the arrival of the settler; 'real' history always starts only with Columbus or Cook or the first European habitation. In each case, economic development, civilized society, and historical progress begin only when the settlers overcome an indigenous primordial anarchy to make the wilderness bloom. In the flurry of amateur and official histories that appeared during the 1880s Home Rule crisis, and that later accumulated to legitimate the new Northern state when it emerged, this characteristic settler trope is certainly pronounced. In these narratives, Ulster's history before the early modern plantations is repeatedly either bypassed or consigned to a summary monochrome 'pre-history', a narrative strategy strikingly at odds with contemporaneous Irish nationalist histories, which always highlighted the achievements of pre-Christian and Christian Irish civilization in the centuries before the Tudor plantations. Thus, for example, Ernest Hamilton's *The Soul of Ulster* (1917) emphasizes the appalling barbarity that prevailed in Ulster prior to the plantations, and concludes that 'no colonization scheme has ever been more abundantly justified, both by antecedent conditions and by results, than has that of Ulster by James I'.[47] Likewise, Cyril Falls's *The Birth of Ulster* (1936) opens with the statement that 'the Birth of Ulster... is what is known to historians as the Plantation: the colonization of the northern province of Ireland with English and Scots, from which had sprung a clearly-defined race, differing markedly from its parent stocks and to a far greater

---

[45] Frank Wright, 'Case Study III: The Ulster Spectrum', in David Carlton and Carlo Schaerf, eds., *Contemporary Terror: Studies in Sub-State Violence* (London, 1981), p. 161.

[46] Frantz Fanon, *The Wretched of the Earth*, trans. Constance Farrington (New York, 1963), p. 51.

[47] Ernest W. Hamilton, *The Soul of Ulster* (London, 1917), p. 3.

extent from its neighbours'.[48] The text sets out to reclaim the legacy of the earliest colonists, their accomplishments too often overshadowed in Protestant history, Falls suggests, by an emphasis on the later Williamite wars.

In keeping with wider imperial discourses of the times, these Unionist histories proudly celebrated Ulster's colonial origins, distinguished between 'colonist' and 'native' racial characters, and chronicled the bitter trials and hard-won achievements of those engaged in Ulster's 'great colonising and civilising mission'.[49] Some, along with W. A. Philips, maintained that '"the solid bloc of Protestant Englishmen and Scotsmen"' had remained distinct across the ages by resisting assimilation into the Gaelic population; while, according to Hamilton, 'present-day Ulster's 800,000 Protestants' were 'standing testimony to the stern resistance of the colonists to the allurements of the native girls'. He lauded their forefathers who had never 'at any time through the centuries yielded to the charms of the native daughters of Erin'.[50] Hamilton also surmised that: 'Behind a ready, but thin assumption of agreement with imported ideas, the basic nature of the native Irish Celt remains today the same as it was in the days of Elizabeth, the same as it was in the days of Strongbow, and probably very much the same as it was in the days of Noah'.[51] Both Falls and Hamilton, incidentally, use the term 'colonists' to refer not only to the seventeenth-century planters, but also to the contemporary Ulster Protestant community of their own day.[52]

Though argument and inflection vary significantly depending on the political sentiments of the historian, many of these Unionist histories rehearse a complex of tropes concerning the taming of the wilderness, the recurrent treachery of the natives, the trials and heroism of the planters under siege, the perfidy of the imperial centre, and the dangers of going native or of society reverting to primordial anarchy in the event of capitulation to native rule. These are the familiar stuff of settler historiography everywhere from the United States to South Africa. This elaboration of Northern Irish history in colonialist terms has not entirely disappeared;

[48] Cyril Falls, *The Birth of Ulster* (London, 1936), p. vii.

[49] Thomas MacKnight, *Ulster As It Is* (London, 1896), cited in Gillian McIntosh, *The Force of Culture: Unionist Identities in Twentieth-Century Ireland* (Cork, 1999), p. 25.

[50] W. A. Philips, *The Revolution in Ireland, 1906–23* (London, 1926), p. 12, cited in McIntosh, *The Force of Culture*, p. 27; Hamilton, *The Soul of Ulster*, p. 71.

[51] Hamilton, *The Soul of Ulster*, pp. 15–16.

[52] See, for instance, Falls, *The Birth of Ulster*, p. 253, and Hamilton, *The Soul of Ulster*, p. 200.

though now professionally discredited, it survives in a still-popular Paisleyite rhetoric which dismisses the pre-plantation populace as 'bog-trotters' and construes the Protestant plantation as an heroic biblical mission to redeem a heathen wilderness.

The poetry of John Hewitt, a presiding presence in twentieth-century Northern writing, offers a sustained analysis of the historical dilemmas of Ulster Protestants, to which the language of colonialism and the memory of the original Stuart and Cromwellian settlements are central. A left-wing writer descended from an English planter family that had settled in Armagh in the seventeenth century, Hewitt produced an extended literary meditation on his own troubled relationship, and that of the wider community to which he belonged, to that colonial inheritance. In his early verse play, *The Bloody Brae* (written in 1936, published and staged in 1957), Hewitt dramatized a confrontation between an English settler and the ghost of a local Gaelic woman whom he had murdered, an encounter set against the background of the 1641 rebellion when the native Irish had almost devastated the new settlements. The themes developed here—Protestant guilt concerning the violence done to the native Irish, a defiant assertion of Protestant right to the land both in spite and because of history, an abiding dread of retributive dispossession, and a plea for Protestants to 'admit our load of guilt' and for Catholics to acknowledge them as 'co-inhabitants' rather than *colons*—would remain fundamental to Hewitt's entire work.

In one of Hewitt's most famous poems, 'The Colony' (1949), the northern Protestant condition is allegorized as that of a Roman colony at the Empire's waning. Balancing a doubled sense of alienation—the colonists feel abandoned by an imperial centre from which they have become distanced by time and residence, but still do not feel at ease in the land where they have settled—the poem voices a late twentieth-century existential dilemma common among British-descended populations everywhere in the Empire as it began to shrink. Acknowledging that 'we would be strangers in the Capitol', it ends with the insistence that 'this is our country also, nowhere else; and we shall not be outcast on the world'. And yet there is also in the poem an equally insistent anxiety about what the wider collapse of Empire elsewhere might augur ('Already from other lands the legions ebb/ and men no longer know the Roman peace'), and an acknowledgement that the dominant community is haunted by the terror of being demographically swamped: 'Also they breed like flies. The danger's there;/ When Caesar's old and lays his sceptre down,/ We'll be a little people, well outnumbered'.[53] Though Hewitt's poetic voice critically distances itself from the communal nightmare it ventriloquizes, the nightmare scenario described is clearly one that directly parallels those that troubled white minority communities in many settler colonies.

In contrast to the triumphantly heroic rhetoric of colonization deployed in many of the early histories of Northern Ireland, Hewitt's language is much more attentive to the enduring and damaging costs, to both communities, of that history. Yet while Hewitt strains valiantly towards some sort of cross-community accommodation, the touchstones and boundaries of his imagination have some things in common with those historical narratives. Hewitt's imaginative reach, like that of the state histories mentioned earlier, can rarely accommodate the centuries before the early modern settlements. His historical essay, 'The Course of Writing in Ulster' (1953), brusquely dispenses with the province's Gaelic literary heritage and commences with 'the experience of the colonists' in exactly the same manner that the aforementioned Unionist histories do.[54] His poetry shares with the histories an insistence that the country was simply a wasteland before the coming of settlers who 'laboured hard and stubborn, draining, planting' and 'made it fat for human use'.[55] Moreover, in his work, as in these histories, the 1641 massacres have the resonance of a primal trauma that no subsequent episode can erase. Terence Brown has remarked that Hewitt's imagination was most deeply stirred 'only by fears of a final homelessness', and if it is the case that colonial settler writing is always involved in a struggle with a landscape that stubbornly defies symbolic inhabitation, then Hewitt's work meets this description.[56] It is to Hewitt's credit, however, that where some would simply deny the salience of any colonial dimension to the Northern Irish situation, his work consistently asserts that both communities must confront that colonial past if they are not to remain prisoner to it.

[53] John Hewitt, 'The Colony', in The Collected Poems of John Hewitt, ed. Frank Ormsby (Belfast, 1991), pp. 76–79.

[54] John Hewitt, 'The Course of Writing in Ulster', in Tom Clyde, ed., Ancestral Voices: The Selected Prose of John Hewitt (Belfast, 1987), pp. 64–76.

[55] Hewitt, 'The Colony', p. 77.

[56] Terence Brown, 'The Poetry of W. R. Rodgers and John Hewitt', in Douglas Dunn, ed., Two Decades of Irish Writing (Cheadle, 1975), p. 94.

Working in the renewed context of the contemporary 'Troubles', many writers from the North of Ireland have continued to develop the analogy between the Roman and British Empires earlier deployed by Hewitt (and by some English writers, such as John Osborne and David Hare) to contemplate British imperial contraction. Where Hewitt focused on the dilemma of the Roman colonist left behind after the imperial legions had departed, however, these writers, mostly of Irish nationalist background, worked in a context where the 'legions' were back again on Northern streets. The trope most consistently worked was a venerable Roman-Carthaginian one: the late eighteenth-century Celtic revivalists, looking to the classical past for precedent, had constructed Irish identity as Phoenician and Carthaginian, in opposition to imperial Rome, with which they identified the British Empire. The association of Britain with imperial Rome was reworked in Seamus Heaney's *North* (1975), and that of the Northern Irish nationalist community with the Carthaginians in Brian Friel's *Translations* (1980) and Frank McGuinness's *Carthaginians* (1988). Despite considerable variation, the Brian Friel and McGuinness works identify Gaelic society with the razed civilization of Carthage and Irish nationalists with those tragically vanquished by history, rather than with either the imperial victors or the bewildered colonists of Hewitt's imagination. Heaney, Friel, and McGuinness all come from the hinterland of Derry, a city where thirteen civilians were murdered when the British Army fired into a civil rights march in 1972. Against that context, the imagery of Rome and Carthage spoke, however discretely, both to an immediate sense of grief and outrage and to a longer history whereby one culture had tried to expunge and overwrite the memory of another.[57]

The ambition to restore eclipsed memory, to excavate buried histories, is fundamental to anti- or post-colonial literatures, and much Northern Irish writing since the 'Troubles' can usefully be considered in these terms. Whereas the official culture of the Northern state, and to a lesser degree even literary histories of the kind sponsored by dissidents such as Hewitt, had been overwhelmingly Unionist in assumption and temper, the period since the sixties has witnessed an ongoing attempt by writers and poets of nationalist background or republican sympathy to recover

---

[57] For a more extended discussion, see Elizabeth Butler Cullingford, 'Romans and Carthaginians: Anti-colonial Metaphors in Contemporary Irish Literature', in Cullingford, *Ireland's Others: Gender and Ethnicity in Irish Literature and Popular Culture* (Cork, 2001), pp. 99–131.

dimensions of Irish history and culture long excised from the established state versions. Sometimes, as in the work of Seamus Heaney or Brian Friel, this project has deployed an overt rhetoric of archaeology and excavation, the writer working to retrieve the multi-layered strata of a usually violent past from beneath the surface landscape. More often, the work of recovery entails translations from the old Irish into modern verse. In the work of writers such as Tom Paulin or Stewart Parker, both of Protestant background, it has involved the retrieval of radical dissenting or repub-lican traditions within Ulster Protestant history that mainstream Union-ism has preferred to forget. Though most contemporary writers have eschewed direct political commitment, their work has effected a dramatic broadening of the northern Irish literary canon, prising it open to accom-modate Gaelic as well as British, republican as well as Unionist, cultural memory. The cohort of writers that made up the Field Day Theatre Com-pany in the 1980s gave this drive a more self-consciously programmatic, and controversial, focus. When Field Day's director, Seamus Deane, asserted that the company viewed the contemporary Troubles as a 'colo-nial crisis', he provoked a welter of criticism, though the language of colonialism was scarcely new to the Northern situation.[58]

That said, most literary deployments of the language of colonialism to the North were extremely guarded and reticent. Colonial parables of Rome and Carthage coded the language of Empire in a polished classical veneer and removed the topic from the dangerous immediacy of the pre-sent, where its currency was most potent. Neither the republican nor loyalist working-class communities at the forefront of the conflict shared this reticence: their indices of reference in the 'colonial world' were much more overt, stark, and contemporary. Northern loyalist paramilitaries shipped arms to the province from apartheid South Africa and openly identified with colonial settler societies from Rhodesia to Israel; Irish republicans were armed by Gaddafy's Libya and their street murals iden-tified the Northern nationalist struggle with those of African-Americans, South Americans, and Palestinians. At the time of writing, five years after the Good Friday Agreement, many loyalist estates in Northern Ireland fly the Israeli flag and republican ones the Palestinian flag. In the segregated working-class districts of Northern Ireland the tendency to map the

[58] Seamus Deane, 'Introduction', in Deane, ed., *Nationalism, Colonialism, and Literature* (Minneapolis, 1990), p. 6.

Northern situation in terms of other late colonial cartographies evidently endures.

Select Bibliography

TERENCE BROWN, *Ireland: A Social and Cultural History, 1922–1985* (London, 1985).

DAVID CAIRNS and SHAUN RICHARDS, *Writing Ireland: Colonialism, Nationalism and Culture* (Manchester, 1988).

JOE CLEARY, *Literature, Partition and the Nation State: Culture and Conflict in Ireland, Israel and Palestine* (Cambridge, 2002).

ELIZABETH BUTLER CULLINGFORD, 'Romans and Carthaginians: Anti-colonial Metaphors in Contemporary Irish Literature', in Cullingford, *Ireland's Others: Gender and Ethnicity in Irish Literature and Popular Culture* (Cork, 2001).

SEAMUS DEANE, *Strange Country: Modernity and Nationhood in Irish Writing Since 1790* (Oxford, 1997).

—— *A Short History of Irish Literature* (1986; Notre Dame, 1994).

—— *Celtic Revivals: Essays in Modern Irish Literature, 1880–1980* (London, 1980).

—— ed., *Nationalism, Colonialism, and Literature* (Minneapolis, 1990).

—— gen. ed., *The Field Day Anthology of Irish Writing.* 5 vols. (Derry and Cork, 1991, 2002).

T. G. FRASER, *Partition in Ireland, India and Palestine: Theory and Practice* (London, 1984).

LUKE GIBBONS, *Transformations in Irish Culture* (Cork, 1996).

GLENN HOOPER and COLIN GRAHAM, eds., *Irish and Postcolonial Writing: History, Theory, Practice* (Basingstoke, 2002).

STEPHEN HOWE, *Ireland and Empire: Colonial Legacies in Irish History and Culture* (Oxford, 2000).

MARJORIE HOWES, *Yeats's Nations: Gender, Class, and Irishness* (Cambridge, 1996).

DECLAN KIBERD, *Inventing Ireland: The Literature of the Modern Nation* (London, 1995).

DAVID LLOYD, *Anomalous States: Irish Writing and the Post-Colonial Moment* (Durham, NC, 1993).

GERALDINE MEANEY, *Sex and Nation: Women in Irish Culture and Politics* (Dublin, 1991).

EMER NOLAN, *James Joyce and Nationalism* (London, 1995).

LIONEL PILKINGTON, *Theatre and the State in Twentieth-Century Ireland* (London, 2001).

INDEX

Lightning Source UK Ltd.
Milton Keynes UK
UKOW040024111012

200354UK00002B/6/P